Palestra
Pandemonium

Palestra Pandemonium

· · · · ·

A History of the BIG 5

ROBERT S. LYONS

Temple University Press Philadelphia

Temple University Press, Philadelphia 19122
Copyright © 2002 by Temple University
All rights reserved
Published 2002
Printed in the United States of America

Library of Congress Cataloging-in-Publication Data
Lyons, Robert S., 1939–
Palestra pandemonium : a history of the Big 5 / Robert S. Lyons.
p. cm.
ISBN 1-56639-991-2 (cloth : alk. paper)
1. Philadelphia Big 5. 2. Basketball—Pennsylvania—Philadelphia—
History—20th century. I. Title.
GV885.415.P55 L96 2002
796. 323'09748'11'0904–dc21

2002020420

To Joan and our children:

Joanne, Bob, Rick, Dave, and Greg.

A man couldn't ask for a better family!

Contents

Introduction
• • • • • • •
Palestra Pandemonium

"Winning the Big 5 championship was more important to me than winning the national championship," said Dr. Jack Ramsay, the Hall of Fame coach who won or shared seven such crowns at St. Joseph's before joining the NBA, where he won a title at Portland.

For more than three decades, Philadelphia's Big 5— La Salle, Pennsylvania, St. Joseph's, Temple, and Villanova—waged college basketball's biggest, most envied, unique, and frenetic, intracity rivalry. No other city in the nation ever had as many major universities competing so feverishly for such a coveted title as did the City of Brotherly Love from 1955 to 1991.

The Big 5 was housed at the Palestra, a venerable red brick building on the campus of the University of Pennsylvania. That building hosted more fans at more games over more seasons than any other college arena in history. This musty, high-ceilinged, 75-year-old arena is still regarded by many people as the best basketball facility in the country.

"The Palestra is to college basketball what Fenway Park and Wrigley Field are to baseball," wrote John Feinstein in his book, *A Season Inside*. "It is a place where you *feel* the game from the moment you step inside."

When Jim Boyle, the former St. Joseph's coach, became Paul Westhead's assistant in Denver, the first person to approach him was one of the Nuggets' players. "He walked up and said, 'Coach, I'm Walter Davis and I'm pleased to meet you, sir,'" Boyle recalled. "Then he said, 'Is it true you that played ball in the Philadelphia Big 5?' I said, 'Yes, I did.' He said, 'Man, I've heard so much about that league!' Here was Walter Davis, a great small-forward from North Carolina and the ACC who played in that year's NBA All Star game, in awe about the Big 5. I'll never forget that. When he said that I was just filled with pride."

It wasn't just the frenzied battles on the court that made the Big 5 unique. The camaraderie between the coaches has never been duplicated. Big 5 coaches honored unwritten agreements not to send game films or scouting reports on their city rivals to out-of-town opponents. Athletic directors wouldn't schedule home games that conflicted with a Big 5 doubleheader at the Palestra. Players would never think of transferring from one Big 5 school to another.

Every Big 5 team has been nationally ranked and has gone to the NCAA Final Four at least once. La Salle won the NCAA championship in 1954, two years before the Big 5 officially started, and Villanova captured the title in 1985 in perhaps the greatest tournament upset in history. Temple won the National Invitation Tournament in 1969 and was nationally-ranked No. 1 for part of the 1987–88 season—the only Big 5 team ever to reach the top spot. Only once in all the years that the teams played under one roof at the Palestra did none of the Big 5 schools fail to make it to a post-season tournament. That was in 1975–76, and it was the only time that the Big 5 schools finished collectively under .500. On the other hand, four of the Big 5 schools have reached post-season tournaments in the same year eight times.

Traditional rivalries like Army–Navy or Harvard–Yale had nothing on the Big 5's fierce battles fought before screaming fans, amidst the colorful streamers, fanatic mascots, often-raunchy rollouts, banging drums, and blaring bands. These games were often decided by a last-second buzzer-beater fired by some obscure walk-on, whose shot sent the Palestra into tumultuous bedlam and gave the winning team's alumni and students bragging rights for another year.

"If you won at the Palestra in the winter, you could talk all summer on the playgrounds," explained Penn coach Fran Dunphy, who played at La Salle. "The Big 5 was part of the fabric of the life in Philadelphia; there's no other way to describe it," said St. Joseph's athletic director Don DiJulia. "The Big 5 intensity level was equal to professional playoff games," added Cliff Anderson, the great Hawks center, who went on to play for four years in the NBA and ABA. "Right down to the last guy on the bench, your heart was in your throat, you were sweating, you couldn't sleep the night before."

"The Big 5 went beyond basketball," said Dan Baker, who served as its executive director for 15 years. "It was a social thing, a source of civic pride. The Big 5 led the way, even before the Civil Rights Movement and other attempts for equality. It was an exclusive club that was open to everybody—black, white, Catholic, Protestant, Jew. People accepted one another. If you loved college basketball you were welcome to be part of it. I don't think some people understand the ramifications of what this tradition meant to the city." The Big 5 took great pride in being a champion of racial harmony long before it became fashionable at many other institutions. George Raveling revolutionized the recruiting landscape for minorities and helped change forever the face of college basketball when he was an assistant coach at Villanova.

Frequently these Big 5 battles, waged between institutions located within a radius of only 17 miles, were renewals of some of the intense rivalries that characterized many of the local Catholic and Public League high school games. Maybe it would be a couple of ex-high school teammates from South Philly facing each other in the Temple–La Salle game or kids from West Philly and the Northeast teaming up to beat their former CYO buddies in the Penn–St. Joe's game. During the summer they would go at it again in pickup games at the Palestra, on the playgrounds, or down at the South Jersey shore.

Certainly no other five-team conference in the universe can match the Big 5's legacy of coaches and players who have found success in the pros. Some of them, like Jack Ramsay (St. Joseph's/Portland), Chuck Daly (Penn/Detroit), and Paul Westhead (La Salle/Los

Angeles Lakers), won NBA championships as head coaches. Others, such as Penn's Jack McCloskey of the Detroit Pistons and Penn's Bob Weinhauer of the Houston Rockets, won as general managers. Four of the five men coaching Big 5 teams in 1973–74 (Temple's Don Casey, St. Joseph's Jack McKinney, Daly, and Westhead) went on to the NBA, and the fifth—Villanova's Rollie Massimino—turned down an offer to coach the New Jersey Nets. Both Villanova's Jack Kraft and Temple's John Chaney have been named college basketball's National Coach of the Year.

And then, of course, there are the players. "The Palestra was one of the places you had to play to become All-America," recalled Raveling, who later coached at Iowa, Washington State, and Southern California. Naismith Hall of Famers like Elgin Baylor, Dave Bing, Bill Bradley, Julius Erving, Jerry Lucas, Pete Maravich, Calvin Murphy, Wes Unseld, and Lenny Wilkens played against the Big 5. The 1957–58 Palestra All Opponent team, in fact, included three of the game's all-time greats—Oscar Robertson, Jerry West, and Wilt Chamberlain.

More than a hundred players from Big 5 schools have been good enough to play professionally in the NBA, ABA, or internationally, and more than a dozen of them were first-round draft choices. La Salle's Michael Brooks and Lionel Simmons were National Players of the Year. La Salle's Ken Durrett, St. Joseph's Matt Guokas, Temple's Mark Macon and Guy Rodgers, and Villanova's Howard Porter were consensus All-Americas. Villanova's Ed Pinckney and Howard Porter and Temple's Hal Lear were named Most Outstanding Players of the NCAA Final Four.

Each Big 5 school produced its share of legendary backcourt combinations. So many of them received national acclaim, in fact, that the term "Philadelphia guard" has long been synonymous with backcourt excellence. Fans everywhere have vivid memories of such intelligent floor generals as Temple's Hal Lear and Guy Rodgers; Bobby McNeill and Joe Gallo of St. Joseph's; Pennsylvania's Steve Bilsky and Dave Wohl; La Salle's Bernie Williams and Roland "Fatty" Taylor, and Villanova's Wali Jones and Billy Melchionni.

A few years ago, the Philadelphia Sportswriters Association honored Guy Rodgers, perhaps the greatest guard not in the Naismith Basketball Hall of Fame, with its Living Legend award. Associated Press sportswriter Jack Scheuer, who played independent basketball with Rodgers on the Philadelphia playgrounds in the 1950s, introduced him as the "classic Philadelphia guard." The next day, Scheuer's telephone rang. "I just want to tell you that was the greatest compliment I ever received," said Rodgers, who had recently retired after a 12-year career in the NBA.

"What people forget is that the Big 5 wasn't just guys going at a hundred miles an hour, frenetic games, and last minute shots," said Bilsky, who is now Penn's athletic director. "It was also real quality basketball being played by real quality players. From Guy Rodgers right on down through the years, there was just some great talent out there."

The Big 5 is also the story of the unsung heroes who provided some of the most thrilling moments in city series history. It's about the infamous Emma Square, comical characters like Yo Yo, and unforgettable events like the "Bomb Scare." It's also about class and sportsmanship. Like the time Howard Porter quickly came to the aid of Penn's Corky Calhoun, who was being taunted by a Villanova fan at the Philadelphia airport after the previously unbeaten Quakers' shocking loss to the Wildcats in the '71 NCAA Eastern Regionals. Or the time that Porter went out of his way to protect the drummer of bitter archrival St. Joseph's, who was being threatened by fans in Kansas.

Quite a few Big 5 players, such as Penn's Rhodes Scholar John Wideman, excelled in the classroom as well. Seven of them were named Academic All-Americas: Tony DiLeo, Jack Hurd, and Tim Legler, of La Salle; Bob Morse of Penn; and Tom Ingelsby, John Pinone, and Harold Jensen, of Villanova. Hurd, Morse, and Pinone were selected as NCAA Graduate Scholars, as was Charles McKenna of St. Joseph's.

Just about every great coach faced a Big 5 team at one time or another—Lou Carnesecca of St. John's, Bobby Knight of Indiana, Al McGuire of Marquette, Frank McGuire of South Carolina, Adolph Rupp of Kentucky, Dean Smith of North Carolina, and John Wooden of UCLA, to name just a few. The late Jim Valvano, who won a NCAA title at North Carolina State, lost the first game ever played in La Salle's tiny Hayman Hall—an East Coast Conference playoff game—when he coached at Bucknell in 1974–75.

Before the Big 5 officially began its round-robin schedule in 1955–56, some of the teams wouldn't even play each other. Penn hadn't played Villanova since 1922, but the Quakers and Wildcats shared the Palestra for doubleheaders, often directly competing for attention with La Salle, Temple, or St. Joseph's, who might be appearing in doubleheaders down the street at Convention Hall. That meant fans would sometimes have to choose between watching Villanova's Paul Arizin or La Salle's Tom Gola, West Virginia's Hot Rod Hundley or Rio Grande's Bevo Francis.

"At the time it seemed like the perfect solution," recalled former Villanova athletic director Bud Dudley, who helped organize the Big 5. For the first 15 years, each school played at least ten games at the Palestra— four against each other and six against outside opponents in doubleheaders. All receipts for the season, including television and radio revenue, were split equally—not big money by today's standards, but a far cry from the $85 profit realized by La Salle, St. Joseph's, and Temple in their final year at Convention Hall.

Gradually, cracks began to appear in the united front of the Big 5. Coaches bickered. Scheduling conflicts became commonplace. Villanova joined the Big East Conference and reaped larger financial windfalls. Other schools like Temple also started looking for greener pastures. In 1986, some Big 5 games were moved to campus sites. By 1991, the round-robin format was abolished and schools were only required to play two Big 5 opponents each year—none of them at the Palestra unless Penn was the host. The Big 5 had become an unfortunate victim of its success.

A few years ago, the Big 5 brought back Les Keiter, a local legend as its early radio and TV voice, to speak at a banquet. "I almost cried when I walked into the Palestra and saw how it's all deteriorated," recalled Keiter, who had become famous with his colorful descriptions of "Palestra pandemonium," "in again, out again, Finegan!," and "ring-tailed howitzers from the sky." "People told me, 'Les, you wouldn't even recognize the Big 5 now.'"

This is their unforgettable story: the coaches and players, the amazing characters, officials, and others vividly describing in their own words the intensity, the exhilaration, the emotion of 36 years of the most memorable and fascinating rivalries of the Big 5 city series, the likes of which we will never see again.

Palestra
Pandemonium

Chapter 1

• • • • • • •

The Field of Dreams

The bus carrying the University of Kentucky basketball team wheeled up 33rd Street and turned into the Palestra parking lot. The Wildcats were in town for the NCAA Eastern Regionals, but the games weren't scheduled for the venerable old red brick and sandstone arena on the University of Pennsylvania's campus. They would be played a few miles away at the Spectrum on that spring weekend in 1992. Duke, the eventual NCAA champs, would beat Kentucky 104–103 in overtime of the regional finals in what many observers consider the greatest college basketball game ever played.

"It didn't matter that the regionals weren't even being played there," recalled *New York Daily News* national sportswriter Dick Weiss, who was on the bus that day doing research for a book on Kentucky coach Rick Pitino. "Rick arranged to have a private workout at the Palestra because he understood how special the building was to the people in Philadelphia when he brought his UMass teams in to play against the Big 5. He wanted his kids to experience the building. I still remember him giving a five or ten minute lecture to his players on what this building meant to college basketball. I know he made an impression on them because they always talked about it afterwards.

"Pitino's talk meant so much to me," continued Weiss, who grew up watching games at the Palestra, took his wife, Joan, there on their first date, and still remembers every good seat he sat in before later covering the Big 5 for the *Philadelphia Daily News*. "It was just a rite of passage. It was a way of growing up. It looked like an old, beat-up gymnasium when you walked in, and when it filled up, it got hot and it got musty, but you could just feel the energy and electricity. I've been to Duke's Cameron, where it's probably as good as it gets, and I've been to the Pit in Albuquerque, the loudest place in college basketball, but the Palestra is still the best place to watch a game. I remember how exhilarating you would feel coming out of there after doubleheaders."

"I remember hearing about Frank McGuire bringing one of his South Carolina teams into the Palestra," said John Nash, the former Big 5 executive director who later became general manager of three different NBA teams. "Some of his players were accustomed to playing in some pretty big venues and started complaining about the locker room facilities. Frank called them together, sat them down, and started reciting the names of some of the all-time greats who had played there, including Wilt Chamberlain, Jerry West, and Oscar Robertson. Basically he said: 'If this locker room was good enough for them, it's good enough for you gentlemen.'"

"Guys coaching in the NBA today still tell me about going to the Palestra to watch Big 5 games," said Jack Ramsay, the former St. Joe's coach who is now an ESPN analyst. "I don't know how many of them would tell me how impressed they were with the whole atmosphere. They'd say, 'After practice we'd always jump in the car and drive down to the Palestra to see you guys play.'"

"I remember how great it was sitting in the Palestra locker room before going out for the game," said Bill Kelley, who played for Temple in the 1960s. "You could hardly hear Harry Litwack talk, the noise was so deafening. Your hands were slick with a little sweat, especially at the Big 5 games. I always led the team out on the floor

▲ The 1958 St. Joseph's–Temple game attracted 9,648 fans, the largest crowd ever to watch a Big 5 game at the Palestra. *(Urban Archives, Temple University, Philadelphia, Pennsylvania)*

because I was the smallest. It always felt great busting through that locker room door and seeing the crowd just rise up. It was so cozy, up-close, personal. Today, it's real lit up but in those days it was a little dim. I liked it better that way."

"I always tell people, whoever designed the Palestra was a genius," said former La Salle basketball coach Speedy Morris, who started taking his players to games when he was coaching CYO teams in the 1960s. "Back then I didn't have a lot of money and I wasn't yet coaching high school where I could call and get tickets. It was tough to scrimp but I made sure to get down there every Wednesday and Saturday night, traveling in my old beat-up car. I had so many bad cars back then, it was lucky that we made it. Sometimes it would take a while to get started or maybe we'd freeze because my heater wasn't working, but somehow we'd get there. I'd take a couple of kids at a time—guys who are surgeons and lawyers today—and I knew it was something they'd look forward to. My wife and I dated 14 years before we got married and lots of times she had to take a back seat because I was taking guys down to the Palestra. I was just a typical Philly guy who loved the Big 5."

"I've coached in the Atlantic Coast Conference and it was loud there, but nothing compared to the Palestra," said Jack McCloskey, who ran the Wake Forest program for a few years before going into the NBA. "The noise was electrifying. It seemed to echo off those walls and just reverberate throughout the whole place. I think that roar made it even more unique."

When McCloskey was coaching at Penn, he followed the same ritual every night after practice. "After they turned the lights out, there was still one emergency light shining up in the corner," he recalled. "As I was walking out of my dressing room, I'd walk across the floor, stop in the middle, and look around. And I would say, 'Geez, how lucky can a guy be to be coaching at a great university and to be in this fantastic basketball atmosphere.'"

"It was the Palestra that made the Big 5 so unique," said former Temple coach Don Casey. "Where else could you get that type of arrangement with everybody playing at one house? For a while it seemed like certain areas of the city gravitated toward St. Joe's, and others to La Salle. Villanova had its section. It seemed like West Catholic was playing South Catholic in high school and then meeting again in college. There was a little bit of pride in your neighborhood. You'd be pulling for one another at times and then at other times you'd think, 'I'd like to see Villanova get whacked tonight.'"

"That's why the Big 5 was so unpredictable," said Jim Williams, the first Temple player ever to score 1,000 points and grab 1,000 rebounds in his career. "All of us played against each other in the summertime. There was nothing that we didn't know about each other's game. It was like, 'I know what you have and you know what I have, so it's going to take your best to beat me.' That's what made the Big 5 so great."

Williams was an all-state star at Norristown High School, outside Philadelphia. His team was eliminated in the state district finals in his junior year, then lost the championship game to Uniontown the following season. "We were all excited not because we were playing for the state championship, we were going to play in the *Palestra*," he recalled. "From the time I was in high school, it was a thrill and a goal for any kid in the area just to set foot on the Palestra floor. If you were privileged enough to suit up there, you had hit the epitome of basketball."

"Even though the Palestra was located on Penn's campus, it belonged to all five teams," said the Quakers' Kevin McDonald, a member of the Big 5 Hall of Fame. "In the summer between my junior and senior year, I had the key. We would open up the doors and everybody would come. If you thought the games during the regular season were good, somebody should have had a camera there during the summer when we were just playing pickup and there was nobody in the stands."

Villanova's Herron brothers—Keith and Larry—were regulars. So were Temple's Tim Claxton and La Salle's Michael Brooks, as well as Duke's Gene Banks. Even people like Darryl Dawkins of the Philadelphia 76ers dropped in occasionally. "The hard part was keeping people out of there," said McDonald.

"We had a fascination with the Palestra from the time we were kids in Southwest Philly, but we didn't have any money," recalled Jim Boyle, who would later play and coach at St. Joseph's. Boyle and a bunch of West Catholic High School buddies like Jim Lynam and Herb Magee, who had a "burning desire" to play there, quickly discovered two ways to sneak into the building. They would scale an outside wall and climb through a window that opened underneath the scoreboard, or arrive at adjacent Hutchinson Gym well before game time and sneak through a door that opened into the Palestra.

"I figured out a third way," said Boyle. "If there were a lot of people moving around near the entrance, you could walk *backwards*."

Pat Williams, the former general manager of the Philadelphia 76ers and Chicago Bulls, never missed a weekend doubleheader at the Palestra from the beginning of the Big 5 in 1955 until he graduated from high school in 1958. "I had an intense love affair with the Big 5," explained Williams, who drove the two-hour round trip from Wilmington with his boyhood buddy, Mike Castle, the future governor of Delaware and now that state's only representative in Congress. Williams still has a copy of *Palestra Illustrated* from every game with his ticket stub neatly stapled to the program. "To this day there is no taste or smell in the world like a boiled Palestra hot dog slathered with yellow mustard," added Williams, who is now the senior executive vice president of the Orlando Magic.

"With the streamers, the rollouts, the mascots, and the bands, the Palestra is an entirely different atmosphere from a professional game," said Harvey Pollack, the nationally-known statistician who has handled Big 5 games since the beginning. "The logistics are great, you can see anywhere and you're right on top of the action. And, besides, every year is different with new players, new faces, new cheerleaders, new gimmicks, and, sometimes, new coaches. I learned early in the game to tune out the noise; that's why they call me the Ice Man. If you get captured by all the noise, you wouldn't be able to do your job." Pollack, a member of the Big 5 Hall of Fame, and his statistical team set a number of unofficial NCAA records back in the 1960s for speed in compiling box-scores after games. That was when everything was hand-written, before the computer age.

Just the sight of the Palestra changed the lives of some players. Dave Wohl, for example, was recruited by

Penn to play quarterback on the football team. One day, shortly after arriving on campus, he took a walk down 33rd Street. "I was just looking for a place to play and walked into the Palestra," the Big 5 Hall of Fame guard recalled. "There was nobody in there but to me it was just magnificent. It was the biggest thing I had ever seen at that point as a player. I just took one look at it and I was sold." Soon Wohl started making daily trips to the Palestra. "I started playing pickup games with all the guys who had been recruited for basketball—guys like Steve Bilsky and all the seniors that I would eventually graduate with. I really liked them and started to feel, 'Hey, these are the guys I want to hang around with.'" When Wohl, who would go on to a successful 27-year NBA career as a player, coach, and general manager, informed the football coaches that he decided to concentrate on basketball, "they told me I'm probably making the biggest mistake of my life."

"Tennis players talk about how they just love to step on Centre Court at Wimbledon," said Matt Guokas Jr., the St. Joseph's All-America who later coached and played for the Philadelphia 76ers. "That's the way I felt every time I walked into the Palestra. Coming out of that locker room, getting into your layup line with the crowd screaming and yelling, literally you got chills. You never walked into that building when it wasn't an event."

One of the most famous events in the history of the Palestra convinced Guokas to transfer from the University of Miami to St. Joseph's. It happened in 1962, in the opening round of the Quaker City Tournament, when St. Joseph's pulled off one of the most riveting upsets in Big 5 history 58–57 over Bowling Green.

Even though he liked coach Bruce Hale and teammates like Rick Barry, Guokas had been homesick from the moment he stepped off the plane in Florida. "I probably changed my mind a hundred times between Thanksgiving and Christmas," he recalled. "Then I came home and went to the Quaker City Tournament. I'm sitting with my mother in the same seat—to the right of the bench—I sat in as kid when my father broadcast Big 5 games on TV or radio. When Jim Boyle hit that winning jump shot, it felt like the roof was going to blow off. My mother turned and looked at me. She could see that I was beaming and I said, 'This is me, mom. I have to come back here.'"

The Palestra even affected Ollie Johnson's career. "The lights on the left side of the basket were much brighter," recalled the former Temple/Big 5 Hall of Famer who played for ten years in the NBA. "When I looked up, I was looking right into those lights. They were always in my eyes because I'm a baseline shooter. It was probably a career decision just because of the Palestra. Whenever I knew we had a game there, I would

practice more from the other side of the court. That's why I think I shoot better from the right side."

To say that some of the nation's greatest players appeared against the Big 5 would be quite an understatement. Take the 1957–58 Palestra All Opponent team, for example—Robertson of Cincinnati, Chamberlain of Kansas, West of West Virginia, Bob Ellis of Niagara and Lou Pucillo, the first player under six-feet ever recruited by North Carolina State. Pucillo was cut two straight years by Jack Kraft at Philadelphia's Bishop Neumann High School before finally making the team as sixth man in his senior year. "That shows you how smart I am," deadpanned Kraft, who later coached at Villanova.

The 1964–65 All Opponent team wasn't too shabby, either, with Princeton's Bill Bradley, Miami's Rick Barry, Davidson's Fred Hetzel, Penn State's Bob Weiss, and Detroit's Dorrie Murray. Nor was the 1968–69 team of Detroit's Spencer Haywood, Western Kentucky's Jim McDaniels, Kentucky's Dan Issel, Princeton's Jeff Petrie, and Columbia's Jim McMillian. Or the 1969–70 squad that included Julius Erving of Massachusetts and Calvin Murphy of Niagara. Other stars who played against the Big 5 at the Palestra included Si Green and Dave Ricketts of Duquesne; Marvin Barnes, Vinnie Ernst, John Thompson, and Len Wilkens, of Providence; Adrian Dantley of Notre Dame; Dave Bing of Syracuse; Bob Lanier of St. Bonaventure; Mike Gminski of Duke; Paul Silas of Creighton, and Rod Thorn of West Virginia. Pete Gent, the author of North Dallas Forty, made the Palestra All Opponent team in 1964 when he starred for Michigan State. Former Boston Mayor Ray Flynn (Providence) and NFL Commissioner Paul Tagliabue (Georgetown) also played at the Palestra, as did Syracuse's Jim Brown, the great Cleveland Browns running back.

But the best of all was probably Bradley, the only Palestra opponent ever to be voted the Outstanding Visiting Player for three consecutive years (1963–65). "I remember when I was working at Villanova," recalled Jim Murray, the former Wildcat sports information director who later became general manager of the Philadelphia Eagles. "George Raveling took me up to Princeton to see this great freshman from Missouri. We stopped at Krispy Creme Donuts on Roosevelt Boulevard in Northeast Philadelphia on the way up and George couldn't stop raving about this kid. It was Bill Bradley."

"That guy came into the Palestra and tormented me for three years," recalled Penn's Jack McCloskey. "He played six games against us and we beat him only once. We tried everything. We would go zone, we would go box-and-one. We'd go man-to-man against him and every time he touched the ball, we had somebody else

running at him. He was such a great player it never bothered him. I used to say, 'Get upset! Be mad that we're doing this to you!' But he was just as calm as could be. He waited until he had that open spot and BOOM, he'd bury that shot. He might have been as good a college player as ever played. And just a great person."

In 1989, after Detroit won the first of two NBA titles under general manager Jack McCloskey and coach Chuck Daly, the Pistons were invited to the White House to meet President George H. W. Bush. Afterwards, the Michigan congressional delegation hosted the champs at a reception in the Senate chambers. New Jersey Senator Bill Bradley came over to say hello. So did Maryland congressman Tom McMillen, who had played

▲ Wilt Chamberlain of Kansas is guarded by Bob Clarke of St. Joseph's in 1957 game at the Palestra. *(St. Joseph's University)*

against McCloskey for the Terrapins. "Every time I saw Bill I reminded him that I was tired of finishing right behind him all the time," said McCloskey. "I told him that I was awfully glad he graduated."

"I don't think there's a place on earth that is comparable to it," said Les Keiter, the voice of the Big 5 during the glory days of the 1960s. "I've broadcasted games all over the world and no matter where I was, I would always say, 'You don't know what it's like until you walk into the Palestra.' You talk about the *Field of Dreams* in baseball, this was my *Field of Dreams*. The mystique and the history of the place are unparalleled. When you first come through the doors there's a certain feeling that you get that just transcends the moment. Then you walk out on the floor and look up at nine thousand people, the scoreboard, the streamers, the fervor and fever in the stands, the intensity of the players and the coaches. There's nothing like it in the world in sports. It almost defies description."

"I've broadcast games in just about every arena in America, and there's nothing louder than the Palestra when it's full," said Al Meltzer, a Philadelphia sportscaster for more than 35 years. "I can still feel the drum which was always underneath the broadcasting booth. I can feel it from my toes right through the top of my head. Every time he hit that drum, you could almost see your brain explode. You had earphones on but it was impossible to shut the noise out. You thought that you lost your mind or something. The intensity was beyond description. You got to such a boiling point, you thought the building couldn't take it any more. I'm surprised it's still standing."

Keiter and Meltzer were part of an impressive list of local sportscasters who broadcast Big 5 games at one time or another—people like recent Baseball Hall of Fame inductee Harry Kalas, the longtime play-by-play man of the Philadelphia Phillies who handled telecasts with future National League baseball president Bill White. Television, in fact, probably did more than anything else to turn the Big 5 into one of Philadelphia's most popular institutions.

"The Palestra didn't lend itself well facility-wise to TV," said Bill Campbell, who did Big 5 telecasts in the 1960s with Richie Ashburn, the late Phillies Hall of Famer, on Channel 17. "It was not the greatest place to broadcast, especially working way up high in the rafters like we did. If you had a guest to interview, he had to climb all the way up on that ladder. It was brutal and a lot of guys would turn you down. They'd say: 'I have to go all the way up there?' It was pretty primitive and it wasn't that easy, but we managed to survive. But that doesn't detract from the mystique that the Palestra has."

"It amazed me the first time I climbed up there and thought, 'Wow! Al Meltzer has to do this every night,'" recalled John Nash. "And what happens if he has to use the restroom and get back in time for the second half? Back in those days, we dictated to television, they didn't dictate to us. The cameras for the most part were all the way up at the top of the Palestra. We did the games initially with one camera. Then we eventually got them on the floor and we'd argue about him standing or sitting because the cameras could be destroying sight lines.

Somehow we got it done. I think the TV people were always a little more willing to accept less at the Palestra than they would, say, at a Pauley Pavilion or one of the bigger arenas because they realized they were dealing with a much smaller situation."

Keiter had been brought to Philadelphia to become sports director of WFIL-TV and radio, then owned by Walter Annenberg's Triangle Publications empire. In 1963, he began broadcasting the entire Big 5 schedule on radio and selected city series games on television. He came from New York, where he had broadcast the old American Football League games of the New York Titans, then owned by Harry Wismer (today they are the New York Jets). He also did the New York Giants football games for seven years and New York Knickerbockers games from Madison Square Garden, where his statistician was a young kid named Marv Albert. Keiter grew up in Seattle, where one of his boyhood pals was Edwin Guthman, later press secretary to the late Senator Robert Kennedy and editor of *The Philadelphia Inquirer*. One of Keiter's first jobs was broadcasting University of San Francisco football (before the Dons dropped the sport). USF's coach at the time was Joe Kuharich, who went on to a long career in the National Football League, much of it cloaked in controversy with the Philadelphia Eagles. USF's publicity man was Pete Rozelle, who would go on to become NFL commissioner.

"When I was in New York, various Philadelphia teams would come into the Garden to play, and there were always references made to the Big 5 and the 'Philadelphia-type' ballplayer," recalled Keiter. "When I arrived in Philadelphia in 1963, I was very curious to see if it were true. And boy oh boy, did I find out in a hurry! I've done 14 heavyweight championships and have been privileged to be part of the Olympics, but the Big 5 was always right up there front and center at the head—at the top. Sitting at ringside with some of the greatest fighters of all time, I'd get that terrific feeling inside of me and I'd always say that it's reminiscent of how I felt at the Palestra in Philadelphia."

Keiter quickly became a favorite among Big 5 fans for his colorful descriptions of players shooting "ring-tailed howitzers"—some of them went "in the air, in the bucket," others "tickled-the-twine" or went "in again, out again, Finegan!" And as a tribute to the 9,200 screaming fans at the Palestra, he would always come on the air saying, "WELCOME TO PANICKSVILLE, USA!"

"I didn't do them consciously," said Keiter of his signature expressions. "In those days announcers had their own styles doing play-by-play on radio. Sportscasters, especially on TV today, are pretty much clones of each other because they're under direct orders not to be flamboyant, not to have a flair. I used many of those expressions when I was doing New York Knicks games in

▶ Les Keiter (right) and his color man, Matt Guokas Sr. (left), shown with the author, prepare for a Palestra broadcast in 1963. *(La Salle University)*

the Garden, long before I came to Philadelphia. I just got caught up in the excitement of a certain player or a given sequence in a game. They came out naturally. They were not contrived."

Keiter's first color man was Matt Guokas Sr., the former Philadelphia Warriors' great and the father of St. Joseph's star Matt Guokas Jr. Soon he brought in Al Meltzer, a young disk jockey from Buffalo, to help with the Big 5 games. The two worked together until 1966, when a struggling new station, WPHL-TV, starting broadcasting on a new, unfamiliar ultra high-frequency channel from an old warehouse in Wyndmoor, Montgomery County, just outside the city. Its first hire was Meltzer.

"I was the only *live* person at the station," Meltzer recalled. "I went over there basically to do all sports all the time but I also did the afternoon movie, all the announcing, and everything else." Channel 17 needed a hot product to fill its airwaves and Meltzer helped talk the Big 5 athletic directors into televising every home game. "That was a miracle in itself because Channel 17 didn't have any money," said Meltzer. "It had a tough time meeting its payroll, as a matter of fact. Luckily the athletic directors bought it." Rights fees were minimal—"maybe ten thousand dollars for each school"—but the telecasts created an entirely new audience for Big 5 basketball. "I don't know if the Big 5 made Channel 17, but it certainly made UHF television. At the time, TV sets didn't have UHF tuners. You had to buy a separate tuner with a circular antenna. That pushed UHF-TV over the brink because people couldn't get the games unless they bought that equipment. We were the ESPN of the mid-'60s but we didn't know it then, nor did anyone else. We like to think we were the forerunners of the basketball TV explosion. The college game down South and in the Far West, except for Kentucky and UCLA, was virtually non-existent. The timing was absolutely perfect. It was great for us because shortly after that college basketball just went crazy."

Although Keiter stayed in Philadelphia for only six years—he left WFIL to return to Honolulu the day they broke ground for Veterans Stadium in 1970—his

name became synonymous with the Big 5. Most fans remember him for one thing. "The first thing they say is 'Remember the Bomb Scare?' I've heard that hundreds of times," Keiter said. "It even happened to me when I went over to London to do the Muhammad Ali–Brian London fight at Wembley Arena. I'll never forget. A couple from Philadelphia came up to me and said, 'Les, do you remember the Bomb Scare?'"

No wonder. It only caused a 40-minute delay, but if there was one singular moment that will always live in the minds of Big 5 fans, it's the "Bomb Scare"—February 20, 1965.

I was La Salle's sports information director at the time. The Explorers had beaten Western Kentucky in the first game and Keiter invited me to join him in his broadcasting perch high above the Palestra for the second game, between Villanova and St. Joseph's. In those days the play-by-play man usually did the color, game-analysis, and halftime interviews, so I guess I gave Keiter's voice a welcome respite for those few seconds when he would call on me for a comment or two. It was halftime and suddenly Mike Morgan, a young Temple student, starts making a startling announcement over the public address system. Immediately 8,735 fans start filing out. I was sitting to the left of Keiter's statistician, Toby DeLuca, the long-time music librarian of WFIL-radio. Toby hears the announcement and turns to his right, where Keiter is interviewing referee Lou

Eisenstein. "Les, Les," DeLuca says, gently nudging Keiter, who does not respond. "LES, LES . . . " Keiter turns to DeLuca, visibly annoyed, and says, "Toby, I told you. Never interrupt me when I'm doing an interview!" "But Les, IT'S A BOMB!"

"My memory," said Keiter, "started with the announcement by that young man who was on the PA system saying 'Will everybody please rise and leave the building.' He must have repeated that a dozen times. I'm up in the booth high up in the rafters looking down and trying to figure out where everybody was going. And why they were all leaving. I could hear in the background his voice saying, 'Please leave . . . Please leave. . . .' And they were all leaving their coats and their pocketbooks and their briefcases at their seats. Everyone went up the steps and filed out of the building. Can you imagine that? People leaving their belongings on their seats and calmly filing out? And then I suddenly saw the police and bomb squad come pouring in from all the exits. There must have been a couple of dozen of them. And they started to search all the coats and the briefcases and pocketbooks, looking under them very gingerly. I'm up there trying to make sense of all of this because our cameras are showing what the police are doing. I'm trying to just ad-lib, saying something to the effect that 'obviously there is something in the building that they're looking for and perhaps it's a bomb and that's why everybody has left the building.' And then I said, 'I'm sure that we'll be leaving now, too, and we'll be returning you to the studios.'"

At that point the phone rang. "Toby DeLuca picked up the phone and I could hear the voice at the other end. It was Tom Jones, who was WFIL's program director. I had just uttered the phrase, 'We'll be leaving . . . ' and I heard Tom saying, 'TELL LES THAT HE'S NOT GOING ANYWHERE. STAY ON THE AIR. EVERY-BODY IN PHILADELPHIA IS BEING CALLED BY OTHER PEOPLE AND KNOWS THAT THIS IS GOING ON BY WORD OF MOUTH. WE'VE GOT THE BIGGEST AUDIENCE WE'VE EVER HAD. TELL LES HE'S TO STAY RIGHT THERE—NO MATTER WHAT HAPPENS!'

"So I said something funny and pointed up to the ceiling and said, 'Well, I guess that we're going to stay right here but the next thing you might see is Toby and me going right through the ceiling if the bomb goes off.' I don't know what else I said for the next 15 or 20 minutes. The next thing I saw was the police officer directing the bomb squad who was giving orders to everybody. He reminded me of one of those red-necked southern cops that you see in the Jackie Gleason movies or something. Anyway, he's pointing up at me suddenly, screaming at me loudly, 'YOU TOO! OUT OF THE BUILDING RIGHT NOW!' So now I'm betwixt and

between. I'm being ordered by the police to leave and I've been told by my boss on the phone to stay put. So I just turned to Toby and said something off the air—but it actually was on the air—to the effect that 'Well they want us to leave but we are not going! We're staying here!' Now the policeman in charge was getting loud-er—yelling at me and pointing. He finally threatened me, saying 'If you're not out of there in five minutes, we're going to come up that ladder and bodily carry you out.' And I invited him, replying 'Come on up!' We were high up on a platform that you could only reach by going up a ladder through a little opening. Climbing all those steps up to the TV booth was like climbing Mount Vesuvius.

"Then I told Toby and our cameraman who was in our booth to cover the opening with some of our equipment so there was no way they could get through. He was just fuming down there. He sent two cops up the ladder and they couldn't get through the opening. So they had to go back down and this guy was just ready to either physically assault me or arrest me. He was ready to explode, he was so mad at me. Then all of a sudden the police left and the people came filing back in and the game resumed. But it was a very traumatic experience."

In 1970 Keiter returned to Honolulu, where he had begun his sportscasting career 21 years earlier, to become owner of a local advertising/marketing agency. Soon he began broadcasting the baseball games of the Triple-A Hawaiian Islanders in the Pacific Coast League (where he succeeded a young sportscaster named Al Michaels), and later became sports director of KHON-TV. He also appeared in a few episodes of the popular TV show *Hawaii Five-O*. But he never forgot the Big 5. "During my nightly sportscast, I'd give the top three or four college basketball scores in the country and then I'd say, 'And in the Big 5 in Philadelphia tonight it was La Salle so and so, Temple so and so.' I had an affinity." Keiter retired from sportscasting in 1993 and is now the special assistant to the manager of Aloha Stadium, the site of the NFL Pro Bowl and various college bowl games.

In the early days, all of the Palestra doubleheaders were played at night. Saturday nights, in fact, were big date nights for local guys and gals. "When you think about it, we were one of the few places in the country that didn't have games on Saturday afternoons," said John Nash, the Big 5 executive director from 1975 to 1981. "I remember it was one of the topics at an athletic director's meeting. One of the reasons we didn't play in the afternoon was television. The people at Channel 17 didn't want to compete for ratings against college football and things like that. Also, our society lived a different lifestyle twenty or thirty years ago. Back in the '50s everybody went home, had dinner, then went to the games. Fast food places didn't exist. Maybe they had a hot dog or popcorn as a snack at the arena, but you went to watch basketball. You didn't go to eat. Today we've become accustomed to going to the game *and* eating at the arena. Then the Palestra doubleheader started at 7:00 P.M. but if the first game went into overtime, the second game might not start until 9:30. You couldn't take grade school kids in the middle of the week because now you're looking at the game ending at 11:30 or 11:45. When I was a kid I thanked my parents for letting me go to the Palestra because they would say, 'you're not going to be home until midnight.' But they had the benefit of being able to turn the game on TV and gauge how much time it would be before I got home." In 1978, Saturday afternoon doubleheaders were inaugurated at the Palestra and quickly became popular. "We had some terrific games," recalled Nash. '"And the best part about it, you could bring kids."

One of the charms of the Palestra was its antiquated scoreboard, which could only be reached by walking up to the top row of the stands, pulling down a set of stairs, and climbing about 15 more feet to a catwalk. The ritual was repeated by a Penn student between games of every doubleheader, when the names of the teams had to be changed on the scoreboard. "I knew a lot of people who did it," said *Philadelphia Daily News* sports columnist Rich Hoffman, who was the sports editor of the *Daily Pennsylvanian* in 1979. "It was a pretty coveted job until they installed the new scoreboard in the mid-'70s. Students would climb up and change the letters with this suction cup contraption that was attached to the end of a long pole. They didn't pay you but you got a season pass to all the games. I always thought it was a great job."

The Palestra is the home of the infamous "Emma Square," which was painted on the court as an aftermath of the longest, perhaps most bizarre, game in Big 5 history. It happened on January 24, 1959, when an unknown Providence team came from behind to upset Villanova 90–83 in *four* overtimes. The game featured tremendous play by John Driscoll, a 6' 8" Villanova sophomore who had 22 points and 23 rebounds. Equally brilliant for the Friars were future NBA stars Len Wilkens and John Egan, who scored 39 points against the Wildcats and was voted that year's outstanding Palestra visitor. But the turning point and the most memorable moment came when George Emma, who was better known as captain of Villanova's baseball team, was inserted into the game by coach Al Severance. "He came somewhere down the line but he sure as heck didn't report to me," recalled Bob McKee, the Big 5's Hall of Fame scorekeeper. "I'm screaming my fool head off, '*Come here! Report! Report!*'"

The Villanova bench was also screaming for Emma to report to the scorer's table, but he ran right onto the floor. "We had no choice but to blow the horn and indicate to the officials that he hadn't reported," said McKee. The crucial technical foul not only enabled the Friars to tie the game and force it into overtime, but also resulted in a permanent white box being painted on the floor in front of the scorer's table. Since then, players have been told, "Look for the square or you're not getting into the game."

One of the most colorful traditions that set the Palestra apart from other college basketball arenas was the ritual enjoyed at the beginning of every game by each Big 5 school. After their team scored its first field goal, students would throw hundreds of colorful crepe paper streamers onto the floor, often completely covering the court in a sea of crimson and gray or cherry and white. Play would stop briefly while the floor was cleared. For the most part, opposing coaches accepted the delay in good spirits. Then around 1985, Princeton fans started to throw out orange and black marshmallows. Soon students in other areas of the country began abusing the privilege by tossing pieces of fruit or heavier items. Predictably, the NCAA stepped in and banned the tradition. "I called the NCAA and requested a waiver," said Dan Baker, the former Big 5 executive director. "But they said that if they granted an exception for one school they would have to do it for others. They were afraid of injury and ruled that a technical foul should be assessed against any team whose fans throw streamers on the court." When the NCAA ruling came down, Baker had to inform the referees working the Big 5 doubleheader that night that they would have to enforce the ban on streamers. The first official he notified was Jim Huggard, the former Villanova guard, who had seen many a blue and white streamer during his playing days.

Penn's Fran Dunphy and St. Joseph's John Griffin wouldn't take no for an answer, however. After making a personal plea to the NCAA to reconsider, and being rejected, the two coaches took matters—and the Big 5 tradition—into their own hands when they matched wits in a Big 5 game in 1994. When the streamers came flying out of the stands after the Hawks scored the first basket, the officials promptly called the "T." But Dunphy told Andy Baratta to deliberately step over the free throw line when he shot his free throw. Rap Curry, of St. Joseph's, was told by Griffin to do the same thing after Quakers fans let loose with their streamers.

And there were the rollouts—those frequently creative, sometimes controversial, often outrageous examples of student resourcefulness. Some of them were relatively harmless, like "HAWKS BANK ON McFARLAND TO CHASE MANHATTAN." Others were often tasteless, containing double entendres or questions about a player's academic ability or sexual preference.

"The rollout would start in the upper stands and be passed down overhead like it was in a mosh pit, down to the front where it would disintegrate," recalled Brother Patrick Ellis, the former La Salle president. "They were a constant series of exchanges that tended to escalate toward the edge of propriety which, of course, is normal undergraduate behavior." La Salle used to sponsor a traditional formal dance on campus, the Blue and Gold Ball, the same colors of the basketballs used in pre-game warms. One night a banner came fluttering out of the St. Joe's rooting section: "LA SALLE HAS BLUE AND GOLD BALLS." The La Salle fans immediately countered with "IS THAT WHAT THE JESUITS TEACH YOU?" As can be imagined, a high-level meeting immediately ensued with the disciplinarians from both schools, and rollouts were banned . . . for about a game.

"When I was coaching I didn't have time to read rollouts during the game," said former St. Joseph's coach Jack McKinney, who also served as the Hawks' athletic director for a while. "Sometimes the students would slip one in that I had censored the day before. Somebody would tell me later, 'Oh that rollout was so funny.' And I'd say, 'Whoops, I think we're going to have a meeting today.' So many of them were so good, so clever. When I was checking them over, I would laugh and say to myself, 'Pretty darn creative, but I don't think La Salle—or Temple—will think so.'"

Villanova's Whitey Rigsby remembers warming up with his teammates before a game at the Palestra. He was standing next to the Herron brothers when the St. Joseph's fans unfurled a rollout that said "LARRY HERRON CANNOT READ THIS." "The younger brother turned to Larry and said, 'Look,'" recalled Rigsby. "He pointed up to it and laughed and started cutting Larry up." And with that, the Hawk fans rolled another banner that said "DON'T LAUGH, KEITH, NEITHER CAN YOU." "Then, of course, we all got on them."

"As an athletic director I was much less enamored and a little more fearful of the rollouts than I was as a student," recalled former La Salle athletic director Bill Bradshaw, who is now the athletic director at Temple University. "Often they were quite ingenious, but you just held your breath when they came out because they would cut to the jugular of the other school."

It wasn't just the rollouts that brought out the best *and* worst from the students at the Big 5 schools. Villanova's Chris Ford sometimes got pelted with miniature hot dogs when he appeared on the court. Students

from La Salle and St. Joe's regularly dribbled basketballs from their campuses to the Palestra as a show of support. Once after a big city series win in 1965, eight carloads of Hawk supporters paraded around Philadelphia's City Hall with their horns blaring. Then they drove right into the courtyard, scattering onlookers and interrupting a murder trial and other court proceedings upstairs before being hauled into a police station, where they were lectured by the cops and their dean of men, the Rev. Joseph Geib.

Some of the pranks were incredibly creative. Like the time the St. Joe's student pretended to be a producer at WCAU-TV and told the Villanova *Wildcat* mascot that sportscaster Tom Brookshier wanted to do an interview at the station on City Line Avenue. "Bring your costume to the studio because Tom might want to take some film of you wearing it," suggested the "producer." "Leave it in your car, drive up to the entrance, run inside, and notify the guard. Tell the guy on the security desk that you're here to see Tom Brookshier. And don't worry—one of our people at the station will park your car for you." The Wildcat did precisely as instructed and some St. Joe's students, waiting in a nearby car, promptly stole the costume. The *Wildcat* went to the St. Joe's game the next night dressed in a tuxedo.

"One day I was scheduled to speak at a pep rally at St. Joe's, but something came up at the station and I sent my regrets," recalled Keiter. "Lo and behold, the entire Hawk student body came out of the gym and marched down City Avenue to WFIL's station. They all moved into the parking lot and started screaming 'We Want Les!' I'll never forget George Koehler, the general manager, hearing all this noise as they were yelling for me. We were in a meeting and he turned to me saying, 'Les, for God's sakes go down there and give them whatever it is that they want, give it to them.'" Which Keiter did with a personal appearance.

One of the most innovative fans in the early days was a La Salle freshman who regularly brought a rather vocal contingent to the Palestra in a retired 1948 Buick ambulance, fully-equipped with the flashing red Pierce-Arrow lights on top. The enterprising young lad had assured his parents that the flashing lights were disconnected, but somehow after Explorer victories they suddenly became operational; during return trips up Broad Street the ambulance would barrel through traffic signals and make it back to campus in record time.

But if the young fans didn't always uphold the highest standards in the early days, there were always people at the Palestra to keep them in line. "I have a buddy whose grandfather had a concession stand at the Palestra," said Jim Murray the former Villanova sports information director. "His name was Eugene 'Onie' Smith. One Friday night a guy comes up in his Hawk jacket and asks for hot dog and Coke. Onie said, "Not here pal.' 'What do you mean?' the kid said. 'You can't get a hot dog here,' replied Onie. 'It's Friday.' And the kid protested and said, 'You don't understand. My name is Cohen. I'm Jewish. I'm just going to St. Joe's!' Onie was unmoved. He said, 'There's no way you're getting a hot dog at this stand.'"

It was a different time, even in the broadcasting world. "I'll never forget interviewing Bob Lanier of St. Bonaventure after a game," said Al Meltzer. "He said live on television: 'We played a *helluva* game.' And I remember saying to myself: 'He said *helluva* game. Oh my God! We crossed the boundary line!' It wasn't that long ago, either."

"I also remember a couple of weird incidents, a couple of death threats at the Palestra," recalled John Nash. Probably the most serious occurred in 1979, when Temple officials received a threat to star player Rick Reed prior to a Big 5 game. After being alerted by Temple's athletic director Ernie Casale, Nash called Mike Chitwood, a friend and Philadelphia police homicide detective, seeking advice. "Would you like me to come up and act as his bodyguard? I could leave the locker room with him, walk with him, and sit behind Temple's bench," said Chitwood. "I'll act like a secret service guy would act protecting the president." Nash then called Casale. "I told him that I had this guy who at the time was probably the most highest decorated police officer in the history of Philadelphia. Today he's the police chief in Portland, Maine. Ernie said, 'fine, let's do that.' So Mike sat right behind the team bench and no one ever knew what was going on. It never got in the papers. They never did tell Rick Reed until after the game what had taken place. I'm not sure if I was his parent how I would have felt about that. It's a tough call."

Although La Salle had the *Explorer,* Temple the *Owl,* Penn the *Quaker,* and Villanova the *Wildcat,* the St. Joseph's *Hawk* was the most notorious of the Big 5 mascots. "That damn Hawk flapping his wings," recalled Villanova's George Raveling. "I can remember many times sitting there and trying to catch him not doing it. It used to really tick me off because they'd always be saying '*The Hawk never dies.*' So one game I said, 'I don't believe that.' I tried to catch him. Even during the game he'd still be over on the side flapping and I would say, 'I'm going to catch him one night.' I never did!"

The unofficial mascot of the Big 5 was the lovable Yo Yo, an unkempt, disheveled, comical figure named Harry Shifren. Yo Yo bummed cigars from Harry Litwack, quarters from everyone else, and regularly shot fouls during halftimes at the Palestra. "We think he was from Brooklyn," said longtime *Philadelphia Bulletin* and

▲ Yo Yo. *(Urban Archives, Temple University, Philadelphia, Pennsylvania)*

Daily News sportswriter Bob Vetrone. "After the games he would mingle with the pressmen at the *Bulletin* building on 30th Street. He had a unique way of speaking—the school in New York was '*Ford-a-ham*' and he liked to see '*cap-city*' crowds at the Palestra."

"I would say that Yo Yo was the most colorful, unique person ever associated with the Big 5," said Dick Weiss, of the *New York Daily News.* "He was unbelievable, like one of those Damon Runyon characters. Here's this hobo who made a living walking two French poodles in Rittenhouse Square. He used to work in the '*Ack-a-me*' and he slept either in the old *Bulletin* building or the Camac Baths downtown. He used to walk into the Palestra like he owned the place. He would always ask people for money to buy hot dogs and everybody used to take care of him. He must have grown up in New York, because he had a great memory for New York teams. He always talked about '*Frank Si-na-tio*' from '*Hok-a-broken*'. Curry Kirkpatrick, the *Sports Illustrated* writer, was covering Villanova and South Carolina one night in the Garden and he said, 'God, is that troll still traveling with the teams?'"

"Some people in the Big 5 tried to get rid of him," recalled retired Villanova athletic director Art Mahan.

"But I used to take care of him. I never knew how he got in the building at Villanova, but the first thing you know he'd be in my office and I'd make him a sandwich and give him a cup of coffee." Once, before a sold-out Holiday Festival game at Madison Square Garden, Mahan was about to catch a train for New York when he received a telephone call from former Villanova assistant coach Joe Walters, a long-time Wildcat benefactor, who said that he needed a ticket for sportscaster Al Meltzer. "Joe I don't have any left but I'll see what I can do," Mahan replied. Just as he was leaving the house, Mahan's daughter said, "Dad I have a paper due tomorrow, why don't you give my ticket to Joe Walters?" Mahan called Walters back and said the ticket would be at the Will Call window. "So I get to the Garden," recalled Mahan, "and my wife is sitting in one of those fancy loge VIP chairs and I have to climb over this guy sitting in the middle seat—which was my other ticket. It's Yo Yo! I said, 'Hey, Yo Yo, you're in the wrong seat.' He says, 'No, No, I'm in the right place.' I said 'Let me see your ticket stub.' Then I said, 'Where did you get this?' He said, 'My friend *Al Meltzer* gave it to me!'"

"Yo Yo used to come up to see me at Villanova and say, 'O'Halloran, take me to dinner,'" recalled former Wildcat guard Fran O'Hanlon. "On game day, I'd take him down to the cafeteria and he'd eat off of my plate before he'd start on his own plate. I'd say, 'Yo Yo, I've got to have some food, you know?' For whatever reason, Yo Yo liked me. Whenever we played at the Palestra, he would come into our locker room, go right to me, and say 'O'Halloran, How you doing?' Then he'd take my Coke and walk away with it."

When Yo Yo died in 1979, the Big 5 athletic directors contributed $300 toward his funeral expenses and the Philadelphia Phillies paid the rest.

The name *Palestra* was suggested by Dr. William N. Bates, a professor of Greek at the University of Pennsylvania. Bates explained that young men in ancient Greece would train for their feats of prowess—wrestling, gymnastics, tumbling, and leaping—in their *gymnasia*. Then they competed in a variety of events and displayed their skills in a rectangular enclosure attached to the gymnasium called a *Palestra*. The organizing committee was satisfied that the name fit all of its specifications—authentic, dignified, descriptive, and novel. "The only deviation was made in deference to Philadelphia's winter weather," explained the late Ralph Morgan, a Penn trustee who served on the Penn athletic council that planned the building. "We put a roof on our Palestra. The Greeks left theirs open in the winter."

The Palestra opened on January 1, 1927—Penn beat Yale 26–15—and immediately became one of the social hubs of the community by regularly sponsoring dances after the games with men attending in tuxedoes and ladies wearing long dresses. By the time the Palestra hosted the Eastern semifinals of the first NCAA Basketball Tournament in 1939, it was a nationally-known venue. Since then it has held more fans at more basketball games than any other arena in the United States.

In 1987 the building received a major $2 million facelift that reduced its capacity from 9,240 to 8,700. The hard wooden bleachers were replaced with more comfortable plastic benches. Rows of seats with backs were added near courtside. Media facilities were upgraded, lighting was improved, and a fresh coating of Carolina blue replaced the brown paint on the walls and ceilings. Still remaining, however, is its distinctive roof braced by ten arched-steel trusses and brightened by rows of skylights on the south side. The building sits next to Franklin Field on the northeastern edge of Penn's campus, tucked behind outdoor tennis courts and adjacent to the Amtrak railroad tracks and the Schuylkill River.

"In today's world it's antiquated," said Fred Shabel, the former University of Pennsylvania athletic director "I find that I don't do a good job verbalizing it so the best way for me to describe the Palestra is to take somebody to a game. I like to sit down on Press Row at the Penn-Princeton game, for example, with friends from places like Fort Worth or Cleveland. Usually they're basketball guys who are just amazed. When you're that close to the floor, right on top of the action, it's a different world."

Shabel didn't always have such a fond appreciation for the Palestra, especially when he was an assistant coach at Duke and head coach at the University of Connecticut. "We had the feeling that the Big 5 was a marvelous concept," recalled Shabel, who is now vice chairman of Comcast-Spectacor in Philadelphia. "But we certainly had the very strong feeling that we didn't like coming to the Palestra to play a game. It was one of those situations where it was very difficult to win."

In 1965, Shabel's U-Conn team won the Yankee Conference title and was rewarded with a first-round game against one of Jack Ramsay's greatest St. Joseph's squads at the Palestra. "I remember calling the NCAA and saying, 'Look, this is a first-round game for us. Why are we playing on their home court?' I'll never forget the NCAA's answer: 'It's not their home court. Their Alumni Memorial Fieldhouse is.' I said, 'You guys have got to be kidding me!'" Connecticut led at intermission but Shabel was whistled for a technical foul in the second half and St. Joe's went on to win 67–61.

"I always thought the officials in the Palestra let you get away with more physical play," said Dave Wohl, the former Penn guard. "So teams would come in from different conferences and they were really almost intimidated. Nothing like the NBA, but you could hold and grab a little more, you could bump a little more, you could bang under the boards a little more. So the Philadelphia kind of style was more accepted and when the city teams would go against each other I thought the officials would even let you go another notch for the college game."

"I loved the Palestra when I was coaching at Villanova," said Jack Kraft. "But when I used to come back to play there with Rhode Island, I didn't think the place was as good. Sometimes it felt as though the people in the stands were sitting right on top of you. Out of bounds on the side, you only had an area of about three feet before you hit the stands. Underneath the baskets, the stands came right up to the braces of the backboard."

Al McGuire, who won a NCAA championship at Marquette in 1977, refused to bring his teams back to the Palestra after Villanova nipped the Warriors 80–78 in 1966. "He told me 'We just can't win there,'" recalled Kraft. Gary Thompson of Wichita felt the same way after St. Joseph's converted 30 of 32 free throws to upset his unbeaten, top-ranked Shockers 76–69 in the championship game of the 1964 Quaker City Tournament. "The conditions were ridiculous," Wichita's coach said after the game. "Our treatment on the floor by the officials and off the floor by those damn, horn-blowing, hollering St. Joseph's fans was atrocious. It was a damn farce."

When John Nash became executive director of the Big 5 in 1975, one of the first coaches he called was Al McGuire. "The answer was 'Never at the Palestra,'" said Nash. "Al was smart enough to recognize the incredible home court advantage of the Palestra. I remember McGuire or his assistant Hank Raymond making reference to the number of nationally-ranked teams that had come in and been defeated. It had been 11 years since Gary Thompson ripped the fans and officials, but the power teams were afraid. They would not come. Notre Dame obviously was a highlight on the schedule, but I couldn't get North Carolina to come in. We did get Ralph Sampson and Virginia to come and play Temple but I couldn't encourage some of the other big powers into the Palestra. Duke (with Philadelphia's Gene Banks) agreed to play La Salle, but only at the Spectrum."

Officials of the Eastern College Athletic Conference had trouble attracting top intersectional teams to the Quaker City Tournament after Thompson's outburst. The Christmas holiday tourney had begun amid considerable fanfare in 1961 and enjoyed its best crowds in 1964, when 34,332 fans watched eight teams competing for the title won by the Hawks in that shocking upset over Wichita. The Quaker City tourney that year actually produced more revenue for its contestants than its New York counterpart, the Holiday Festival in Madison Square Garden—much to the embarrassment of the ECAC. The Garden matchups featured Bill Bradley's Princeton team and a University of Michigan powerhouse led by Cazzie Russell. But the Quaker City Tournament was moved from the Palestra to the Philadelphia Spectrum in 1967, then was discontinued after 1973.

The Minneapolis-based Jostens Ring Company made a five-year commitment to sponsor a four-team Holiday Tournament at the Palestra beginning in 1985. Featuring an opening-round match-up between two Big 5 schools—thus guaranteeing a local team playing for the championship—it enjoyed one sellout when Villanova's defending NCAA champs made an appearance in 1985. However, the final year was canceled after Loyola Marymount, coached by Paul Westhead and featuring Bo Kimbel and the late Hank Gathers, was ordered to withdraw by the university's new president because the tournament conflicted with study time before final exams. "Jostens invested about $100,000 a year to sponsor the event but realized more than $1.5 million in free publicity," according to Bob Kane, a former La Salle tennis player, who ran the company's Mid-Atlantic college division and served as the tourney's executive director.

Palestra appearances by nationally-ranked powerhouses afterwards were tougher to arrange. Arkansas came in to play Villanova one Sunday afternoon and Razorbacks' coach Eddie Sutton raved about the atmosphere of the Palestra. La Salle hosted Western Kentucky and Florida State, and Penn did the same with Atlantic Coast Conference opponents Duke and Virginia. But the other big names usually belonged to traditional Big East teams like Syracuse and Georgetown—and most of those games eventually ended in the Spectrum. Denny Crum, who had vowed never to return, changed his mind in 1984 when he brought his Louisville team with Camden High products Billy Wagner and Milt Thompson in to play La Salle in a game won by the Cardinals 93–88. Dean Smith scheduled one of his North Carolina teams against La Salle as a personal favor to Explorer coach Lefty Ervin, but by the time the game was played—and won by the Tar Heels 79–72 in 1987, Ervin had been replaced by Speedy Morris.

However, the mystique remains. As sportswriter Bob Vetrone said wistfully: "If they hadn't built the Palestra, maybe there never would have been the Big 5."

Chapter 2

• • • • • • •

Just One Big Happy Family

One day in the early years of the Big 5, Villanova was getting ready to play Penn at the Palestra. "Just before they went out on the floor," recalled sportscaster Bill Campbell, "Al Severance is giving his pre-game talk in the locker room—and he was pretty loud as he always was. He said, 'Now in this situation, Ramsay will do this and Ramsay will do that, and when that happens look for Ramsay to do this.' Finally, David, his son, put his hand up and said, 'Coach,'—he always called him coach around the team—'We're not playing St. Joe's and Jack McCloskey is Penn's coach, not Ramsay.' And Al bellowed, 'Oh, what the hell is the difference—Ramsay, McCloskey—they're all the same. They eat the same, they walk the same, they talk the same . . . Ramsay, McCloskey, they're no different!'"

Indeed, no coaches or players epitomized the warm camaraderie of the Big 5 family more than did Ramsay and McCloskey, who had become close friends back in the 1950s while traveling every weekend to Sunbury, where they were teammates in the Eastern League for five years. As young high school coaches, they shared dreams of moving up to the collegiate ranks. Their families socialized together and they became godparents of each other's children—McCloskey to Sharon Ramsay and Ramsay to Steve McCloskey.

"Severance used to call Ramsay and me the *Bobsey Twins*," said McCloskey. "He just laid it on: 'You guys are always together. What are you doing? Are you sleeping together?' We don't see each other much now at all but in the early days we were very, very close. We wouldn't do it for Big 5 games, but if my team was playing Princeton or something like that, we'd meet underneath the stands at halftime and I would say to Jack, 'What do you think?' And he might suggest something. And I would do the same thing when St. Joe's was playing. We helped each other that way."

"We became close friends and always hoped the other would succeed," recalled Ramsay. "Of course, we were also rival coaches. We never talked about the game we were going to play against each other, before or afterwards, really. It was kind of hard because here you were coaching against your friend. You wanted your team to win, but you didn't want him to lose. But we always tried to help each other out as much as we could. We went to clinics and would ride to games together. In the summer we would do basketball camps together."

Such warmth characterized the Big 5 like no other college basketball conference in the country. "It was like a sacred trust," said Jim Murray, the former Villanova sports information director. The coaches, for example, had an unwritten agreement never to schedule home games that conflicted with a Palestra doubleheader. They would never consider allowing a player to transfer from one Big 5 school to another and wouldn't share game films or scouting reports with outside teams preparing for a Big 5 opponent. "There was never any question of that," said McCloskey. "But if one of the teams was playing Detroit, for example, you'd give your Big 5 compatriot as much information as you knew. I remember passing on information to Villanova about a team we played, and La Salle's Dudey Moore helping me out when we were playing in the Holiday Festival."

One time before facing each other for the Middle Atlantic Conference championship that would decide an NCAA tournament berth, coaches Paul Westhead of La Salle and Jack McKinney of St. Joseph's flipped a coin to determine whose assistant would scout the game that was likely to determine the winner's post-season opponent. Westhead won the toss but McKinney won the game—and agreed to pay the Explorer assistant coach's scouting expenses.

Some of the family connections in the Big 5 are uncanny. Ramsay, the legendary St. Joseph's coach, played for Severance at Villanova for a year during World War II. Two of his Hawk players—Dan Dougherty and Harry Booth—later became assistant coaches on Villanova's NCAA Final Four teams. Villanova coach Jack Kraft played for Billy Ferguson at St. Joseph's. La Salle hired another former Hawk, Paul Westhead, as head coach. Jim Henry, La Salle's athletic director when the Big 5 was formed, played football at Villanova.

Villanova's Hank Siemiontkowski knocked St. Joseph's out of the 1971 NCAA tournament with 23 points and 11 rebounds in a first-round game at the Palestra. A few months later, the Wildcats' center found himself replacing Olympian Mike Bantom as St. Joseph's took a goodwill tour of Europe. "I'm a Hawk now," the future Big 5 Hall of Famer exclaimed as he joined his new teammates for games against Olympic squads from Russia, Czechoslovakia, and Italy.

Mike Mulquin, who played for Villanova, married Kathy Byrne, the sister-in-law of his teammate, John Pinone. Another Wildcat, Tom Ingelsby, married Rose Hastings, the sister of his teammate, Ed. La Salle's Joe Bryant married Pam Cox, the sister of Chubby, the former Villanova player. Jack Ramsay's daughter, Sharon, married former Hawk player Jim O'Brien, the head coach of the Boston Celtics. St. Joseph's athletic director Don DiJulia married Pat Lynam, the sister of Jim, a teammate under whom he had served as an assistant and whom he later hired as the Hawks' coach. Lynam's daughter, Kath, married James Jude Boyle, the second son of his St. Joseph's teammate, Jim Boyle, who succeeded him as Hawks' coach. Jim Boyle's daughter, Tracie, married one of his Hawk players, Brian Daly. Boyle's other daughter, Kelly Ann, married Mike Doyle, who served as his graduate assistant coach after playing at Philadelphia Textile for his buddy, Herb Magee. "Some of the best recruiting I've ever done," quipped Boyle. "A Boyle and a Doyle in the same year."

Bruce Moore captained the 1966–67 Pennsylvania quintet about 30 years before his son, Eric, played for the Quakers. Curt Fromal played in La Salle's backcourt, just as his son, Steve, did 30 years later. Mike Arizin played for a year at La Salle about 25 years after his dad, Paul, was named an All-America at Villanova. Dave Bednarik played basketball for La Salle about 20 years after his brother, Chuck, tore up the Franklin Field gridiron at Penn. Jim Lynam's brother, Kevin, played at La Salle. So did John Beck, whose brother, Ernie, was one of the all-time greats at Penn. Bob Mlkvy,

of Penn, is the younger brother of Bill, Temple's famed "Owl Without the Vowel"—a named coined by Associated Press sportswriter Ralph Bernstein in a *Sport* magazine article. Jack McCloskey's daughter Molly played basketball at St. Joseph's. The father of Penn's great shooter Bobby Morse was the head librarian at Temple University. Harry Carpenter, who played at La Salle, has spent his career working at Temple. La Salle guard Chip Greenberg's dad, Hank, was a member of La Salle's first NIT team in 1948. His uncle, Charley, played on La Salle's 1954 NCAA championship team, and his sister, Kelly, is the women's coach at Penn.

Tyrone Pitts, one of Penn all-time leading scorers, later served as one of Speedy Morris's assistants at La Salle. One of Pitts' coaches at Penn was Craig Littlepage, who played for Paul Westhead, the former Hawk player and Explorer coach, in high school and who later worked as Rollie Massimino's assistant at Villanova. Villanova's Fran O'Hanlon had some memorable one-on-one games against La Salle's Fran Dunphy, then became his assistant at Penn. Former St. Joseph's coach John Griffin played for La Salle's Speedy Morris as a kid in the CYO and later at Philadelphia's Roman Catholic High School. After he left La Salle, Dudey Moore became Jack Kraft's top scout at Villanova. Also helping Kraft while he was in Villanova's law school was Bob McAteer, who had been one of Dudey's guards with the Explorers. Even the Big 5 mascots got into the act. Joe Cassidy jumped out of his St. Joseph's Hawk costume into college coaching as an assistant to former La Salle player Eddie Burke when he coached at Drexel. Phil Martelli, the current St. Joseph's coach, played for Burke in high school at Philadelphia's St. Joseph's Prep.

Former Temple coach Don Casey played basketball at Camden Catholic High School for Charles McClone, who preceded Ken Loeffler as coach at La Salle. When Casey got the job at Bishop Eustace, he hired one of his old high school high teammates, Ralph Bantivoglio, the former La Salle guard, as his assistant coach for a year. Casey's best player at Eustace was Billy Melchionni, the future Villanova and NBA star. When Casey left Temple, Paul Westhead, his coaching rival at La Salle, brought him into the NBA as an assistant at Chicago. Rollie Massimino was Chuck Daly's assistant at Penn before he went to Villanova. Jack McCloskey brought Daly and Dick Harter, his only full-time assistant at Penn, into the NBA with Detroit. He also hired Penn's Bob Weinhauer at Minnesota. Harter, who coached the Charlotte Hornets, worked as Jack Ramsay's assistant with the Indiana Pacers, then was hired by Jim O'Brien, Ramsay's son-in-law and coach of the Boston Celtics. Penn's Corky Calhoun played for Ramsay's NBA championship team at Portland. Michael Brooks, the 1980 College Player of the Year at La Salle, played for Lynam in the NBA at San

Diego. Temple's Terence Stansbury played on a team in France with Brooks, his boyhood idol, for two years, and coached the former La Salle All-America there a third season. Tony DiLeo, the former La Salle guard, coached Bryan Warrick and Rodney Blake of St. Joseph's in Cologne when he was Germany's Coach of the Year in 1987. The first coach that Temple's Ollie Johnson had in the NBA in Kansas City was Penn's McCloskey. Matt Guokas Jr., the former Hawk, was one of his teammates.

"When you go back far enough, you find out that these coaches have known each other forever," said John Nash, the Big 5's former executive director. "They criss-cross, they're intertwined. We see it even in the NBA." In 1999–2000, when Nash was general manager of the New Jersey Nets, his head coach was Temple's Casey. Don's top assistant was former Hawk Lynam, who had once hired Casey as *his* assistant in San Diego. The team's director of scouting was former Penn guard Ed Stafanski, who had been Nash's first student assistant when he took over as director of the Big 5. One of New Jersey's top players was Kerry Kittles of Villanova. And handling the broadcasts for the NBA team was Bill Raftery, who played for La Salle. The same goes with the Big 5 players. In 1970–71, for example, the Philadelphia 76ers' roster included Cliff Anderson and Matt Guokas of St. Joseph's, as well as Wali Jones and Jim Washington of Villanova.

In the late 1950s and early 1960s, dozens of Big 5 players spent their summers playing basketball at the South Jersey shore. Many of them, including Hawk teammates Westhead, Lynam, Boyle, Bob McNeill, and Joe Gallo, worked as lifeguards in North Wildwood. Their captain was Richie Phillips, the Villanova football player who later became head of Major League Baseball's umpires' union. Their first lieutenant was Bob McAteer, the La Salle guard. "Even though there was an intense Big 5 rivalry, it didn't matter because you were often a stand partner with a guy from another school," recalled Westhead. "Then everything changed when it became September and October."

La Salle's Joe Heyer spent a summer working with McNeill at an all-night food drive-in, then played basketball during the day at Pop Kenney's spacious home in Wildwood. "Every college player you could think of was there," he recalled. Even players like Niagara's Jim Maloney, who had gone away to school, were regulars. La Salle's Tom Gola and Villanova's Paul Arizin still stopped in occasionally. "Mr. Kenney was an old man by that time," said Heyer. "He was a casket maker who had made his money in the flu epidemic of 1918. We played in his driveway where he had baskets attached to two trees at each end. He sat at half-court in a big high chair

and kept score. It was twenty points a game and you had to win by four. Lose, you were out and five more guys would take your place." Bucky Harris, who later coached for many years at Philadelphia Textile, lived across the street. "Bucky was a tough guy right out of the Marines and you wanted him on your side," said Heyer. "You could see him come out of his doorway. We would always wait when we were picking teams and as soon as we saw Bucky come out that door, we'd yell, 'He's on our team!'"

McAteer and Temple guard Bruce Drysdale waged some furious one-on-one battles in Big 5 games, then worked together during the summer in a hotel in Wildwood Crest owned by Curt Simmons, the Phillies pitcher, and Pete Retzlaff, the Philadelphia Eagles tight end. Once after scoring 30 points to beat the Explorers, Drysale spent the night in the La Salle dorms with McAteer, who had unsuccessfully defended him a few hours earlier. "It was fun hanging out, playing chess, and goofing around" recalled Drysdale, now a Philadelphia dentist. "It was just a great thing to have that camaraderie." Onc spring when Drysdale played in a varsity golf match against La Salle, McAteer *caddied* for him.

When Drysdale was younger, one of his first coaches at the Shelmire Playground in Northeast Philadelphia

▲ **M**att Guokas Jr. played for St. Joseph's, as did his father, Matt Sr., and his son, Matt III. *(St. Joseph's University)*

at La Salle and head coach at Pennsylvania, where his boss is athletic director Steve Bilsky. Dunphy and Bilsky had gone head-to-head during classic Big 5 matchups between the Quakers and Explorers in the late 1960s.

Another typical Philadelphia/Big 5 kind of guy is La Salle's former coach Speedy Morris, who has lived all his life in the same Manayunk neighborhood and who coached two of Ramsay's sons at Immaculate Heart of Mary Parish in Roxborough. "I remember Jack Ramsay watching our CYO games in the afternoon and then seeing him coaching that night at the Palestra," said Morris. "That was like seeing God twice in the same day." Speedy didn't realize how close

was Matt Guokas Sr., who had played for St. Joseph's and the old Philadelphia Warriors. "He used to take me and his son, Matty, to see NBA doubleheaders at Convention Hall," said Drysdale. "Then we'd walk across the street to catch another doubleheader at the Palestra. Mr. Guokas was broadcasting the games and at halftime he would have them point the camera at me to tell my dad at home that I was okay."

Probably no one epitomizes the Big 5 family more than Dan Dougherty. In addition to playing for Ramsay at St. Joe's, Dougherty served as an assistant at Villanova to Jack Kraft and coached players like La Salle's Dunphy, Penn's Jerome Allen, and St. Joseph's Bruiser Flint in high school. Dougherty, who also played against Villanova in 1956 in the first Big 5 game in history, grew up in the Olney section of Philadelphia in a row house next door to Ed Givnish, who played for La Salle. One time when the Hawks and Explorers met at the Palestra, Dougherty checked Givnish under the basket. Givnish went flying in the air and broke his shoulder. Directly across the street from Dougherty lived La Salle's Joe Heyer. Dunphy, who was Heyer's only recruit during his two-year coaching stint at La Salle, played for Dougherty at Malvern Prep and later spent a year as Dan's assistant coach at Army. That was before he became an assistant

Big 5 people were until he started coaching at Roman Catholic High School. "I came up to visit Paul Westhead at La Salle one time on the day of the Temple game," he recalled. "His secretary told me that Paul was downstairs playing squash with Don Casey. They were going to be killing each other that night at the Palestra and here they were, two really good friends playing a game of squash."

The relationship of the coaches was absolutely unbelievable," said Ralph Bernstein, who covered sports in Philadelphia for the AP for 50 years. "They respected each other and went out of their way to help each other. I think that, more than anything, helped to keep the Big 5 going for so long."

"We were like a family," said Temple's Harry Litwack shortly before his death in 1999. "All the coaches became very close to each other. We would take personal pride in beating each other and we'd want to kill the other's team during the game. But afterwards we would go out to dinner, go to the races, have get-togethers with our wives, and just be good friends."For some coaches, however, it took a little longer to crack the Big 5 family circle. "I felt as an outsider for a long, long, time," recalled Chuck Daly, who came to Penn from Boston College in 1971. "Not because of the coaches—Jack Kraft, Harry Litwack, and Jack McKinney couldn't have been nicer. This was influenced by the Catholic school mentality from high schools on up. There was a barrier there. If you went to recruit at a Catholic school, you were fourth in line. But in time, as the coaching changed—when Westhead, Casey, and Rollie came in—I thought that in our own way we protected each other as much as we could."

No matter what happened in the Big 5 games at the Palestra, you could be sure that the friendships would almost certainly be rekindled at the weekly Philadelphia Basketball Writers' luncheons the following Thursday.

"You really looked forward to those lunches," recalled Penn's McCloskey. "Al Severance was as funny as the devil and there was tremendous mutual respect with people like Harry Litwack, Dudey Moore, Jack Ramsay, and myself. You might be playing one of them that night and the jokes would be flying around but there was no animosity."

La Salle's Dudey Moore, who had been a coaching legend a few years earlier at Duquesne, found the weekly gatherings to be a little bit of an adjustment, however. "Out in Pittsburgh, I was the big shot at the luncheons," he once told sportswriter Bob Vetrone. "Here I'm the last paragraph."

Temple's Casey, who loved to "mix and mingle," remembers the time he jumped all over his buddy Paul Westhead after the La Salle coach, a Shakespearean scholar, announced at one of the luncheons, "Like an almond tree that bears its fruit in silence, I'm not going to talk today."

"I'd get up to speak and Casey would just kill me," recalled Westhead. "He'd rip me apart: *'Oh we got old Hamlet over here with that knife of his, To be or not to be.'* Casey would say, 'Paul, don't you understand, nobody knows what the hell you're talking about?'"

"I think some of the coaches—not me, of course—prepared for those luncheons as much as for the games," said former Hawk coach

Jack McKinney, laughing. "I remember Ramsay, McCloskey, and Kraft just picking on Harry Litwack every time he got up to say something. They always had some wisecrack to say about Harry, but he'd just sit there chomping on his cigar. You always just had to say something funny to loosen things up. They were fun times. The warm feelings the coaches had for each other were prevalent throughout the Big 5. That's what made it so special."

"One time in the early 1970s we were playing in a tournament down South and Chuck Daly was an assistant at Duke," recalled Villanova's Kraft. "I happened to be sitting next to Chuck at a banquet." This, of course, was before Daly got the Penn job. "Chuck said to me, 'How do you guys do it? How can you be so friendly and talk to each other? I wouldn't even think about sitting next to Dean Smith of North Carolina, or talking to anyone else in the ACC. We just don't do that down here.' Frank McGuire of South Carolina always marveled about the same thing and said it's really unique that we got along so well together. Coaches down there were always at each other's throats."

"It was really fun listening to the coaches needling each other and throwing barbs at each other," said sportscaster Al Meltzer, who is now a host on Philadelphia's Comcast SportsNet. "One thing would

▶ **B**ig 5 Hall of Famers (from left): sportswriter Bob Vetrone, La Salle's Alonzo Lewis, and sportscaster Al Meltzer. *(La Salle University)*

lead to another but it was done in a really nice way. I used to think to myself, 'God, this is wonderful! Can you imagine all those ACC coaches getting together down in Carolina each Thursday? No way.'"

"Meltzer used to tell me that his week was ruined if he missed a luncheon," recalled Temple's longtime sports publicist Al Shrier. "It was like show time. I remember one week the Big 5 coaches all agreed secretly among themselves that they would imitate another coach. It was hysterical, one of the best luncheons we ever had."

Early in the 1990s, however, the weekly luncheons—at one time eagerly anticipated by coaches and players—became monthly affairs. Then they were held just a couple of times a year, and gradually they disappeared completely from the basketball calendar. So did the traditional pre-season get-togethers of coaches, players, administrators, student leaders, and law enforcement officials. They featured people like Philadelphia Police Commissioner Thomas J. Gibbons, who discussed "Gambling, Riots, Hooliganism Control and Prevention" at the very first meeting on Penn's campus in November 1955. Penn served as host for about a dozen years. After that each school took turns as host.

"I always thought it was a great idea," said Kraft. "You had a chance to meet the players and administrators from the other schools and the law enforcement and security people let you know what was going on about gambling. They described how most gamblers would approach you, and that's something I didn't have any idea about."

"The security aspect was important," said McCloskey. "Players learned how they should tell their coach if they were approached by gamblers or anybody suspicious. It's something that should be done by every school in America. We do it in the NBA."

"The Big 5 was the fabric of the culture of Philadelphia, especially during the magical times of the 1950s and '60s," said DiJulia, who experienced the phenomenon as a player, coach, athletic director, and commissioner of the East Coast and Metro Atlantic conferences. "Philadelphia was a city of neighborhoods and the culture at the time was the spirited rivalry among friends who could relate to their teams. It was like Saturday morning on the playgrounds."

"To this day I can walk down the street in Philadelphia and say hello to people who recognize me from my days at Penn," said Joe Sturgis, who later practiced law in Center City for more than 35 years. "One time I made a presentation to the state legislature in Harrisburg and the speaker of the house stopped the program to introduce me as a member of the Big 5 Hall of Fame. I've had people in Pittsburgh and as far away as Florida asking about Penn or the Big 5."

"It was almost like the intermarriage of the royal family," recalled Meltzer, the only sportscaster in the Big 5 Hall of Fame. "You even got to know the basketball referees because they all came from around the tri-state area." Some of them like Villanova's Jim Huggard and Temple's John Koskinen had played in the Big 5. Others like Duke Maronic and Alex Wojciechowicz had strong local connections. Both played football for the Philadelphia Eagles. John Stevens was a well-known American League baseball umpire, Steve Honzo regularly worked the big national games, and referees like Len Toff and Dan Smeddy were familiar faces in Philadelphia's Catholic League.

A few years ago, former La Salle athletic director Bill Bradshaw bumped into Henry "Hank" Nichols, the supervisor of college basketball officials, during a coaching clinic at the Final Four. "A couple of referees saw Henry and I talking," recalled Bradshaw. "We were having a serious, passionate conversation. We were really animated and I was saying, 'No, that's not right, Henry!' And he said, 'Bill, I'm telling you!' One of the referees said, 'What are you guys talking about . . . the block/charge? Are you talking about the hand-check rule?' I said, 'No, Henry's a Villanova grad and he can't believe that only three Villanova guys made the all-time Big 5 team in the *Philadelphia Daily News* poll. He can't understand how John Pinone didn't make it when four La Salle guys got in.' They were certain that I was arguing about a call that some referee made and here is Henry telling me, 'Bill, you can't tell me that John Pinone doesn't belong on that team.' And we stopped ourselves and looked at each other and I said, 'Isn't it just unbelievable what a grip the Big 5 has on both of us?' I said, 'I didn't even go to school when you did, Henry. You were there with Wali Jones and I remember Johnny Jones.'"

Bradshaw and Nichols were discussing the 40th anniversary Big 5 team that appeared in the *Philadelphia Daily News* in 1995 after the newspaper published a ballot for ten days listing twelve candidates from each school. Some 4,500 fans responded. "It was really the first time we used the newspaper as a ballot," said Mike Rathet, the *Daily News* sports editor at the time who ran with the idea after it was proposed by Dan Baker, the executive director of the Big 5. "I don't know that the Big 5 sells a lot of newspapers, but everybody in the city seems to have an attachment one way or another. It worked out well for us." The team included La Salle's Larry Cannon, Ken Durrett, Michael Brooks, and Lionel Simmons; Penn's Corky Calhoun; Temple's Guy Rodgers and Mark Macon; Cliff Anderson of St. Joseph's, and Villanova's Wali Jones and Howard Porter.

The *Daily News* team, of course, didn't include some of the legendary names that played *before* the Big 5 was

▲ Five outstanding players who performed before the Big 5 was formalized were inducted into the Big 5 Hall of Fame in 2000. They are (from left): Villanova's Paul Arizin, Temple's Bill Mlkvy, Penn's Ernie Beck, La Salle's Tom Gola, and St. Joseph's George Senesky. *(Big 5—Ed Mahan)*

formally organized. Five of them were inducted into the Big 5 Hall of Fame as old timers, including Tom Gola, who had previously been enshrined as coach of the great 1968–69 La Salle team. Paul Arizin was Villanova's inductee. *The Sporting News* Player of the Year in 1950 and the Wildcats' first 1,000-point scorer, Arizin's 85 points against the Naval Air Material Center in 1959 is the highest single game performance in Big 5 history. Penn's selectee was Ernie Beck, the Quakers' leading career scorer and rebounder, who still held eight other school records. His best single game was 47 points against Duke in 1952. From Temple came All-America Bill Mlkvy, who set the Owls' all-time scoring record with 73 points against Wilkes College in 1951. He still holds school single-season marks for field goals and rebounds.

St. Joseph's was represented by George Senesky, a two-time All-America and the Helms Foundation National Player of the Year in 1943. He led the nation in scoring as a senior with 515 points and went on to establish himself as a great *defensive* player for eight years in the NBA. Mlkvy played in 31 games for the Philadelphia Warriors in 1952–53 while attending Temple University Dental School. Arizin, Beck, and Gola were teammates on the Warriors' NBA championship team that was coached by Senesky in 1955–56.

Arizin, the Villanova All-America who later was elected to the Naismith Basketball Hall of Fame after a brilliant NBA career with the old Philadelphia Warriors, actually convinced Frank Blatcher, his neighbor in South Philadelphia, to go to *La Salle*. Blatcher had won a couple of championships in the Navy and had been recruited by Josh Cody to play for Temple "One day, Paul and I were playing one-on-one," recalled Blatcher. "He asked me where I was going to school and I told him I was all set to go to Temple." "Did you ever think about La Salle?" Arizin asked. "There's this young kid up

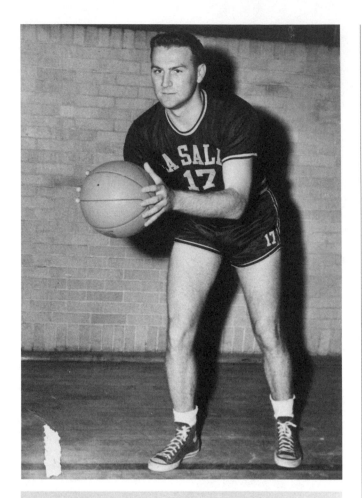

▲ Frank Blatcher was convinced to attend La Salle by former Villanova All-America Paul Arizin. *(La Salle University)*

there who's a helluva player. His name is Tom Gola and I think that you'd really blend very well with him." As they say, the rest is history. Blatcher and teammate Charley Singley were the top scorers when La Salle beat Bradley for the 1953–54 NCAA title.

Long after he left the Big 5, Digger Phelps remained one of its biggest boosters when he got the head coaching job at Notre Dame. Phelps had been Harter's assistant at Penn and always made sure to bring the Fighting Irish into the Palestra once a year to play La Salle or Villanova. Phelps also stuck up for his Big 5 brethren, as La Salle's athletic director Jack Conboy well remembers. In 1977, Conboy was a member of the NCAA Basketball Tournament committee and was supervising Eastern Regionals games played at the University of Maryland. Notre Dame was there, and so was Kentucky. "We had a meeting with the coaches about television," said Conboy. "The TV people had a new innovation that year. They wanted to introduce individual players from one team, then another, and

have them shake hands at mid-court. Joe B. Hall, Kentucky's coach, refused to do it. 'Well then don't bother bringing your team out on the floor because I'm going to forfeit the game,' I told him. 'You can't do that,' Hall said. Digger then stepped in. 'Hey, I know this guy from Philly. If he tells you he's going to punch you out, he'll punch you out!' Hall backed off and the next day the players went out and shook hands. I said, 'Thank you, Digger,' and he replied, 'What the hell, I knew you weren't going to let him get away with it.'"

Considering the heat and passion generated by the city series games, it's quite amazing that players rarely lost their tempers or fought with each other on the court. "In the years I was there, I never remember a fight among Big 5 teams," said Ramsay.

But there were a few major skirmishes between the mascots. The most memorable occurred between the La Salle *Explorer* and St. Joseph's *Hawk* at halftime of a Drexel–Marist game at the Palestra. The brawl was witnessed by more than a dozen pro scouts—including Jerry Krause of the Chicago Bulls—who were on hand to see players like Rick Smits of Marist, Tim Legler and Lionel Simmons of La Salle, and Rodney Blake of St. Joseph's. But no one at home saw it because Philadelphia's Prism-TV had cut away from its telecast during halftime. "All three major networks called wanting to know if we had film of the fight," said Vetrone, who was handling Big 5 publicity at the time. "We told them, 'No, but we have some great *game* footage.'"

Occasionally the coaches had their differences, but matters were usually resolved later that night over a few brews at Cavanaugh's on Market Street or at the writers' luncheon the following Thursday. Most of them involved—surprisingly—Pennsylvania and Kraft's Villanova teams. One time Penn slowed the game down before losing to the highly-favored Wildcats. "I shook Jack's hand afterwards and complimented him on his kids' composure," recalled McCloskey. He said, 'I don't think you should have played like that' and walked away. I thought about it for a while, then went right into the Villanova locker room and yelled, 'IF YOU WANT THE DAMN BALL, GO OUT AND GET IT!' Afterwards we became good friends. It was just a moment of frustration on both parts."

In 1968, Harter accused Kraft of running up the score after the Wildcats won 75–46, a charge that the Villanova coach vehemently denies. "I can honestly say that I've never run up the score on anybody in my life," Kraft said later. The following year, the Quakers held the ball and pulled off a big upset, 32–30, when Bilsky hit a long jumper at the final buzzer. "We let them dictate the tempo of the game which turned out to be a mistake because they took us out of our rhythm," recalled Kraft. Afterwards, he told Harter, "Gee, that's a helluva way to play a basketball game," and the Penn coach replied, as Kraft remembers it, "It's my team and I can do what I want." "We got together later that week at the luncheon and I said, 'Look, I wasn't demeaning your coaching. It's too silly to get involved with anything like that. So let's just forget it and get back to our normal playing.'" That truce lasted until 1971, when Villanova shocked the previously unbeaten Quakers 90–47 in the NCAA Tournament.

Even the freshman games between Big 5 schools were highly competitive affairs before the NCAA declared first-year students eligible for varsity play in 1973. "Those freshman games," said Harter, "were as important to me as any games I've ever been involved in. Ever! They were huge. God they were big. They were so important to me." Harter recalled his early days at Penn when McKinney was coaching at St. James and Casey was building his program at Bishop Eustace. "Jack and Don came up with their high school teams and beat our freshman team before we started getting players," he said. "They were better than we were."

Bill Cosby, the famous comedian, played a few Big 5 freshmen basketball games for Temple in 1960–61. "We started the season with ten players, but five had failed off the team at mid-term," recalled Skip Wilson, the Owls' freshman coach at the time. "We were all set to go to West Point with five players, a trainer, and myself. I saw Cos and I said, 'Come on out for the team,' and he makes the trip to West Point. Then we played against Delaware. Bill played maybe five or six games."

One of those games was against Villanova with Cosby drawing the unenviable task of guarding Wali Jones, who would go on to have a great career in the Big 5 and NBA. Today he handles community relations for the Miami Heat. A few years ago Cosby brought some Philadelphia Legends basketball players down to Florida to help out with Wali's "Stay in School" program. "We had some good times talking about that," Jones recalled. "Bill talked about guarding me and told the kids how fast I was. He said I just went by him."

Although Big 5 rivalries sometimes got quite bitter— especially some of Villanova's games with St. Joseph's and Penn—Villanova's Howard Porter actually found himself coming to the aid of his beleaguered foes a couple of times. The first incident happened in 1970 when the Hawks and Wildcats were playing in a tournament at the University of Kansas. "We had played Houston in the first game," recalled Villanova's Kraft. "We got dressed, came up, and were sitting in the stands right behind the St. Joe's rooting section. Their drummer was drumming

▲ Villanova's Howard Porter (left) and La Salle's Ken Durrett get together at the Wildcats' post-season basketball banquet after Durrett was honored as Villanova's Most Valuable Opponent. *(Urban Archives, Temple University, Philadelphia, Pennsylvania)*

furiously as usual but the Kansas fans had never experienced anything like that. Some of their people became very agitated and a few of them came right up to him and said, 'Hey, stop beating that drum!' Howard Porter came down to the kid and says, 'Sam, you just go ahead and keep beating that drum. Don't worry. We're right here to help you.' Not that Howard would have been able to do anything with all those Kansas fans, but that shows how Big 5 people stand up for each other."

It happened again at the end of the season after Villanova had shocked Penn in the NCAA Eastern Regionals. As luck would have it, both teams returned to Philadelphia on the same plane. When the players were waiting in the baggage-claim area of Philadelphia International Airport, a teenager in a Villanova T-shirt began taunting Penn's Corky Calhoun. Porter immediately rushed over and chased the kid off.

"I remember going to dinners with the coaches," said Nash. "These guys were very competitive and yet they really enjoyed each other. Seldom did it deteriorate into a battle between them—maybe occasionally for short periods." At one of their dinners, Temple's Casey got into a heated argument with Massimino. "It was maybe my first year with the Big 5," recalled Nash. "While they were having their animated discussion, Rollie's assistant Mike Fratello walks in. In those days, Fratello, who was a pretty fiesty guy, himself, did a lot of driving for Rollie and had come to pick him up. After a few minutes, Mike tried to enter the fray and said something to Casey. I remember Casey turning and pointing his finger at him and saying, 'When I need to hear from the chauffeur, I'll call on you!'" Years, later, of course, both Casey and Fratello ended up coaching in the NBA.

Dick Weiss, the sportswriter, remembers Casey as the "Peacemaker," who started the annual tradition of hosting other Big 5 coaches and their wives at their homes for dinner or taking them out after the season. "Back in the '70s when all this in-fighting was going on in the Big 5, he was the guy who was always making phone calls trying to hold it together. He was the guy who would be calling Rollie. He'd be the guy calling St. Joe's. He'd be the guy always trying to patch up the problems because he understood that the Big 5 was bigger than any one team, any player, or any coach. He grew up with the Big 5."

"Everybody likes Don Casey," said Ramsay. "He doesn't have an enemy in the world. I remember he used to come and watch us practice at St. Joe's when he was coaching at Bishop Eustace. I got to know him well and would go to his summer day camp for high school kids, which he operated on a veritable shoestring. He would say, 'Just come over and talk to the kids a little bit. Give them fifteen minutes.' You'd end up being out on the floor for an hour and a half. He'd be sitting over there on the sideline and you would look over at him and he'd nod as if to say, 'You're doing good!' Then he would say, 'Let's have a bite to eat.' I'd say, 'Where are we going?' and he'd reply, 'Right here! Dwynne's getting it ready.' And you'd go into the cafeteria and his poor wife would be cooking hot dogs. The kids would be lined up, the perspiration running down her face. Then after lunch he'd say, 'Why don't you stick around? Maybe you could talk to the kids one more time.' So before you knew it you spent the whole day there. And then when it was over he'd say, 'I have your check.' It would be for $25 or something like that."

McCloskey also got to know Casey when the young Bishop Eustace coach asked to attend Penn's practice sessions. "He would be taking notes about things we tried to do," recalled McCloskey, chuckling at the memory. "He would ask about this offensive set or some defensive drill. Then one day he calls me and said, 'You've got to come over and see my team play.' So as I'm walking in to Eustace, one of his kids is shooting and said to me, 'Coach McCloskey, coach Casey told me that you're using all our drills.'"

McCloskey also remembers Casey's summer camps. "One day he called me and said, 'We ought to get together.' It was probably the first summer basketball day camp ever in the area. Casey thought it would be a good idea if he would keep the books and I would do a lot of the teaching. One day, we sat down and I said, 'Case, let's go over the books and see how many people we're getting and how we're doing financially.' In those days we charged something like $25 for the whole week. Now it's $25 a minute. We were bringing in college guys to lecture and paying them something like a hundred dollars. Now they get five thousand. But anyway, I go over the books and say,' Case, it says here that some kid's coming in for ten dollars.' 'Oh yeah,' he said. 'That's my butcher's kid.' And then there was his tailor's kid who was paying $15. I said, 'Case, how many guys do we have like this?' And he said, 'Oh, there's a few more.' I said, 'Hell, we're losing money!' Even today, every time Casey sees me he talks about the camp and says, 'I still owe you a little bit of money.'"

"I don't know what I would have done without the help of the McCloskeys, the Ramsays, the Litwacks, the Harters, and the McKinneys," said Casey, who got his big collegiate break when Litwack hired him as an assistant at Temple. "I just thought it was so tremendous of those guys to take the time to expose me to their coaching philosophies, to allow me to know the game, and to get into a position where I am today in the NBA. I don't know if I was capable of doing anything else. I think they probably would do it for anyone, but they picked up my eagerness. They thought maybe I had ability and was interested enough so they shared their time."

Members of the Big 5 family extended themselves in many ways off the court as well. One year Temple was in Seattle for the NCAA tournament and John Chaney learned that the father-in-law of Speedy Morris had passed away. "So John sent Speedy a Mailgram, then called him at La Salle," recalled Bob Vetrone, who was working in the Big 5 office. "He said, 'I want to make sure that you're all right and Mimi is okay,' and all that stuff. Speedy couldn't get him off the phone for fifteen minutes. 'John, you've got to get off and get your team ready for Michigan,' the La Salle coach told him. Chaney was so concerned about the well-being of Speedy's family. Not a whole lot of people would have been thinking about anything except Michigan in that situation."

Sometimes, though, the Big 5 family got, perhaps, a little too cozy. Like the time nationally-ranked Princeton came into Villanova's old Fieldhouse to play the Wildcats the year that Bill Bradley's Tigers went to the NCAA Final Four. "Jack Kraft was coaching against

Butch Van Breda Kolff and my position was way up on a running track above the floor," recalled Les Keiter, who was broadcasting the game. "I had to look through a couple of posts down to the scorer's table directly below me. To my right was Princeton's bench and to the left was the home team. In the final minutes of the game with the score tied, Princeton called a time out. When Bradley was playing, he was like a coach on the floor. Now he's huddling with the team and Van Breda Kolff gets up from his bench and walks right in front of the scorer's table. He's standing in front of Kraft yelling something out at his team. Lou Bonder was the referee and was bent over the scorer's table going over some detail. Remember, I'm on the air broadcasting. I turned my voice away from the mike and leaned over, screaming 'Lou, Lou,' and he looks up at me and I'm pointing to Van Breda Kolff. I said, 'He can't be there.' I put my hands together and said, 'That's a technical foul. Call a technical on him. He has no right to be on the Villanova side and out on the floor.' The next thing you know, Bonder looks up, nods to me, walks out, blows his whistle, and signals *technical foul* against Van Breda Kolff.

"Well Van Breda Kolff became enraged. And he was a big, burly, aggressive kind of a guy. I knew him only casually. And he looks up at me and he's got his fists clenched like, 'I'll punch you in the nose for that!' And he's yelling and screaming at Lou Bonder: 'How can you let this announcer call a technical?' And of course the game was riding on it. The technical foul was the decisive point." Bill Melchionni made it and Villanova won. "Now it's a month or so later and I was broadcasting one of the games at the NCAA Eastern Regionals in Blacksburg, Virginia. I walked in to a pre-game reception with a couple of writers from Philadelphia. There's a cluster of people talking and drinking in a room full of people and I hear this loud voice as I'm walking in. It's Van Breda Kolff saying, 'And can you believe this damn announcer calls a technical foul from his position way up. And Bonder goes along and calls the *T* and I lose the game. If I ever see that sportscaster I'm going to give him a fist full of knuckles.' So I walked over to him and I said, 'Butch, do you want to give me that bunch of knuckles? I'm Les Keiter.' And he turned to me and said, 'How could you do such a thing?' berating me in front of everybody. Later that year I was the MC of the Philadelphia Basketball Writers' banquet when we honored Bradley and Van Breda Kolff. I repeated this whole litany from the podium and Van Breda Kolff came up and was very warm and said, 'Oh, that was one of those things' and so forth. But I'll never forget that incident."

The Big 5 meetings were always "very businesslike, but sociable," according to Ramsay, who also served as St. Joseph's athletic director for a few years. "They were very high level kinds of gatherings focusing on good competition and good sportsmanship. The athletic directors were primarily interested in having the Big 5 continue on a very productive basis. I don't ever

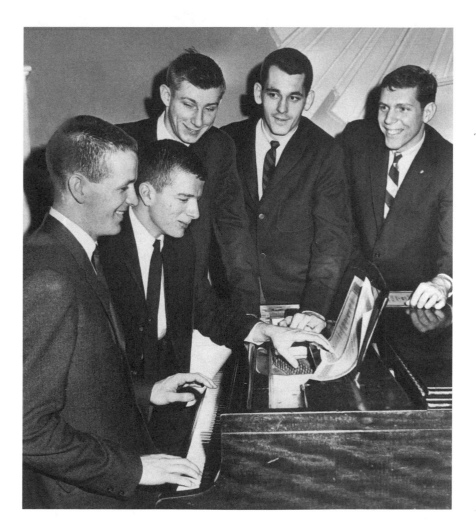

◄ The Philadelphia Basketball Writers honored an "Unsung Hero" from each Big 5 school at the end of every season. The 1963–64 group included (from left) Joe Cunnane of La Salle, Bill Melchionni of Villanova, Bob Harrington of Temple, Jim Boyle of St. Joseph's, and Bruce Moore of Penn. *(Urban Archives, Temple University, Philadelphia, Pennsylvania)*

recall any serious disruptions. Once I remember Ernie Casale having a problem with someone—I don't remember who—and walking out of a meeting. But it was over quickly."

"I'll never forget my first Big 5 meeting," said McKinney. "I was only twenty-nine or thirty at the time. I came walking in and this AD came up to me and said, 'Hey Jack, how are you?' It was La Salle's Jim Henry and he said, 'Don't let these guys rattle you or upset you. You just stay near me and ask me if you're not sure what to do. But just follow my lead today. And after that, just go on and take over if you want to.' He was my guiding light at my first meeting and after that I felt comfortable because they were terrific people. There were a lot of arguments—little things like the 7 o'clock and 9 o'clock starting times—but the majority prevailed. Just great motives, great goals, great people."

"You had Jerry Ford, a rather quiet, Ivy-League type," recalled Villanova's Art Mahan. "Jack Ramsay was a wonderful fellow but very tense, all business. Jim Henry was the same. He wasn't a barrel of laughs but a good fellow with honesty and integrity. Then you had Ernie Casale. He was like the Pied Piper or whatever. So I was the only one there who had a little sense of humor. But I couldn't tell jokes to myself. We used to rib Ernie at the meetings. You could always play some kind of joke on him and he wouldn't get it." Casale and Mahan had been longtime adversaries from their days as baseball coaches and Mahan had been unsuccessfully trying to convince Casale to schedule a football game between the two schools. "Ernie didn't like Yo Yo," said Mahan. "One time he complained about seeing Yo Yo on television shooting baskets. Jerry Ford said, 'The guy is harmless, really. What do you think, Art?' And I said, 'I think the Big 5 needs characters like that. They need a Yo Yo! They need an Ernie Casale!' And everyone laughed, then Ernie said, ' . . . What . . . ?' Nobody would explain it to him and I was afraid to explain it to him. I didn't want to get punched in the nose."

"Ernie Casale was like a parliamentarian," recalled Conboy, who succeeded Jim Henry at La Salle. "He would say, 'Now we can't do it this way because . . . ' But he always had a real valid reason. We did have our problems and we would get hassles, but they were always resolved and there would be no hard feelings by the time we left. You might get a little peeved, but everybody shook hands."

"Ernie was the best," said St. Joseph's DiJulia. "When La Salle's Bill Bradshaw and I were the new kids on the block, he invited us to his golf course and became our mentor. We were new, young, and dumb and sometimes would think, *'oh, no, that's crazy,'* but later we would appreciate that he had so much experience. He was focused and opinionated, but the way he looked at things made sense. But Ernie's way was the *only* way and I say that with respect."

"Ernie Casale was like a father to me," recalled Baker. "He took me under his wing. He would scold you but he was as honest as the day is long. He loved Temple, of course, and would always do what was best for the Owls but he loved the Big 5."

Baker is credited with the almost-insurmountable task of single-handedly keeping the Big 5 family together when he served as its executive director from 1981 to 1996. "My memories go back much further," recalled Baker. "I remember following Rodgers and Lear at Temple in the 1950s. As a student at Audubon High School in the 1960s, I arranged bus trips from New Jersey to 13th and Filbert in Philadelphia. Then we would walk or take public transportation to the Palestra for Big 5 games." Baker began his professional associa-

▲ **D**an Baker served as executive director of the Big 5 from 1981 to 1996. *(Dan Baker)*

tion in 1977, when he started producing Big 5 radio broadcasts. That venture continued until 1998, shortly after he resigned his Big 5 position and joined Drexel University's athletic department. Baker, who estimates that he did play-by-play on more than a thousand high school and college games, always wanted to be a sportscaster. He started out broadcasting West Philadelphia High School's Public League games when Gene Banks was a senior and recalled walking up and down 52nd Street soliciting advertising from the local merchants and "selling time for fifty dollars here and a hundred dollars there." Baker, who was teaching in the Philadelphia School District at the time, also coached the sixth grade basketball team at Landreth Elementary School, where Banks, later a Duke All-America, had been his top player. Today he is also the public address announcer for the Philadelphia Phillies and Eagles.

"The meetings weren't too bad, but philosophically the institutions started going in different directions," said Nash, who preceded Baker as executive director of the Big 5. Nash was highly regarded as a diplomat and dealmaker during his six-year tenure—traits that served him well later when he became a general manager in the NBA with the Philadelphia 76ers, Washington Bullets, and New Jersey Nets. Probably the only person to wear both NBA and NHL championship rings, Nash was ticket manager for the Philadelphia Flyers during their Stanley Cup years in the 1960s and GM of the 76ers when they took the NBA title in 1983. He also managed advertising and promotion for the Atlantic City Race Course in the late 1970s.

"Scheduling was the biggest difficulty," Nash recalled. "Often you came to the point where you had a terrific game available or you were trying to finish out the Big 5 schedule. Temple, for example, might be scheduled to play Villanova on January 19th and all of a sudden we find out that Ralph Sampson and Virginia are available. *Will Villanova move the game? All right, let's look at some dates. We could play this game on February 12th but Villanova has a game on the 11th and can't play back-to-back.* There were always those kinds of difficult decisions. Everybody was so competitive that nobody wanted to give an inch. I understood that because I wasn't a commissioner. I was

▲ John Nash was the first executive director of the Big 5 and served in that capacity for six years, until 1981. *(Urban Archives, Temple University, Philadelphia, Pennsylvania)*

▶ St. Joseph's University athletic director Don DiJulia, who also played for the Hawks, began his association with the Big 5 in 1964. *(St. Joseph's University)*

just a coordinator and didn't have the authority to say, 'Well, we're going to do it here or there.'"

Most of the petty arguments over starting times, bench assignments, ticket allocation, or the order of appearances by cheerleaders were resolved quickly at the monthly meetings. But one of the biggest issues that confronted the athletic directors concerned the increasing presence of women sportswriters in the late 1970s. Reporters like Mary Flannery of the *Philadelphia Daily News* had been covering college athletics periodically, but Gail Shister of the *Philadelphia Inquirer* was the first local woman to be assigned to the Big 5 on a regular basis. "I remember being in a brouhaha with Gail about her need for immediate access to the locker rooms because she was writing on deadline," recalled Nash. "We spent a lot of time talking about that. This was during the early days of Title 9, so the athletic directors didn't want to develop a policy that was going to fly in the face of the women on the campuses. On the other hand, they didn't want to develop a policy that would be viewed critically by parents and, especially, some of the religious schools. Today it almost seems tame and harmless. Rollie, of course, viewed her as trying to stir up a hornet's nest and Villanova wasn't going to comply the way the rest of the schools did. I think Villanova brought robes for the players and tried to make some other accommodations. I remember having discussions with the sports editor of the *Inquirer* and assuring him that we would do our best to get Gail equal access. Frankly, at the time I wasn't all that sympathetic to her plight. I found it difficult to accept that the *Inquirer* had assigned her to this beat. But, of course, today it's commonplace."

"Everybody was on the same page at the beginning," said DiJulia, who served as St. Joseph's athletic director from 1976 to 1981, then returned again in 1988. "There was more camaraderie earlier. The world was different. The institutions weren't competing in the business of higher education at the time. We knew that some students were going to go to this school and others would go to that school so there was a terrific cooperative spirit. That changed through time."

Chapter 3

• • • • • • •

"It Will Never Work!"

It was all Bob Paul's idea!

For six years, the University of Pennsylvania and Villanova had been sharing doubleheaders at the Palestra while La Salle, Temple, and St. Joseph's played some of their major opponents in twin bills a few blocks down 33rd Street at Convention Hall. Fans were often forced to decide whether they wanted to watch popular hometown All-Americas like La Salle's Tom Gola or Villanova's Paul Arizin, who sometimes played in different arenas virtually next door to each other on the same nights.

"We were dying at the gate with Villanova," said Bob Paul, then Penn's sports publicist, who suggested the idea to John Rossiter, the school's business manager, one spring day in 1955. "I said, 'John, what would be wrong getting the five Philadelphia schools together because the other three are dying at Convention Hall as well?' John liked the idea and suggested that we talk to Bud Dudley, who just happened to be coming to Penn later that day for a meeting on a different topic." When Villanova's athletic director was approached by the two Penn officials, he said, "It's a helluva idea. Why don't we see Jerry Ford about it?" Later that day they talked to Penn's athletic director. "I was shocked because Jerry thought it was a great idea, too, but he told us that he would have to discuss it with Penn's president, Gaylord Harnwell," recalled Paul.

Penn athletics' financial situation had been shaky for a few years since Harnwell's predecessor, Harold Stassen, had committed the university to the Ivy League, which prohibits athletic scholarships and insists on higher academic standards. The Quakers had recently de-emphasized their football program and were no longer playing the Notre Dames and Ohio States on a regular basis. The university had just won a bitter battle with the NCAA, which had tried to prevent the Philadelphia Eagles from renting Franklin Field, the splendid football stadium located adjacent to the Palestra, for National Football League games. But Harnwell was looking for other ways to generate revenue by renting out Penn's facilities.

Two weeks later, Penn's president gave the go-ahead and Dudley was given the task of getting the other three schools to agree. Villanova's AD was well respected around town as a bright, creative promoter. He had recently attracted national attention when his "Grocery Bowl" football games (so-called because of a tie-in with the Acme supermarket chain) drew more than 90,000 people to Philadelphia's old Municipal Stadium (where the First Union Center now stands), matching the Wildcats against teams like Georgia and Mississippi. Later, after leaving Villanova, Dudley introduced the Liberty Bowl game in Philadelphia in 1959 before moving the contest to Atlantic City in 1964 and Memphis the following year.

◀ **B**ig 5 athletic directors (from left): Jim Henry of La Salle; Bud Dudley of Villanova, and George Bertlesman of St. Joseph's. *(Urban Archives, Temple University, Philadelphia, Pennsylvania)*

"Penn didn't talk to anyone at that time, but they thought the Big 5 was a great idea," recalled Paul, who later served for 29 years as media relations director for the U.S. Olympic Committee. "Jerry Ford always used to say, 'How do I convince those Papists to come along with us Ivy Leaguers?'" said Fabricius, who succeeded Paul as Penn's SID. "Bud's biggest sale came with St. Joe's and La Salle and he convinced them. I think Temple was left without much choice but they were a little hesitant about it."

Even though they had shared the Palestra since 1949–50, Penn and Villanova had not played each other since 1922, and had met only once before that. Longtime *Philadelphia Bulletin* scholastic sports editor Jack Ryan had been a Wildcat participant in that game. Penn was forced to vacate the Palestra in 1943 and 1944, when the Navy used it for dining facilities for its V12 program during World War II. The Quakers played some of their home games as part of Convention Hall doubleheaders during that period, but their only other game with Temple had been in 1921. Villanova hadn't played St. Joe's or Temple since 1939, even though the Wildcats had joined in occasional Convention Hall doubleheaders in the 1935, '38, and '39 seasons. In fact, the only Philadelphia schools that met faithfully every year had been La Salle, St. Joseph's and Temple, which had cooperated in Convention Hall doubleheaders since the 1930s.

"I can remember as a kid at Coatesville High School, I never knew that Convention Hall and the Palestra were only a block apart," said Paul Rubincam, who played baseball and basketball for Jack McCloskey, later served as Penn's athletic director, and is now executive director of the Big 5. "I had gotten two sets of directions from two different people. One set had me coming down Haverford Avenue to Convention Hall. The other had me coming down Lancaster Avenue to the Palestra. Don't forget, this was the late 1940s when there were only about ten red lights between Philadelphia and Coatesville and there were no turnpikes or expressways."

Home facilities on the campuses for some of the Big 5 schools bordered on the ludicrous. Villanova had its old 3,000-seat Fieldhouse and St. Joseph's played in its

"The Big 5 idea came out of the blue and was a great surprise," said Dudley, who retired in 1994. "I was kind of shocked because Penn was always way above us at that time. Being in the Ivy League they were the kings. But the idea of playing under one roof at the Palestra made sense." Dudley arranged a meeting with his counterparts—La Salle's Jim Henry, George Bertlesman of St. Joseph's, and Temple's Josh Cody. "At first they weren't quite sure that Penn was sincere about the thing," said Dudley. "Looking back, I think they were a little bit uncertain. But after several meetings, we finally got everybody together."

"They knew they were going to have problems," said Ed Fabricius, who was the sports editor of *The Daily Pennsylvanian* at the time and remembers Jerry Ford calling him into his office and telling him: "This is going to be one of the biggest things ever for Penn and for the city of Philadelphia in college basketball."

One of the major problems was communication. Temple and Villanova, in fact, weren't even speaking to each other. "I guess that stems more from football than basketball," said Dudley, "but there wasn't a great friendly relationship there."

"Back in those years, Temple didn't want to get beaten by a smaller school," said Art Mahan, who served as Villanova's athletic director from 1961 to 1978. "We beat them a couple of times and they didn't want to play us any more."

La Salle and Villanova weren't exactly on friendly terms, either. That's because of a controversial 22–21 basketball loss at Villanova in 1935, the last year the schools had faced each other. Explorer partisans accused the timekeeper of keeping the clock running until the Wildcats managed to score the winning basket.

cozy 3,200-capacity Alumni Memorial Fieldhouse. La Salle played the last game in its 1,400-seat Wister Hall gymnasium in 1952 and moved its home venue to Lincoln High School in Northeast Philadelphia for about ten years before opposing schools started to balk about playing on a slippery floor.

Temple had also used Lincoln High School once for its 1950–51 season opening win over Delaware. Now it was playing its home games on the third floor of South Hall, the old Turners' Gymnasium that the university had recently purchased on its campus at Broad Street and Columbia Avenue. "Maybe I'm exaggerating a little, but I think we had maybe 275 seats for home games," recalled former Owls coach Harry Litwack in 1998. "We had a great time trying to coach basketball. If you can visualize it, one side of the gym had rows of seats. On my left was the upstairs balcony and on my right was a stage. Many a time a basketball player ran right into that stage. Often the band and the wrestling team would be there at the same time."

Bob Vetrone, who covered college basketball from 1948 to 1965 for the old *Philadelphia Bulletin*, remembers the night he sat in South Hall with Adolph Rupp's assistant coach Harry Lancaster, who was scouting the Owls prior to their game at Kentucky. "Harry mentioned Kentucky's 13,000-seat coliseum and said, 'Bobby, this gym is the size of our training room. In fact, our training room is bigger than this place.'"

One reason, possibly, for the Owls' reluctance to join the Big 5 was the fact that Cody had been arranging Convention Hall doubleheaders with Edward "Ned" Irish, a 1927 Penn graduate, who had been promoting college twin-bills at Madison Square Garden since 1934. Irish, who helped organize the first National Invitation Tournament in the Garden in 1938, had been using Convention Hall as the second stop on an East Coast swing that he arranged to attract top intersectional opponents. In fact, when Bob Paul traveled to New York to inform Irish about the impending announcement of the formation of the Big 5, his response was simply: "It will never work!" The reason was obvious. "It was money out of his pocket," said Paul, who recalled the big fees Irish would charge the Philadelphia schools for the privilege of hosting nationally-known opponents. "Josh Cody told us that each school (La Salle, St. Joseph's, and Temple) got paid only $85 from Madison Square Garden for the games they played in the last year of Convention Hall doubleheaders," explained Paul. It

▲ Former Penn athletic director Paul Rubincam has been the executive director of the Big 5 since 1996. *(University of Pennsylvania)*

▲ Temple University athletic director Josh Cody. *(Urban Archives, Temple University, Philadelphia, Pennsylvania)*

didn't take Cody long to come around, however, especially after learning that La Salle and St. Joe's were coming aboard.

"When Jim Henry told me about the possibility of the Big 5, I was very much in favor of it," recalled Dr. Michael Duzy, who was the president of La Salle College at the time. Dr. Duzy, then a member of the Christian Brothers who was known as Brother Erminus Stanislaus, said that the unique arrangement not only enabled schools like La Salle and St. Joseph's to upgrade their schedules, but kept a number of local high school basketball players in the city. "To play in the Big 5 was something that these boys looked forward to. It was a significant boon for the city of Philadelphia, too."

There were, however, a few people, mainly from Penn, who opposed the Big 5 concept. One was Ralph Morgan, the 80-year-old trustee who had founded the Intercollegiate Basketball Rules Committee back in 1908 and later served as one of the key members of Penn's Athletic Council that had planned the Palestra. "This trustee, who was my mortal enemy from then on, felt it would be degrading for Penn to let them play these teams," Jerry Ford told *Philadelphia Inquirer* columnist Frank Dolson from his home in Jasper, Arkansas, in 1989.

"There were a lot of staunch Pennsylvania people who were opposed to the Big 5," said McCloskey, who had just joined the Quakers' athletic program. "They didn't want to be part of something that looked so commercial." But, said Dolson, "The idea of the Big 5 was not to sell out every game. They never expected to. It was to put all major college basketball games in this area in one place and share the expenses."

"You would have thought that there would have been all kinds of bickering getting those five schools together," recalled Bob Paul. "But really there was nothing to it." Except maybe the matter of sharing expenses. "That was a little bit of a sticky point," said Dudley. "It was Penn's playing field and they were the kings so we had to work hard to negotiate and come out of the thing with everybody happy. There were some interesting meetings to decide how to best spend and share the money." Amazingly, there was no written contract in those early days, only a handshake agreement that was finally hammered out to share the revenue five ways and pay Penn a maintenance fee of $400 to open the Palestra for each doubleheader. That enabled its lighting and locker room facilities to be upgraded. Although some of the smaller schools like Millersville would come in for as little as $125, the quality of opponents improved considerably when the Big 5 was formalized. That's because it was now able to pay higher guarantees to attract some of the bigger name teams—like Oklahoma City and its colorful coach Abe Lemons—for

back-to-back weekend games. Kentucky commanded the largest guarantee in the early years—$3,000 to play Temple in 1956–57, the same season Indiana agreed to meet La Salle for $2,500. Within three years, the officiating also improved when the athletic directors agreed to increase the fee from the Eastern Collegiate Athletic Conference standard of $25 to $40, the going rate for major conferences like the Atlantic Coast. "We were probably the only place that gave each referee two complimentary tickets," said Paul.

The agreement was announced at Penn's Houston Hall on November 23, 1954. The name "Big 5" was coined shortly afterwards by *Philadelphia Inquirer* sportswriter Herb Good, one of Philadelphia college basketball's most ardent supporters. Good died suddenly of a heart attack on August 29, 1967 which, ironically, was both his 57th birthday and 33rd wedding anniversary. The weekly basketball luncheons were later named in his honor.

"It was amazing that five schools with various philosophies, budgets, and facilities were able to get together," said Vetrone. "We would bring the idea up occasionally at the weekly writers' luncheons but we thought it would never happen." "It worked immediately," recalled Temple's publicist Al Shrier, who is now in the Big 5 Hall of Fame. "We had no major problems at all. It just seemed to all blend together. We started to produce some unbelievable basketball and the atmosphere was terrific."

When it began, the Big 5 athletic directors met once a month. "The schools learned a lot of respect for each other," said Fabricius, who handled the advertising and shared publicity duties with Shrier while Rossiter took care of all the business matters. "There was some give and take when somebody would occasionally get upset. Maybe there'd be a few shots back and forth, but the one thing that always stood out in my mind was the ability of these divergent personalities to work together and get it done. I never remember any antagonism over the type of athlete anyone was recruiting. Another unique thing was that the presidents never dictated policy. I remember going to a couple of meetings with president Gaylord Harnwell. The Big 5 program was running and that's all he cared about. He thought it was wonderful that Penn could be host to all these schools in the city. It's amazing how simple it was to do things back then, especially when you stop and think of how the sports world has changed so dramatically today. I remember Jerry Ford used to rely on Jim Henry. They had a very good relationship and Jim would say, 'I'll take the lead on this because you wouldn't want the other athletic directors to say that Penn is dictating anything.'"

"John Rossiter was the one who gave us all lessons in diplomacy," said Mahan, the former Villanova athletic

▲ University of Pennsylvania athletic director Jerry Ford.
(Urban Archives, Temple University, Philadelphia, Pennsylvania)

director. "There were no flareups, because he knew how to make everyone get along. He kept everyone on an even keel. He handled the scheduling, but he would always consult you."

But not everybody was all that impressed when the Big 5 was formed. In fact, it wasn't until the 1960s, when television started carrying the games into everyone's homes, that the Big 5 began to reach its legendary popularity. "We all tend to think that every game was a sellout, but it wasn't," said Ramsay, who began his Hawk coaching career the year the Big 5 began. "There were some days when there just weren't many people in the Palestra."

Ramsay is absolutely correct. The 30 doubleheaders that first year drew a total of 104,461 paid admissions and the ten city series matchups averaged only 3,703. The only sellouts the first two years of Big 5 action came in the two games between Temple and St. Joseph's. Crowds for city series games dipped as low as 1,181 for Villanova's 63–47 win over Penn in 1956–57. It wasn't until the 1961–62 and 1963–64 seasons that as many as five city series games were played before full houses. There were five sellouts again in 1971–72, and a sixth doubleheader came within 100 fans of capacity. In 1982–83, half of the eight Palestra doubleheaders sold out. But the final two city series matchups that year were

played at the Spectrum in South Philadelphia and attracted a total of 35,643 fans, including the largest college basketball crowd ever in the Commonwealth of Pennsylvania—18,060 watched Villanova beat St. Joseph's 70–62.

"To me it was no big deal," recalled Hal "Hotsie" Reinfeld, who was a senior at Temple when Big 5 play began. "I was from the old school. My goal as a kid was to play at Convention Hall and Madison Square Garden. To me the Palestra was just another place to play but it did have a totally different feeling because Convention Hall had all the tradition of the (NBA's old Philadelphia) Warriors and a lot of great sporting events."

Frank Blatcher, one of the returning players from La Salle's NCAA Tournament teams, was also a senior. "I don't remember it really being such a big deal then. Nobody did. It wasn't ballyhooed at all. It was just like two more schools were coming into the city championship."

"I don't think any of us thought the Big 5 would be so successful," said Litwack shortly before he died. "We were just looking for a good place to play. I never thought it would turn out to be so big, but it was a good selling point, especially for me, because I had to depend on the local public high schools for talent."

Dan Dougherty, a walk-on, was in his senior year at St. Joseph's. "I thought it was great because I never had the opportunity to play in the Palestra," he recalled. "There was sort of an elitist feeling about Villanova and Penn playing in the Palestra when the three city teams were playing at Convention Hall. People had a difficult time trying to decide which doubleheader to attend on a Saturday night. There was no TV in those days so we never saw Villanova or Penn in action. And now we had the opportunity to play with them."

"I thought it was a great idea," said Joe Sturgis, who had been recruited at Penn by former Quaker All-America Howie Dalmar, who later coached at Stanford. "We looked forward to playing the other Big 5 teams. We held our own." So did Sturgis, who, at 6'4", was one of the nation's leading rebounders as a senior co-captain of Penn's first Big 5 team.

"There was a little bit of indifference," remembers Jack McKinney, who was a sophomore at St. Joseph's when the formation of the Big 5 was announced. McKinney had played basketball under Ramsay at St. James High School in Chester, Pennsylvania, but had been recruited for track by the Hawks. Later he would succeed Ramsay as coach. "It was not a super thing, but it was something to look forward to. We all thought that it was a good idea because now we'll get a chance to play against Villanova and Penn. But even more exciting for me was the fact that my high school coach was coming to be my coach in the first year of the Big 5.

"But we liked the idea of playing in the Palestra. It was a lot different from Convention Hall. It had a lot less space. In Convention Hall, it felt like you were in the Los Angeles Coliseum because it seemed to go into the stands forever. And they had all those back rooms at Convention Hall. Every once in a while we'd get lost trying to find our way into our locker room. The Palestra was all condensed and confined in space and area. The locker rooms were small and the crowd was on top of you, which seemed like a hindrance. But the Palestra grew to be the best thing about the whole Big 5 because the fans were right there. The St. Joe's fans could talk across the court to the La Salle people."

McCloskey, who had just been hired out of Collingwood High School in New Jersey as Penn's freshman coach, had mixed emotions when he heard the announcement. "I thought it was great," he recalled. "But there weren't any athletic scholarships at Penn and I knew it would be hard competing against these teams. I thought 'God, we're going to get our tails beat. We're going to have to work so hard. If we can only win a game once in a while.'"

"When the Big 5 started I really didn't think about it one way or another except to say, 'well it's nice that everybody's getting together,'" said Jack Kraft, who would later enjoy a brilliant coaching career at Villanova. Kraft was coaching in high school and officiating in the Boathouse Row League ("for $7.50 a doubleheader") on the Schuylkill River at the time. "Early in the 1950s I had heard coaches complaining that they weren't getting the top sportswriters for their games at the Palestra or Convention Hall and asking 'Why can't they get together?'"

A cultural pecking order seemed to prevail, even among the athletes, according to Temple's Reinfeld. "The Jewish kids out of the Public League went to Temple. Kids out of the Catholic League went to La Salle, Villanova, or St. Joe's. That was a foregone conclusion except for Norm Grekin, who went to La Salle [where he was co-MVP with Gola of the '52 NIT]. A lot of schools out of town didn't recruit Jewish kids and certainly blacks were few and far between."

One of the few exceptions to Reinfeld's theory came in 1963–64, when Litwack dug deep into Philadelphia's Catholic League to recruit four players who joined Jim Williams, an All-State high school star from Norristown, Pennsylvania, in helping the Owls win the Middle Atlantic Conference championship. Temple then qualified for its first NCAA appearance since the 1958 team went to the Final Four. Three of the Catholic Leaguers were from Cardinal Dougherty High School: Bob Harrington, the captain, who played courageously all year with a painfully sprained left ankle, Dan Fitzgerald,

and Vince Richardson. Bill Kelley came from Roman Catholic via La Salle College; he had been one of the few players to transfer from one Big 5 school to another. The NCAAs were short-lived this time, however, as Connecticut, coached by Fred Shabel, won 53–48 in a first round game at the Palestra. Temple had won an earlier Palestra game with U-Conn 53–45.

Only four black players got significant playing time in the first year of the Big 5—La Salle's Alonzo Lewis and Temple's Guy Rodgers, Hal Lear, and Jay Norman. Of the 65 players listed in the first Big 5 media guide, 50 were from the Philadelphia area. Bob Maples, a military veteran from Elmhurst, Illinois, who played for La Salle, came from the farthest away. If you wanted to see players like Earl Monroe, a Philadelphia high school legend who wasn't recruited locally but later starred in the NBA, you had to go to the Gold Medal Tournament run by the city's Department of Recreation after the season. Or visit one of the summer basketball leagues at A Street and Champlost Avenue in Philadelphia or in suburban Narberth, before such leagues were outlawed for college basketball players by the NCAA after the 1960–61 basketball scandal.

"Everybody in the Big 5 played there except for the guys from Penn," recalled Temple's Bill Kelley, who was one of the benchwarmers. "Sometimes it was like an extension of the Palestra when guys like Temple's Pickles Kennedy would go against St. Joe's Bob McNeill. It was such a small court, it was like a matchbox. But when the blacks played the whites, that's when the crowds really came because, as you know, basketball in those days was pretty much a *white* sport. There was a silent quota in college and the pros. There'd be three thousand people standing around an hour before game time. They were wars. Tee Parham [a local Public League high school legend] was like a black Bob Cousy. He did everything that Cousy and Guy Rodgers were doing—behind his back, between his legs. He was unbelievable and he was at his best when he went up against Kennedy and McNeill because those guys were getting all the ink."

Indeed, it would be another decade before college basketball began recruiting minorities aggressively. And perhaps no coach had as much impact in that regard as George Raveling, who was a young high school player in Washington, D. C., soon to attend Villanova when the Big 5 started. "George was the first person to realize the impact that black athletes from the South would have on college basketball at a time when Southeastern and Atlantic Coast Conference schools weren't into recruiting minorities like they do today," said Herb Hartnett, a Villanova grad who later became Penn's sports information director. After he graduated, Raveling went into business with the Sun Oil Company, then became one of Kraft's assistants at Villanova, where he was arguably the most effective recruiter in Big 5 history. With players from the Deep South like Johnny Jones, Sammy Sims, and Howard Porter, he changed the face of recruiting forever.

In many ways, the problems faced by young black players in the early days of the Big 5 were no different than those of their counterparts across the country. Because of an unwritten racial "quota system," Temple's current coach John Chaney never had the opportunity to play for a Big 5 school despite being the Most Valuable Player in the Public League the same year La Salle's Tom Gola was MVP in the Catholic League.

"In my senior year," recalled Reinfeld, "Jay Norman, Guy Rodgers, and Hal Lear were the first blacks to stay in a Lexington hotel when we played Kentucky. When we went to play at North Carolina State when I was a junior, our black players were forced to eat in the kitchen and they had to stay at a local black college. They wouldn't even let them stay at our hotel. And our guys, we hated that. We all said, 'Why are we coming down here?' People today don't realize that. They've heard about it but they never felt it."

"That's how I met Sam Jones, the great Boston Celtic guard," recalled Lear. "When I was a sophomore, blacks sometimes couldn't even come to see the games. When we played at North Carolina State, we had to stay in the dorms at North Carolina College, a black school where Sam played. The coach would drive us to the game and then came back to pick us up." Lear still has a copy of the *Lexington Herald Journal's* December 11, 1955, edition where Ed Ashford's lead paragraph said: *"Paced by a pair of dusky sharp-shooting guards—Hal (King) Lear and Guy Rodgers—Temple's Owls turned in a major upset of the young basketball season by thumping the University of Kentucky Wildcats, 73–61, before 11,000 fans in Memorial Coliseum."*

"I remember when we were out on the floor warming up for that game, they played the national anthem faster than I had ever heard it in my life," recalled Rodgers. "They just *raced* through it. Then after it was over, they proceeded to play 'Dixie' and the people stood solemnly with their hats in their hands and palms of their hands over their hearts like we do for the national anthem. We just kept warming up while the Kentucky players stood at attention. As soon as they finished playing 'Dixie,' the fans started booing us because we were shooting around while they played their sacred song. It was unbelievable. Then during the game I walked over to the side and grabbed a towel while I was talking to coach Litwack. Right after I finished using the towel, one of my teammates came over, grabbed it, and started using it. Then I started drinking some water and some-

one in the stands said, 'Those niggers and whites are using the same towels and drinking out of the same cup! Do you believe that?' I remember coach Litwack turning red in the face and just saying, 'Let's go to work.'"

"Alonzo Lewis was my roommate," recalled La Salle's Blatcher. "I remember when we played in the Kentucky Invitational in 1954, he had to stay with a black family in Lexington. They told us that Adolph Rupp wouldn't even let his players shake hands with CCNY's [City College of New York] black players a few years before that."

Big 5 players were still feeling the pain of discrimination after they graduated. Penn's Sturgis remembers the time in 1957 when he was playing weekends in the Eastern League and making the five-hour drive to Sunbury with teammates John Chaney and Bob Gainey, who had led Ben Franklin High to the Philadelphia city title a few years back. "I'd sit back in the car and laugh at their stories the whole time," recalled Sturgis. But the fun stopped one time in Harrisburg when the teammates pulled over for a milkshake. "They refused to serve the black guys," said Sturgis. "You had to be careful what you did because in that area, upstate Pennsylvania was as red-necked as can be. But a couple of times we had little situations where we told people, 'you serve them or you'll get something over your head!' It was quite a learning experience."

Coaches came from a different mold in the early days of the Big 5. At Villanova, Al Severance, the loquacious justice of the peace and college professor, was winding down a colorful career. Temple's Litwack was a junior high school teacher in Philadelphia. Penn's Ray Stanley was a local businessman working for General Refractories Co. McCloskey, who was being groomed as Stanley's successor, and Ramsay, of St. Joseph's, had both fought in World War II. McCloskey had been a Navy officer participating in the first wave invading Okinawa and was on the beach when they brought back the body of famed war correspondent Ernie Pyle. Ramsay, a Navy frogman working on an underwater demolition team, was in the Pacific, heading toward the invasion of Japan, when they dropped the atomic bomb on Hiroshima. He was in his first year at St. Joseph's. Also making his coaching debut was La Salle's Jim Pollard, the former NBA All Star with the Minneapolis Lakers, who had just succeeded Ken Loeffler, a Yale University Law School graduate who shared an apartment one year in New Haven with future President Gerald Ford. Loeffler was also a talented pianist. "People used to come to the basketball writers' luncheons early so they could hear Ken play classical music," said Vetrone, a member of the College Basketball Writers' Hall of Fame who later worked for Big 5 executive director Dan Baker from 1982 to 1990.

Vetrone grew up in a South Philadelphia row house five doors away from Arizin, the future Villanova and Philadelphia Warriors' Hall of Famer. He first became interested in college basketball in December 1937 when his uncle took him to Convention Hall to see the great Stanford All-America Angelo "Hank" Luisetti, the college game's first real national hero. The game, won by Temple 35–31, was sold out and Vetrone was among the thousands of fans turned away. "I figured then that this has got to be a helluva sport," he recalled. "Here it is in the cold of winter and all these people are trying to get into a game."

Recruiting was much more innocent in those days, primarily because coaches often worked two or three other jobs to make ends meet. In fact, three of them—Pollard, McCloskey, and Ramsay—also coached their college baseball teams. McCloskey also handled Penn's 150-pound football squad while he was serving as Stanley's freshman coach. None of them had full-time assistants. That's probably why McCloskey, who was paying his part-time assistant $500 a year, once recruited a player named Jimmy Day, a 6'4" forward from Mt. Vernon, Washington, after reading about him in the *Street & Smith Basketball Yearbook*. "I saw this guy's name and saw that he was an outstanding student, so we wrote letters and eventually he came to Penn," said McCloskey. Day played in a few games as a sophomore in 1959–60. A few years later, when he was recruiting for Jack Kraft at Villanova, George Raveling found Johnny Jones' name in "Faces in the Crowd" in *Sports Illustrated*. Jones went on to become MVP of the Big 5 in 1968 and is a member of the Big 5 Hall of Fame.

Litwack enjoyed telling people how he recruited players like All-America Guy Rogers over milkshakes and hamburgers at Mike's Broad Tower, a popular student hangout on Temple's campus. "Actually it was a milkshake and a PTC bus token," recalled Bill Kelley, who was also recruited there by Litwack and later married Eleanor, the daughter of the proprietor, Mike Tolia. "Guy Rodgers came down on the bus to meet Harry. They met in Litwack's office and Harry said to him, 'Come on, kid. I'll buy you a milkshake.' He talked to Guy about the program and the school and so forth, then handed him a token and said something like 'Here kid, get home with this.' That's how he got the greatest player in Temple's history. That's not exactly how it's done today."

Even the athletic scholarships were primitive by today's standards. "You'll laugh at this, but I'll never forget when we came back from the NCAA Tournament in 1956," said Reinfeld, the former Temple player. "I was going through the cafeteria line with Hal Lear, the MVP of the Final Four. After he got his food and went to get checked off, the cashier said to him, 'I'm sorry, Harold,

but you're off the meal list. The season's over.' Lear knew that his scholarship included tuition, books, and one meal only during the season. So he never complained. He just laughed."

"I was so naive, I had no idea that there was such a thing as a scholarship," recalled Raveling, who had been recruited by Jack Ramsay of St. Joseph's before deciding to attend Villanova. "When my high school coach explained it to me, I thought he was putting me on. I said, 'Honestly do you mean you go to school for free and just play basketball?' I couldn't comprehend that because I thought he was teasing me. That changed my whole life because if it wasn't for basketball I probably would have ended up in the Air Force or the military."

There was only occasional television and sporadic radio coverage in the early years of the Big 5. Wilmington's WPFH-TV paid $1,000 a night to carry the second games of doubleheaders with Matt Guokas Sr. handling the play-by-play and Bill Pfeiffer the color. Bill Campbell, who was the city's best-known sportscaster, mainly during his 17 years with WCAU, did some Villanova games on radio. "For a ridiculous fee," he recalled. "Less than a hundred dollars, maybe seventy-five." But the entire Palestra schedule that first season was broadcast on Penn's FM radio station, WXPN, by a young undergraduate, Eddie Einhorn, who would soon be personally responsible for elevating college basketball to unprecedented national popularity. Today he is the vice chairman of Major League Baseball's Chicago White Sox.

"That's how I learned the business," recalled Einhorn, who grew up in Paterson, New Jersey, not far from fabled Madison Square Garden. "I broadcast 30 doubleheaders all by myself. In fact, I did both games for two years without a color man. I was a young guy—about 19 years old and, obviously, I thought the Big 5 was a fabulous idea. I was impressed because now they had all the Philly schools playing together and I was seeing every top player in the country come in. They didn't have to go to New York for exposure. College basketball at the time was a little dormant after the scandal in New York. The Big 5 revitalized the game. You could say that it was the start of its whole rebirth."

If the Big 5 began the rebirthing process of college basketball, Einhorn certainly was the person who later took the game to astonishing popularity. After graduating from Penn in 1957, Eddie completed law school at Northwestern University, then started his own television production company, TVS. By the early 1960s, he had convinced the Eastern Collegiate Athletic Conference (ECAC) and the young chairman of its broadcasting committee—Connecticut basketball coach Fred Shabel—to put a TV package together for Saturday afternoons. He used sportscasters like Philadelphia's

Jim Leaming and Les Keiter and often persuaded athletic directors to move all of the fans to one side of the arena so that the place wouldn't look empty for the TV cameras. His standard rights fee for each school in those days was $2,500.

On January 20, 1968, Einhorn changed the perception of the college game forever, transforming it from a regional event into a national spectacle. Paying an unheard-of fee of $27,000, he produced and packaged the first nationally-televised prime time college basketball game in history. And what a game it was! UCLA, the defending NCAA champs, had its 47-game unbeaten streak snapped 71–69 by undefeated Houston, as Elvin Hayes scored 39 points and outplayed Lew Alcindor.

It was the first national TV exposure for a young sportscaster named Dick Enberg. Even during the game, which was carried by 150 stations in 49 states, Einhorn was on the phone writing ten second spots and having Enberg read them on the air. The last station wasn't cleared for broadcast until less than two hours before tip-off. Not only did interest in college basketball immediately skyrocket, but the game provided an astounding boost for integration, especially in the southern part of the United States. Southeastern and Southwest Conference schools, in particular, opened their doors wider to black players after seeing that game on prime-time TV. College basketball was no longer a regional event to be handled as an *independent* production in the eyes of national networks and their advertisers. NBC bought the rights to televise the game nationally the very next year.

Only 2,553 fans were on hand for the inaugural Palestra doubleheader hosted by the Big 5 on Saturday night, December 3, 1955. Muhlenberg handed Pollard his first defeat as La Salle's coach 69–58, then Ramsay made his coaching debut a success by guiding St. Joseph's to an 84–72 win over Rhode Island.

Eleven nights later, on December 14, the Hawks met Villanova in the first Big 5 game ever played. Students from both schools were on Christmas break, however, and only 2,636 fans showed up. "I remember the Palestra being relatively empty, but I think St. Joe's had a pretty good following for that game," recalled Ramsay, who went head-to-head for the first time with his mentor, Severance.

"I think that all the intensity and tenacity of the Big 5 started with those two," recalled Marty Milligan, the 6'1" senior guard from Villanova. "They really went at it

from a coaching standpoint, using their benches, shuffling players in and out throughout the game. There was a lot of strategy, a lot of thinking involved. Right from the beginning, when you were playing another Big 5 school, you got up much higher for the game than if you did when you were playing a team from New York or Virginia or someplace."

Milligan will always be remembered for his last-second layup in overtime that beat Rio Grande and the fabled Bevo Francis 93–92 at the old Philadelphia Arena during his sophomore year. One of the referees in that game was longtime Phillies baseball scout Jocko Collins, who would later help Bob Walters as an assistant coach at La Salle.

Milligan may also go down as the first member of the Big 5 to have family ties severely tested by one of the city series matchups. "My older brother, Jerry, went to St. Joe's on the GI Bill and was the Hawks' basketball manager," Marty recalled. "I kind of think he might have been rooting for me a little bit but there was some competition, family-wise. I was hoping my dad (Edmund) would be rooting for me, but to this day, underneath it all, I don't know."

Dougherty, the St. Joseph's senior who had been nursing an injury, will never forget his pre-game "introduction" to the Big 5. "I parked my car and was crossing 34th Street on the way to the Palestra," said Dougherty, a blue-collar player who had worked his way into the starting lineup. "There was a big traffic jam and lot's of people were heading to the game. A car with a Villanova sticker on the windshield stopped, a guy rolled down the window and said, 'Doc, are you playing tonight?' Before I could answer, he snarled, 'I hope you break your leg!'" Al Juliana came off the bench that night to score 22 points to lead the Hawks over the Wildcats 83–70.

The Big 5 gauntlet had been dropped. The first shot had been fired in what would become one of college basketball's fiercest rivalries. At the end of the 1955–56 season, each team received $9,744.78 as its share of the proceeds from the 30 doubleheaders. Ramsay and Litwack were well on their way to future Hall of Fame coaching careers after finishing 1–2 in the first city series round-robin competition. That they reached Final Fours of the NIT and NCAA Tournaments was almost anti-climatic.

For the Hawks, it would be the first of seven Big 5 titles won or shared by Ramsay. But on the national stage, the first years of the Big 5 belonged to "The Chief," Harry Litwack.

Chapter 4
• • • • • • •

Hail to the Chief

A number of years ago, Philadelphia sports-caster Al Meltzer was having breakfast with Harry Litwack at a motel in Wildwood, New Jersey. Harry was in town helping Scoop Taylor run his summer basketball camp, one of the more popular off-season fixtures among local high school coaches. "All of a sudden the door swings open in the coffee shop and this guy comes sliding into the booth," recalled Meltzer. "He literally bounces me out of the way and grabs hold of Harry and for the next hour or so they're writing all over the table and everything else. Papers were flying everywhere." The intruder was Bobby Knight, then a young coach at Army. "I knew who he was at the time because I had broadcast the NIT the year before and his team was there. Mike Krzyzewski, the Duke coach, was still playing for him. Bobby Knight was picking Harry's brain about the box-and-one and triangle-and-two. All they talked about was defense, but Bobby was taking notes like crazy. He had not been coaching long but you knew right then and there that this was someone very special. And Harry, always the gentleman, gave him all the answers. Bobby Knight was the antithesis of Harry Litwack. He was obsessive and we all know that Harry was quite the opposite."

Obsessive or not, Bobby Knight knew that when he was picking Harry Litwack's brain, he was picking the best. In a career that spanned almost half a century as a player and coach, the distinguished-looking, immaculately-dressed, white-haired, cigar-smoking Litwack made Temple a household word throughout the basketball world. Twice he guided the Owls to the Final Four in the NCAA Tournament. One of those teams won 25 consecutive games, a Big 5 record that stood for 13 years. His 1969 team won the National Invitation Tournament in a memorable upset. His overall won-lost record of 373–193 from 1952 until he retired in 1973 doesn't really give proper justice to the genius of the man, because so many of his teams overachieved tremendously against stronger opponents but just fell short in the win column. Still, 13 of his teams played in post-season tournaments, a fact not lost on his peers, who elected him to the Naismith Basketball Hall of Fame in 1975. Harry died at age 91 in August 1999.

"Whenever you went to the NCAAs, you'd see guys like John Wooden, Hank Iba, and Pete Newell talking to Harry about basketball," Temple's current coach John Chaney once told Mike Kern of the *Philadelphia Daily News*. "They respected him that much. That told me all I needed to know. He didn't have a lot of superstars, but he made his players great. He would arrive at the least common denominator very quickly, always find his best players, highlight them, and have everybody work around that."

One of Litwack's finest talents was finding hidden potential in a high school prospect and developing that player into a very good—sometimes great—college performer. Sometimes he even did it with players with absolutely no high school experience. Take Ollie Johnson, for example. A graduate of South Philadelphia High School, Ollie didn't play organized basketball until he was 19 years old and made the team at Philadelphia Community College (where he currently serves as the school's assistant athletic director). The following year, Johnson was playing major college basketball. He led the Owls in scoring as a junior and senior and played on Temple's 1971–72 team that snapped Penn's record-breaking 48-game regular-season winning streak. By the time he was 23, he was a second round draft choice of the Portland Trail Blazers.

Johnson, who only started playing the game when he grew about six inches after graduating from high school, has collected a roomful of trophies from his playing days. But he keeps only one on display. "It's for being the most improved player in the Big 5. For me that trophy was a reward for all the hard work and frustration. When I was seventeen, I couldn't even make a layup. But I had good coaches who helped me in my development."

▲ Temple coach Harry Litwack was inducted into the Naismith Basketball Hall of Fame in 1975. *(Urban Archives, Temple University, Philadelphia, Pennsylvania)*

Johnson spent ten years as a small forward in the NBA with Portland, New Orleans, Kansas City, Atlanta, Chicago, and Philadelphia. "Because I wasn't a prolific scorer, my thing was basically defense," he said. "I was well taught in Harry Litwack's system. If you didn't play defense, you just didn't play. Learning Harry's matchup zone helped me a lot because even in a zone, you have to play your man in front of you. Even though the pro game is supposedly man-to-man, knowing how to help out and where to be and all those things were just stamped on my mind."

Other coaches who respected Litwack tremendously included Kentucky's Adolph Rupp and John Wooden of UCLA. "Adolph Rupp said that he always liked to play Temple in Philadelphia for two reasons," recalled sportswriter Bob Vetrone. "Number one, he wanted to see Harry Litwack, and number two, he always liked to go to Bookbinders Restaurant."

"John Wooden and Harry Litwack used to room together and do clinics together," said Guy Rodgers, one of the All-Americas developed by Litwack. Before his fatal heart attack in 2001, Rodgers lived in Los Angeles and kept in contact with the retired UCLA coach. "John Wooden to this day still holds Harry in high esteem and he still talks about Harold Lear and myself in the backcourt," Rodgers recalled a few years ago.

Temple won the NIT in 1969, which was also one of the years that UCLA won the NCAA championship. "Wooden was more pleased and more happy about Temple winning the NIT than he was about UCLA winning the NCAA," said Rodgers. "He talked about Harry Litwack constantly. He told me that he considered Harry one of the five best coaches ever. I don't know whether people even knew about it, but their friendship was just beautiful. He would always ask me, 'Have you talked to Harry recently? Well, you better talk to him!' Here you have two men who were like fraternity brothers from different parts of the country who had such great admiration and respect for one another."

"Harry sponsored me when I was inducted into the Basketball Hall of Fame," recalled Jack Ramsay. "He was a special guy, a first-class gentleman. His teams were very fundamentally sound. He played the combination defense better than anybody, so you were hard-pressed to figure out how to get good shots for your players against his teams. Defense was their main weapon, but they always had great perimeter shooters like Hal Lear and Bruce Drysdale and you were virtually powerless to stop them from getting the kinds of shots that he wanted."

A native of Poland, Litwack came to the United States when he was five years old and grew up in South Philadelphia. After starring at Southern High School, he played in the backcourt at Temple from 1927 to 29 and was co-captain his junior and senior years. He was the Owls' freshman coach and assistant varsity coach for two decades before succeeding Josh Cody in 1952. During that time he still taught in the Philadelphia Public School system and served as a high school referee. He played professionally for a brief time with the old Philadelphia SPHAs (South Philadelphia Hebrew Association). He coached and taught physical education at Philadelphia's Fels Junior High School and Simon Gratz High School. For 29 years, he owned and operated one of the nation's first summer basketball camps, Camp Sun Mountain in Pennsylvania's Pocono Mountains. His partner was Bill Foster, who later coached at Rutgers, Duke, South Carolina, and Northwestern. Foster had begun his career coaching basketball and teaching typing classes at Abington High School, in Montgomery County just outside of Philadelphia. One of his students was Litwack's daughter, Lois. It was through her, in fact, that Foster and Litwack became friends and business partners. This venture became so successful that it was one of the main reasons why Harry declined a number of offers to coach in the National Basketball Association.

"Twice Eddie Gottlieb offered me the opportunity with the Warriors and once, later, the 76ers approached me with an offer," recalled Litwack. "But in order to take that job, I would have had to put all the work and responsibility on my two assistants in the camping business. I didn't think it was fair. My wife didn't want me to live on airplanes and we had young children at the time. I said to myself, 'What if I get a lousy team? How long would I last in the NBA?' I never had any pressure with the college job and I worked for good guys like Jimmy Usilton and Josh Cody. Besides, I had a taste of that type of life as a pro player in the early '30s playing for the Philadelphia SPHAs. We always had nice guys on our team who did a good job, but I saw too many players on other pro teams at the time spending all the money they made in the game afterwards at a bar."

The only camp that Villanova's Chris Ford ever attended was Litwack's. It happened when Ford was in high school and was being recruited by Temple, among a number of other schools. Since Chris couldn't afford to pay the fee, he worked as a waiter. "The first day I got there my Chuck Taylor's blew a hole," recalled Ford, who later played and coached in the NBA. "They took me into town to get me a new pair of sneakers. They cost seven dollars and I think they took it out of my wages." Later, Ford became good friends with Litwack and Foster, as well as Harry's young assistant Don Casey. "I did their camps forever, and Casey later became my assistant all five years with the Boston Celtics. He used to say, 'Always be good to your recruits because you never know. Even if they don't come, they may give you a job later in life.' We had a great relationship. Case brought me into the inner circle of the Big 5 people when we got together in the NBA."

Years later when the Celtics were playing in Miami, Ford and Casey called Litwack and invited him to the game. "We said, 'Come to the hotel and we'll give you a ride over on the team bus.' So Harry shows up for the bus. He's got a little brown bag with him. Case and I put him up front on the first seat. We get him over to the gym and we said, 'Come on, let's go in the press room and get you a bite to eat.' And he said, 'Oh, no. My wife packed me a little something to eat.' He was such a great guy."

In 1938, the year before the NCAA Tournament began, Temple went 23–2 and won the first NIT at Madison Square Garden. Harry had rejoined his old college coach, Jimmy Usilton, as freshman coach three years earlier (at a salary of three hundred dollars a year) and had quickly developed a reputation for his defensive expertise. Earlier that season, the Owls made headlines by beating national powerhouse Stanford in a major upset at Convention Hall 35–31. The game drew 11,793 fans and another 10,000 were turned away. All the cred-

it for the victory went to Litwack, who devised a remarkable new defense—the box-and-one—that not only neutralized the nation's highest scorer, Hank Luisetti, but later paved the way for the triangle-and-two and various matchup zone defensive alignments so prevalent today.

"Stanford came into Madison Square Garden for games on Friday and Saturday, and we were scheduled to play them on Monday," Litwack recalled. "Jimmy asked me to go over to the Garden to scout Hank Luisetti. After the first game in New York, I came back and met the group over a cup of coffee at the old railroad station at Broad and Market. They asked me what I thought of this great player from Stanford and I said, 'To tell you the truth, this guy's phenomenal.'

"'How are you going to stop him?' 'We're going to be in a zone defense and I'm going to have the middle man playing man-to-man,' I said. 'What do you mean by that?' I pointed it out on a napkin with Xs and Os. 'He's going to be guarded by Howie Black and I'm going to tell Howie: He's your man. If he runs out towards the toilet, you follow him. Stay right on top of him and keep the ball away from him.'"

Utilizing Harry's revolutionary defensive scheme almost to perfection, the Owls held Luisetti to 11 points. The great Stanford star, who had already scored 1,200 points in less than two years, missed part of the game with a cut over his eye. "After the game I explained to a writer that we were using our regular zone defense," said Litwack. "But we had Howie Black playing Luisetti tight with instructions not to leave him and to keep the ball away from him. So the defense ended up being two men up front and two in the back with Howie trailing him all over. It made a box. And that's how the name came about. But I didn't give it that name. I didn't call it a 'box-and-one,' I just said four men were playing a zone defense and Howie was playing Luisetti man-to-man. Later somebody came along and called it a box-and-one but it was a while before people picked up on it after that."

"I guess we should really call it the 'Litwack Defense,'" said Meltzer, " because Harry really was an innovator and a man before his time. He was the first guy to really take advantage of the zone because, in those days, no one played zone defense. I mean you just weren't a *man* if you couldn't play man-to-man defense. And you couldn't coach if you couldn't teach macho man-to-man defense—toe-to-toe, belly-to-belly and all that kind of stuff."

"Harry did nothing fancy but you knew you were in a cyclone trying to go against that zone," recalled Jack McKinney, the former St. Joseph's coach.

"A lot of the offense and a lot of the plays you see in the NBA today are actually derivatives of Harry's plays," said Rodgers, who is considered the best playmaker and ball-handler ever to come out of the Big 5. Rodgers certainly knew what he was talking about. He played for 12 years in the National Basketball Association, was named to the NBA All-Star team four times, and set the standard for the *point* guard position long before it was given that designation. He was also the first player to win the Big 5 MVP award three consecutive years.

Rodgers and Hal Lear had been Litwack's first great recruits. Like so many other high school prospects, Harry had convinced them to attend Temple after taking them for a bite to eat at Mike's Broad Tower, the popular campus eatery.

Rodgers played at Philadelphia's Northeast High School, less than two miles from Temple's campus. Coached by Ike Wooley, who had been one of Litwack's teammates at Temple, Guy found himself doing virtually everything in high school—bringing the ball up, especially against the press, and playing the pivot even though he was barely six feet tall. "I wasn't a great shooter, but I could score," he recalled.

One Saturday, Wooley took Rodgers to watch pickup games at local playgrounds. Then he took him to lunch at Horn and Hardart's. "What did you see?" Wooley asked his young playmaker. "Before I could answer," said Rodgers, "Mr. Wooley, who was very philosophical and extremely professorial in his manner, continued speaking: 'You saw all these ballplayers and they all wanted to shoot. You never saw anybody setting up other ballplayers. I think that's going to be the key for you.' They didn't call the position 'point guard' then, but Mr. Wooley said, 'If you create and play-make and learn to do all the things I taught you—all the different things like penetration and kicking the ball out, I think you will be in the NBA.'

"In those days," added Rodgers, "there weren't many blacks in the NBA, and there were a lot of schools that black players couldn't go to. We didn't have too many choices but Temple was one of them. I was young and impressionable. Even though I was All-Public, everybody said I was too short to play in college, but Wooley told me: 'No! Just remember, when you have the ball you are ten feet tall.' Then when I got to college, people said I was too short to play pro. There was still a quota in the NBA and the league had only eight teams. Every time I heard I was too short, Ike Wooley and Harry Litwack encouraged me. The two of them had a great deal of influence, not only in my ball-playing but in my life."

Lear had played at Philadelphia's Overbrook High School for Sam Cozen, who would later coach at Drexel University for many years. "He actually arranged a scholarship meeting with Harry Litwack," Lear recalled. "Otherwise, I don't know what I would have done. Before I went to Temple I hadn't even been out of my neighborhood." Lear's uncle, Charles Baker, worked for the City of Philadelphia for many years and founded the popular Charles Baker Summer League that for decades has provided an off-season basketball showcase and training ground for hundreds of high school, college, and professional players.

Lear was two years older than Rodgers, but they quickly became friends after getting to know each other as opponents in Public League high school games. Soon they started traveling around to all the local schoolyards, taking on challengers, often playing two-against-eight and winning most of the time. When Rodgers arrived at Temple, Litwack wasted no time in pairing him with Lear, another lefthander, in the backcourt. Soon they were working together to perfection and virtually destroying opposing zone defenses with their quickness, speed, ball-handling, and shooting ability.

"Certainly for one year in 1956, they were as good a backcourt as you'll ever see," said sportswriter Bob Vetrone. "It was the *perfect* backcourt. Lear could shoot the eyes out of the basket. And Rodgers, in some of our minds to this day, is the best guard Philadelphia has ever had. He's one of the best guards ever. When you see things like passing off the dribble being done today, he and Bob Cousy did those things thirty, forty years ago. I was watching an NBA playoff game on TV recently and the announcer said, 'Oh, that was a great pass.' Guy used to make them every game." Eddie Gottlieb, who owned and coached the old Philadelphia Warriors, once compared Rodgers to Cousy, the great Boston Celtics guard. "That was like comparing him to Babe Ruth," explained Vetrone.

"Basketball players are like musicians and everybody is a virtuoso," said Lear. "People do different things in different ways and have their own strengths and weaknesses. It's hard to say that this guy is better than that guy. It's like apples and oranges. That's why I don't compare players except for Guy Rodgers, who was the greatest. Guy was so good when he was 15, you'd go to the schoolyard and he would be playing *one-against-five.* Dribbling up and down the court was a very simple thing for him. He'd just love it when people would try to press him and he'd put on a little show. He was the consummate ball-handler. All I had to do was just run to spots and take the easy shots."

The players who usually got the ball to Rodgers and Lear were either Tink Van Patton, a 6'8" center who had

▶ **T**emple's Hal Lear is guarded by Bill Lynch of St. Joseph's in the first Big 5 game between Owls and Hawks in 1956. *(Urban Archives, Temple University, Philadelphia, Pennsylvania)*

▲ Jay Norman played for Harry Litwack, then served as a longtime Temple assistant coach. *(Urban Archives, Temple University, Philadelphia, Pennsylvania)*

been Litwack's first "big" recruit; Jay Norman, an Army veteran who came to Temple on a football scholarship; or Fred Cohen, who still holds the Palestra and NCAA Tournament single-game rebounding record. Litwack considered Van Patton one of his "luckiest" recruits. "I never had anyone that big," Litwack said about Van Patton, who had been originally offered a scholarship by a Big Ten school that reneged when Tink suffered a leg injury. Norman had grown up in Bowman, Georgia, a rural town about 40 miles from Atlanta. As a child he remembers plowing fields with a mule. "I thought that this was going to be my life," he recalled. " At the age of seven he moved to Philadelphia, where he later played basketball at Mastbaum High School. The big star across town at Ben Franklin High was a kid named John Chaney. After playing freshman football at Temple, Norman was drafted into the Army where he ended up playing basketball at Fort Belvoir, Virginia. One of his teammates was Dick Groat, the former Duke star and Pittsburgh Pirates shortstop. By the time he returned to college, Lear, Fred Cohen, and Hotsie

Reinfeld, a set-shot artist from Philadelphia's Frankford High School, were seniors. So was Mel Brodsky, a high school teammate of Lear's who walked-on to play for Temple. Rodgers and Tink Van Patton were sophomores.

"With guys like Jay Norman to set screens, we were really in tune," said Rodgers. "We just could read one another real well, and, of course, I was always passing. If you weren't ready for it, you might get hit in the head. Hal Lear always told everybody to constantly have their hands in position to catch the ball because 'if you get open, Guy will get the ball to you.' The guys knew what to expect and they knew if they got the ball and we went on a fast break, it was like two-on-*none*."

Reinfeld remembers a game against Holy Cross in Madison Square Garden. "At one point Guy ran after a loose ball. The ball wasn't bouncing. It was rolling. He never broke stride. He just hit the ball with his fist. He hit it enough to get it dribbling and just kept on going. I don't think he slowed down for a second. We wound up with a layup on a fast break. Here I'm playing with him and I'm applauding him on the floor. I never saw anything like it." When Rodgers was playing defense in practice, added Reinfeld, "he would slap at the ball and try to hit you in the hands. It was like getting stuck with a knife, that's how quick his hands were."

Lear, who now lives in Scottsdale, Arizona, still holds the all-time Temple record for points in a single season (745), an amazing feat considering the number of outstanding three-point shooters in the college game today. "But the proudest thing of my career," he said, "was that as a junior I led the team in *rebounding*." Lear, who was only 5'11", averaged eight rebounds a game that season. At the end of the year he was the first round draft pick of the Philadelphia Warriors but, because of the quota system, his NBA playing career lasted a total of five minutes before he was released about four games into the season. "As a number one draft choice I had to fight to get three thousand dollars," Lear recalled. "Years later, that would have been worth five or ten million dollars. But I have no regrets. I made more money playing in the Eastern League and working than I could make in the NBA at that time."

"A lot of people don't realize it because he didn't play in the NBA," said Rodgers. "But Hal Lear just may have been one of the greatest shooters ever. It's true that we were really good, but we *worked* at it. We worked *hard* to be good. I don't think either one of us thought that we would later be considered the best backcourt when we were playing. We wouldn't have been the top backcourt if we didn't have Jay and Freddie, and Tink—guys of that ilk."

"For me," Lear explained, "the key was always knowing how to get the shot that you want in the position that

▲ **G**uy Rodgers led the Owls to three post-season tournaments, including a pair of NCAA Final Four appearances.

against Kentucky, in Lexington. It was the Wildcats' worst opening-game home loss in 29 years, and it was the first time that Adolph Rupp, who had been coaching at Kentucky since 1930, had ever been beaten in a home opener. Afterwards, Rupp paid Rodgers and Lear a supreme compliment—calling them the best guard combination he had ever seen.

"Before they knew what hit them, we were up by 26–5," said Reinfeld, who vividly remembered a trip to Kentucky the previous year when Cliff Hagan had triggered an 86–59 blowout with 52 points. "It was unbelievable. You could hear a pin drop in that place, the fans were so shocked at what was going on. If you could have seen what Lear and Rodgers did in that game, it was something to behold. They put on such a show. They ran a fast break clinic for those people. After the game, Happy Chandler, the governor of Kentucky, came into the dressing room and congratulated us."

"We probably would have beaten them by more but Harry pulled us out of the game," recalled Rodgers, who scored 24 points while Lear added 19. "We did what no one thought would ever happen. It was very much an emotional game for all of us. A lot of guys had played the year before when Kentucky just whipped our ass (twice in back-to-back games; the second time 101–69 in Convention Hall). I remember Tink Van Patton just crying his heart out with joy. He couldn't control himself."

At least this time Temple's black players were able to stay together with their teammates at a hotel in Lexington. They were, in fact, the first blacks ever permitted to do so. "When I look back on it," said Lear. "Here we are—18-year-olds subject to this kind of behavior. When we met the Kentucky players like Cliff Hagan, Frank Ramsey, and Lou Tsioropoulos, we were scared to death. Then you go to the gym. People are screaming and hollering and calling you all kinds of names. Just the fear of being in an environment where you couldn't concentrate totally on basketball because of all these surrounding issues. Then you had all kinds of referee intimidation where guys would knock you all around and nothing would be called. It wasn't easy to keep your game at the top. So when we beat Kentucky down there it felt pretty good."

The winning streak ended on February 1 against Muhlenberg in Allentown, Pennsylvania, of all places, when the Mules inexplicably were able to slow down Temple's offense and win 67–66. Years later, Jay Norman learned how they did it from Clint Jeffries, one of his teammates in the Eastern League. Jeffries had played for Muhlenberg that night. It seems that someone had tied a string to the bottom of the net that kept the ball from coming out after a basket was scored. It was so small that it wasn't visible, but every time the ball went

you want it. It's what they call *getting your shot.* You develop skills of quickness, of crossover dribbles. I would always watch a guy's foot and if I saw one foot go up on his toes, I'd go the other way. He could never catch you because the guy had to be a step behind because he'd have to bring his foot down and then cross."

In the first year of the Big 5, Litwack's Owls went unbeaten for the first two months of the season with 13 straight victories. Game three was one of the most stunning upsets in Temple's history—a 73–61 shocker

in, someone had to jump up and pull it out. "That just killed our fast break," Norman recalled.

No one was more surprised than Litwack when the Owls made it to the 1955–56 NCAA Final Four on their way to a 27–4 record. "After the third or fourth game we started to realize that we had a pretty fair team, but I never thought we were good enough to make the Final Four," Harry said. "I was just tickled to death to be in the tournament." The Final Four was held in Evanston, Illinois, outside of Chicago. Temple lost to Big Ten champion Iowa 83–76 then beat Southern Methodist 90–81 for third place.

Getting to the Final Four 46 years ago, however, was nothing like it is today. "In 1956 it was just another game," said Norman. "Now it's a happening. I couldn't even give my tickets away in Evanston. I gave them to a friend and said, 'If you can sell them, fine.' He couldn't even sell them."

Temple beat Holy Cross and its All-America Tom Heinsohn 74–72 in the first round at Madison Square Garden. Lear scored 26 points. Then the Owls came back to the Palestra where they took the Eastern Regionals by beating Connecticut 65–59 and edging Canisius 60–58 after trailing by 13 points early in the game. Cohen's 34 rebounds against Connecticut still stands as a NCAA Tournament record. Lear scored 40 against Connecticut but was held to 14 against Canisius.

Late in the Canisius game with the score tied, Norman forced a turnover. "Everyone in the gym knew that the ball would be going to Lear," Norman recalled. "So Lear drove to the basket and got fouled with about ten seconds left. I'll never forget Harry. He calls a time out and after we come over to the huddle he said, '*After* Lear makes those two shots drop back into a zone.' He didn't say '*If* he makes one, do this' or '*If* he misses, do that.' He said *after* Lear makes those two shots.' So, of course, Lear (who was suffering from the flu) makes the two free throws and we go back into the zone. They got a good shot at the basket but it rimmed and came out."

The Iowa game left a bitter taste for the Owls. "We outscored them by seven field goals and still lost the game,"said Litwack. "Every time we did anything they would call a foul." "I remember a bad call where a guy actually kneed Hal Lear in the groin as he was driving the baseline," said Rodgers. "And they called the offensive foul on Harold." "We thought we could beat anybody so we still feel that we got cheated," added Lear. "They called eight charging fouls on us and none of them were charges."

San Francisco, which had dethroned La Salle for the 1955 NCAA championship, repeated easily by beating Iowa 83–71 in the title game. The Rodgers-Lear backcourt stole the show, however, with Guy breaking the NCAA Tournament record for assists and Hal smashing the tournament scoring record. He had 32 points the first night and 48 the second. He was easily named the tournament MVP over Russell even though the Owls didn't make it to the finals. Lear's five-game total of 160 points has been exceeded only twice in almost a half-century of NCAA Tournament action—by Princeton's Bill Bradley (1965) and Houston's Elvin Hayes (1968). "You should have seen him running down the floor," recalled Reinfeld. "Breaks, jumpers, lay-ups, unbelievable!"

In 1956–57, the Owls finished with a respectable 20–9 record that included a 57–50 win over St. Bonaventure for third place in the NIT. The following season, Litwack again had the Owls fighting for a NCAA title. This time the dream for what might have been Temple's greatest team ended in the national semifinal game against Kentucky, in Louisville, when the Wildcats eked out a controversial 61–60 victory. Beating Kansas State, 67–57, for their second national third place finish in three years was little consolation for the Owls. Especially since they had already beaten Seattle, the NCAA runner-up, decisively two months earlier while winning the Holiday Festival in New York.

With Bill "Pickles" Kennedy, a highly-touted sophomore from Philadelphia's Lincoln High School, joining Rodgers in the backcourt, Temple's 1957–58 season got off to a slow start. The Owls won their opener against Delaware, then dropped a pair of games at Kentucky and Cincinnati before rebounding to win 25 straight, only to come up short again against Kentucky in the NCAA Tournament. "It's always nice to have a winning streak," Rodgers said. "But, you know, going into the NCAAs it might have been better for us if we had won maybe 22 or 23 in a row and lost one or two games. Sometimes a shock of reality is good. Pickles was an outstanding all-around athlete. Probably in a lot of ways he was almost as good to play with in the backcourt as it was with Hal Lear and myself. I don't think personally that Pickles ever really got the credit he deserved. Of course, that following year, Temple had a disastrous season (6–19). Unlike myself, Pickles didn't have the ballplayers to be on the same page or at the same stage. I was fortunate."

The first Kentucky game, in Lexington on December 7, was a classic, three-overtime, 85–83 heartbreaking loss for the Owls. Vern Hatton won it with a shot from half-

> ▶ Temple's Bill "Pickles" Kennedy was Guy Rodgers's backcourt running mate as a sophomore and later was the Big 5 MVP as a senior in 1960.

court at the buzzer. "It was *after* the buzzer," recalled Rodgers, "but they said it was good. We should have won that game." Two days later, Temple traveled up to Ohio to face Cincinnati and got blown out by the Bearcats 80–57. "We were totally exhausted and they just overwhelmed us," said Rodgers. "We just weren't good enough that night." Norman and Brodsky played the entire 55 minutes. "I had no legs and neither did Melvin," recalled Norman.

During a practice session before the Cincinnati game, though, the Owls learned another valuable lesson from *The Chief*. The players were standing around talking about Hatton's shot when Litwack walked in, gathered them around in a circle and said, "I want to show you guys something. That shot's not so amazing. To make a shot from halfcourt when nobody has a hand up on the guy's face is not that difficult." Then he suddenly took his suit jacket off, grabbed a basketball, walked to the half-court circle, and threw up a two-hand set shot that hit nothing but net. Harry was 50 years old at the time. "The guys' eyes got *that* big," said Norman. "He made believers of us," added Kennedy.

Litwack's shooting exhibition didn't surprise Guy Rodgers, however. "A lot of people don't know this, but Harry had a fairly decent two-hand set shot," recalled Rodgers. "He could teach you in the most subtle ways. He had a sense of humor and he would do some things that were funny as hell. When people gathered around him they heard a lot of wisdom. He just had this knack."

One of Temple's most memorable games that year came at the end of the regular season when the Owls played St. Joseph's for the second time in one of the Big 5's short-lived "rematch games." They had already clinched their first outright Big 5 title and had beaten the Hawks 73–58 earlier in the year. They won easily again this time 91–77 but played the game without Rodgers, who had gotten poked in the eye in the previous game at Lehigh. Jay Norman picked up the slack, scored 22 points and grabbed 24 rebounds in one of the finest individual performances in city series history— especially since Norman was only a little over 6' 2".

"People always underestimated the value of Jay Norman," said Kennedy. "Not taking anything away from Guy's greatness, but Jay was that fiber that held us together, really the backbone of our team. He was the guy that made our zone work. He had everybody moving in the right direction, switching, and doing whatever we were supposed to do. He would say, 'Go through with him' or 'Pick him up' or 'You take him.' I think that if we had lost him we wouldn't have been as good."

The NCAA Eastern Regionals were scheduled for Charlotte, North Carolina, a city that had not yet completely embraced the notion of equal housing for minorities. Norman was concerned and went to see

Temple's athletic director, Josh Cody, a man for whom he had a tremendous amount of respect. Three years earlier, Jay had played on the Owls' freshman football team with a pair of sore knees. After the season, he asked Cody if he could just concentrate on basketball. The athletic director replied, "I would rather have you play one sport that you enjoy and get something out of, rather than force you to play a sport you didn't want to play and get nothing out of it." This time, Cody was just as responsive. He immediately wrote a letter to the mayor of Charlotte and said that if Temple's basketball players could not *all* be housed together and treated as a family, the Owls weren't coming. The mayor assured his friends from Philadelphia that there would be no problem. And there wasn't.

"I'll never forget what Mr. Cody did for us," said Norman, who later served for 21 years as an assistant coach under Litwack, Casey, and Chaney. "I loved that man. Here was a southern gentleman, a man from Tennessee who was just a great humanistic person." The impact of Josh Cody's influence hit home later that year when the Boston Celtics traveled to Charlotte for an NBA exhibition game. "Bill Russell couldn't stay with his team," said Norman. "He was a very proud man and didn't play in that game."

The national semifinal game against Kentucky was played in the Louisville Fairgrounds, which had been the Wildcats' home court a few times earlier that season. Rodgers, playing with a tightly-wound corset to support his ailing back, led all scorers with 22 points. But the contest was largely decided by two plays involving Kennedy, who was Rodgers's superb sophomore running mate.

At the beginning of the game Kennedy suffered a broken nose when Hatton went up for a jump shot and caught him with his elbow. A doctor came out of the stands and pushed it back into place. "It didn't bother me so I went back in and played, " said Kennedy. "When I got back home and went to Temple Hospital, they told me it was the best thing that happened to me because, otherwise, they would have had to re-break it and set it again. So I was lucky."

Temple had a six-point lead with less than two minutes to go. "Then somebody stole the ball and passed it to me," recalled Kennedy. "I started going down on a fast break. Guy Rodgers was on my left. Somehow, Adrian Smith, the Kentucky guard, got between us. I faked because I was going to pass it to Guy and he went for the fake. He twirled all the way around underneath me and I went over him and they called me for a charge. I've seen that film many many times and I still can't see a charge. Smith came back and made the one-and-one to cut Temple's lead to four points. Then with Kentucky leading by one point, Temple had the ball at midcourt and time for one final shot. Litwack called a time out and set a play for Kennedy. "I remember I was surprised because I thought he'd give it to Guy Rodgers," said Pickles, who was supposed to pass the ball to the corner and then go and get the ball back. "The best I can remember—and it's been on my mind for a long time—I made the pass to Brodsky in the corner and I came over to get the ball from him. I don't know whether I was caught off guard or it was too fast. When I watched the films of it, I could see my head snap back and the ball went right through my hands and out of bounds. So we never got to attempt the shot. It was a horrendous end to the game."

Kentucky won the national championship the next night by beating Seattle. Elgin Baylor was named the tournament's MVP. "After the season, Mr. Litwack told us that all the coaches had met at dinner after the NCAA championship game," recalled Kennedy. "He said that they told him that they thought we had the best team in the country that year."

During the three-year Guy Rodgers era, Temple compiled a 74–16 record with nine of the losses coming in 1956–57 when the Owls lost Tink Van Patton with a broken wrist and were forced to play the season without a legitimate center. "The things that I cherish the most from my career at Temple," said Rodgers, "wasn't really the basketball, it was the people. Winning the Big 5 MVP three times was really an honor and something that I will always cherish. But you don't do that by yourself. And if it hadn't been for a guy named Al Shrier (Temple's long-time sports information director), it never would have happened. I don't take losing my loved ones and friends too good. I went through a period one month before I went to college when I lost my mother. It was so devastating and so difficult for me. Then about six months later, I lost my grandfather. Then after I got to Temple, my grandmother had a stroke when I was going to class. I remember just breaking down and crying my heart out and I went to Al Shrier's office. He knew what I had gone through with my mother and my grandfather. He just tried to calm me down the best that he could. Then he called one of the assistant coaches who was my advisor and said 'Guy just can't go to class.' Al just stayed with me and comforted me. It wasn't just that he put Temple and me on the map as publicity man—and he certainly did a great job at that—but it was his caring. Those memories really stay with you because Al and Harry and the guys on the team pulled me through a lot of hard times."

In 1959–60, Kennedy found a new backcourt partner, Bruce Drysdale, a 5'10" set-shot artist. Both had played for another former Owl, Harry Silcox, at Philadelphia's Lincoln High School. "Bill and I knew each other from the time I was twelve or thirteen," said Drysdale. "He was

▲ Temple's Al Shrier has been associated with the Big 5 since its inception in 1955 and is a member of its Hall of Fame. *(Urban Archives, Temple University, Philadelphia, Pennsylvania)*

one of my favorite people. He was a little older but he would always pick me in the playground games. I was recruited by all of the Big 5 schools except St. Joe's, but Bill was probably the reason I went to Temple."

Temple went to the NIT all three years of Drysdale's career. In 1961–62, the Owls beat Providence in the NIT before losing to Loyola (Illinois). The following season, Providence won the NIT and Loyola became NCAA champions. Kennedy was named the Big 5 MVP in 1959–60, and Drysdale got the nod the following season. "Bill and I could both pass or shoot," said Drysdale, who was named to one of the last "Little All-America" teams (for players 5'10" or under). "We could score and we could set up the other guys. He was so unselfish and just a great player."

One of the few times that people saw Litwack angry came early in the 1968–69 season, when the Owls lost an unbelievable overtime game to Bobby Knight's Army team 60–59 at West Point. Temple appeared to have won in regulation when Jack Kirschling stole the ball and was hit by a cross-body block as he attempted a layup. Not only did he miss the shot, he was called for charging on

▲ Temple's Bruce Drysdale, the Big 5 MVP in 1961, was named to the Little All-America team for players 5'10" or under. *(Urban Archives, Temple University, Philadelphia, Pennsylvania)*

the play. Army then scored eight points *without a field goal* to win the game. Ernie Accorsi , who is now the general manager of the New York Giants, was covering the game for *The Philadelphia Inquirer*. "I was on deadline," he said. "So I jumped on the floor and said to Harry, 'Coach I know it's a tough loss but can you give me a quick quote?' 'It isn't the first time I was screwed by the U.S. government,' he replied."

Later, that 1968–69 season appeared to end on a heartbreaking note for Temple's seven seniors. John Connolly followed up a missed shot by Dave Pfahler at the buzzer to give St. Joseph's a 68–67 overtime victory in the Middle Atlantic Conference championship game to knock the Owls out of an NCAA Tournament bid. What made the loss even more devastating was the fact that Temple had crushed the Hawks 79–59 earlier. With

a 17–7 regular season record, the Owls had been completely overshadowed in the Big 5 by nationally-ranked La Salle and Villanova, and now, even in the MAC by the Hawks.

"Our kids were very disappointed," recalled Litwack. "In the dressing room, I said, 'Well okay, boys, what do you want to do?' The said that they wanted to continue practicing even though we knew that we might not get a bid to the NIT." The National Invitation Tournament was a lot more prestigious in those days. The NCAA Tournament field consisted of only two dozen schools, so the NIT had the pick of more quality teams who welcomed the chance to play in Madison Square Garden. As time went on, though, it appeared that Temple would not be one of them.

"It was tough practicing," said John Baum, the team's captain that year. "Here we were seniors thinking, 'if we don't go, what's the use?' We were getting down to the last day and I didn't think we were going to make it. Then on my way to practice I got the word: 'You're in!' It was so exciting I couldn't believe it. I probably just shouted wherever I was on campus. We all got to practice and were hugging each other." Temple had been the last team selected for the NIT.

Joining Baum, a 6'5" forward, in the starting lineup for Harry Litwack's seventh NIT appearance were 6'9" center Eddie Mast, 6'5" forward Joe Cromer, and 5'11" ball-handler Tony Brocchi, who averaged 38 minutes a game playing on a painfully sprained ankle. Bill Strunk, a 6'3" guard who had led the Owls' freshman team in scoring the previous year, was the only non-senior in the group.

Naturally, the Owls were underdogs every game. The first challenge was nationally-ranked Florida with its All-America Neal Walk. Temple won 82–66 as Mast scored 20 points. Then came St. Peter's, the local favorite from nearby Jersey City. The Owls won that one handily 94–78 behind Baum's 31 points and 23 rebounds. Next in line in the semifinals was Tennessee, one of the nation's top defensive teams. Temple pulled that one out 63–58, blowing the game open in the final six minutes with its zone press.

In the championship game, Boston College was sky-high emotionally for what would be Bob Cousy's final game as coach. The former Boston Celtics' Hall of Fame playmaker, a hometown legend, had already announced his retirement. And it was the first time that any Temple player would appear on national television. Temple won 89–76, snapping the nation's longest winning streak.

"That was the happiest day of my coaching life," said Litwack. "I probably got more satisfaction from winning the NIT than from both of my NCAA Final Four teams. We were the last team selected and I really thought that

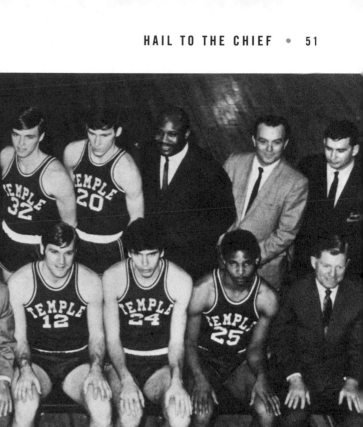

we were going to get knocked off early. I didn't think we would get past the first two rounds because Florida and Tennessee both had outstanding teams. They were really good but we got lucky and won. Afterwards, I really never saw such a happy bunch of basketball players. They believed in themselves and had the chemistry to be a good team."

"We didn't have all the national exposure that the other teams had," recalled Baum. "But we weren't intimidated. We knew that Harry Litwack was a better coach than Bob Cousy. We knew that BC had won 19 straight games, but we believed in Harry and Don Casey. We felt that with our zone, if we do what we're supposed to do, we'll be fine."

At halftime, Boston College appeared to be in complete control, especially up front, where the Owls were getting hammered on the boards and Baum was not doing much to help the offense. As the Owls were getting ready to go back out onto the floor for the second half, Norman confronted Eddie Mast. "Eddie was maybe a little too tentative," Baum remembers. "Jay grabbed him and said, 'Hey, I don't like what you did out there. We need you to play better this half.'" Mast was a terror

on the boards after intermission, finishing with a career-high 22 rebounds.

Baum ended up shooting 10-for-17 from the floor and 10-for-13 from the free throw line. Not only did he grab ten rebounds and outscore Terry Driscoll, 30 to 18, he completely outplayed the BC All-America. But midway through the second half, Boston College was still in control. So much so, in fact, that when the MVP ballots were collected from the writers with ten minutes to go in the game, Driscoll had the most votes.

Right at that time, however, in an effort to spark the struggling offense, Casey urged Litwack to replace Strunk, who was hobbling on a bad ankle, with Tom Wieczerak, a "spot-up" type shooter. The young transfer from Trenton State immediately hit three in a row. Baum blocked a lay-up attempt by Driscoll and the Owls were off on a 14–3 run, took the lead, and put the game away. "We kept creeping up point by point," Litwack recalled. "Everything we threw up went in. Everything they threw up missed."

Afterwards, Baum, who averaged 21 points and 14 rebounds over the four games, was named to the All-Tournament team. Joining him were Mast, who later played for three years in the NBA with New York and Atlanta, and Cromer, the most consistent Owl offensively with 19, 23, 15, and 19 points, respectively, in the four games. Brocchi scored 15 points in the championship game—twice his regular-season average.

When Driscoll was announced as the MVP, there was a stunned silence, then a cascade of boos from the fans. "Driscoll was an All-American but he didn't deserve the MVP that game," said Litwack. "John Baum should have been named Most Valuable Player. My God, every time that ball was up for grabs, he got it."

Baum, who would go on to play for five years in the NBA, still thinks about that MVP award that got away. "The public won't allow me to forget about it," he said. "I got more notoriety for *not* getting the MVP award than I would have if I had gotten it. I remember the next day *The New York Times* talked about how I was robbed. Afterwards I received letters from all over the country. Even when I was playing for the Bulls and Nets, people sent me letters. I got a lot of mileage out of that. Maybe if I had gotten the award, people would have forgotten about it. In fact, a lot of people think that I *did* receive it. I'll be interviewed by ESPN or something like that and the announcers will quickly try to remember without checking their notes. They'll just say, 'Here's John Baum, the captain of Temple's NIT team and the MVP of the tournament.'"

Baum, who also had been recruited by Litwack over a cheeseburger, Coke, and french fries at Mike's Broad Tower, really had no interest in basketball at West Philadelphia High School. Instead he concentrated on soccer and baseball. The latter was his best sport. He had played against future Hall of Famer Reggie Jackson in American Legion ball and had turned down an offer to sign a minor league contract with the Pittsburgh

◄ John Baum, Temple's all-time leading rebounder, was a three-time All Big 5 selection. (Urban Archives, Temple University, Philadelphia, Pennsylvania)

Pirates in 1965. That fall, he enrolled in Philadelphia's Peirce Business School, where he quickly emerged as the team's best player. One night, Peirce played at Philadelphia Textile. Temple's freshman basketball coach Skippy Wilson was moonlighting as a referee.

"Skippy had never seen me play," Baum recalled. "He was probably saying to himself, 'Who is this guy with all this raw talent jumping over everybody and doing real well?' So during the game whenever there was a stoppage of play, Wilson came up behind me and asked me a question: 'Who are you? . . . Are you interested in going to college? . . . Did you take the SATs? . . . What's your major?' I'm wondering why is this official asking me all these questions. I had no idea who he was. So when the game was over, I was in the shower and I got a message from the manager who said 'there's an assistant coach from Temple here to see you.' And I thought to myself, 'that's strange.' Then I said, 'Okay, tell him I'll be right out.' And the manager said, 'No, he's coming in!' It was Skippy Wilson. He came right in and took a shower with me. By the time I walked out of the shower, we had an appointment with Harry Litwack. And when I got out of the shower, I had another message from the manager that Bucky Harris, the coach of Textile, wanted to talk to me. After I got dressed, I told Mr. Harris that I was scheduled to meet coach Litwack tomorrow. And when he heard that, he just ended the conversation and said, 'Thanks, but if you're going to meet with coach Litwack, we have no shot at you!'"

Clarence Brookins, the MVP of the 1967 Quaker City Holiday Tournament, was Baum's roommate for two years. "I would have to attribute a great part of my success to Clarence's work ethic because he ate, slept, and drank basketball," said Baum. "Clarence would say, 'OK John. I'm going to go and work out.' I didn't particularly want to go and work out, but he would insist. So I would go with Clarence and I got better and better and better. We would exercise, work on our drills, play one-on-one and concentrate a lot on defense. Clarence had all kinds of drills. I was a guy who never played much organized basketball before Temple so I needed to get caught up and Clarence was a big part of that.

"Clarence Brookins was the first *big* guard," recalled Baum. "He could shoot and handle the ball well and play defense. I don't think there were any big guards then who could shoot the ball as well as he could. You hear about guys today creating their own shot but Clarence, at 6'4", could jump over you and get his own shot. He could go behind his back. He was just a sound player. There weren't too many 6'4" guys in the 1960s who could do those things as well."

Brookins, like Baum a member of the Big 5 Hall of Fame, averaged 24 points and 12 rebounds when the

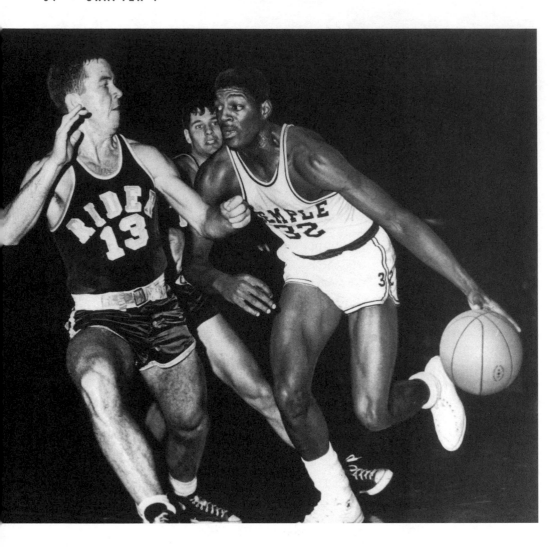

in the NBA for a decade; Duane Causwell, a 7-footer playing with the Miami Heat, and 6'10" Lamont Barnes, a two-time Big 5 first team selection. But no one has broken Baum's record of 1,042 rebounds.

Williams, a member of the Big 5 Hall of Fame, played for the Owls from 1963 to 1966. He was drafted in the fourth round by the Chicago Bulls in 1966, but decided to forgo the NBA to play professionally in Naples, Italy, for six seasons. He also coached the U.S. Marines basketball team for a while. "People thought I was such a great coach," Williams recalled. "I said I couldn't help to be halfway decent because I learned so much from Harry Litwack. I learned from the best."

One night, Williams had a spectacular performance in a pre-season game against a team of touring American college players. Afterwards, he sat down and wrote Harry a letter, thanking him for his advice and guidance. It was in 1969, the year the Owls won the NIT. Later, Joe Cromer, one of the stars of that team, was barnstorming through Europe with another All Star squad and stopped to see Williams. "He told me how Harry started reading the letter to the team one day before practice, but he couldn't finish it. He was so overcome with emotion that he handed the letter to John Baum and John finished reading it. They said that it had an impact."

As one of Harry Litwack's first big men, the 6'10" Williams had a brilliant career for the Owls. He was the first Temple player to score a thousand points (he finished with 1,306) and grab a thousand rebounds (1,031). "It was not a goal of mine to become the all-time leading scorer in Temple's history," he explained. "But I so admired Russ Gordon and the rebounding job he did that one of my goals was to break his record. That means much more to me than the thousand points. I was always in awe how Russ Gordon could control those backboards." Gordon, one of the last of the 6'4" centers, grabbed 995

▲ **T**emple's Clarence Brookins was MVP of the 1967 Quaker City Tournament. *(Urban Archives, Temple University, Philadelphia, Pennsylvania)*

Owls beat Providence, Wisconsin, and St. Francis (Pennsylvania) for the 1967 Quaker City title. Before the Providence game, Brookins asked Litwack to play forward, where he felt he could be more effective against the heavily-favored Friars. He responded with 16 points and a game-high ten rebounds against Providence, then scored 28 points in each of the next two games.

Only two players in Temple's history have scored 1,000 points and grabbed 1,000 rebounds in their careers—Baum and Jim Williams. What makes this feat so remarkable is that both played only three years. Quite a few bigger, taller, and quicker athletes have passed through Temple in the thirty intervening years. Many of them played four years. Players like Tim Perry, who later played

rebounds from 1959 to 1962 and is third all-time behind Baum and Williams.

Williams played in a number of big games for the Owls but none more memorable than a gigantic 73–59 upset over Villanova in 1965. The Wildcats, who later finished the season 23–5 and reached the semifinals of the NIT, were heavily favored. A friend of Williams had a next door neighbor, an eighteen-year-old girl named Betsy Schulz, who was in Delaware County Hospital suffering from a rare blood disease. At the time, she had survived longer than anyone in the world had from this mysterious ailment. Williams was asked to visit her. When he saw her in the hospital, it was quite an eye-opening experience for the young Temple junior. "She was a tiny little thing, just so effervescent," Williams recalled. "She just loved Temple basketball. I took her some mementos from the team. I thought, 'Wow, and I complained many a night because Harry Litwack worked us so hard at practice.' I'd be asleep at my desk studying and sort of feel sorry for myself. But, I tell you after that experience, seeing how courageous this little girl was fighting that disease, it did more for me than it did for her. People thought I was such a great guy for visiting her. I said, 'You got it all wrong—I was the beneficiary of that visit.' We dedicated the Villanova game to her and Les Keiter mentioned her on the air. It was unreal because we beat a Villanova team that was much better than we were. The next week, Betsy died."

The point totals achieved by players like Baum and Williams are even more significant because Harry Litwack's defense-oriented teams usually kept scores down. Furthermore, Harry would always yank his starters when the Owls got a big lead. "As players, we used to hate it," recalled Baum, who finished his career with 1,544 points. "But if you didn't get your

stats by the time we had a twenty-point lead, you wouldn't get them because you'd be coming out of the game. Harry never wanted to embarrass another coach. Even in the NIT championship game he started pulling guys with four minutes to go. That was Harry."

Indeed it was. But before he retired following the 1972–73 season, Litwack still had some magic left. He guided the Owls to a 23–8 record and a share of the Big 5 title with Penn in 1971–72. The highlight came in the very first Big 5 game when Temple snapped the Quakers' 48-game regular-season winning streak—35 in a row at the Palestra—with a 57–52 upset. Harry devised a brilliant box-and-one defense with Mike Jones doing the chasing and holding Penn's Bob Morse to the worst shooting night of his career (2-for-10 for 5 points). Ollie Johnson had 15 points including a couple of key second half baskets that helped thwart a furious Penn comeback. Johnson's finest all-around game came at the end of the year in Litwack's final post-season appearance, a heartbreaking 53–51 loss to South Carolina in the opening round of the NCAA Tournament. Kevin Joyce won it for the Gamecocks with a 20-foot jumper at the buzzer. Hobbling on an injured right ankle, Johnson, the kid who once couldn't make a layup, finished his solid career with 16 points. Another fitting tribute to *The Chief!*

▶ Temple's Jim Williams grabs a rebound away from La Salle's Walter Sampson during a 63–57 win over the Explorers in 1964. *(Urban Archives, Temple University, Philadelphia, Pennsylvania)*

Chapter 5

• • • • • • •

Dr. Ramsay's Hawks Come Marching In

Steve Donches was talking to Cliff Anderson a few years ago at a St. Joseph's University basketball team reunion. "You know, I'm a little bit irritated," said Anderson, the former Hawk All-America. "I went to Hawaii not too long ago and bumped into Les Keiter. Les couldn't remember my name but he said, 'How's Steve Donches doing?'" Anderson was, of course, one of the greatest players ever to wear a Hawk uniform. And he had a big smile on his face when he greeted Donches, his former teammate. But the message was clear: Steve Donches, who came off the bench and out of obscurity to score perhaps the most stunning game-winner in city series history, epitomized everything about the mystique of the Big 5, the Hawks, and Dr. Jack Ramsay, their Hall of Fame coach.

Ramsay, the intense, soft-spoken educator who won or shared seven Big 5 titles in his eleven years as coach, is the man credited with elevating St. Joseph's to the big time. The Hawks had never been to a post-season tournament before Ramsay arrived. By the time he left, they had been to either the NCAA or NIT ten times. Cheered on by some of college basketball's most boisterous fans and a rambunctious perpetually-flapping mascot, Dr. Jack inspired a hustling bunch of overachievers—most of them from Philadelphia's Catholic High School League—to a host of thrilling comebacks and major upsets, including surprising third-place finishes in the 1956 NIT and the 1961 NCAA Tournament. He did it consistently with neither depth nor size—just solid, well-executed fundamental basketball. And he did it while moonlighting at various times as the Hawks' athletic director, baseball coach, and chairman of the college's Education Department.

Later, in 20 seasons with Buffalo, Philadelphia, Indiana, and Portland in the National Basketball Association, Ramsay guided his teams to 16 playoff appearances. In 1977, he coached the Trail Blazers to a NBA title, making him the only coach in history to have directed a college team to the NCAA Final Four *and* a NBA championship. Not only did he silence the critics—who denigrated his "Rah! Rah!" collegiate style—by winning 864 games to become the league's winningest active coach when he retired in 1988, he finished his career with more victories in college and professional basketball (1,098) than anyone. Today he is a familiar face on national television as an analyst for ESPN.

"In a way we were spoiled," said Jim Boyle, one of Ramsay's former players and a later successor as coach of the Hawks. "We were used to good coaching in high school, but when we got to St. Joe's I knew immediately that I was in the company of a master. His concentration, his clarity, his focus, his enthusiasm were clear. We absorbed his basketball principles completely. We were like soldiers in his army. It was a wonderful experience and one of life's blessings for me to be on teams that Jack Ramsay coached. He's been an important part of my life. In fact, as time went on he has become maybe even more special than as a coach. As a friend, as a mentor, he taught us loyalty, commitment, camaraderie. He taught us everything about life."

Ironically, early in his coaching days when he was earning a master's degree and a doctorate in education from the University of Pennsylvania, Ramsay did not consider himself a good teacher. "I thought I was a pretty good player and because I could play, I thought I could automatically coach," he recalled. "When I think back on it now, I didn't do enough teaching at all. I really didn't know how to break the game down to teach it to players. After the first year of high school coaching, I got my ears whacked. These guys were playing zones and combination zones, and were doing things, and I didn't have the same level of players that they had. So I knew if I was going to compete with them, I had to really do a good coaching job with my players." Ramsay started attending coaching clinics conducted by people like La Salle's Ken Loeffler, San Francisco's Phil Woolpert, and California's Pete Newell. "I would really study them and listen how they teach their players. I became a better coach from that point on. Teaching was always a big part of it to me after that first disastrous season."

One vivid Ramsay teaching moment stands out in the mind of St. Joseph's athletic director Don DiJulia, one of Jack's former players. It happened before the championship game of the 1964 Quaker City Tournament against Wichita State, the nation's No. 2 team. "The weekend before the game, we had a walk-around in the Fieldhouse in street clothes with the shoes off so you wouldn't scuff the floor," he recalled. "Wichita State played a 2-2-1 zone press. We had just played Lehigh and as we were walking through, he gathered everybody together and said, 'This is how we'll attack that zone. It's no different than what happened against Lehigh. They're no better. This team doesn't have a chance. It's that simple.' And he was right!" With Marty Ford outscoring 6'7" All-America Dave Stallworth 27–26 in a classic one-on-one duel and Billy Oakes adding 21, the unbeaten Hawks won their tenth straight game 76–69.

That's the game that triggered the outburst by Wichita coach Gary Thompson, who vowed never to return to Philadelphia. The Shockers had eliminated previously unbeaten Villanova 88–74 in the semifinals. Meanwhile, the Hawks were ousting a talented, sixth-ranked Illinois team that had already beaten defending NCAA champion UCLA as well as Kentucky. St. Joseph's displayed one of the most balanced attacks ever seen in the Big 5 that night with five double-figure scorers and four double-figure rebounders. Some observers feel that the Big 5 had real trouble attracting major intersectional teams to play in the Palestra after that. Incidentally, the Hawks were a perfect 15–0 at the Palestra that year.

"He was like a conductor leading his symphony," explained former La Salle coach Speedy Morris, who recalled Ramsay as the coach who had the most profound influence on his career. "He put his whole person into the game, running up and down the sidelines, taking his jacket off. He was sweating, he was hot. He was into it with his arms waving and directing. He was the first guy that I thought, *'That's what I would like to be. I would like to coach in the Big 5.'* When freshmen were ineligible for the varsity and they had freshman

teams, I thought it would be great if I could just be a freshman coach and be a part of a Big 5 program. I used Ramsay's 1-2-1-1 zone press, that I learned from *Pressure Basketball,* which I read a plethora of times. I did that from eighth grade through high school and still use it today, although that press is not as effective as it used to be because kids today are throwing diagonal passes and long baseball passes and it's a little easier to beat."

It's difficult to imagine another coach who displayed as much emotion and intensity as Ramsay. "You always got the impression that if you touched him he would explode," said sportscaster Al Meltzer. "I mean every muscle. From the time the game started until the time it ended, I believe that every muscle in his body was like this."

Sportswriter Frank Bilovsky learned just how much Ramsay allowed himself to become emotionally involved after he stepped into the St. Joseph's locker room following the Hawks' big upset over Wichita for the 1964 Quaker City Tournament championship. "That was a scene I'll never forget. He couldn't talk to us because he was sitting in the corner just weeping into a towel. His whole emotions were releasing. He completely lost his composure because he was so overwhelmed by the victory. And then when he got his emotions under control and he was ready to be interviewed he was his usual great, eloquent interview. That was my most vivid memory of Jack. And, of course, those two fists in the air whenever a St. Joe's player made a great play."

"I was unreasonable about the importance of winning," Ramsay explained. "In hindsight, I overdid that by a great margin. It's hard to divorce yourself from that altogether, but I think as time went on I got better and more determined. I was never good at it but I got better anyway."

"Jack was very competitive, very dedicated and really instilled the same feeling in his players," recalled Bob McNeill, the All-America guard who played on some of Ramsay's early teams. "The way you played kind of demonstrated the kind of person you were. He really got that message across. Even in practice when he would challenge you one-on-one, I mean you'd come out of there bleeding. He'd make sure that you didn't beat him in a one-on-one game. Nobody wanted to play him. You know you'd be on the injured list. When he lost the game it was like you lost someone in your family. He took it so hard. It was tough, particularly when you had a long bus ride back."

▶ **St.** Joseph's coach Jack Ramsay celebrates a Hawk victory with players Bob Gormley (left) and Steve Courtin.

Ramsay was quite obsessed with physical conditioning. In an effort to achieve an edge, he regularly consulted German military manuals in his early days at St. Joseph's. "I found some interesting stuff," he explained. One tidbit, for example, was that the Germans had been using what we now know as Gatorade as an energy drink for their pilots. "I got the components and mixed it up myself. The first Gatorade in this country was probably in the St. Joe's fieldhouse." Ramsay and assistant coach Jack McKinney formed a faculty basketball team and played regularly against the students. "Before these games I would mix this stuff up, drink it, and test it out to see if this really did something for me."

Ramsay also learned that the Germans experimented by running cold water over the stomachs of their fighter pilots to heighten their intensity, mental acuity, and visual sharpness. "I would test this on myself when I played to see if there were any benefits," Ramsay recalled. "I couldn't get the players to subscribe to it but I thought it helped me."

Ramsay made the St. Joseph's varsity as a freshman in 1942–43, playing for Billy Ferguson, who coached the Hawks for 25 years. At the time, Jack wanted to be a medical doctor. "I had chemistry labs that kept me late for practice and Billy always said not to worry because studies came first," he recalled. "But it bothered me. I really felt bad about missing practice and said to myself, 'Look, if you don't want to be a doctor more than you want to practice basketball, than maybe it's not for you.' That's when I started thinking about coaching." Then came a three-year stint as a Navy frogman during World War II. When the Navy assigned Ramsay to Villanova for officer-training, Jack found himself starting at guard on Al Severance's varsity. The Wildcats weren't very good that year, finishing with a 9–11 record and getting blown away in their final game by the Norfolk Naval Training Center, led by Red Holtzman, 69–19. "It was an interesting year," said Ramsay, who recalled averaging "maybe ten points a game."

Later, as a member of an underwater demolition team training for the invasion of Japan, Ramsay was riding in the Pacific heading for the Land of the Rising Sun when the U.S. dropped atomic bombs on Hiroshima and Nagasaki. "We turned around and came back home," Ramsay recalled. "I was actually disappointed that we didn't get a chance to finish what we had been trained to do." Ramsay resumed his studies at St. Joseph's, graduated in 1946 and began his coaching career at St. James High School, in Chester, Pennsylvania, then at Mt. Pleasant High School in Delaware. In 1955, he was back on Hawk Hill as head basketball and baseball coach, studying for his doctorate in education at the University of Pennsylvania, teaching a few classes on the side, and serving for a few years as the school's athletic director.

In Ramsay's college coaching debut, the Hawks upset nationally-ranked Fordham in New York 89–71. The Rams had been picked as best team in the East in pre-season polls. "A huge win," he recalled. "I think it helped them believe that I could help them to be a good team."

"I was a sub in that game," said Jack McKinney. "Not only was it an important game for us, but it was particularly important to him because he proved to us that 'he's the man.' The whole school was going crazy the next day talking about the game."

The Hawks went 23–6 that year and knocked off Temple 77–68 to finish with a perfect 4–0 record in the first Big 5 round-robin competition. The game with Harry Litwack's eventual NCAA Final Four team attracted 9,387 fans, the only Big 5 sellout that year. The fans also got an early glimpse of Ramsay's defensive philosophy expressed in his definitive book, *Pressure Basketball*, which went through five printings after he wrote it in 1963. "Then it went out of print," recalled Ramsay. "Then I had so many requests for copies that weren't available that it was reprinted by another publishing company. It's still selling."

Ramsay had picked up pressure basketball concepts back in his high school coaching days from Woody Ludwig, the long-time football and basketball coach at Pennsylvania Military College in Chester. "We scrimmaged them one time and we were doing pretty well," Ramsay recalled. "Suddenly he put on this full court zone press and we started throwing the ball all over the place." Ramsay soon began tinkering with Ludwig's defensive scheme. "When I started coaching at St. Joseph's, we would use it when we thought it would be effective. Some games we played it for the whole forty minutes. Other times we just used it when thought we could get some benefit to it. It's an energy-consuming defense—you've got to keep going, going, going. Even in the NBA, my teams won a lot of games with it. But your players have to be willing because it's almost constant running, effort, positioning, anticipation, and reaction."

Four of the players Ramsay inherited that year made the first All Big 5 team. They included All-America Kurt Engelbert, who led the Hawks in scoring; Bill Lynch, the team's top rebounder, who had played for Ramsay in high school; Mike Fallon, the team captain; and Al Juliana, who came off the bench to trigger the 83–70 win over Villanova in the first Big 5 game ever played. Juliana was known for his line-drive jumper, a shot described by Matt Guokas Sr. on early Channel 12 telecasts as "Al Juliana's trolley wire jump shot." At the end of the year, Ramsay and St. Joseph's fans were outraged

▲ **D**an Dougherty (left) and Kurt Engelbert were members of the first St. Joseph's teams to play in the Big 5. *(St. Joseph's University)*

when Fallon was left off the NIT All Tournament team after he came off the bench to score a total of 46 points, triggering the Hawks to a third place finish in their first ever post-season appearance. After beating Seton Hall handily 74–65 in the opener, they dropped an 89–79 decision to Louisville and then rebounded to beat St. Francis (N.Y.) 93–82.

Fallon's backcourt running mate was Dan Dougherty, who made All Big 5 the following season. Dougherty, a junior, had been a bit apprehensive when he learned that Ramsay was coming to St. Joseph's. A few years earlier, during a game between his school, St. Joseph's Prep, and Ramsay's high school team, a St. James player piled on top of Dougherty's best friend during a scramble for a loose ball. Dougherty jumped in to help his teammate when someone grabbed him from behind. It was Ramsay. "I had no idea who it was," recalled Dougherty. "I turned around, threw a punch and missed him. I got thrown out of the game and so did the kid from St. James." During one of Ramsay's first practices on Hawk Hill, the new coach called for a one-on-one drill. "He blows his whistle and it was just Ramsay and myself," said Dougherty. "I go to the basket. He

drills me, I mean really good, and says, 'That's for two years ago. Now it's forgotten.'"

At the end of the season, Yale University tried to lure Ramsay to the Ivy League. "I had grown up in Milford, Connecticut, not far from the university, and entertained the idea," he said. "I only had a one year contract at St. Joseph's but when I told them about it, they doubled my salary to $7,000. I thought I was in hog heaven. We had next to nothing budgeted for recruiting—I think $300 or something like that—and $150 for game films that were done for a ridiculous rate in eight-millimeter color by Lou Tucker. He was good. He started with me and I think everyone else in the Big 5 then used him."

The only time Ramsay really lost his cool happened the following season against Auburn in the semifinals of the 1956–57 Carousel Tournament, in Charlotte, North Carolina. This happened to be the first in-season tournament appearance ever for a St. Joseph's team. The Hawks had gotten off to a great start that year by reeling off six straight wins, including an upset over Davidson in the opening round. Now in a nip-and-tuck game against Auburn, Ramsay had been off the bench several times complaining that the officials were disrupting the Hawks' motion offense.

"Their players would step in front, fall down, and draw the offensive charge," he recalled. "We had never seen that before. These guys were jumping in front of us on our cuts, falling down on contact, and getting the foul calls. I had a hard time accepting all that." What was absolutely impossible for Ramsay to accept, however, came on the last play of the 66–64 Auburn victory when referee Al Kluttz waved off the potential game-tying field goal by Ray Radziszewski, who later played for a season with the Philadelphia Warriors. The official claimed that Engelbert had tapped the ball into the basket after the buzzer. Ramsay and some of his players had to be restrained after confronting the officials at midcourt, arguing that no one touched the ball. Inflaming the situation, Lou Bello, another referee working the tournament, came rushing out of the stands to join in the argument.

"Bello comes out of the stands shouting, 'What a great call. The best call I've ever seen,'" said Dan Dougherty, who recalled being grabbed around the neck and whipped away by a Carolina state trooper during the fray. "Fans were yelling 'Kill the Papes!' from the stands."

"The entire St. Joseph's entourage charged the officials with the outrage of kamikaze pilots," wrote Bob Quincy in the next day's *Charlotte News. "Quick thinking by fellow official Red Mahalik, who grabbed his partner in square-dance fashion and sashayed him to the safe confines of the dressing room, probably prevented a full scale battle."*

Now fast-forward 24 years to October 1980. Dougherty's son, Dan, is playing football for Wake Forest against Duke, and dad makes the trip to Durham. Before kickoff, he visits Cameron Fieldhouse just as the Blue Devils' alumni vs. old-timers basketball game is ending. He bumps into Mike Krzyzewski, who once worked for Dougherty as the prep school coach at Fort Belvoir and later succeeded him as coach at Army. They chat for a while, then walk into the locker room. Who is sitting there but Lou Bello, who had officiated at the old-timers game. "Dan, this is Lou Bello," says Coach K. "I looked at him," recalled Dougherty, "and said, 'Charlotte, North Carolina. Carousel Tournament. The shot was good!' He goes, 'The shot was not good! And Ramsay knows it was not a good shot!'"

Despite his intensity, Ramsay never gave a poor rating to basketball referees when he filled out their evaluation forms at the end of each game. "First of all," he explained, "I felt that the officials overall were very good. I never wanted my players to feel that the officials either won or lost a game for us. Except on very rare occasions are officials going to determine who wins— maybe a bad call at the end of the game. I wasn't trying to be soft on them. The ECAC at that time had a great system of selecting and training officials, then observing them and critiquing their performance."

The only time Ramsay got ejected from a game came in the NBA when his Portland Trail Blazers were playing in Denver. Ironically, the official who gave him the heave-ho was none other than one of his former Hawk players, Billy Oakes, who played in the St. Joseph's backcourt from 1964–66. "I deserved to get thrown out. There were a couple of calls that I thought were not good. I had gotten a technical earlier and, in hindsight, I deserved both of them. I made some disparaging remark. Billy was a very competitive, non-stop type of guy who loved to referee, even in college. At practice, he would say to me, 'Let me call them while I'm out of the scrimmage.' You could tell that [famous NBA referee] Mendy Rudolph was his idol. He would mimic Mendy's actions."

In 1957 and 1958, St. Joseph's took their first overtime games in Big 5 history—both over La Salle. The Hawks overcame an 11-point second-half deficit to win the first one 97–85. Then Bob McNeill triggered an 82–77 triumph by scoring 30 points, including 18-of-22 free throws, in the final city series game of the 1958 season. McNeill, who still holds the Hawks' career assist average of 5.46 per game, joined sharpshooting Joe Gallo, his teammate at Philadelphia's Northeast Catholic High School, to form one of the earliest—and finest— backcourt combinations in the city, first in the Catholic League, then in college.

▲ **A**ll-America Bob McNeill holds the St. Joseph's career assist record. *(Urban Archives, Temple University, Philadelphia, Pennsylvania)*

"I remember that game playing against kids you grew up with," said McNeill, who led the Hawks in scoring for three years. "La Salle had Hugh Brolly and Joey Heyer. When we finally took the lead, they started pressing us so every time we got possession, Jack would give me the ball and they just kept fouling me. I remember I could have won it in regulation but I missed the second part of a one-and-one." McNeill, who never missed two foul shots in a row, won it from the free throw line in overtime. "Bobby was as close to unflappable as you could get," recalled Ramsay. "He was very skilled, very confident, very sure of his game. He looked like he wasn't quick enough but he would get by you with a great first step. He was a quiet guy but very intelligent."

In their previous Big 5 game, the Hawks had battled back from a 17-point deficit to beat Villanova, 86–82. "I remember for some reason I decided to take a 25-foot

▲ Joe Spratt had the opportunity to display his defensive skills against three of the nation's top players—Wilt Chamberlain, Oscar Robertson, and Jerry West. *(St. Joseph's University)*

shot at a critical stage in the game and Jack yelling, 'No! No! No!'" recalled McNeill, who is one of the best players *never* to be named Big 5 MVP. (Guy Rodgers, Joe Spratt and Pickles Kennedy received the honor during McNeill's career.) "Then it went in and he yelled, 'Atta Boy!' or something like that. It was a dumb shot to take but it was one that just happened to go in at the right time."

Ramsay guided the Hawks to their first NCAA Tournament appearance the following year. The reward for a 22–3 regular season record and the Hawks' second outright Big 5 title was a game against West Virginia in the Eastern Regionals, in Charlotte, North Carolina. The Mountaineers won 95–92 thanks to one player. "I knew all about Jerry West," said Ramsay. "I had

scouted him and recognized him as a great player. But I had a player who was a terrific defender, Joe Spratt. In the first half he did a terrific job. They only allowed four personal fouls in those days and Spratt had two at the half. I could hear their coach, Fred Schaus, complaining to the officials the whole game about Spratt fouling West. They finally fouled him out and when that happened, West just took the game over. He was blocking shots and scoring and rebounding. We had opened with a pretty good lead, but we had no answer for him." West finished with 36 points and the Mountaineers went to the NCAA championship game, where they lost to California and Darrall Imhoff 71–70. West was named MVP of the Final Four.

Coming the season after he had drawn the assignment of guarding Wilt Chamberlain of Kansas and Oscar Robertson of Cincinnati, Spratt's effort against Jerry West climaxed the most challenging defensive trifecta ever attempted by a Big 5 player. "You can't compare Wilt with the other two because he was one of a kind," explained Spratt, who had guarded Chamberlain twice in Philadelphia city championship games when their respective high schools, West Catholic and Overbrook, split the two victories. "Oscar was more of a pure shooter but Jerry did everything. He was a shooter, he was a rebounder, he was a defensive player. He had more of an all-around game." Although St. Joseph's held Chamberlain to 13 points and led the Jayhawks 26–23 at halftime, Wilt finished with 31 points and 22 rebounds to lead Kansas to a 66–54 win over the Hawks early in the 1957–58 season. Robertson was even more awesome later that year, scoring 43 points to trigger a 100–78 Cincinnati rout and setting a single game Palestra record by an opponent that stood for more than a decade. "I remember Ramsay saying to me before we went out on the floor, 'Joe, make sure you don't foul Oscar.' We go out for the center-jump, the ball goes up, the whistle blows, no time had clicked off the clock, and I had a foul called on me. Ramsay just turned and his eyes went to heaven."

Spratt later had the opportunity to display his offensive talents in his senior year when he was named Big 5 MVP. He hit 10 of 16 field goal attempts and scored 25 points in an 82–70 win over Villanova that helped insure a perfect 4–0 Big 5 record for the Hawks. "Villanova had two players from my neighborhood—Jim Huggard and John Driscoll—and everyone was saying that they were going to beat us," said Spratt. "We opened up by outscoring them something like 22–3 and won easily."

In 1960–61, three St. Joseph's starters were implicated in a point-shaving scandal that involved a total of 37 players from 22 institutions nationwide. Ed Bowler, a seldom-used reserve player at La Salle, was also involved. The St.

Joseph's players—Jack Egan, Vince Kempton and Frank Majewski—had each received $2,750 for conspiring to shave points in games against Dayton, Xavier, and the second of two contests that year against Seton Hall. They were not asked to lose the games, only to control the point-spread so gamblers could make a financial killing. St. Joseph's lost to Dayton and Xavier and beat Seton Hall in overtime at the Palestra. Like the others involved, the St. Joseph's players were never prosecuted. Although they were suspended from the college, they were permitted to return later to earn their degrees.

The Hawks had gone unbeaten in the Big Five for the second time and had lost only two other regular-season games that year. They easily eliminated Princeton and Wake Forest in the Eastern Regionals in Charlotte to advance to the Final Four in Kansas City. The regional final was carried on closed-circuit television in the St. Joseph's Fieldhouse and college officials arranged to have the sounds of 3,000 cheering Hawk fans piped into the Charlotte Coliseum. When Wake Forest coach Bones McKinney heard the "Go, Hawks, Go!" cheers reverberating throughout the arena, he reacted angrily, saying, "I've never heard anything like this!" and ordered that the sound be turned off.

Even without their cheering fans, the Hawks quickly took control of the game and led by 20 points at the half. The St. Joseph's and Wake Forest locker room were located adjacent to each other. "All you could hear was Bones McKinney screaming and yelling, 'How can you let a team like this possibly beat you? Nobody's ever heard of this team,'" recalled Tom Wynne, a sophomore. "Ramsay just said, 'OK, guys, you just heard what you have to do in the second half.'"

Even today, Ramsay, who was also the Hawks' athletic director at the time, finds it difficult to rehash that devastating season. "I'd rather not talk about it because I like to remember all those guys as the players and the people they were," he explained. "It was an unfortunate situation that I had some responsibility for not supervising them more closely—for again putting winning ahead of what was more important than their individual development as people. It was a great team—Lynam and Wynne, Egan, Kempton and Majewski. It's just unfortunate that it didn't have a chance to be recognized for being as good as it could be."

Egan had led St. Joseph's in scoring with a 21.9 average, including a 47-point outburst against Gettysburg earlier that season, a Hawk single-game record that stood until Tony Costner matched it 22 years later against Alaska-Anchorage. He also was named to the NCAA All-Tournament team after scoring 50 points and grabbing 21 rebounds in the two Final Four games.

Harry Booth, who later coached at St. Joseph's, was one of Egan's teammates that season. "There was no doubt in my mind that Jack Egan would have played ten years in the NBA," said Booth about the No.1 draft choice of the Philadelphia Warriors that year. "He was a 6'5" player who could handle the ball, could score, could rebound. He would have been an outstanding player." "In my opinion he was as good as Paul Arizin," said Wynne, a member of the Big 5 Hall of Fame.

Jim Lynam, then the team's sophomore playmaker, was relaxing in his dorm room the morning after returning from the NCAA Final Four in Kansas City. With Jerry Lucas scoring 29 points and grabbing 25 rebounds and John Havlicek holding Egan to six points, the Hawks had been eliminated by unbeaten Ohio State 95–69 in the national semifinals. They bounced back to upset Utah 127–120 in four overtimes for third place (which was later vacated by the NCAA) as Egan closed out his career with 42 points.

Later, reflecting on the Ohio State game, Lynam said, "Men against boys. They were just too good. Sometimes, circumstances are there that you did everything that you could. You take your whipping and go on. Obviously before the game we thought we had a shot. It was the first time we played against a team like that. They had four future pros and one of them is a Hall of Famer. The only real recollection that I have of the game was like 'Man, I'm back here by myself.' They were fast breaking and laying it up. It was like a pregame layup drill all game long. They were so dominant in every area. Jerry Lucas gets every rebound and outlets the thing practically to half court. I never saw the tape of the game but we were outmanned. We were unable to control or set any kind of tempo, they were so good."

Lynam lived on the ground floor of a converted Main Line mansion. Suddenly the pay phone outside his room rang. Jim Boyle, his buddy and a red-shirt freshman, was on the other end. "He's hysterical and he's yelling and whatever he's saying is incomprehensible," Lynam recalled. "I hear words and high volume. I said, 'Bo, slow down!' He said something to the effect like 'Horse, Frank and Vince.' We called Egan '*Horse*,' and my first thought was that they were in a car accident. And whatever he then said, it obviously wasn't a car accident. You hear words but you can't form that thought—what the words mean. So it took like seconds and I asked a question and I'm sitting in a phone booth in a closet and I'm by myself and I'm just holding the phone. It was like 'What have these three guys done?' And my next thought was. 'Your life's over. You've ruined your life.' And literally I had a visual impression of sitting in a cave. It was weird. It was like sitting somewhere in this remote

God-forsaken *nowhere*. I've never forgotten that. And I liked those three guys."

"Jack Ramsay was so depressed when I got in that morning," recalled Jack McKinney, who also served as assistant athletic director. "He spent the whole day just shaking his head and saying 'I just can't understand it.' We would talk about particular games with the telephone constantly ringing. I was like the blocker or security guard and no one was allowed in to see him. His secretary was channeling off phone calls. We just sat there and talked and tried to console each other. He'd break down once in a while and just shake his head. Then his secretary came in and said, 'There's a reporter here to see you. It's [*Philadelphia Inquirer* sportswriter] Herb Good.' Jack had a great amount of admiration for Herb, someone who understood everything that was going on. He said, 'Okay let him come in.' I left and Herb went in and consoled him for almost a half an hour. He told him, 'It's not your fault. You didn't do it. These things happen in life.' I know Herb made a big impression on Jack then. I'm sure he helped Jack make a decision because, at that point, Jack was thinking about not coaching. Herb told him that the game needed him. He had all the right things to say. I know that he strongly urged Jack not to quit coaching."

Two nights later, college officials—at Ramsay's urging—decided to go ahead with the annual basketball awards banquet. Ramsay asked Lynam to get there a little early. "We're having some pictures taken, and you're the MVP," he said. "It's tough to define one's feelings but there was a turmoil within that I could not reconcile—like something is not right about this" recalled Lynam of that moment. "You can paint it, you can perfume it, but you know what it is. I'm not the MVP. I'm pretty good. I'm the point guard of a team that just went to the Final Four. A seven-foot guy, Billy 'The Hill' McGill, who's going to go high in the NBA draft—I just drove his face for 31 in a four-overtime consolation game. Nobody has to tell me I'm a decent player, but I'm not the MVP of this team. Egan's the MVP."

Lynam never had a feeling like he did sitting through that dinner. "And when they called my name to go up and get the award, I saw that it said *for outstanding player, etc.* And at the bottom of the gold plate where they inscribed the words, there's a cut and it says *James F. Lynam*. And I said to myself, 'Boy, you talk about simplistic things speaking volumes for eons. As long as that thing is still with us on the earth, *that* will tell the story of what really happened.' And I remember I had it in my arms. As I was walking down the little platform from the end of the stage, I walked down the steps and as I was walking back to my seat, I said to myself, '*I would like to take this and throw this on that wall so that this gold ball shatters into as many pieces as it possibly can.*'"

"One day during the Eastern Regionals in Charlotte, we were having breakfast on the veranda of the hotel with the three guys who ended up being involved in the situation," recalled Boyle. "I had a newspaper and I said, 'Look at this. Two guys from Seton Hall are accused of fixing basketball games and one of them was against us.' Somebody took the paper out of my hand, looked at it and the three guys got up and left instantly. It didn't register with me. These guys were friends of mine. It was just a tragic mistake by young kids. It was shocking, it was devastating, it hurt the feelings of Coach Ramsay immensely, and it hurt us all. But now as a guy that's been around the block a few times, I just see it as a mistake that guys made when they were young kids, twenty years old, or so. I wish it hadn't happened. And their lives would have been different—it had a nasty impact on these guys for sure. It was a sad moment in St. Joe basketball history, really. But even sadder, from a personal point of view, these guys made a mistake. But everybody makes mistakes. Everybody! We're human and we falter from time to time. They faltered in a public way in a sacredness about competition and that's what made it so awful at the time. But I'm sure they've gotten absolution."

Lynam, Boyle, and Wynne, who turned down a football scholarship to the U.S. Naval Academy to play for Ramsay, helped St. Joseph's recover from the trauma of the scandal the following two seasons. Although the Hawks tied Penn for last place in the Big 5 in 1961–1962 (their only losing season in city series play under Ramsay), they did manage to set a single-game Palestra rebounding record (83) that still stands today as Larry Hoffman pulled down 31 during a 99–72 win over St. Peter's. They finished 18–10 and returned to the NCAA Tournament where they lost to Wake Forest and NYU in the Eastern Regionals. Lynam shared Big 5 MVP honors with Villanova's Wali Jones.

"Jimmy Lynam was the coach on the floor—a very intelligent guy who knew his game and everybody else's," recalled Ramsay. "He knew what the opposition was trying to do and how he could beat it. A great clutch guy." Also a guy who almost didn't get recruited by the Hawks because Ramsay confused him with Jimmy's West Catholic High School backcourt running mate, Herb Magee.

"I went to see their game," explained Ramsay. "I'm standing in the aisle, looking out, peering around people. The best kid who was really playing well turned out to be Magee. Because there's no program and no P.A. system—and I had never seen any of these guys before—I assumed this is Lynam." Ramsay had made an appointment with West Catholic coach Jim Usilton to meet with Lynam and his parents after the game. "So the game ends and this kid comes walking over with a big smile on his face. I thought to myself, 'N*o, this isn't Magee.*' I find out that I had been watching the wrong guy."

Did Ramsay admit that he had confused the two players? "No, I faked it. Then I asked Usilton about Magee. I said, 'this kid can really shoot.' I entertained the thought of taking them both but thought, 'I can't have two little guys.' But I should have taken them both. Herb loves the story. He is a great guy. If you ask him, who is the best shooter in the game, he says 'All time? Other than me?'" Magee became Philadelphia Textile's all-time leading scorer, then went on to a highly successful coaching career at the school now known as Philadelphia University.

The Hawks finished with a 23–5 record and returned to the NCAA Tournament in 1962–63, a season that was highlighted by the most stunning upset of the Ramsay era—a, 58–57 win over unbeaten Bowling Green on a desperation 18-foot shot at the buzzer by Jim Boyle in the opening round of the Quaker City Tournament at the Palestra. The Hawks were unable to stop the Falcons' talented 6'11" center Nate Thurmond, who had 23 points and 23 rebounds, but got a tremendous performance from tournament MVP Steve Courtin, who scored 22 and grabbed seven crucial rebounds. Courtin, a sophomore, shot 28-for-51 from the field and ended up with 64 points for the tournament.

"I will always remember that game, probably because the first eight guys out of the Bowling Green locker room were able to dunk," said sportswriter Dick Weiss. "St. Joe's comes out in terry cloth warm-ups looking like they belonged in a Catholic League playoff game. No one believed St. Joe's could stay close to this team. You always remember things magnified, but I still have a feeling in my gut that everyone in the Palestra stood up and was singing the Hawk fight song. I mean I get goose bumps thinking about it. After Boyle's shot, I still think the ball moved around the rim for at least two or three seconds before it dropped in. I still remember Jack Ramsay throwing his sport coat into the stands. That was just a classic example of what it was like to be in the Big 5 because basically Big 5 teams back in the 1960s were Catholic League graduates or local kids who had come together as a bunch of over-achievers playing for outstanding coaches and basically taking on the rest of the country."

"When that game started," recalled Boyle, "I looked down the other end of the court and I saw Nate Thurmond. I thought 'Man, I've never seen a guy who looked like that.' I never saw a guy that athletic-looking and that tall. I was thinking, 'I've heard this guy was good but I never played against a guy *this* good before.'

I wouldn't say that I was intimidated but I was very curious to see how this guy played basketball. And he was awesome. Howie Komives was also great. He showed that when he later played on the Lakers' NBA championship team."

"We knew they had the potential to blow us out," recalled Ramsay, whose Hawks were still reeling from a heartbreaking 78–77 loss to Penn four days earlier. "But we played a very effective game at both ends of the floor. We kept it close. We were trapping to get the ball because they had the lead in the dying seconds of the game and all they had to do was hold the ball out. But Tom Wynne finally got an interception out of the pressing defense and called a time out. We got the ball at half-court with three seconds left and I remember setting up a play to get a quick cut with Wynne taking the ball out of bounds."

Boyle was supposed to come to the ball and hit Jim Lynam, cutting to the basket, with a pass. "Which I did," recalled Boyle. "But, unfortunately, he couldn't get the shot and just flipped it back to me. It was only a reflex. I knew that time had run out. I just caught it and shot it and the next thing I knew the ball was bouncing, bouncing, it just kept bouncing on the rim. I was looking at the ball and saying, 'I hope it goes in.' It seemed like an eternity. And then the ball finally fell in and we had beaten the No. 1 team in the country." The Hawks went on to edge Villanova 59–54 in the semifinals, then defeated Brigham Young 76–64 for the first tournament championship in the school's history.

At the end of the season, St. Joseph's battled back from a 12-point deficit to nip Princeton 82–81 in overtime in a first round NCAA Tournament game at the Palestra. Bill Bradley was spectacular as usual with 40 points and 16 rebounds before fouling out. That came after John Tiller, a 6' 8" junior center playing the game of his life, came out of nowhere to block one of Bradley's shots. Tiller made four crucial steals in the game and grabbed ten rebounds. After putting on its best offensive show of the season and beating West Virginia 97–88 in the Eastern Regionals behind 23-point efforts by Boyle and Wynne, St. Joseph's faced Duke for the right to go to Final Four. It was a one-point game at halftime but the Blue Devils won handily, 73–59. "Actually I can laugh about it now but it took me a long time to get over the fact that I shot 0-for-14 in the second half," recalled Boyle.

▶ Jim Boyle grabs a rebound during a 53–49 win over Temple as St. Joseph's teammate Bob Dickey watches in a 1962 game. *(Urban Archives, Temple University, Philadelphia, Pennsylvania)*

Steve Donches recalled sitting in class one Friday anticipating the game that night pitting his freshman team—arguably the strongest in St. Joseph's history—against the Hawks' varsity that included players like Boyle, Courtin, and Oakes. The varsity always won these traditional games to kick off the season, but Donches and his teammates—who included Cliff Anderson, Vince Curran, Al Grundy, and Roger Harrington (whose brother, Bob, played for Temple)—felt that they had a shot to make it a game. "We were feeling pretty good about it," recalled Donches. But the game was never played. It was November 22, 1963.

With Courtin averaging better than 20 points-per-game in 1963–64, the Hawks came on strong at the end of the season to finish with an 18–10 record and play well in the NIT. They upset Rick Barry's Miami Hurricanes, one of the highest-scoring teams in college basketball history, 82–76, before dropping an 83–81 heartbreaker to Bradley, the eventual tournament champion. Courtin's 31 points against Bradley and 30 against Miami are still the best individual post-season tournament performances ever registered by a St. Joseph's player.

"Courtin was a clutch player, fearless and fazeless," said Ramsay. "And, boy, he could jump. I'll say he was one of the first ordinary 6'2" or 6'3" guys who could go over the rim. He was a little undisciplined but he just had unbounded confidence and turned out to be a really good college player."

Courtin, who was known to his friends as the "Woodlyn Weaver," also held the St. Joseph's free throw shooting records for a while. "That came from my dad," he explained. "His philosophy was, '*This is going to be the easiest shot you're ever going to have because there's nobody guarding you. So take advantage of it.*' That really sunk in with me and I worked at it and took pride in my foul shooting. During one stretch in his senior year, Courtin didn't miss a free throw for nine straight games. At one point he made 39 in a row, missed one, then made 28 more.

Courtin, who shared Big 5 MVP honors with Villanova's Wali Jones, also sparked a late-season 69–63 win over a nationally-ranked Wildcat team that had lost only two games up to that point. Before the game, in which he scored 23 points, he made one of his weekly visits to a local steak shop, located about a mile from the

St. Joe's campus and across the street from Overbook High School, where Wali Jones had starred a few years earlier.

"You were supposed to write your pick for the game and high scorer on the wall," recalled Courtin, who had played in the backcourt with Don DiJulia at St. James High School. "Whoever picked the closest won a cheesesteak. I wrote down St. Joe's and put my name down as high scorer. I came back a week or so later and Larry, the owner, said, 'Hey were you in that pool?' I said, 'Yes.' He said, 'You're the guy who picked St. Joe's and this Steve Courtin guy. You won. What's your name?' I said. 'Steve Courtin.' He said, 'Do you mean you've been coming in here for four years to get a cheesesteak? Why didn't you tell me?'"

In 1964–65, the Hawks finished with a 26–3 record. Two of the defeats came in the NCAA Tournament, to Providence (81–73) and North Carolina (103–81). Twice that year the Hawks scored 117 points, the second time setting a Winston-Salem Memorial Coliseum record as they registered the most points ever against a Wake Forest team in a 117–91 win.

The Hawks wrapped winning streaks of ten and sixteen games around their only regular season loss, 65–61 at unbeaten Providence four days after their stunning Quaker City Tournament upsets over two of the nation's top teams, Illinois and Wichita. Their third-place finish in the AP and UPI polls was the highest national ranking up to that point by a Big 5 team.

Returning basically the same team in 1965–66, St. Joseph's put on an awesome season-long offensive show. Averaging 91.1 points-per-game—which still stands as the Big 5 scoring record, all five starters averaged in double figures: Cliff Anderson (17.9), Matt Guokas (17.5), Tom Duff (14.8), Billy Oakes (13.5), and Marty Ford (11.0).

"That was my best team," said Ramsay. "A unique team." What made it so unique? "I think the overall skill of the players. They played so well together. There was no jealousy or animosity among any of them. They had unbelievable harmony on that team. And except for Oakes who went about 5'10", Ford, Duff and Anderson, who were all 6'3" to 6'7", could all run, could all pass, and could all defend. The big guys could all rebound. They were willing to play together as a team at both ends of the floor."

"It was a strangely configured team in sizes and shapes because we had no center and no *real* point guard," explained Guokas. "We had good chemistry amongst our top six or seven guys. We all kind of shared being the floor leader. I got a chance to make plays, but I wasn't like a ball-handler type of guy. And Jack wisely

▲ St. Joseph's Cliff Anderson was consistently outstanding against Big 5 opponents, such as this game against Penn in which he scored 31 points. (Urban Archives, Temple University, Philadelphia, Pennsylvania)

didn't try to make me one. He used me in positions where I could catch the ball and then make a play for somebody rather than do it off the dribble. And Cliff, at 6'3", was in effect our big man because he played such a big game and he wasn't an outside shooter. He kept himself around the basket. He was a good scorer, a good rebounder and very tough, very physical, as both our forwards—Duff and Ford—were."

"I remember vividly like it was yesterday standing on City Avenue right before the 1965–66 season," said Don DiJulia, who had just returned to St. Joseph's after studying for three years at St. Charles Seminary. "Matt Guokas and I were saying 'This team is really good.' We had a copy of the schedule, and we went down game-by-game and honestly we didn't think that this team would lose a game. Somebody named Anderson was a freshman nobody knew about but I think Jack Ramsay knew that this was a special group." And for good reason. The Hawks had just been picked as the nation's No. 1 team by *Sports Illustrated*.

From the moment he first set foot on the Palestra floor with an amazing 21-rebound performance to lead the Hawks to a 77–64 upset over top-ranked Davidson in his second collegiate game, Anderson was arguably the best player ever *in Big 5 games*. During his three-year college career from 1964 to 1967, he led the Hawks to a 66–18 record, scored a then-school record 1,728 career points, and grabbed 1,228 rebounds, which is still the Hawks' best ever. As a senior All-America, he scored a Big 5 record 116 points in the four city series games (eclipsing 30 points three times) to earn Big 5 MVP honors going away. His 26.5 point-per-game average that year still stands as a St. Joseph's record, as does his single season point total of 690 and single-season rebounding mark of 450 set in his sophomore year.

"Cliff was an amazing player when you consider his height," recalled Guokas. "They say he was 6'3" but he probably played like he was 6'9" or 6'10" and I'm not exaggerating. He had those long arms and big hands. He was slinky around the basket, deceptively strong, had the ability not only to get his shots off in and around the hoop, but to draw fouls. You felt comfortable giving him the ball either in the post or down in the baseline and he could make something happen." Guokas frequently brought Palestra fans to their feet oooiing and ahhiing with anticipation when he quickly moved the ball upcourt on a fast break and fired an outlet pass to Anderson streaking under the basket.

Many observers consider Anderson's 36-point, 24-rebound effort in a 69–61 win over Villanova the night of the Bomb Scare on February 20, 1965, the greatest individual Big 5 performance in history. What made the feat even more incredible, it came against one of the best defenders in college basketball, Big 5 MVP Jim Washington, who fouled out midway through the second half.

"I had a great deal of admiration for Jim and I was really inspired for that game," recalled Anderson, who was only a sophomore but wasted no time challenging the Wildcats' senior All-America candidate. "I drove down the middle, went right under the basket in front of him. I knew he could jump high so instead of jumping, I faked and sure enough it looked like he jumped out of the building. I mean I thought I saw the bottom of his sneaks. I'll never forget that. Because he went so high, as he was coming down I started going up and scored. I think that set the tone for the game. I was really surprised being able to get 24 rebounds against Jim Washington. As most people will attest, rebounding is mostly intensity and the will. Every ball I considered mine and if he got one I felt like he stole something from me."

"Clifford had incredible leaping hang time, great hands to catch and finish a play," said Ramsay, who later called Anderson his greatest player *ever*. "Just an amazing athlete with excellent basketball instincts. Smaller guys he'd jump over. Bigger guys he was too quick for. He would just outmaneuver guys. Almost all of his scores took place within six feet of the basket."

Anderson was briefly reunited with his college coach at the end of his professional career in 1970–71 when he joined the Philadelphia 76ers, at the time coached by Ramsay, for five games. "My knee was all banged up and I had an operation," he recalled. Cliff had been drafted by the Los Angeles Lakers. Later he played for Cleveland as well as Denver, in the ABA. "I really felt like I let Jack Ramsay down. Jack was the epitome of class and I really wanted to help him out. I wanted him to be proud of me and I wanted to show him that I was able to make the transition from center to guard. I thought I was well on my way but then my knee injury just ended it all. I remember I was in Portland or Seattle and I went to a doctor who was taking fluid out of my knee, and the doctor said, 'Listen if you want to be able to walk later on in life, you better find something else to do.'"

Ramsay had attempted to recruit Guokas when he played at Philadelphia's St. Joseph's Prep, but Matty decided to attend the University of Miami. "I thought that was the end of it," recalled Ramsay. But after his freshman year, Guokas's dad, Matt Sr., told Ramsay that young Matt was unhappy in Florida and wanted to transfer.

"I knew I had to make room for him," recalled Ramsay. "Matty was like Jimmy Lynam in having a great feel for the game, except he was Jim Lynam *and* six or seven inches. He was a terrific asset. He had great vision of the floor, was unselfish, and saw himself as the guy who was the focal point, the crux of the team. He didn't have great speed and wasn't a great perimeter shooter, but at the college level he could do so many things. He would sometimes play a high post position, where we would get the ball to him and he would relay it underneath to Anderson or Duff or whomever. He was another unflappable player who played with great confidence and poise—almost mistake-proof.

A *Look Magazine* All-America, Guokas helped the Hawks to a 50–8 won-loss mark. He still holds St. Joseph's career (5.7 average) and single-season assist records (176). Later, he was a member of two Philadelphia NBA championship teams as player and assistant coach and he also served as head coach of the 76ers and Orlando Magic. Today he is a basketball analyst for NBC-TV and the Cleveland Cavaliers.

Two of the Hawks' four regular season losses in 1965–66 came on a road trip to Brigham Young (103–83) and Wyoming (99–92). "They were good and we had no chance out there," said Guokas, who hit six straight jump shots at one point in the second half to bring the Hawks back from a big deficit to tie the Cowboys. "Normally on trips like that, we would take a referee from the East. This trip we did not, but it wouldn't have mattered if we had a hundred referees."

"It was a trip from Hell," recalled Ernie Accorsi, who was then the Hawks' sports information director. "For a number of reasons." After the Wyoming game, the Hawks slogged through snowdrifts ten to twelve feet high during a heavy blizzard and boarded a bus in Laramie headed for the Denver airport where they had booked rooms for the night. It was December 23 and everyone was anxious to get home before Christmas. "Now it's the middle of the night and the bus is crawling through the snow near Fort Collins," recalled Accorsi, who went on to a long career in the National Football League, most recently as the general manager of the New York Giants' 2001 Super Bowl team. "The Colorado Highway Patrol came out at a crossroads and said, 'The roads are too treacherous. You can't go any further. You have to turn off and find a place in town to stay.' Jack Ramsay asked the bus driver, 'What's the problem?'

And the bus driver explained that the police wouldn't let us go through. Ramsay said, 'Go!' And the bus driver said, 'Sir, but the policeman said . . .' and Ramsay screamed, GO!!!' The bus driver took one look at those eyes and that vein popping out of his neck and that was the end of it. It was another 90 miles or so but we got there at four in the morning."

The Hawks demolished Niagara, a good Minnesota team with Archie Clark and Lou Hudson, and previously-unbeaten Temple by an average margin of 27 points to easily repeat as Quaker City Tournament champions. "We weren't cold, we just panicked," said Minnesota's shell-shocked coach John Kundla after St. Joseph's romped in their semifinal matchup 91–66.

"People weren't prepared for our explosiveness," explained Cliff Anderson. "Jack Ramsay was very innovative when it came to devising defenses against certain teams. At the same time we could always just explode on offense. We could play ten minutes of good defense, then have a two-minute explosion of 20 points. That's what gave us the confidence to feel like we could play with anybody."

Again, the Hawks went unbeaten in city series play—and, in fact ran off ten straight Big 5 victories from 1964 to 1967. But that 1965–66 season will forever be remembered for one thing.

The Shot!

Launched by seldom-used reserve Steve Donches at the final buzzer of the first Sunday afternoon game in Big 5 history, the 29-foot-desperation heave did much more than give St. Joseph's a 71–69 victory. In addition to shattering Villanova's hopes for a major upset over the fourth-ranked Hawks, it probably did more than anything else to engrave *Big 5* on the consciousness of the Philadelphia sports fan. The game had been televised by Channel 17 and that's all they talked about the following day in offices and schools throughout the Delaware Valley. No one will ever know how many people actually watched the game, but the only thing that prevented phenomenal rating numbers was the fact that not everyone in those days had UHF converters.

A former all-state guard from Bethlehem Catholic High School, Donches had always wanted to play for St. Joseph's. As a youngster, he recalled sneaking into Grace Hall to watch the Hawks play Lehigh. He had missed his entire sophomore year recuperating from torn leg muscles, and had only made the team after impressing Ramsay with his play as a last minute replacement for Steve Chapman on a State Department–sponsored trip to South America the previous summer. He had won the Most Improved Player award as a freshman but hadn't expected to make the varsity when Matt

Guokas transferred from Miami and Don DiJulia joined the team.

The Hawks lost only one of 18 games during the 30-day tour to Brazil, Argentina, Uruguay, and Chile, where they conducted clinics and faced national teams, some of them composed of Olympic players. But it wasn't the most pleasant of journeys. In Chile, relations with the United States weren't good and there was rioting in the streets. The games were played outdoors and started as late as midnight. "One basketball court was surrounded by a chain link fence," recalled Donches. "When you were shooting foul shots, fans would light coins with lighters and flip them at you." It was winter in South America, and except for a few days in Rio, some of the hotels were so cold that the players constantly ran hot water showers in their rooms to generate heat. "But I played well enough to catch the coach's eye," said Donches.

Ironically, Donches was in the Villanova game only because Oakes had picked up his fifth personal foul

with less than two minutes left and the Hawks trailing by five points. St. Joe's battled back to tie it at 69, then Villanova had the chance to hold the ball for the last shot. But with 38 seconds left, Donches flicked the ball away from a Wildcat into the hands of Guokas, who called a time out. Then, following a broken play, Donches picked up a loose ball with four seconds left, dribbled once to his right, and let go. "I turned and I saw Chuck McKenna under the basket but I let it fly," explained Donches. "As it was going up I said to myself, 'too short,' but I really meant that it was too low. It was not an arching shot and it was obviously not my normal range, but it was pretty much on line. The buzzer went off and it hit the bottom of the net. When I turned around—because it was right in front of our bench—all I could hear was Ramsay screaming, Whoooaaa! Whoooaaa!' I turned to him and said, 'We did it!' There was a momentary pause to see what the officials were calling. Then, of course, there was pandemonium with people coming out of the stands. After the game, one of

the things I said to Ramsay was 'Thank you for the South American trip!'"

Probably the most relieved person in the Palestra was Guokas, who felt nauseous and couldn't sleep well the night before. "People don't believe this, but I lost like 15 pounds overnight without getting sick," he recalled. "In the layup line I felt weak and could barely move. I had to get safety pins to keep my pants bunched up so they wouldn't fall down. We start the game and I have nothing. I can't run and I'm kind of delirious. We're about five minutes into the game and I'm standing at the foul line bent over. I see Jack Ramsay get our backup guard Steve Chapman up. He starts taking off his warmups. I whirled around and glared at Jack and I shook my head and said, 'No! I'm not coming out!' I could tell he didn't like that but he pulled Steve back. A little bit later, I ran by the bench and said, 'Just give me a few more minutes and I'll be able to get going.' And he said, 'That's all you're going to get, a few more minutes.' It was one of those things, you start going on adrenaline, but I finally got involved in the game, played the entire 40 minutes, and, of course it turned out to be a classic." When Donches put his shot in the air, Guokas was swooping underneath the net, hoping for an offensive rebound. "I was thinking if that ball did not go in, there's no way I could play five more minutes of overtime," he said. Guokas played the next two games, but then spent a week in the hospital being treated for a stomach disorder.

The Hawks, who had suffered two of their three losses to Providence the year before, handled the Friars relatively easily in the opening round of the NCAA Tournament 65–48, even though coach Joe Mullaney had a much stronger team this time around. The game was played in Blacksburg, Virginia, and the Hawks almost didn't make it. "At first, Jack Ramsay said we're not going to go," recalled Guokas. "He said there's no way we can go and get back in time to get to class. I remember there was a big meeting on campus and, as a compromise, the administration chartered a plane for the team. We flew down the evening before, played the game, and flew home in time for class the next day. I think Jack was just trying to make a statement with the powers-to-be."

But any dreams for a national championship ended in the Eastern Regionals in Raleigh, when that perennial post-season nemesis, Duke, won another heartbreaker 76–74 to snap St. Joseph's ten-game winning streak. Playing on a court where they had won 19 of their 20 games, the Blue Devils couldn't stop Cliff Anderson (20 points, 15 rebounds) but held the Hawks overall to 32 percent shooting from the field. "Duke had all the pieces," said Guokas, who had his usual steady game with 19 points before fouling out. "We felt that we were as good as them but knew we would have to have a perfect game to beat them."

"That was disappointing," recalled Ramsay. "I thought in hindsight I respected Duke too much. If I had to do it again I would have let it all go. We played too conservatively. We should have run at them. We should have trapped them, gotten them into a running game. I felt I should have done more to help the team than I did. That was a team capable of winning a national championship. They were explosive. We could trap full court,

half court, play man to man, play zone—we could do everything with that team. But I think I didn't do enough to help them in that final game."

Anderson was forced to endure even more serious obstacles in North Carolina. "Times were different back then," he explained. "I don't think they were accustomed to having many black players come into their stadium. People used the 'N' word a lot and they spit at me, but it didn't really bother me. I don't think it affected my game. I tend to think that I just took it out on the other team. Sometimes the security wasn't what it should be and some of the more rabid fans got a little close. Being from North Philly, I didn't really care. I just pushed them out of my way. We never did anything to exacerbate the situation. It's not that we were soft or that we didn't feel anger, but I thought we handled everything with a lot of class."

As it turned out, it was the final college game for both Guokas and Ramsay. Guokas decided to forgo his final season of eligibility and was drafted by the Philadelphia 76ers. During the season, Ramsay had developed an edema on the retina of his right eye that obscured his vision to the extent that he could only see around the edges and couldn't read or see anything directly with that eye. His doctors said it was a condition brought on by stress.

"There were instances where it affected first one eye and then the other, and then I couldn't see at all," recalled Ramsay. "That was a little unnerving for me. I didn't want to lose my vision. I knew I was putting a lot of stress on myself to win, more than I should have, to be sure." While he was getting medical help in the beginning of the summer—without satisfaction—Ramsay started thinking of the possibility of life without basketball. "I had gotten my doctorate. I was taking on more responsibilities with the education program at St. Joseph's, and I was thinking at some point I would get out of coaching and just do the other work—maybe stay on as athletic director and work in the Education Department or maybe do education full time. I had been thinking long term when I started graduate work, with the idea when I finished coaching that I would have this to do."

That's when Irv Kosloff, the owner of the Philadelphia 76ers, approached Ramsay about becoming the team's general manager. "It suddenly clicked," Jack recalled. "I'd get a chance to get out of the pressures of coaching and stay in basketball in an interesting job. I would try it and if I didn't like it I could always go back to coaching." By September, the eye condition had cleared up and Dr. Jack was on the way to the NBA.

Chapter 6

• • • • • • •

Finally Some Respect for the Quakers

The University of Pennsylvania's quest for respectability in the Big 5 succeeded primarily through the efforts of two excellent coaches, Jack McCloskey and Dick Harter. Unfortunately, one found his NCAA championship hopes denied, the other destroyed.

The Quakers went winless in Big 5 games that first year in 1955–56 under the coaching of Ray Stanley, but it was obvious that Penn's athletic director Jerry Ford was grooming McCloskey for the head job. Jack had spent a year at the University of Pittsburgh on a football scholarship, but came to Penn when he enlisted in the Navy's V12 program during World War II. Afterwards, he was signed to a baseball contract personally by Connie Mack, the venerable owner of the Philadelphia Athletics, and pitched in the minor leagues for four years before tearing his shoulder.

"My mother made me get down on my knees and promise her that I would complete my college education," McCloskey recalled. "My dad was a coal miner from the day he was 12 years old. They both knew how important an education was." Once when McCloskey was a teenager not doing as well as he should in school, his dad took him down into the mines. "He said, 'I want it to be the last time you're ever down here.' It was so miserable. I couldn't believe my dad went through all the hardships he suffered. He was red from his knees to his ankles because of the dampness down there. His legs were raw. My mother would put Vaseline on his legs, wrap them in wax paper, and then tie them up with some sort of sheets. He never missed a day at work. He never complained. But he taught me a lesson."

McCloskey made good on his promise and earned a degree in education from Penn in 1948. He played for eight years in the Eastern League with the Wilmington Blue Bombers, then coached at Philadelphia's Germantown Academy and Collingswood (New Jersey) High for five years before joining the Quakers as Stanley's assistant and freshman coach, lightweight football coach, and head baseball coach. "I think I was making about $6,500 and I thought I was stealing money," he said.

McCloskey took over as Penn's head basketball coach for the 1956–57 season. After finishing with a 7–19 record and going winless in the Big 5, Jack knew that he needed help. He called on one of the nation's top defensive gurus, Penn State's John Egli. "After 15 minutes I realized I didn't know anything about playing the zone defense," McCloskey recalled. "He gave me all the rules, all the slides, everything that they did. We added a few new wrinkles and John said to me after watching us play, 'Hey, you got it pretty good. I like this thing you're doing.'" Egli's lessons paid off in 1957–58. The Quakers used a 3-2 zone effectively and finished with a winning season (13–12). They also picked up their first Big 5 triumph, 67–66 over La Salle, when John Saxenmeyer, a sophomore playing in his first city series game, sent it into overtime with a last second steal and layup and then clinched it with a couple of jump shots.

▲ Joe Sturgis was co-captain of Penn's first Big 5 team in 1955–56. *(Urban Archives, Temple University, Philadelphia, Pennsylvania)*

"I really didn't think we were going to win too many games that year," said McCloskey. "We used to pray that nobody would press us. Fortunately not a lot of them did, although the teams in the Big 5—teams that knew us—came after us pretty good."

"Jack McCloskey was ahead of his time in a lot of things," recalled Joe Sturgis, a member of the Big 5 Hall of Fame who with Francis Mulroy co-captained the Quakers in 1955–56. "He was one of first coaches who taught *hands on.* He was big on pushing people. He understood basketball. He liked talking about it, thinking about it, and trying to get better, and I think that was reflected in his career. He was one of the first promoters of the use of contact lenses and was always after players to use them."

Dick Censits, a 6'4" forward, made the team as a walk-on in 1955. He credits McCloskey with developing his game so well that he became the first Quaker to be named All Big 5 for three straight years. "After every practice, Jack stayed with me and helped me considerably to understand that it wasn't just shooting," recalled Censits, who later served on Penn's board of trustees. "Jack taught me more about the game, specifically the ability to go by my man on a drive." Censits came off the bench to score 29 points against Duke in Penn's third game that year and was never out of the starting lineup afterwards. A member of the Big 5 Hall of Fame, he is one of only a half-dozen Quakers to average double figures in both scoring and rebounding for their career.

Even though Bob Mlkvy, Penn's hottest prospect in almost a decade, went down with a thigh injury the first day of pre-season practice in 1958–59, the Quakers were gradually improving. Building his team around players like George Schmidt, the team's leading scorer that year; John Canzano, a scrappy 5'10" guard; and Stewart Greenleaf, a 6'4" forward with a deadly left-handed jumpshot from the corner, Penn picked up its first victories over Temple and Villanova in the next two seasons and won 16 games in 1960–61, the most triumphs the Quakers' had recorded since the Big 5 was formed.

Canzano once sprained his ankle racing to get into a game. It happened against Duquesne in the opening round of the Keystone Classic in Harrisburg. Yet he toughed it out to score 15 points and trigger an upset win over the Dukes. Greenleaf, who went on to become a Pennsylvania state senator representing Montgomery

◀ Dick Censits walked on to become the first Quaker to be named to the All Big 5 team three times. *(University of Pennsylvania)*

▶ **B**ob Mlkvy overcame a serious thigh injury to lead the Quakers in both scoring and rebounding twice. *(University of Pennsylvania)*

County, recalled that McCloskey grabbed him after practice one day and worked for hours on his shooting technique. The next night, with time running out against Brown and the Quakers trailing by a point, Greenleaf found himself all alone in the corner as the entire Bruin team swarmed all over Mlkvy. "Clearly we were trying to get the ball to Bob," Greenleaf explained. "They pounded all over him. Fortunately, I put it in. I could have easily been the goat instead of the hero."

Just like his famous brother, Bill—the "Owl without the Vowel"—Bob Mlkvy had been an All State star at Palmerton (Pennsylvania) High School. As a little guy—they were eight years apart—Bob remembers many a night at Convention Hall where he sat on Temple's bench and watched his All-America brother shatter a host of Owl scoring records. A 6' 4" forward, Bob had been recruited by more than 85 schools, including Duke, Miami, Maryland and a number of Ivy League institutions. Like his brother, he wanted to play in Philadelphia. He chose Penn because of its combination of academics and athletics. He liked the way Jack McCloskey presented himself. And he wanted to break away from his brother's shadow.

"It was very difficult," Bob recalled. "I could never get away from it, really, but I tried to put that behind me. From the day I started high school, everyone wanted me to score and shoot and all of my brother's records were always in front of me. But I loved the game so much, I just played an all-around game and tried to be comprehensive in my play. We were two different kinds of players. My brother was more an offensive-minded player. I was aiming to be a complete player like Tom Gola. He did everything well. He hit the boards strong, contributed his points, and played tough defense. Not that I didn't admire my brother—I always followed him and was really proud of him in all that he accomplished."

Bob Mlkvy's basketball dreams were almost shattered before they began. Going in for a layup in only his second day of varsity practice as a sophomore, he was kneed in the right thigh by a teammate. The pain was excruciating and by the next morning he couldn't lift his leg to get out of bed. Doctors described it as a severe hematoma, but the calcium deposits quickly shot through the muscle so Mlkvy could not bend his leg. "It was like a board, just so stiff and hard," recalled McCloskey. Mlkvy returned to the lineup for the last nine games of the season. "I could barely move," he recalled. "I must have had at least six inches protecting my thigh. Even that hindered me. If I had fallen and turned my leg back, I would have torn my muscles to shreds. I would have done anything to play, I was so anxious to start my career. It hindered me later. I was a little shy making contact with it, especially the following year. No question, it curtailed my effectiveness. Not so much physically as mentally trying to avoid contact in certain situations."

"Because of that injury he was never quite the great player that he looked liked he was going to be," recalled McCloskey. "But he was outstanding—a great outside shooter like his brother. He was so unselfish, really a great passer for a guy his size." Still, Mlkvy was able to score 25 against his brother's alma mater and played well enough for the next two seasons to be named to the

All Big 5 team. Today, like his roommate Canzano and his brother Bill, he's a dentist. Both Mlkvys are members of the Big 5 Hall of Fame, the only brother combination to hold that distinction.

In 1958 McCloskey brought in the only full-time assistant he ever had, Dick Harter, an ex-Marine who had played on Penn's 1952–53 Ivy League championship team. Since McCloskey was still coaching baseball, Harter handled the freshman team and took care of most of the recruiting. That paid considerable dividends, especially in 1962–63 when the Quakers finally were able to grab a share of their first Big 5 title with Villanova.

Only a 63–62 loss to the Wildcats kept Penn from winning the Big 5 crown outright. "We had the game won," recalled Ray Carazo, who was known as McCloskey's "Steady Eddie guard." Penn led 29–23 at halftime and was still up by two points until the closing seconds when Wali Jones put the Wildcats ahead with a three-point play. "Wali used to kick his feet out and lunge forward when he shot that jumper," explained Carazo. "Sid Amira had put his hand up and Wali came forward and landed on him. The referee called the foul but there was no foul. McCloskey went berserk in the locker room. Jack was not a happy camper."

"Harter meant a great deal to me," said McCloskey. "Dick is a very intense guy, but like all the younger coaches at the time, we were all like that. Harry Litwack came up to me one time and said, 'Young fellow, you got to learn to relax and take it easy. You're not going to live very long if you get this emotionally involved.' It was good medicine. Harter was very demanding, but he was a hard worker and an outstanding coach and over a period of time he calmed down a little bit. He had excellent thoughts, particularly on the defensive end."

Harter's first significant recruit for McCloskey was John Wideman, a 6'3" forward from Pittsburgh, a future Phi Beta Kappa, and the Big 5's only Rhodes Scholar. Wideman, a member of the Big 5 Hall of Fame, was captain of the 1962–63 city series co-champions and always seemed to excel in Big 5 games. As a sophomore he scored 25 points to spark a 63–62 upset win over Villanova. As a senior, his layup with 18 seconds left in the third overtime gave the Quakers a 78–77 win over St. Joseph's in one of

▶ John Wideman, the captain of Penn's 1962–63 Big 5 co-champions, later became an award-winning author.
(University of Pennsylvania)

the most exciting Big 5 finishes in history, and his 18 points triggered a 59–53 victory over Temple in the game that gave Penn a share of the Big 5 crown. "Wideman was a very aggressive individual, very strong physically and defensively one of the better players I've been associated with," recalled McCloskey. "He really wanted to compete. At his height he played a little out of position at small forward, but he could do a lot of things real well. Boy, did he attack the boards."

Had it not been for "another twist of the gods," said Harter, Penn might never have gotten Wideman, who went on to become an award-winning novelist. "I was driving out on the Pennsylvania Turnpike to recruit him and it was snowing so hard you couldn't even see the road. I finally went through a tunnel and said to myself, ' If I get through this tunnel and the storm is still this bad, I'm turning around and going back.' I went through the tunnel and the weather was absolutely clear. It was a true omen. I kept going for another two hours."

From 1963 to 1966, the Quakers displayed one of the most explosive fast-break combinations ever seen in the Big 5, with Stan Pawlak, a 6'3" forward who led the team in scoring three straight years, and Jeff Neuman, a steady playmaker. "They were so exciting because Jeff was a great ballhandler and Stan was just a tremendous all-around player," said McCloskey. "Jeff was as good a middle man on the break as any player that I've ever seen in college." Years later when he was in the NBA, McCloskey assembled some grainy, eight-millimeter films showing Pawlak and Neuman running the fast break. "I would tell the players, 'This is the way it should be run,'" he recalled. "I still remember Dennis Rodman in Detroit saying, 'Those guys are pretty good, coach.'"

"Jeff was really well ahead of his time in terms of his ability to do things on the basketball court," said Pawlak. "He was a point guard before there were point guards, just an amazing player for that time. In today's world he would be a commodity because he could do things that a lot of guys can't do today. He was an exceptional ball-handler and passer, particularly on a fast break."

"Stan was very tough-nosed," recalled Neuman. "You just knew when you got him the ball something was going to happen. Either he'd get fouled or he'd score. He had very good hands. I always knew that he would be there. It made doing what I did easier because sometimes you'd throw passes and they'd bounce off guys' chests. But Stan was like a vacuum cleaner."

McCloskey's Quakers put it all together in 1965–66 with a 19–6 record. Pawlak was spectacular in the Quakers' two Big 5 victories that year, scoring 24 points in a 73–60 win over Villanova, and the most points ever scored by a Penn player in the Big 5 (37) in a 90–76 rout of La Salle. "That was my favorite Big 5 game of all time," explained Pawlak. "I had 26 in the first half. It was as good as it could get. I think in the second half, I said to myself, 'I'm shooting too much,' or something."

Pawlak experienced a real eye-opener before the season started. "It was Bobby Knight and Jack McCloskey, who were of the same ilk, almost getting in a fist fight at a Thanksgiving scrimmage at the Palestra. Army had a young sophomore center who was really a tough guy and Bobby was preaching his typical defense. Of course, you can't foul out of a scrimmage so these kids were absolutely killing us. Jeff and I were tough kids, and we did some killing back, but it got to the point where the fouling was so flagrant that Knight and McCloskey confronted each other. It was unbelievable. I'm not sure which one of them was tougher. It finally calmed down but there was no love lost for the rest of that scrimmage."

After winning the Ivy League title that year, McCloskey resigned to become head coach at Wake Forest. Not because he didn't think that he could ever win a national championship at Penn, as many people speculated. It was because his *own administration* wouldn't allow him to compete in the NCAA Tournament.

▲ Stan Pawlak and Jeff Neuman formed one of the great early fast-break combinations in the Big 5. *(University of Pennsylvania)*

The NCAA had just passed legislation requiring athletic directors to confirm in writing that their students predicted a minimum 1.6 grade point average. Penn's academic requirements were much higher than that, but as a matter of principle, athletic director Jerry Ford refused to sign the necessary documentation. Penn's opposition was based on the principle that a national organization should not determine institutional policy. As a result, the Quakers were barred from the tournament. "We really had a fine team and this denied these guys the opportunity to do something that they worked for a long time," said McCloskey. "It crushed me because I know it crushed them when I had to tell them. Yet there's not a day that goes by that I don't think about them as a team because they were denied something that was so ridiculous. It was difficult for me to live with the athletic director under those conditions. I really believe that maybe the athletic director didn't want us to win some basketball and football games when Penn got into the Ivy League. He wanted to show the Harvards, the Princetons, the Yales, 'Okay, we're doing things the right way according to the rules.'"

Pawlak remembers that the team had a feeling that it wouldn't be going to the NCAA Tournament after clinching the university's first Ivy League title. "We had a practice with the idea that we might play but kind of knowing that we weren't," he explained. "We were one of the nicest bunch of college kids that you could ever have. There wasn't a rabble-rouser in the whole group. We were all very dedicated basketball players who minded our Ps and Qs. In fact, when we were told, we put our tails between our legs and I don't think we reacted as strongly as we should have."

The Quakers would have played Syracuse in Blacksburg, Virginia, in the first round. Neuman and Pawlak had nice basketball reputations in the East, but were not really considered outstanding NBA prospects. That game, however, may have given them some national exposure and the chance to do something special. "Looking back on it, I think it hurt Jeff and me pretty badly," said Pawlak. "Suppose I go in that game and get 30 against Dave Bing, who is now in the Hall of Fame. I'm not predicting that I would have, but the opportunity was taken away from us. In today's world, that would never happen. At that time we didn't complain. It was a strong-willed athletic director trying to make his point and his point to him was more important than us having the opportunity to play in that basketball game. It never happened again. There was never another Ivy League team that stood on that ground. So it was kind of fruitless."

Pawlak and Neuman are both in the Big 5 Hall of Fame. Stan later assisted his former high school teammate Gary Williams at Woodrow Wilson High School in Camden, New Jersey, then took over as head coach when Williams, the coach of Maryland's 2001-02 NCAA champions, moved into the college ranks. He also played for 12 years in the Eastern and Continental Leagues and was named to the starting backcourt on the combined league's 25th Anniversary team. The other guard? Jack McCloskey.

McCloskey had considered leaving the Quakers earlier in his career when he met with Ike Richman, the owner of the Philadelphia 76ers. "He asked for a certain price, which would be like meal money today," recalled Bob Vetrone, who was covering basketball for the *Philadelphia Bulletin* at the time. "He asked for a five-year guarantee and Richman replied, 'Jack, the only thing I can guarantee is that someday I'm going to fire you.' I don't know whether Ike was smiling or not when he said it but Jack decided to stay in college basketball for a while."

At least until the Demon Deacons beckoned and McCloskey's former assistant, Dick Harter, took over. Harter had left Penn to take the head coaching job at Rider College the year before, and had compiled a respectable 16–9 record with five of the losses coming in overtime. "I probably wouldn't have gotten the Penn job if I hadn't gone to Rider," he recalled. "I had no idea Jack was going to leave. I could picture him staying at Penn forever."

Joining Harter as his full-time assistant with the Quakers was Digger Phelps, a young coach at St. Gabriel's High School, in Hazleton, Pennsylvania, who had played at Rider before Harter arrived. "I only knew Digger from saying hello to him once or twice when he came back to visit," Harter said. "Tom Petroff, Rider's baseball coach, absolutely convinced me. He kept saying, 'You've got to hire Digger Phelps.' He shoved that down my throat. It was a good shove." Phelps went on to become head coach at Fordham in 1970–71, then spent 20 years at Notre Dame. Today he's a basketball analyst on ESPN and ABC-TV.

"Digger did the bulk of the recruiting and proved to be a great asset," said Harter. "He had a great perspective about recruiting. Maybe at Penn we were too local. We thought going to Pittsburgh was a long recruiting trip. Maybe because he wanted to go out to Chicago and visit with the Notre Dame people, or whatever, but he said, 'Let's spread out,' and that helped."

"We just really worked very well together," recalled Phelps, who coached the Penn freshmen to an unbeaten 21–0 record in 1968–69. "I always thought, once I got Harter into a home, he would win over the family. He always had the right suit and tie on, the right presentation. He always looked good. I think Dick Harter and I could sell the Brooklyn Bridge back to the Indians if we had to."

more responsible than anyone else to sell me on the merits of 'Let's just play straight up man to man,'" recalled Harter. "As we had success with it, I'd give lectures at basketball camps saying, 'My idea of heaven is a place where everyone plays zone because you'd never lose to them.' Our guys took pride in that. In all my years as a college coach I don't think that I played zone for more than one half a game."

Wohl, who had originally come to Penn to play football, recalled Phelps and Harter as the most demanding coaches he'd ever seen. "They ran the hardest practices I've been involved with my entire life," he said. "They found a way to motivate guys. Digger was in his first big-time coaching job. His indoctrination was kind of like Parris Island. It was truly a love/hate relationship with him but he was a very pivotal figure in my development. Then when I moved up to the varsity, Dick was tougher and in many ways even more demanding and exacting. They did not settle on you having pre-conceived limits on what you could achieve. That's probably one of the reasons I was able to play professionally because hard work carried you a long way."

"Digger was more of a yeller-screamer whereas Harter was more of a demanding coach, very much of a perfectionist, hard-nosed, dive-on-the-floor type coach," explained Bilsky. "Dick wasn't as intimidating and not as demonstrative as Digger."

The Penn players did not always appreciate Harter's coaching style, especially in 1970–71, when the Quakers went unbeaten during the regular season. "We were clearly going to be an upper echelon team, but after about ten or twelve games, Dick wasn't letting us enjoy it," recalled Wohl. "We'd win by 20 and he thought we should have won by 30. He was almost demanding perfection and I remember the players came up to us and said, 'You and Steve have to go talk to him.' We didn't really envy the idea of standing in front of Dick and saying, 'Well, you've got to let us enjoy this.' I remember Steve and I were kind of like, 'You go.' . . . No, you go!'

Soon more good players started gravitating to Penn, and that paid enormous dividends by 1970–71. That's when the Quakers started four future Big 5 Hall of Famers and achieved their highest national ranking ever—third. Harter's last two teams won 48 straight regular season games at one point, went unbeaten in the Big 5, and compiled an overall 53–3 record. What made Penn's performance even more impressive was the fact that every Big 5 team except Temple was ranked nationally in the top 25 that year. The Quakers went on to become the nation's third winningest team of the 1970s (behind UCLA and Marquette), taking 79.9 percent of their games.

Harter's first solid recruits were a pair of quick little guards, Steve Bilsky and Dave Wohl, who formed one of the most electrifying backcourts in Big 5 history. Then came Jim Wolf, a 6' 9" center from Cleveland who chose Penn despite pressure from the governor of Ohio to attend Ohio State. In 1969, it was Bobby Morse, who would start slowly, then blossom into one of the Big 5's greatest shooters, and Corky Calhoun, who grew three inches to 6'7½" between his freshman and sophomore years. "Those three inches, you just can't coach," recalled Harter, who was quickly establishing a reputation as one of the nation's better man-to-man defense-minded coaches at a time when the Big 5 was very heavily zone-oriented.

"Ray Edelman, my part-time assistant coach, was

◄ **D**ave Wohl turned his back on football to team with Steve Bilsky in the Quakers' backcourt and go on to a successful NBA career. *(University of Pennsylvania)*

So we finally both said, 'Coach we will do anything you want. If you want to practice five hours, we'll practice five hours. You want to practice 24 straight hours we'll do it. We'll do anything you want, but when we win the game you've got to let us enjoy it!' I think it was a wake-up call for Dick. And the rest of the year, without being any less demanding, he let us enjoy the fact that we played basketball and were passionate about it."

Bilsky, who was runner-up that year for the Naismith Award, given to the nation's best player under six feet, and Wohl, the Quakers' all-time assist leader for three seasons, are both members of the Big 5 Hall of Fame. "We had an instant chemistry together as players," recalled Bilsky, who is now the Quakers' athletic director. "It wasn't as it is today with one guy being the point guard and the other guy the shooting guard. We both perceived ourselves as being ball handlers *and* shooters and scorers, and we played off each other very well. I think we both were thoughtful players, typical 'Philadelphia guards.' We played heady games and I think in that regard we matched well. We were constantly thinking about the right things to do on the court. Our styles just meshed. Dave was very strong and a good jump shooter. I was more of a player who liked to drive and penetrate and create things. After a while we developed an instinct of where each other was going to be at some point."

Many observers believe that Bilsky made the shot in his sophomore year that turned Penn's basketball program around. It came against eighth-ranked Villanova in January 1969, when the Quakers were struggling to

▲ Steve Bilsky, who is now Penn's athletic director, made the shot that turned the Quakers' basketball fortunes around. (*University of Pennsylvania*)

establish themselves. They were coming off two straight losing seasons and had dropped 16 of their previous 20 Big 5 games, including nine of their last ten against the Wildcats.

"We definitely had the sense that it was the Big 4 *and* Penn," recalled Bilsky. "That had to do with the quality of the Big 5 teams at that point—they were really strong. One of Harter's goals was to beat a team that was either nationally-ranked or perceived as being significantly better. All he wanted to do was win. He didn't care if it was 5–4, 32–30, or 90–80. He basically said the best chance we have to beat this team is to slow it down, *'Don't shoot unless you know you can make it.'*"

With the score tied at 30, Villanova's defense was content to let Bilsky and Wohl play catch for 4:40 before calling a time out with 20 seconds to go. Harter then called a play designed for Bilsky to take a shot off a pick by Wolf. But Villanova's 6'8" Howard Porter suddenly

switched off Wolf with his big hands towering over Bilsky. "Here's this guy coming out lunging and doing the right defensive play," the 5'10" guard recalled. "So I kind of like just veered a little bit further out—it probably was 23 or 24 feet. The adrenaline was flowing. As soon as I shot it I knew it was in. There was never a question in my mind because I had taken that shot a million times in practice."

Penn's 32–30 victory was its only Big 5 win that year. But after dropping their next two games to La Salle and Princeton, the Quakers went on to win eight straight games and compile a 15–10 record for their first winning season under Harter. Respectability had returned to the program.

Morse, a 6'8" forward, had not been heavily recruited in high school. But he went on to lead the Quakers in scoring for three years and make the Big 5 Hall of Fame. "He was the best shooter I've ever seen," said Bilsky.

Wohl recalled that none of Morse's teammates would play "HORSE" with him in practice. "All Bobby would do is shoot jumpers and because he made almost every one of them, it was no fun. So at shoot-arounds, he would be wandering around the side baskets waiting for the games to get over." One night Wohl was rooming with Morse on a road trip. "We come back after the game and Bobby can't sleep. He's on his bed tossing and turning and I wake up and said, 'What's the matter?' He goes, 'I never shot 4-for-12 in my life!' I started laughing and said, 'Don't worry about it. Hey, if I had a dollar for every 4-for-12 night, I could retire.'"

One summer after Morse had graduated, Harter was coaching at Oregon and running a basketball camp in the Pacific Northwest. He invited Bobby to come out and give a lecture. "He said that he was happy to come but didn't want to talk," recalled Harter. "So I suggested, 'Why don't you just shoot the ball.' Now he had just driven across the country and had not slept for three days. All he had were these rubber basketball camp balls, not even good-quality basketballs, but I swear he made at least 48 out of 50 shots as we did this lecture. He was just drilling them. No one ever shot a basketball as well as he did that day. I've never seen anything like it. An 18-footer to him was a layup."

"I'll never forget one game," recalled Fred Shabel, the Quakers' athletic director at the time. "Penn is beating Southern Cal and Morse is bombing away from the corner. At least three times, people jumped off the bench screaming, 'WHAT ARE YOU DOING?' Then they clapped their hands and sat down when his long shot went in." Morse later earned a medical degree but never practiced medicine. A third-round draft choice of the NBA's Buffalo Braves, he decided instead to play for

nine years in Europe, where he became a national celebrity in Italy and France. "Driving down highways outside of Rome, I've seen billboards with Bobby Morse's picture," said Shabel. "Bobby was the Michael Jordan of Italy for a stage, a hero of Italian basketball."

"Bobby 'One-Step' Morse, that was our nickname for him," said Villanova's Chris Ford. "He would only take one dribble, one step, but he'd nail you with a jumper."

Morse and his classmate, Corky Calhoun, the Big 5 co-MVP (along with Chris Ford) in 1972, helped the Quakers register the best record in the East in each of their three varsity seasons. Calhoun, who is also a member of the Big 5 Hall of Fame, was Penn's top rebounder his first two seasons, then moved to the backcourt as a senior. "He could have been a tremendous offensive player because he could shoot and handle the ball," recalled Wohl. "But he was just content to blend in and be a great defensive player. I don't think most people had any idea how good a defender he was."

"I guess maybe to a fault I was too unselfish," said Calhoun. "I thought that everybody wanted to share the ball, wanted to score a little bit. I remember Phil Hankinson said it correctly one time that I didn't have a strong scoring ego. That was probably an accurate way to describe myself because the guys who

◀ **B**ob Morse led Penn in scoring three times and later became one of the top professional players in Europe. *(Urban Archives, Temple University, Philadelphia, Pennsylvania)*

score a lot do have a scoring ego. I guess that wasn't part of my makeup coming to Penn. Defensively, I took it as a personal challenge because I thought that certainly would contribute to victory."

Calhoun, who grew up in a suburb of Chicago, had followed the careers of Bill Bradley and Cazzie Russell in the Ivy League and Big Ten. He chose Penn over Michigan because of its academic reputation and also because he thought he'd get to play sooner. Corky was only 5'2" in seventh grade. He had grown a foot by his sophomore year in high school and was listed as 6'4" when Digger Phelps came calling. When he graduated from Penn, he was 6'7". All seven members of the Big 5 team that season went on to play professional basketball but Corky had the longest NBA career of any Quaker—eight seasons. His Penn quintets went 78–6 overall, 11–1 in the Big 5, and won a record 48 regular season games. "My class likes to think of it as 99–6 because we went 21–0 in my freshman year," he explained. "We were one game away from the Final Four two years in a row."

Also quite instrumental in Penn's success was its tremendous bench strength, with players like Phil Hankinson, who would later make the Big 5 Hall of Fame and play for two years with the Boston Celtics; Craig Littlepage, a future coach of the Quakers; Ron Billingslea; and Alan Cotler. "We always said that our greatest competition was in practice when we scrimmaged," explained Bilsky. "All of them could have started for just about any other team in the country"—which they eventually did for the Quakers.

Hankinson, who led the team in scoring in 1972–73, saw his NBA career end when he hurt his knee in a summer league game in California. Tragically, in November 1995, he took his own life. "Phil was a guy with talent, both as a player as well as a person," recalled Littlepage, his college roommate who delivered a eulogy at his funeral in South Carolina. "What he did on the floor pretty much speaks for itself. He was part of our family; I felt a part of his family. We were the best of friends in many regards. He just had this manner about him. He maximized the experience of a student athlete. He was always the life of the party. He loved being a Celtic. To be playing on championship-level teams

▶ **C**orky Calhoun, co-MVP of the Big 5 in 1971–72, twice led Penn in rebounding. *(Urban Archives, Temple University, Philadelphia, Pennsylvania)*

was a big thrill for him. And then having his career cut short—not being permitted to blossom the way he would have wanted—that was the factor that put him on a downward spiral, not only physically but I think emotionally, from which he never recovered."

The Quakers' only regular-season loss in Harter's final two seasons was an 88–85 heartbreaker to Purdue in the Holiday Festival, in Madison Square Garden, in 1969. Wohl got into foul trouble on some questionable calls as he was guarding All-America Rick Mount. They also dropped a 79–69 decision to Niagara in the first round of the NCAA Tournament. "Niagara beat us because I just couldn't play Calvin," explained Wohl, who later became Murphy's teammate in the NBA. "When I first got traded to Houston he wouldn't talk to me. I finally went up to him and asked him why. Calvin said, 'It's that letter you wrote.' I said, 'What letter?' 'The letter you wrote me before you played me in college.' I never wrote you a letter, Calvin. Why would I write you a letter?' Here someone wrote a letter to Calvin, signed my name, and said all these things we were going to do to him—we were going to kick your ass . . . you aren't anything. Calvin said, 'I was so pumped for your game. Just going head-to-head with you.' I told him, 'Remind me if I find that person to just strangle him.' Calvin and I became very good friends. He's a great guy."

In 1970–71, the Quakers ran the table by winning 26 straight games. Then disaster struck after the Ivy League champs had swept aside Duquesne and South Carolina in the first two rounds of the NCAA Tournament.

The infamous 90–47 loss to Villanova!

"The only explanation I can give for it was that we had such an overpowering season," said Harter. "We never really faced any deficits, had never fallen behind, and suddenly here we are in the biggest game of our lives, and they jumped on us. We just did not respond well to it. I think it was very hard to be behind by 15 or 20 points the first time ever. We just didn't play and they did. They beat us fair and square. We knew that if we got by South Carolina, the next game was going to be an emotional deal. We had beaten Villanova a couple of times and we didn't want to play Digger and Fordham. After beating South Carolina, we watched the Villanova-Fordham game and we didn't want it to end. We would have liked to play any team in the country other than one of those two teams. But that's basketball."

Bilsky was not playing at full strength because he had injured a knee in the last regular season game at Columbia. He remembers Villanova players being just as puzzled as the Quakers about the shocking turn of events in the game. "Everybody was kind of in a fog, even in the beginning of the second half when we were down 20, 25 points," he recalled. "Although Villanova played with much confidence and poise, they looked as quizzical as we looked. Then all of the sudden, somewhere near the middle of the second half, that look changed to something like, '*We're going to pay you guys back for three years of being beaten.*' Then the look went to '*Let's go!*' and they then played the last ten minutes of the game even more flawlessly. They weren't trashy, they weren't talking, but you could sense that many years of frustration were being let out. But I do remember all of them looking like they were scratching their heads and asking, 'What's going on here? What's wrong here? This game should be close.'"

Even if the Quakers had been at their best, Calhoun doesn't think that they wouldn't have beaten Villanova that day. "Maybe we had a little bit of an emotional letdown," he explained. "But Villanova played outstanding and had UCLA not held the ball, they probably would have beaten them. They were in a zone certainly, but still even if we played our normal game, I don't know if we could have won that game."

But even more discouraging, especially after Villanova had come within six points of winning the national championship, was the fact that the Quakers felt that they matched up perfectly against UCLA. "It was like two almost similar teams," said Wohl. "Knowing that we were better than Villanova, we thought we could beat them. Both backcourts were pretty good with different strengths, so it was really going to hinge on some

of our frontcourt matchups. But we felt that they had never seen a shooter like Bobby, and Corky was a good enough defender to play any of those three guys that got hot. With Phil and Craig, we felt our bench was a lot deeper. All of us felt in our heart of hearts that we could have won the title. We had something and we just couldn't hang on to it. It's probably the most disappointing moment I've ever had in my athletic life."

A few days after the tournament, Harter received a phone call from a University of Oregon booster. His name was Henry Hood and his only connection to the Quaker coach was the fact that they used to play cards in a fraternity house at Penn during their college days. As Harter recalled the conversation, "Hood said, 'Hey Dick, this is Hen—Henry Hood. I'm out in Oregon now and I got you the Oregon job.' And I said, 'Oh, yeah, sure!' I was really down from the Villanova game, so I was willing to listen to anything. I said, 'Why don't you have the Oregon athletic director call me up, Henry.' I figured I was brushing him off. I hung up and a minute later, the athletic director of Oregon calls and says, 'We've heard all about you and you are our choice if you'd really like this job.' I said, 'I don't know,' and he said, 'Well at least come out and look at it.' That's a true story. Hood had the thing arranged. He was just a big donor to their program."

"Dick was really thinking about leaving anyway," recalled Shabel. "He came out of the Villanova game and said he could never win big without having grant-in-aid, without having scholarships. He said there's lots of kids you can't get. I remember seeing him when we were loading the bus to come back. He said, 'I can't get it done nationally here.' I felt at that moment that they weren't being given enough credit for what they did accomplish. They got killed at the end but I thought that they had an unbelievable season."

Harter insists that the Villanova loss was not the main reason why he took the Oregon job. "I left Penn because there was a lot of talk of how the Ivy League was going to retrench," he said. "There was even talk about making you stay in dormitories when you were going on the road to play, say, Harvard or Dartmouth. Then you always had the disadvantage of recruiting under the *needs* factor, and I thought if I could coach at a school where you could give full scholarships you'd never lose any games. Those two factors combined with the devastating loss and the fact that talented guys like Wohl and Bilsky were moving on. Yet, when I look back at it, we left a lot of very good players there. But I don't regret it because as great as the Big 5 was, Oregon proved to be the same. Our court there was very similar to the Palestra. It seated ten thousand but we turned that town on. We couldn't catch UCLA because they were too good and we didn't get into the NCAA Tournament because at the time they only took one team. But as far as turning on an area, that was unbelievable. You can't believe how hard my guys there played."

They certainly did. Especially in the famous "Payback Game" two years later when Rollie Massimino brought his young Villanova team out to Eugene and got crushed 116–77. "I remember Rollie was dreading going out there," said Frank Dolson, who had recently joined *The Philadelphia Bulletin*. Dolson and Harter had been classmates at Penn and the two were close friends. Oregon's best player, Ronnie Lee, had played for Massimino in high school.

"Rollie told me that everybody at Villanova told him what a no-good SOB Dick was, and I'm saying, 'You can't listen to these people, Rollie. Dick is a great guy. Judge people by the way they treat you. Take my word for it.'" Dolson flew out for the game and caught up with Massimino at practice. "Rollie comes bouncing over and says, 'Frank, you were right. Dick has been terrific. He took me to a boosters' club luncheon today and said all these great things about me. Like you said, he's a great guy.' I said, 'I told you, Rollie. You can't find a better guy than Dick.' So now they play the game. Harter had a pretty good team and the lead gets up to 30 or 35 in the second half. With about ten minutes to go, Dick calls time out and puts them into a full court press. He's standing there directing traffic as if it's the final minute of a tie game. He went nuts. Villanova called time at one point. Craig Littlepage, who played for Dick and was now one of Rollie's assistants, stood there staring at him. But Dick was oblivious to all this. All the kids were in shock. There were tears in the locker room afterwards. It was really bad and now the game is over and I've got to write a column. I was staying at Harter's house and that didn't make the situation any easier. After the game I started over towards the Villanova locker room. Rollie was waiting for me in the corridor. He said, 'What are you going to write? Are you going to write the truth or you going to cover up for your friend?' I said, 'Rollie, relax!' When I got to the Oregon locker room, we got into an argument. Dick said, 'Wasn't that great? We really put it to those bastards,' something like that. And I said, 'It's a damn disgrace, Dick, you ought to be ashamed of yourself.' He said, 'how can you say that? You were there when they . . .'"

Dolson stayed at Harter's house that night where he wrote a column "just ripping the hell out of Dick." Afterwards the two went out to get something to eat. "We were still arguing with each other. I kept telling him, 'Dick, that's not Jack Kraft. All you are doing is hurting Massimino. He had nothing to do with that game. He wasn't there at the time.'"

The next night Dolson was eating dinner at Harter's house. The phone rang. "It was Dick's mother, calling from the Philadelphia area, and she obviously said to him something like, 'Did you see what that so-and-so friend of yours wrote?' because I heard Dick say, 'Yeah, and he's eating dinner right now at my table.'"

Chapter 7

• • • • • • •

The Year the Champs Stayed Home

It's probably never happened before. Certainly not in the Big 5. The All-America leads his team to a pair of national championships. Then, 15 years later, he returns as coach and restores dignity to a program that has fallen on hard times. That's precisely what Tom Gola did at La Salle. As a freshman in 1952, Gola led the Explorers to a NIT title. Two years later, they won the NCAA championship. The following season, Gola's senior year, La Salle returned to the NCAA finals and finished runner-up to unbeaten San Francisco. And then, in 1968–69, Gola coached the best team in the Explorers' history to a 23–1 record, good for second place in the final Associated Press poll. The period between La Salle's glory runs, however, was characterized by a parade of coaches—five in seven years at one point—and an embarrassing NCAA probation. La Salle also produced a number of outstanding individual performances by some of the finest players the Big 5 has ever seen.

La Salle's two appearances in the NCAA Final Four occurred in 1954 and 1955, the year before the formal start of the Big 5. That's why Gola is the only person to have been inducted *twice* into the Big 5 Hall of Fame—as an Old-Timer and as coach of that great 1968–69 Explorer team, generally considered the best ever in the Big 5. After La Salle beat Bradley 92–76 for the NCAA title in 1954, Yogi Berra of the New York Yankees called Gola "the Joe DiMaggio of basketball." Ken Loeffler, who had turned in a great coaching job with his sophomore-laden Explorers, said simply, "Gola is the best in the world." Fittingly, Tom's three-point play had put the Explorers ahead for good in the championship game as he finished with 19 points and 19 rebounds.

Everyone except La Salle's captain and playmaker, Frank "Wacky" O'Hara, returned the following season. The Explorers finished 26–5 and came within 15 points of becoming only the third team in history to win consecutive NCAA titles—San Francisco ended the dream with a 77–63 win in the championship game. After the season, Loeffler resigned to become basketball coach at Texas A&M, where he toiled in the shadow of famed football coach Bear Bryant. The new coach at La Salle was Jim Pollard, who had just retired after a brilliant NBA career with the Minneapolis Lakers but who had no experience handling a college program.

Pollard's coaching debut coincided with the start of the Big 5 in 1955–56. With all of the starters except Gola returning, La Salle struggled to a 15–10 record and failed to make a post-season tournament for the first time since 1949. The loss of Gola, who still holds the NCAA career record for rebounds (2,201), was incalculable. "Tommy made everybody on the team stronger," said Frank Blatcher, who had come off the bench to score 23 points and share game-high honors with Charley Singley in the NCAA title game against Bradley. "There haven't been too many players in the history of the game that had Gola's talent. It was like Pavarotti being able to sing." Still, the Explorers had a formidable lineup. "In my mind, we had a fantastic team," said Blatcher. "La Salle should have won the Big 5 that year."

Besides Blatcher, an excellent set-shot shooter, and Singley, who had made the NCAA Final Four All Tournament team in 1954, there was Charley Greenberg, the club's best defensive player; Fran O'Malley, who would become La Salle's first member of an All Big 5 team, and Alonzo Lewis, who had replaced Wacky O'Hara in the starting lineup in 1954–55. Also returning were Bob Maples, an occasional starter from Elmhurst, Illinois (the only member of the NCAA champs who was not from Pennsylvania), and Bob Ames, who would later become one of our nation's top

▲ Fran O'Malley was the first La Salle player selected to the All Big 5 team in 1955–56, when he led the Explorers in rebounding. *(La Salle University)*

Middle Eastern experts for the CIA, only to be murdered in the terrorist bombing of the U.S. Embassy in Beirut, Lebanon, in 1983.

Lewis will never forget the night before La Salle's NCAA title showdown with San Francisco. As was its custom, the entire Explorer team went to see a movie after practice.

"I was the first one up at the box office and they wouldn't let me in," Alonzo recalled. Segregation was still flourishing in Kansas City. "I hailed a cab and told the driver, 'Take me to the black pool room.' I got to the pool room and inside were Bill Russell, K. C. Jones, and the other San Francisco players as well as two black play-

ers from Iowa. We played a couple of eight-ball games. I was probably a better shooter than all of them."

Although he still wasn't permitted to stay at the same hotel with his teammates, Lewis had been the center of a historic civil rights breakthrough earlier that season. When he took the floor in La Salle's 85–71 win over Loyola, in New Orleans on December 5, 1954, Alonzo became the first black player ever to participate against whites in an athletic event in the state of Louisiana. Moreover, for the first time in history, Loyola officials ignored a state law prohibiting mixed races to mingle and allowed black fans to sit anywhere in its Fieldhouse to watch the game. As a private Roman Catholic institution, Loyola was not bound by state law. Lewis scored the first basket of the game and finished with six points. "I know there was pressure," said Lewis, "I just don't recall how it affected me. I don't remember all that fanfare. I know I've been more nervous at other games, like Big 5 games. I remember we were getting ready to go out on the court before the Temple game and Jim Pollard asked me, 'How do you feel, Al?' and I said, 'I'm cool as calm.' I meant to say, 'I'm as cool as a *cucumber.*' The guys really got on me about that."

Lewis, a member of the Big 5 Hall of Fame, was La Salle's high scorer with 20 points when the Explorers dropped their rematch with San Francisco 79–62 in the opening round of the 1955 Holiday Festival in Madison Square Garden. He scored 16 in the first half, but didn't see the ball much after that when K. C. Jones was assigned to guard him. O'Malley had 18 points and also figured in the turning point late in the game. With La Salle trailing 58–55, Fran stole the ball and was racing in for a layup when Russell caught him from behind and pushed him into K. C. Jones. It would have been Russell's fourth personal, but officials called an offensive foul on O'Malley. "This will give you an idea about our lack of size," said O'Malley, the Explorers' best rebounder, who was guarded throughout the game by Russell. "Here's a guy that's 6'9" watching a guy 6'3". I certainly was not going to take him in the pivot because he'd beat me up." After La Salle beat Syracuse in a consolation round, Lewis came back to light up the Garden in the fifth place win over St. Johns, hitting 16 of 21 shots, all of them long distance jumpers, for 32 points.

La Salle beat Syracuse twice that year, and Blatcher found himself going head-to-head with a guy named Jim Brown. "We had a war physically but he was a great basketball player," Blatcher recalled about the future NFL Hall of Fame running back, who was also an All-America lacrosse star for the Orangemen. "Brown and I were beating the hell out of each other. He was a strong guy. On one of the last plays of the game, he gave me a bang and a half. I had banged him down at the other end. I went baseline on him and had no chance to make the

ment, the Richmond Invitational, by beating Virginia and Richmond. Bill Katheder, an Army veteran who had played on the 1952 NIT championship team, took MVP honors. Garberina didn't even play in the Virginia game but made the All Tournament team when he scored 13 points in the last seven minutes against Richmond. Two weeks later, La Salle and Villanova tangled in the longest and highest scoring game in the history of the Big 5. When the three-overtime classic was over, the Explorers, who had blown an 18-point lead in regulation, had won 111–105.

shot, but I threw the effort up and he fouled me." Blatcher made both free throws to clinch a 75–72 win. Brown finished with 15 points and came off the bench to score 10 points two weeks later at the Palestra as La Salle won again 71–64.

In 1957, the Explorers upset Temple 63–61 behind Lewis' 26 points, to grab a share of their first Big 5 title. Tom Garberina, a 6-foot junior who made the All Big 5 team that year, learned first-hand about Guy Rodgers' quickness when he raced down the court on a fast break with only Guy standing between him and the basket. "I decided to put the ball between Rodgers' legs because he was playing me perfectly defensively," Garberina explained. "I had it between his legs and went to run around him. He was so quick, he turned around and just picked it up out of the air. The average guy would have just stayed dumbfounded on the spot. I never tried that again when we played him."

The following year, La Salle was picked to finish seventh nationally. But the Explorers' 1957–58 season was virtually ruined before it began when tiny Millersville State Teachers College pulled off an 80–70 upset in the opening game at the Palestra. It was the most embarrassing loss ever suffered by a La Salle team and it marked the beginning of the end for Pollard, whose contract was not renewed at the end of the season.

There were some bright moments for the Explorers, however. They won their first regular season tourna-

Garberina had 24 points including a dramatic, last second tip-in that sent the game into the third overtime. "The noise level at the Palestra that night was uncanny," Garberina recalled. "It was almost charismatic." Bob Alden, a 6'7" sophomore who would make the All Big 5 team two years later, scored the game-winner on a lay-up after Hugh Brolly threaded a perfect pass to him through traffic.

Garberina, the first Big 5 player to shoot 50 percent from the field (50.3 percent), had scored a career-high 30 points the previous season against North Carolina State. Everett Case, the longtime coach of the Wolfpack, remembered that performance a year later and invited Tom to play in the North-South All-Star game in Raleigh. Case couldn't coach that night, but he told Joe Lapchick, who had come down from St. John's to handle the North squad, to be sure to start the kid from La Salle. Hal Greer, a hot-shooting guard from Marshall College who later became an NBA All Star with the Philadelphia 76ers, came off the bench to replace him. "I tell people that I started in an All-Star game ahead of a Hall of Famer," said Garberina.

Succeeding Pollard in 1958–59 was one of the most respected coaches in the game, Donald "Dudey" Moore, who had built a solid program at Duquesne University. "Dudey was the John Wooden of the '50s in Pittsburgh," recalled Bill Raftery, who was Moore's most

step away and altered everything. It slowed him enough to change his shot. If nothing had ever happened to him, I seriously believe that he would have been a great pro." Abbott, who played at St. James High School in Chester, Pennsylvania, got a shock his first day of practice when he walked-on as a freshman. "Everybody talked about the Philadelphia Catholic League being great," explained Abbott, who later served for a year as Joe Heyer's assistant coach at La Salle. "But those guys from North Jersey were spinning my head around. I was running into picks and walls. I thought that I was going to have a concussion. Bill was far more advanced. He already had experience that I didn't have."

The other guys from North Jersey that impressed Abbott were a pair of transfers, Bob McAteer, a 6-foot guard from the U.S. Naval Academy, and Ed Bowler, a 6'3" forward who had briefly attended Virginia Tech and St. Peter's. McAteer, a member of the Big 5 Hall of Fame, led the Explorers in scoring as a senior when he had a career high 42 points against Millersville. He also contributed to La Salle's most dramatic win that year, 78–76 at Georgetown, when he scored 33 points, including the game-winning jumper with two seconds left. Starting at forward for the Hoyas was Paul Tagliabue, the future NFL commissioner, who scored 12 points. Two years earlier, Tagliabue had come off the bench to score two points and grab five rebounds at the Palestra as the Explorers pulled out another heart-stopper, 80–79. Joe Heyer teamed with Ralph Bantivoglio to score the game-winner on a fast-break layup.

Bowler, who had been a High School All-America in Jersey City, was 23 years old, married, and had twins by the time he became eligible in 1960–61. At the end of the season, he was dismissed from school after being implicated in the nationwide betting scandal that rocked the college basketball world. Like the other play-

highly touted recruit. Raftery, a *Parade* magazine High School All-America from Kearny, New Jersey, had been labeled as the "next Tom Gola" and had made a recruiting trip to La Salle's campus with North Jersey's other hot prospect that year, Vinnie Ernst, who decided instead to attend Providence College. Neither Raftery nor Moore achieved the lofty expectations that greeted their arrival. Bill suffered a devastating knee injury during a pre-season scrimmage at NYU before the start of his junior year and played only 18 minutes before undergoing surgery in January. He had first injured the knee when he crashed into a pole during a summer league game after his freshman year. He played his first varsity season in considerable pain, but still led the Explorers in scoring as a sophomore. Although he came very close to making the New York Knicks after graduation, he was never quite the same player.

"Raftery was *Bradleyish,*" recalled Tony Abbott, who was Bill's backcourt running mate for two seasons. "He could rebound, pass, and shoot. He was still a great ballplayer when he graduated, but that injury took a

ers, he was never prosecuted, having been granted immunity for his testimony before a grand jury. According to Manhattan District Attorney Frank Hogan, who headed the investigation, Bowler had accepted $1,000 to see that La Salle lost by more than eight points in a game at Niagara University. That was one of his few starts for the Explorers that year. He shot one-for-ten from the field and scored two points as the Explorers lost 77–71. Midway through the second half, Dudey Moore replaced Bowler with Abbott and La Salle quickly cut into the lead with a full-court press. But because he wasn't in the game at the end, and La Salle lost by only six points, Bowler had to return $800 to the fixers.

Nobody from La Salle had any idea that one of its players was involved, although Moore frequently complained: "Bowler never misses in practice, but once I put him in a game he doesn't do anything." Abbott recalled a road trip that the Explorers had taken that season. "I was sitting on the airplane with Bowler and he started showing me an article in *Sports Illustrated* about the tenth anniversary of the 1951 college basketball scandal. I was 20 years old and said I never even knew anything about it. Then he told me how it worked. I didn't think it was strange at the time. Then a couple of months later he gets taken out of class."

"Eddie's specific responsibility was to get Bill Raftery and Bob McAteer involved because they had been friends from North Jersey," recalled Frank Corace, who was on La Salle's freshman team that year. "Ed, being the type of guy he was, felt that he couldn't jeopardize their friendship. I think the people who were paying this money were very upset with Eddie because he refused to get Mac and Bill involved in the thing. You can't condone stuff like that, but at least he felt strong enough that he wasn't going to get them involved."

Moore never quite achieved the success that he had enjoyed at Duquesne. Raftery, the player closest to him, thinks that Dudey's "Coach of the Year" reputation was unjustly tarnished in Philadelphia. "We weren't as good as everybody thought we were," Bill explained. "We weren't as serious as we should have been in some cases, myself included. Basketball wasn't as important to some of our guys as it was to him. And yet in his last year he got La Salle to its first tournament since Gola's time. He probably should have never left Pittsburgh. When we played out there, it was like the Messiah had come. Everybody—the redcaps and the cab drivers—all knew him. When he came to Philly, there were some people on our own campus who didn't know him."

It almost seemed that Dudey Moore was snake-bitten. In 1960, La Salle won its first nine games, then fizzled after Bob Herdelin, an All Big 5 selection and the team's top rebounder the previous year as a sophomore,

was dropped from school after running into some off-campus problems. The following year in the Holiday Festival, the Explorers almost beat top-ranked Cincinnati, the defending NCAA champs, but played the game without Corace, their high-scoring sophomore, who was out with the flu. Another time, La Salle had a 12-point lead late in a game against St. Joseph's when the Explorers' 6'7" center George Sutor bent the rim like a pretzel. "I remember going to the huddle and you could hear Jim Lynam saying. 'Come on, let's go. Jack will tell us how to beat these guys,'" recalled Raftery. "That was partly for us to hear and partly bravado, but we never scored a basket the rest of the game." Corace also remembers the Hawks' 66–49 win that night. "It took 25 minutes for Palestra officials to install a new rim," he explained. "Meanwhile St. Joe's is down the other end, shooting hoops and going through their warm-up drills. When the game resumed, we were all cold."

Sutor was coached at Philadelphia's Father Judge High School by Buddy Donnelly, the playmaker of La Salle's 1952 NIT champions. George had the dubious distinction of ripping down another rim, this time at Miami Beach Convention Hall in a game against the Hurricanes. Although only 18 minutes had been played, officials declared halftime while they went scurrying around for a replacement. They couldn't find one. Miami shot the daylights out of the twisted rim in the second half and won, 121–99. It was the most points ever scored against La Salle. "George was a lovable guy, a real good center for us," recalled Corace, who outscored Miami's Rick Barry 35 to 32 in that game. "Not a serious bone in his body."

Arguably the strongest player ever to wear a Big 5 uniform, Sutor led the Explorers in rebounding all three seasons. His best game—26 points and 27 rebounds—came against Western Kentucky in the opener of the famous "Bomb Scare" doubleheader. He held La Salle's record in the shot put for 31 years, and could do leg presses at 1,400 pounds. "Gyms used to hate to see me come in because I used to bend their bars," he explained. George had never played football, but parlayed his strength into a NFL tryout with the Philadelphia Eagles, where he played one exhibition game as a defensive end against the Washington Redskins. Although he had impressed the coaches by swatting away a number of field goal attempts in practice, Sutor had difficulty handling the Eagles' All-Pro tackle Bob Brown. "I thought I had him beat one time but he stopped and just lifted his hands up and literally lifted me off the ground," George recalled. "He didn't *break* my jaw but I could not eat for three days."

Sutor who was dyslexic, struggled with reading but still managed to earn a pre-law degree by attending classes, day, night, and summer, for five years. Later he got his teacher's certification at Glassboro State. "When Brother Aloysius gave me that reading test at La Salle, he said, 'George, you're dyslexic.' I didn't know what it was and I said, 'am I going to die?'" Sutor played for two seasons in the ABA with Kentucky, Minnesota, Carolina, and Miami and spent a season with the team that traveled all over the world playing the Harlem Globetrotters. "I played in Monaco before [Philadelphia's] Princess Grace and carried her son, Prince Albert, on my shoulders," recalled Sutor. He frequently found himself guarding Wilt Chamberlain, who joined the tour in the major European cities. "I met the Pope in Rome, played before 150,000 people in a soccer stadium in Barcelona, and couldn't imagine how big an aircraft carrier was when 5,000 people watched us on the *Enterprise.*"

When Dudey Moore was coaching, the Explorers always seemed to fall one victory short—usually against Temple or St. Joseph's—of grabbing the automatic NCAA bid or impressing the NIT selection committee. La Salle's only post-season tournament in his five years as coach came against St. Louis in the 1963 NIT. It was the Explorers' first national TV appearance since their NCAA championship days, and the result was a heartbreaking 62–61 loss.

La Salle had the ball and a one-point lead in the closing seconds when Raftery took a long jumper from the corner that fell short. "All of a sudden this crack opened up and unfortunately I went up when I shouldn't have and took this bad shot," he recalled. "We could have locked the game up by not shooting." St. Louis then came down and scored the winning basket. "It was devastating because we had a chance to move on. I was broken-hearted like any kid. I remember putting my head in a water fountain in the back of the Garden where nobody could see it and crying before I went into the locker room. Then I went home and my father's dying in bed. Here I take the worst shot in the world, go home and, of course, being from the background I was from, we didn't have a family doctor but I got a doctor to come up to the house. My father had a totally collapsed lung and said to the doctor with his Irish accent, 'I've got to go to work.' The doctor said, 'If you go to work, you're going to die at work.' My dad survived and he lived another twenty years. It was funny because you go from a bad mistake that cost your team a chance to move on, and then you go home and that hits you. Bang, bang, bang! It was a pretty interesting reality check. At that age, I never thought of stuff like that."

The NIT was not a total loss for Raftery, however. Bob Wolff, the veteran CBS sportscaster, spent a few days at La Salle before the St. Louis game and Bill showed him around campus. Wolff was quite impressed with the Explorer co-captain and told him that he should consider a career in broadcasting. After graduating, Raftery frequently sat in with Wolff, who was doing play-by-play for the New York Knicks. The two struck up a lifelong friendship. "He sort of planted the seed," recalls Raftery. "I never thought of broadcasting as a career. I thought I was going to be a coach." Both things, in fact, happened. After coaching for 16 years at Fairleigh Dickinson (Madison) and Seton Hall, Bill has spent the past 20 years handling telecasts of the New Jersey Nets games, working as an analyst on ESPN and CBS-TV, and broadcasting the NCAA Final Four on CBS radio.

During his senior season, Raftery became the bizarre target of a fan's wrath. It happened during a 79–76 loss at Niagara, where Dudey Moore was locking horns with one of his best friends in the coaching profession, "Taps" Gallagher. The Explorers implemented their usual opening tip-off play. Walter Sampson, the center, tapped the ball to Corace, with Frank tapping it over his head to Raftery. The play worked perfectly and Bill scored an easy layup. "At that point, a lady comes out of the stands under the basket and hits Bill across the back with her umbrella," recalled Corace. "All of a sudden the game stops. Dudey jumps off the bench, 'Who the hell is this woman?' She was probably about 70 years old at the time and never missed a Niagara basketball game. Before the game could resume, they had to usher her over to the side. Taps and Dudey got together. No fouls were called and the game resumed."

Curt Fromal, who had grown up learning the game on the playgrounds near Chester, Pennsylvania, with players like Tom Wynne and Steve Courtin, of St. Joseph's, averaged better than 20 points a game for La Salle's freshman team. But when he moved up to the varsity with Raftery and Abbott in 1961–62, he found himself buried deep on the bench. "I went in and asked Dudey why I wasn't playing," the 5'8" guard said, "and he told me that I was too small to play Big 5 basketball." A few weeks later, however, Fromal started against Villanova. Assigned to cover Hubie White, Curt did a fine job denying him the ball. He held the Wildcat star to six points as Villanova coughed up a big lead late in the game but still hung on to win 65–63. After the season, Fromal was called out of class. His sister was on the phone. "We've had a small fire," she said. "I arrived home and couldn't get within two blocks of my house," Curt recalled. "It was completely gutted." Fromal's father suffered a stroke trying to put out the flames and died three days later. Curt withdrew from college and spent the next year working to help support his family.

By the time Fromal returned in 1963–64, Bob Walters, a former La Salle captain who led the team in scoring all four years of his varsity career, was coaching

► **H**ubie Marshall (left) and Curt Fromal formed a potent backcourt combination for La Salle in 1964–65. *(La Salle University)*

the Explorers. The one-time assistant to Ken Loeffler was running a successful Philadelphia plumbing, heating, and air-conditioning business with his brother, Joe, the man-behind-the-scenes at Villanova. Fromal led La Salle in scoring and made the All Big 5 team as a senior in 1964–65. His career high of 34 points came in a 93–85 loss to St. Joseph's, and one of his finest all-around games (26 points) came in a losing effort against Detroit in the opening round of the NIT. But his most satisfying game was a 29-point effort in an 81–74 win over Temple. "I remember glancing up during warm-ups and Dudey Moore was sitting at the press table," Fromal recalled. "I hadn't seen him in two years. I was really hot that night and I played extremely well. Coming off the Palestra floor after the game, I stopped and stared at him. I looked him right in the eye. No words were exchanged. He looked at me and I just smiled at him and then walked away. I never saw him again."

Corace had been highly recruited after leading Monsignor Bonner High School to the Philadelphia city championship. But even though the 6'6" forward had chosen La Salle, he actually found himself dressed in a St. Joseph's Hawks' uniform before he ever wore the blue and gold. This meant he had a little explaining to do to La Salle's athletic director Jim Henry when he arrived on campus to begin his freshman year. "Jack Ramsay was writing his book, *Pressure Basketball,* and needed some photographs of players," recalled Corace, who was playing summer pickup games at St. Joe's. "He asked me to hang around one day because he wanted to photograph somebody shooting an underhand foul shot. Jack put a St. Joe's uniform on me and that's how I'm pictured in the book."

A two-time All Big 5 selection, Corace twice led the Explorers in scoring and had a career-high of 40 against Utah State. He had a number of outstanding games against Big 5 rivals, but the most memorable was a 32-point explosion in a win over St. Joseph's that helped La Salle grab its first Big 5 crown, in 1963–64. Corace and Steve Courtin of the Hawks were old friends. They faced each other in high school when Monsignor Bonner and

St. James played for the Philadelphia Catholic League title. Years later they were teammates in the Eastern League. After one of their games in Wilmington, they stopped for a few beers. Corace recalls the conversation. "Steve said, 'Frank, I've got to tell you something. Remember the St. Joe's–La Salle game?' I said, 'Sure. We beat you 80–70. I remember the numbers.' Then he said, 'We were practicing our man-to-man defense before the game and Jimmy Boyle says to Jack Ramsay, 'Coach, I've played against Corace for so many years. I played against him in high school, in the sandlots, in college. I know exactly what he's going to do.' So Jack Ramsay says, 'All right, Jimmy, you take care of Corace.' The game starts and at the end of the first half, I have 19 or 20 points. Steve Courtin said, 'I have never seen Jack Ramsay so mad in my life as he was after the first half of that game. He said to Boyle, 'Jimmy, you have no clue at all what Corace is going to do. We're changing our defense.'"

Corace was MVP of the Quaker City Tournament in 1963–64. Georgetown paved the way for La Salle's first major regular-season tournament title by upsetting No.1 Loyola (Chicago), the defending NCAA champions, in

▲ **F**rank Corace twice led La Salle in scoring and was MVP of the 1963 Quaker City Tournament. *(La Salle University)*

Although Walters called Corace "definitely the outstanding pro prospect in the East," Frank decided to forgo the NBA for a career in business, even though he was the second-round draft choice of the Philadelphia 76ers. It was a good decision. Today, the Big 5 Hall of Famer is a successful investment manager for a suburban Philadelphia firm whose Institutional Management Division is chaired by Tom Gola.

Walters stayed for only two years as coach of the Explorers. He resigned the day before the start of the 1965–66 season, citing ill health and business pressures. He also hated to fly, and the Explorers had a number of intersectional games looming on their schedule. But the real reason he quit was that he wanted to make sure that former La Salle guard Joe Heyer, his part-time assistant, got the job. In 1959, Heyer had been La Salle's top scorer. He broke Gola's school record and Oscar Robertson's single game Palestra record with 17 field goals against Lehigh. Both marks were eclipsed by Ken Durrett's 20 against Lafayette ten years later. "As a player, I was hot and cold," Heyer recalled. "One night that basket looked like it was two bushel barrels wide. Other nights it looked like the size of a coffee cup."

Now at the age of 28, Heyer was the youngest head coach in major college basketball. He was also the busiest. In addition to handling both the freshmen and varsity, Heyer taught full-time at Philadelphia's Cardinal Dougherty High School—which meant that he had to call in sick whenever the Explorers had an overnight road trip. Two nights a week he attended classes at St. Joseph's, studying for his master's degree. Facing a rugged schedule, La Salle had the nation's most exciting 10–15 team that year. The Explorers won only three of their first ten games but then upset four nationally ranked tournament-bound teams—Brigham Young, Temple, Villanova, and Louisville. In between there was a killer road trip to Duquesne, Creighton, Utah State, and Seattle, where La Salle came up exhausted and empty.

A week before its 1965 Quaker City Tournament opener against La Salle, unbeaten BYU had demolished St. Joseph's 103–83 in a showdown of top-ranked teams. No one gave the Explorers a chance. George Paull, who had also played for Heyer in high school, found some added incentive for La Salle's 71–69 victory. "Before the game both teams were out on the floor warming up," Paull recalled. "Bill Ring, our center, said, 'Did you hear that?' They had three 7-footers standing out at half court. The next time I went back into my layup line, I just went a little bit slower. And one of their big guys turned and said, 'I thought we were playing the varsity team tonight. What are you guys, the junior varsity?' I guess it was a form of intimidation but we were too stupid to be intimidated."

the opening round. La Salle won its opener against Northwestern, then took care of Georgetown 80–69 behind Corace's 29 points and a brilliant defensive effort by Joe Cunnane, who held Jim Christy to two points after the Hoya sharpshooter had scored 30 the night before. The Explorers then beat St. Bonaventure 83–80 for the crown. Harry Carpenter, a walk-on who played for Villanova's Jack Kraft at Philadelphia's Bishop Neumann High School, made some big plays underneath for La Salle in the tournament. But he suffered a separated shoulder in the closing seconds when he got tangled up with Fred Crawford, the Bonnies' All-America, who shared game scoring honors with Corace with 28 points. "I don't remember us winning it," said Carpenter. "I didn't remember a thing until the next day."

La Salle's best player that year was Hubie Marshall, one of the Big 5's most prolific shooters ever, who triggered the big 96–92 win over Louisville with 42 points. "Hubie had as good a game as any guard has ever played in the Palestra against a major opponent," said Heyer. "He was on fire that night. I would say that Hubie and Hal Lear were the two best long distance shooters in the history of the Big 5. As far as just shooting the jumper from outside, Hubie was probably better than Lear, who got a lot of his points on fast breaks and drives. If Hubie got one from ten or twelve feet it was in the bank."

Marshall's backcourt running mate, Ed Burke, who later coached at Drexel University for 14 years, remembers "taking it to Wes Unseld" in the Louisville game. "I gave it that Overbrook shuffle taking it to the basket," Burke recalled. "I didn't know whether to throw it down or just lay it off the glass. I heard the roar of the crowd and the ball was 30 rows up in the stands. He just took that thing and threw it!"

Despite being out-rebounded by 27, La Salle beat Villanova 78–70 as Burke hit six straight long-range jumpers, finished with a career-high 18 points, and held Bill Melchionni to one field goal in the second half. Less than a week later the Explorers nipped Temple 86–85, as Marshall scored 31 points and Dave "Lefty" Ervin, a transfer from Salem Junior College, added 23, including the game-deciding free throw with 29 seconds left. A few weeks earlier, Ervin had given Big 5 fans a taste of his exceptional scoring touch when he shot 15 for 16 from the field and outscored Dave Bing 31 to 30 in a losing effort against Syracuse at the Palestra.

Marshall, a two-time All Big 5 selection and a member of the Big 5 Hall of Fame, went over the 40-point mark two other times that season. He set a La Salle record for points in a half (33) during a 42-point outburst against Albright in Heyer's first game as coach, and had 40 against American U. He also holds La Salle's career record for free throw shooting (84.6 percent).

Heyer made another significant move that year, one that has had a lasting impact on the Big 5. His only "recruit" was Fran Dunphy, a relatively unknown guard from Malvern Prep, who came highly recommended by his coach, Dan Dougherty, the former St. Joseph's player who grew up in Heyer's neighborhood in Philadelphia. Dunphy, who had an excellent playing career for the Explorers and is now the coach at the University of Pennsylvania, was given a half-tuition scholarship for baseball and basketball. "A half scholarship to me meant that I got one of the semesters for free and would have to pay for the other one," he recalled. "It cost $1,100 a year to go to La Salle in those days, so I had $550 in cash when I went up to register. Actually I put a hole in my suit coat pocket and had the cash stuffed in the lining of my jacket—not in the pocket, itself—as I took the Broad Street subway up to campus."

Meanwhile, Walters was working behind the scenes assembling the nucleus of arguably the best team in Big 5 history. "He was an amazing guy," said Heyer, "a go-getter who was always thinking ahead. He was a great recruiter. He would just jump into his big Cadillac and go anywhere at any time to recruit guys." From Philadelphia's Lincoln High School, Walters brought in 6'5" guard-forward Larry Cannon, a *Parade* magazine All-America whose single season scoring in the city had been surpassed only by Wilt Chamberlain. From Washington's DeMatha Catholic High came Bernie Williams, one of the smoothest shooters ever to play in the Big 5. And from Mahanoy City, Pennsylvania, at the recommendation of George Senesky, the former St. Joseph's and Philadelphia Warriors' star, it was Stan Wlodarczyk, a gifted but soft-spoken 6'6" forward who would have a tremendous impact on La Salle's frontline, as would Ed Szczesny, a 6'8" center from Plymouth-Whitemarsh High in suburban Philadelphia, who transferred from the University of Oklahoma.

Despite all the talent, however, the Explorers struggled in 1966–67, winning only 14 of 26 games. Although there were some impressive triumphs over teams like Nebraska, Oklahoma City, and Bowling Green, La Salle's only Big 5 victory came over Penn 85–83 when Marshall scored 31 points. Cannon had two of the best games of his career that year, with 32 points against Oklahoma City and 25 rebounds against Western Kentucky.

"We expected that Bob would be the coach," recalled Cannon, who later became the first La Salle player selected for the Big 5 Hall of Fame. Like all of Walters's recruits, Larry ended up playing for a different coach in each of his three varsity seasons. "There was never any mention at that time that he didn't like to fly," Cannon recalled. "There was so much publicity about the high school All-Americans and there was a lot of friction around the school because the veteran players did not know what to expect." Heyer refused to let La Salle's talented freshman team play the varsity in the annual preseason scrimmage, preferring instead to mix the lineups up. "It was like the old joke about UCLA being No.1 in the country and No. 2 on campus," recalled Cannon after Kareem Abdul-Jabbar's freshmen team had beaten the defending NCAA champions by 20 points.

"I think that Joe more than anyone felt this friction that existed between the upper class players and the younger players," added Cannon, who led the Explorers in scoring that year. "It was a difficult situation for him. His way of handling it was, understandably, to side with the veterans, so to speak, in terms of protecting them and bringing us along slowly. I remember that Bernard and I didn't start our first game as sophomores. He did bring us off the bench and it was hard to keep us out of the game after that. It was not a real comfortable season. Of course, we were not an easy bunch to handle, I'm sure."

At the end of the season, Heyer found himself fed up with all the pressure and resigned. He moved to Florida where he taught in a junior high school for a year before returning to North Penn High School, in Lansdale, Pennsylvania, where he coached basketball for a while and taught for 30 years. His replacement was Jim Harding, an outspoken Jekyll and Hyde-type personality who created more controversy in one year than all of the other Big 5 coaches combined. Harding had previously coached at Loyola University (New Orleans) and at Gannon College and had been highly recommended to La Salle's president by his counterpart at Gannon. He charmed La Salle's athletic selection committee with his warm, friendly gregarious personality. Then when he got the job, he terrorized the team with threats and insults.

"Playing for Jim Harding was a phenomenal experience," recalled Dunphy. "It was tough, no question about it. He was very demanding. It was almost surreal in so many ways. Nobody was prepared for how hard we had to work. I can remember Stanley Wlodarczyk going into his room one night. He had a ten-pound weight and he said, 'Here's my hand. Just drop the weight on there. I just don't want to play any more.' But as you look back on it, he taught us a tremendous amount of basketball. I'm not sure I learned more basketball in any one season in my career. He was unbelievable. Every little detail was covered. He was just so hard on everybody. I would almost like to sit down with him today and say, 'You just can't be that demanding on everybody. Everybody's trying their best. They're not cheating you out of effort or anything.' But that's what you did in those days. You got away with that for the most part."

"To me he was like a military guy," said Cannon. "I don't think that he was a real creative offensive coach, but defensively he knew the fundamentals and we worked at them all the time. Basically, offensively he just let you play. He was such a DI [drill instructor] type character that the players were afraid of him. They didn't play in a relaxed fashion. They played nervously and anxiously and, of course, you can't play the game like that."

Harding brought in another key player that year, Roland "Fatty" Taylor, a 6'0" guard from Washington, D. C., who transferred from Dodge City Junior College in Kansas. By the time he graduated, Taylor became the finest defensive player in Big 5 history. He later played professionally for eight years with Washington, Virginia,

and Denver. Twice he was named Defensive Player of the Year in the ABA and four other times he made the league's All Defensive team. "When he would guard me in practice, he would hold me to *no dribbles*," recalled Lefty Ervin, who later became head coach of the Explorers. "I couldn't even put the ball on the floor because he'd be gone. He was the greatest defender of all time."

One of the most memorable offensive *and* defensive performances ever seen at the Palestra occurred during the 1967–68 season when Niagara's Calvin Murphy scored 52 points against the Explorers *despite* Taylor's brilliant defense. "I had never seen Calvin play," recalled Taylor. "One day before practice, Jim Harding grabbed me and said, 'Fatty, I've got enough confidence in you to pick Calvin Murphy up baseline to baseline, no help, no switch for 48 minutes.' I was really psyched up, but the whole week Kenny Durrett and Bernie Williams kept telling me, 'You can't do it.' I kept thinking about the guys I played against on the playground—people like Dave Bing and John Austin—and thought, 'He's no better than they are.'"

The game started and Niagara won the opening tap. "I was at the foul line defensively waiting for Murphy," Fatty explained. "He blew by me so fast and laid it up before I could even turn around. I just heard the crowd go '*OOOHHH!*' I looked at the scoreboard and it said 2–0. That's the only time I ever played basketball that I got scared. He came down a couple of times, took me to the corner, shot over me and missed a couple of times. Once I think I deflected the ball. I said to myself, 'I've got him going now.' The next time he came down like he had a Gatling gun. *Boom! Boom! Boom! Boom!* They were setting high picks, low picks on me. I fouled out and after the game Bernie and Kenny said to me, 'Fatty, you played good defense on him.'"

La Salle would go on to win 20 games for the first time in 13 years, but by the end of the season, Taylor and Harding were not seeing eye-to-eye. The defense-minded coach ended up running the nation's best defensive player off the team. "He completely destroyed me that year," said Fatty. "I was giving that man everything I had and he treated me real bad. Nobody ever treated me like that. I was an All-American in junior college and led the conference in scoring, but Harding didn't like how I shot the ball. He told me the only shot he wanted me to take was an uncontested layup. So any time I thought about taking a shot, he would holler and

▶ La Salle's Roland "Fatty" Taylor and Bernie Williams (right) combined for one of the finest backcourt tandems in college basketball in 1968 and 1969. *(La Salle University)*

scream at me and degrade me. I completely lost all my confidence." It all came to a head the week after season ended. "Harding called me in his office and said, 'Fatty, if you don't average ten points a game next year, you're not going to be in the starting lineup.' I said, 'Coach if you give me a free hand, I'll average 15 or 18 points a game for you. But you're telling me only to take uncontested layups.' We really got into it. Bernie was there and he had to come over and get between us. I was so mad, we were ready to fight.' Bernie broke it up and after that Harding said, 'You're off the team!'"

Then there was the mid-season episode at the Boston Garden Invitational, when Harding erupted after the Explorers dropped the opening round game to Providence 77–56. Ernie Accorsi of the *Inquirer* and Frank Brady of the *Bulletin* were the only Philadelphia writers covering the game. "We went to the locker room and heard yelling and screaming," recalled Accorsi. "Then Harding comes out and says, 'I'm revoking scholarships.' We went back to the floor. I don't think this would happen today, but I looked at Frank and said, 'This is devastating.' He said, 'Yeah, let's give him a chance to get off the hook here.' I said, 'Fine.' Now we're sitting in the third deck watching the second game. We approached Harding and said, 'If you want to retract what you said, it dies with us.' 'ABSOLUTELY NOT!' he replied. He was even stronger." Accorsi and Brady had no choice but to write the story quoting Harding: "Unless some guys show more aggressiveness, I'm going to drop them from the squad. . . . I'm going to drop them right off the team and you can quote me on that. . . . Tomorrow is the turning point. *Either they produce or they go—and with them go the scholarships.*" By the next morning, a sizable Philadelphia media contingent had swarmed to Boston where the Explorers won a meaningless consolation game over North Carolina State.

"When Jim talked about taking scholarships away, it was just madness," recalled Cannon. "I think that we were all just stunned. Who had ever heard of such a thing? It wasn't even in the vocabulary. You simply don't do something like that. To sit back and watch the scenario develop between Harding and the media was a surprise every day. We used to laugh about it."

A month later, Fran Scott, a 6'8" reserve forward, quit the team and told *Philadelphia Inquirer* columnist Frank Dolson that not only had his scholarship been taken away, but that other team members were being paid for work that they did not perform. Dolson investigated the charges and turned his findings over to the National Collegiate Athletic Association.

La Salle lost its final game that year to sixth-ranked Columbia 83–69 in the first round of the NCAA Tournament in College Park, Maryland. The Ivy League champs had a pair of All-Americas in Heyward Dotson and Jim McMillian, but it was obvious that the Explorers were a distracted bunch of players. "I remember us being psychologically oppressed," said Ervin, their captain. "I remember us as a team thinking *'We're burned out a little bit here.'* That was a shame. It's almost like I had a feeling that we didn't want to play. When it was over there was a big sigh."

As it turned out the Columbia game was the last time that this great Explorer team would have a shot at a national championship. On October 30, 1968, the NCAA placed La Salle on two years probation, thus declaring the basketball team ineligible for post-season tournaments. In a cruel irony, several La Salle administrators, including the author, were present when the NCAA's 18-member council announced the sanctions at a hotel in Kansas City—a hotel located right across the street from Convention Hall, where the Explorers had enjoyed their greatest moment 14 years earlier when they had won the NCAA title.

The NCAA charged La Salle with five violations of "principles governing financial assistance" and two violations of "principles of ethical conduct." The financial aid violations involved (1) the improper termination of scholarships on the recommendation of basketball coach Jim Harding; (2) six cases in which athletes were paid for "some hours they did not work"; (3) failure of the college to provide scholarship athletes with "a written statement describing the amounts, duration, conditions and terms of the awards"; (4) token payments to freshman players for outstanding performances; and (5) threats by Harding to terminate scholarships for poor performances in basketball. The ethical violations included charges that (1) La Salle's basketball coaches established an incentive rewards system for outstanding performances and threatened to terminate institutional financial assistance for poor performances in the sport of basketball, and (2) a basketball coach at the college advised at least one student athlete to withhold information at the time the student was to be interviewed by a representative of the NCAA Committee on Infractions.

According to the NCAA, La Salle revoked scholarships for Scott and Jack Lawlor, a senior reserve, when they quit the team. But, said the NCAA, once college officials became aware that this action was in violation of NCAA rules, the grants were reinstated. La Salle officials confirmed that the players had been employed part-time to clean heating and air conditioning filters by "A to C Housecleaning Services, Inc.," a company operated by Frank Loughney, a former Little All-America football player at La Salle. The players included Cannon, Wlodarczyk, and Williams, as well as Durrett and Bill Pleas, who were yet to play their first varsity game, and a member of the swimming team. The amount of the weekly payments varied according to various sources. La Salle officials said that records for one week showed that the pay ranged from ten to fifteen dollars. "I think we were getting $25," recalled Cannon. Fran Scott told the *Philadelphia Bulletin* that $60 "was more like it." The basketball coach who established the incentive rewards system—"50 or 75 cents to the kid who got the most rebounds," according to Harding's comments to the *Philadelphia Bulletin* at the time—was Bill Wilson, La Salle's freshman coach. Wilson was also charged with advising the student to withhold information.

Harding and Wilson were long gone by the time that La Salle went on probation. Harding had resigned two months earlier to take the coaching job with the Minnesota Pipers, which had just relocated its American Basketball Association franchise from Pittsburgh. The job of restoring respectability to the Explorers now rested on the shoulders of Gola, who had retired in 1966 after ten years in the NBA with the Philadelphia Warriors and New York Knicks. Gola had exactly one month to get ready for the 1968–69 season, and he was commuting at least two days a week between Harrisburg, where he served as a member of the state legislature, and Philadelphia. "I had two good assistant coaches—Eddie Altieri and Curt Fromal—and I didn't miss any games," he recalled. "They were two good guys who knew the system and I could depend on them if I was going to be late."

No one was more relieved than Taylor when Gola took over as coach. "We loved how Tom Gola carried himself," Fatty recalled. "He came in and said, 'Hey, you guys have talent. I'm going to put in the five-man weave and all I want is for you guys to play defense, play together, and respect one another.' We loved hearing his little conversations about what it was like in the pros. He made us believe that we could win. There was no stress, no pressure. Everybody was relaxed. We could play our game. We didn't have to look over our shoulders. He treated us like men. He was a good example for us as a human being."

With Gola employing the same system that he had learned under Ken Loeffler, the Explorers lost only one of 24 games, went unbeaten in the Big 5 for the first time ever, and finished with its highest national ranking in history. La Salle beat Temple's soon-to-be NIT champs 101–85 as Durrett made his Big 5 debut by hitting 12 of 17 field goal attempts and scoring 27 points. Other victims included Indiana, when La Salle scored its season high in a 108–88 triumph, Miami, Syracuse, Western Kentucky, Creighton and Detroit. The Titans were the only one of those teams to make a serious run before falling 98–96 in the Explorers' finale at the Palestra, when Spencer Haywood scored 30 points and grabbed 30 rebounds.

La Salle's fast break was absolutely devastating, especially over a four-game stretch when the Explorers averaged 102 points in blowouts over Temple, St. Francis (Pennsylvania), Loyola (New Orleans), and Lafayette. "Tom brought that break in from the NBA," said Ervin, who also served as one of Gola's assistants that year. "It was maybe the best fast break in the history of the entire region." When they were playing for the Philadelphia 76ers, Wali Jones and Archie Clark used to tell Fatty Taylor, "You had a helluva team. We'd be practicing and we'd be looking at the clock and we'd say, 'Hey man, we have to hurry home and see La Salle play.' We just loved how you all ran and how you played. We'd used to run home to catch you on the tube."

"When I played at La Salle, I thought that Kenny

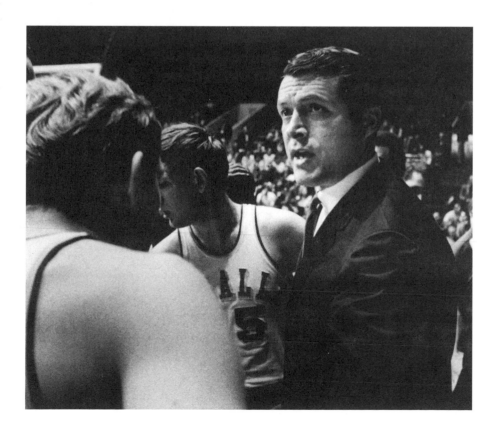

► La Salle All-America Tom Gola returned to coach the Explorers to a 23–1 record and second place in the final 1968–69 AP poll. *(La Salle University)*

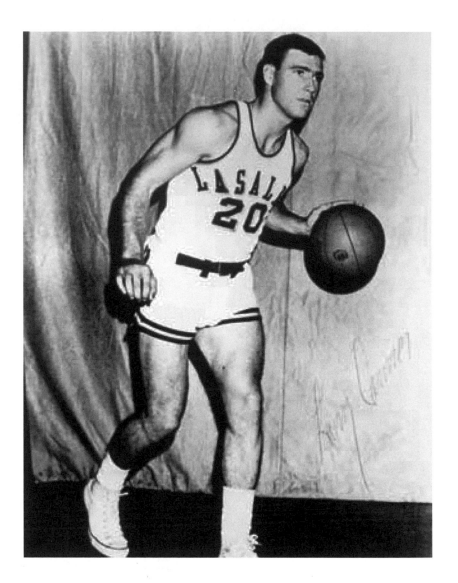

► Larry Cannon was the first La Salle player elected to the Big 5 Hall of Fame and the fifth player selected in the 1969 NBA draft. *(La Salle University)*

Loeffler's five-man weave was the greatest thing since apple pie," Gola explained. "Even our big guys could move the ball. They could all shoot so we had a very easy time playing against opponents with one or two big men because they were used to guarding big men. Everybody handled the ball, and when I coached I used the identical same system. It allowed all of them to have fun. It wasn't like a one- or two-man show. There were times if guys started to get a little crazy, I would call for the ball to be touched by five guys before anything happened."

Williams, a member of the only team to defeat Lew Alcindor's Power Memorial High School powerhouse, later played for five years in the ABA with San Diego and Virginia. "When I first saw Bernard, I thought that he was the best player that I had ever seen," said Cannon. "You don't see too many players who were as fluid as Bernard coming down the floor, handling the ball, and shooting his jump shot. He could shoot the ball from great range so effortlessly. And what jumping ability! I had never seen anybody dunk the ball like that. He was a little older and probably a little more mature than us. He was always the voice of reason when we were being kind of crazy kids."

The highlight of the year, of course, was La Salle's 74–67 win over Villanova in the most anticipated showdown ever waged in the Big 5. It was the only time that two Big 5 teams faced each other when they were ranked nationally in top ten. The Explorers were seventh and the Wildcats eighth. Ken Loeffler, who coached La Salle's NCAA championship team, was there. The game was broadcast worldwide by Jim Murray, Harry Anger, and the author over the Armed Forces Radio Network. And it featured the much-heralded matchup between the spectacular sophomores—Durrett, La Salle's 6'7" former high school All-America from Pittsburgh, and Villanova's Howard Porter, who would share Big 5 MVP honors.

"We prepared extremely well for that game and knew exactly what we wanted to do," recalled Fromal. "We wanted to run but we didn't want to make it a matchup of Durrett and Porter. We made sure that Kenny stayed away from him as far as foul trouble was concerned. That was the biggest thing we worried about. We couldn't afford to lose Kenny." Wlodarczyk and Szczesny shared the defensive chores on Porter with Durrett helping out from the weak side. Porter, who played spectacular defense with eight blocked shots, had 21 points, as did teammate Johnny Jones, but Taylor did a pretty effective job denying him the ball before fouling out. Williams kept the Explorers in the game early by scoring 14 of his 18 points in the first half. Durrett led La Salle with 20 and broke the game open with a three-point play that gave the Explorers a 68–61 lead with 2:27 left.

"Bernie was so pumped up and so excited, he ran over Fran O'Hanlon twice and got three fouls in the first four minutes," said Taylor, who knew that the Explorers needed Williams' long-range shooting to bring the Wildcats out of their zone defense. "Gola called a time out and Bernie comes over and says, 'Don't take me out, coach! Don't take me out! I'm all right.' So Gola left him in the game and Bernie started shooting that jumper from the corner, opening everything up."

"I thought we matched up with them pretty good," said Gola. "I remember at one point in the game when Taylor fouled out, Larry Cannon came up to me and said, 'Let me guard Johnny Jones.' I shivered because Larry wasn't the best defensive player because he concentrated more on offense. But he had his heart in it and he was ready to win that game. I just said to him, 'Larry, if you're going to do it, you've got to concentrate on the guy.' He guarded Johnny Jones and did a great job. He made it look easy."

Cannon, who is ambidextrous, actually switched his glove and pitched with both hands in Little League baseball games. "I also applied that to basketball," he recalled. "My ability to use both hands and go to my left just gave me so much more diversity. I remember Jim McMillian saying after that Columbia game that he thought I was left-handed." Larry was the fifth player taken in the 1969 NBA draft (by the Chicago Bulls), but went with the Miami Heat of the ABA, where he played a few games for former La Salle coach Jim Pollard. Unfortunately, his five-year professional career was cut short by a blood clot following a collision when he was playing for the Indiana Pacers.

"Without a question, Larry was probably one of the top five players in the history of the city," said Lefty Ervin, Cannon's former teammate and coach. "He would have been a marvelous pro because he did everything. Just seeing him go up the court and penetrate the defense, drive to the basket in the most efficient manner, and deliver those passes, it was just picture perfect. He was a very fine shooter and was wonderful around the basket."

La Salle's only loss came against South Carolina, 62–59 in the championship game of the Quaker City Tournament at the Spectrum. The Gamecocks were headed by Frank McGuire, who had coached Gola for a season with the Philadelphia Warriors. Bobby Cremins, the future coach of Georgia Tech, was the only returning starter, but a pair of sophomores played surprisingly well. John

Roche did a masterful job controlling the ball, and 6'10" Tom Owens took care of the rebounding. "I think we were a little overconfident and they just controlled the whole tempo of the game," said Dunphy. "It seemed that they would hold the ball for 30, 40 seconds at a time. Then we would rush down and try to shoot it right away because we were frustrated after having been on defense for so long."

"I remember that Gola said, 'That loss was my fault,'" recalled Jack Conboy, La Salle's athletic director at the time. "Tommy said he would have played his starters longer without going to the bench. 'I didn't realize that those guys were as strong as they were,' he told me. 'I could have played them harder and we could have won that game.'"

▶ La Salle's Fran Dunphy, the MVP of the 1969 Quaker City Tournament, went on to become head coach at the University of Pennsylvania.
(La Salle University)

In addition to the formidable starters—all except Wlodarczyk played in the NBA or ABA, and he was a late cut by the Milwaukee Bucks—the Explorers had an impressive bench with such players as Szczesny, Dunphy, and Larry Cannon's younger brother, Greg, a 6-foot guard, who led the team in assists in 1970–71. "That was the best team that La Salle ever had, including all the teams that I played for," said Gola. "I thought that we would have had a great shot against Lew Alcindor and UCLA. With the pressure that we could have put on defensively between Fatty Taylor and Bernie Williams, we could have contained them from getting the ball to Alcindor."

Three starters from that squad—Cannon, Durrett, and Williams—later became Big 5 Hall of Famers. But instead of facing UCLA in the NCAA championship game in the Louisville Fairgrounds before a national TV audience, the best Explorer team *ever* ended its season at West Chester State College's tiny Hollinger Fieldhouse, winning a meaningless game 91–73. "To end it there was really difficult," said Dunphy. "We had been through a lot. We had achieved great success but you couldn't prove it to anybody. Everybody had to take our word for it that we were pretty good."

The Explorers struggled to a 14–12 record and went winless in the Big 5 the following year, but co-captains Dunphy and Durrett provided some exciting highlights. Dunphy was named MVP of the Quaker City Tournament after La Salle won the title by sweeping by Georgia, Cornell, and Columbia. He had 24 points against the Lions in the title game. Durrett, the Big 5 MVP, became the fastest Explorer in history to reach the 1,000-point plateau, doing it in his 46th game.

"Kenny Durrett was better than me," explained Gola, a member of the Naismith Basketball Hall of Fame. "He could do more things with the ball than I could and he could rebound. He had all the moves before Dr. J. He had such a fluid motion. He was just a great ballplayer."

After the 1969–70 season, Gola resigned as La Salle's coach, shortly before being elected city controller of Philadelphia. His running mate, who became the city's new district attorney, was Arlen Specter, now in his third decade as U.S. senator from Pennsylvania.

Chapter 8

• • • • • • • •

The 'Cats Run with the Ball (Defense)

One night in the late 1980s, John Nash, then the general manager of the Philadelphia 76ers, was sitting in a hotel lounge in Orlando when Milwaukee Bucks coach Don Nelson walked in. "He's had a few drinks and he wants to start poking some fun at me," recalled Nash. "I had only been a GM for a couple of years so I was kind of the new kid on the block. He was there with some veteran guys like Bob Ferry and he starts, 'Oh, you guys from Philly, you're all soft. You don't know how to be tough. You think you're from the inner city and you're tough but you're not tough.' I let him go on for a while, then finally I said, 'Nellie, let me ask you a question: 1961 Quaker City Tournament. You came in with Iowa and I watched a 6-foot-3-inch Hubie White kick your ass.' He was startled. And then he turned to me and said, 'I was sick that night.' Then he left. But, do you know what happened? From that moment on, I gained his respect because he realized that my basketball experience went back a little bit further than he would have expected."

Nash was referring to one of the great moments in Villanova basketball history, when the Wildcats and their new coach Jack Kraft caught the attention of the nation by upsetting the heavily-favored Hawkeyes 69–56 for their first-ever regular-season tournament championship. For Kraft, the surprise choice to succeed long-time coach Al Severance, it was the first of dozens of significant victories over a 12-year period that saw his Wildcats compete in 11 post-season tournaments, including a run to the NCAA championship game against UCLA in 1971. Kraft, who was named National Coach of the Year that year, guided the Wildcats to 20 or more wins in a season seven times and registered a 238–95 career record for a .715 won-lost percentage, easily the highest ever at Villanova.

Severance, a loquacious attorney who preceded Kraft for a quarter of a century, had, in fact, coached in the first NCAA Tournament game ever played, on March 17, 1939—when his Wildcats defeated Brown University 43–30 at the Palestra. Villanova made it to the Final Four that year before losing to Ohio State 53–36 in the first of four NCAA tourney appearances under Severance. As an undergraduate, he captained the Wildcats' 1928–29 basketball quintet, ran on the track team, held Villanova's 135 and 145-pound boxing titles, and graduated as class valedictorian in 1929. A long time business law professor at Villanova and a justice of the peace in Chester County, Pennsylvania, Severance was also known as an entertaining raconteur and the subject of countless humorous anecdotes during his colorful career.

"Everybody used to ridicule his coaching ability, but Al was a very bright guy, very interesting, never boring, very amusing," recalled Bill Campbell, who broadcast Villanova games back in those days. "Al was a real character. His classes were jammed. Everybody wanted to hear him."

"One year, Villanova stayed at a hotel in midtown Manhattan and took the subway to Madison Square Garden. I'm one of the last ones to get on this crowded subway, but I got caught on the platform," George Raveling, the team's leading rebounder, recalled. "The door shuts and I don't get on, so I'm knocking on the door, saying, 'What should I do, coach? What should I do?' And Al says, 'Turn yourself in to Lost and Found!'"

"I remember he once quit right in the middle of a game," recalled Maje McDonnell, who played for Severance and later served as his assistant. "It was in 1947, I was co-captain, and we were getting beaten badly up in West Point. He said 'I quit. You're the coach.' Then he went up and sat in the top of the stands. So I put myself into the game. 'What are you doing?' he

▲ **J**im Huggard never played basketball in high school but went on to become one of Villanova's best playmakers and a top college referee. *(Urban Archives, Temple University, Philadelphia, Pennsylvania)*

▲ **V**illanova coach Al Severance with his 1959–60 captain George Raveling, who later became an assistant to Jack Kraft. *(Urban Archives, Temple University, Philadelphia, Pennsylvania)*

yelled. 'I made my first move,' I said. In the second half, I sat on the bench without playing and we started to come back. The closer we got, he started to come down the steps. By the time we went ahead, he was back on the bench." Villanova pulled the game out 45–42.

Severance shared his only Big 5 title with St. Joseph's in 1959–60, when the Wildcats went 20–6 and won their first ten games before losing at unbeaten West Virginia 89–81. They lost despite 27 points and numerous steals by Jim Huggard, a 5' 10" guard who had never played while a student at Philadelphia's West Catholic High School. Also participating in that game against the Mountaineers was Hubie White, a talented sophomore, who, like Huggard, would eventually be named to the Big 5 Hall of Fame.

"Jerry West walked on water down there," recalled Huggard, who later became a Division I basketball referee for 22 years. "He was fouling the hell out of White and nothing was called. Hubie was really upset after the game and I said, 'You're down South, pal. They don't even want to see you.'"

As an All Public League star at West Philadelphia

High School, White had been heavily recruited. One night, Severance invited Hubie and his dad to dinner at the old Ben Franklin Hotel, in Philadelphia's Center City. "This was a time when black people were not treated as well as maybe they should have been," recalled White. "I remember my father feeling so great that he was sitting in this elegant dining room with me and the coach of Villanova. Finally at the end of the dinner, Al Severance said to my father, 'Mr. White—he said that very clearly. *Mr. White*—would you like a cigar?' And my father, leaning back beaming, said, 'I don't mind if I do.' That was one of the greatest things I've ever experienced. Because of the way he treated my family and the way he treated my father particularly, I decided that Villanova was the place I wanted to go. Al was really a good guy, one of the greatest guys I've ever met."

Villanova missed a chance to win the Big 5 championship outright that year when St. Joseph's guard Joe Gallo scored 24 points and hit a pair of free throws with one second left to seal a 78–75 win. The Wildcats came back the following week to grab their share of the title when Huggard, who still holds the Wildcats' single game assist record (16) with Fran O'Hanlon, scored 22 to trigger a 68–52 win over La Salle.

Severance, who coached for the first six years of the Big 5, also guided Villanova to back-to-back appearances in the National Invitation Tournament. The Wildcats lost to St. John's 75–67 in 1959. The following year they defeated Detroit, headed by Dave DeBusschere, 88–86, but got eliminated in the quarterfinals by Utah State 73–72. White dazzled the Madison Square Garden crowd by combining for 50 points, 17 rebounds and 9 assists in the two games. Dick Kaminski added 23 points against Detroit and 17 against Utah State. The Wildcats clinched the Detroit game when Bob Liberatore came off the bench to score nine quick points in the second half.

The Utah State game was Villanova's first ever appearance on national television. "I'm originally from Athens," said White. "My mother called every relative in Georgia and said, 'Turn on the TV because Junior is going to be on. He's playing in the NIT.' Everybody thought it was fantastic and they couldn't believe this guy who came from Athens when he was a little seven-year-old was now on television playing for Villanova. Utah State really had a good team, but we got so preoccupied with the fact that we were going to be on national television, we forgot that we had to play the game. Guys would be in front of the mirror getting ready, fixing their hair and making sure their uniform was just right, and they forgot that we had to win it in order to move on. But we were cool."

▲ **V**illanova captain Joe Ryan led the Wildcats in scoring in 1958–59. *(Villanova University)*

Another Big 5 Hall of Famer from the Severance era was Joe Ryan, captain of the 1958–59 team which missed a chance to grab the Big 5 title when St. Joseph's won 82–70. Ryan led the team in scoring that year with 384 points. "We used to beg him to shoot the ball against the Big 5 particularly," said Huggard. "On any given day he could drop 30 on anyone. He could have been an All-American but he got beat up pretty good by guys he played with his first three years. He could jump and rebound and pass. He was the whole package."

When the time came to anoint a successor to Severance, Jack Kraft's name was not on the list of candidates compiled by Villanova's officials. Their first choice was Eddie Donovan, who had built St. Bonaventure, a tiny university in Olean, New York, into an Eastern basketball power. Donovan had not only verbally committed to take the job, he had begun house-hunting on the Main Line with his wife and father-in-law. The Bonnies were playing in the NIT at the end of the 1960–61 season when Villanova athletic director Art Mahan and longtime Wildcat basketball consultant, Joe Walters, traveled to New York to close the deal. Instead, Donovan hit them with a bombshell: he had just accepted a better offer to become coach of the New York Knicks of the NBA. "It was a total surprise," recalled Walters, a Villanova benefactor, volunteer assistant coach, and advisor to the university's senior-level administrators on basketball issues who had, according to several Wildcat officials, "monumental influence" on the program.

A graduate of St. Joseph's College, where he had played for Bill Ferguson from 1940 to 1942, Kraft had been coaching high school basketball for 12 years. He was also respected as one of the better basketball officials in the area and was one of the referees on the floor when Wilt Chamberlain, the 7-foot-1 center from Overbrook High School, scored 90 points in a Philadelphia Public League game at Roxborough High School in 1955. "Poor Roxborough didn't have a kid over 6' 2"," recalled Kraft. "Here's Wilt up in the stratosphere. He'd get the ball and he's just hold it up there and those poor little kids, they're jumping up trying to get him. They were hitting him but I told the other official, 'We can't be calling fouls on that because, my gosh, we'd be living at the foul line all the time. Just as long as they don't disrupt and disturb him and get him upset. Of course if he's shooting and so forth, and it's costing him points, that's a different story,' After a little while, Chamberlain looked over and realized what we were doing and he gave us his approval. He said, 'Okay, I understand. That's okay by me.' Which showed what a great guy he was."

When it became apparent that Donovan and some of the other rumored candidates were out of the running, Kraft sat down and wrote a letter to Art Mahan. About a month later, Jack was hired. "Of course, I knew what the alumni were saying," he recalled. '*Who the hell is Jack Kraft? . . . Oh my God, we're getting a high school coach and a St. Joe's grad at that!. . . What's going on out there?*'"

It didn't take long for the Villanova faithful to find out. Combining a confusing *Ball Defense* with the splendid talents of White and some promising newcomers, Kraft came out of the gate on fire—winning his first 12 games.

Kraft learned the *Ball Defense* from Ed Hickey, the long-time coach at St. Louis University, who guided the Billikens, led by future Hall of Famer "Easy" Ed Macauley, to the NIT championship in 1948. The two quickly became friends when Kraft, an officer assigned to preflight school at the Naval Air Training Station in Iowa, played for the base basketball team coached by Hickey.

On the first day of tryouts, "Hickey said to me, 'Oh, you're from St. Joe's. Did Bill Ferguson coach you? I remember playing St. Joe's in that tiny gym one New Year's Day when I was coaching Creighton.' I told him I was there watching the game as a high school junior because I lived only a few blocks away." Hickey then described how the referees allowed the St. Joseph's players to swat the ball underneath the protective mats on the walls behind the basket every time the Hawks scored a field goal. As a result, Hickey's players were unable to get their patented fast-break working. "I named the referees and said, 'They worked all the St. Joe's home games. One had crimson eyes, the other had gray eyes. There's no way you were going to win. You were a dead pigeon coming in from out there in the Midwest.' He said, 'At least you're honest about it.' We laughed and had a great time and developed a nice relationship."

"I thought that college coaching was the easiest thing in the world," said Kraft of his first season. "I mean, 'This is so easy it's not even funny.' We beat Princeton at Princeton. We beat both Canisius and Niagara in Buffalo. We won the Quaker City Tournament. They gave me [Eastern] Coach of the Year that season. They thought I was a genius. The only thing was I had good players that nobody knew about."

Kraft soon realized that he had potentially one of the finest backcourt combinations ever in the Big 5 in Wali Jones, a flamboyant guard from Philadelphia's Overbrook High School, and George Leftwich, who had been recruited out of Washington, D. C. In addition to Hubie White, he had a pair of hard-working forwards, Jim McMonagle, from Philadelphia's La Salle High School, and Jim O'Brien, who had played for him at Malvern Prep. "Hubie probably had more talent per foot than any player that I've seen for quite a while," said Kraft. "He was just out of this world. I don't know of any other 6'3" center who could do the things that he did. He was tremendously quick, could leap right up there with the 6-foot-7s and 6-foot-8s. He didn't have to concede anything."

White was matched against Iowa's 6'8" center Don Nelson in the finals of the Quaker City Tournament that season, "Nelson was a good ball player," said Kraft, "but he was so frustrated in the first half because he never got the ball. They tried to throw the ball into him and Hubie kept stealing it on them. He couldn't understand why they never got it in there. He couldn't figure how anybody could be that fast to get around him and get his

hands on the ball, whether it be intercepted or tapped to one of our guards or our outside guys in the zone." Nelson finished with 19 points but most of them came after the game was decided. The Wildcats led by as many as 19 points in the first half.

"The one thing that I remember about that game is a move that Nellie made on me," recalled White. "It was one of the most incredible moves I'd ever experienced because I always considered myself as a really great defensive player. He caught the ball near the top of the key and I went up with him. He did a little bit of a head fake to his left, and the next thing I knew he had spun around me and gone in for a dunk shot. I couldn't believe it. I had never had anybody do that to me and I was really upset after that. After that, my game got a little bit stronger."

After the Quaker City, the Wildcats remained unbeaten by blowing away Seton Hall 99–67. "Then we went to West Virginia and got knocked down to earth," said Kraft. "It was an awakening to me of what happens when you go down South or to some of these far away places. You better be 20 points ahead or you've got problems."

With the aid of some questionable officiating, West Virginia won 88–82. But the Wildcats would get revenge later by beating the Mountaineers in a first-round NCAA Tournament game in the friendly confines of the Palestra 90–75. Villanova earned that bid by finishing with a 19–6 record that included a 4–0 city series sweep for its first outright Big 5 title and its first win over St. Joseph's since the Big 5 was formed. White, the MVP of the Big 5, set a city series record that stood for 17 years by scoring 38 in an 81–54 rout of Pennsylvania, then triggered a 66–59 victory over the Hawks with a game-high 23 points and 17 rebounds.

After that first round NCAA win over West Virginia, the Wildcats stunned NYU 79–76 in College Park, Maryland. "I was sitting behind the NYU bench," recalled Ken Mugler, who was Villanova's sports information director at the time. "They had two great players, Barry Kramer and Happy Hairston, but nobody could handle Hubie. They're arguing among themselves and Hairston says, 'I want White.' Hubie pump fakes, goes around him, and scores and that ended that. It was amazing. We were playing with five guys." The following night, the Wildcats ran out of gas with about six minutes left against a much bigger and deeper Wake Forest team and lost 76–69 despite a marvelous 25-point effort by Jones. Wali later became the inspirational leader of the great Philadelphia 76ers' 1966–67 NBA championship team during a brilliant 12- year professional career.

"Wali Jones was the greatest guy you ever wanted to coach," said Kraft. "There was nobody like him. If we were ahead by a few points with five minutes to go, people left the game because Wali would control the ball. They'd foul him and he'd go up and shoot two free throws. The other team might come down and get a field goal but he'd go back and hold the ball and get fouled and shoot two more foul shots. Opposing players, especially in the Big 5, didn't really like Wali. Not so much personally, but they didn't like playing against him and I could never understand why."

Kraft found out the reason why one year when he bumped into Jim Boyle, the St. Joseph's player, at the Philadelphia Basketball Writers' banquet. "He said, 'The next time you're playing, watch Wali,'" recalled Kraft. 'When someone is on the foul line and the referee hands him the ball, Wali walks from one side of the foul line to the other. Then he steps on your foot. He distracts you. And then he says, Excuse me. You know he didn't do it accidentally. You know he did it intentionally. And that's disturbing when it happens.'"

Although Jones was hampered all year by a cartilage injury to his right knee that necessitated post-season surgery—Duquesne coach Red Manning described him as "the best one-legged backcourtman in the country"—Wali figured prominently in Villanova's three city series wins that gave them a share of the Big 5 title with Penn in 1962–63. He hit a pair of foul shots with two seconds to go in a 63–62 win over the Quakers, passed to Eric Erickson for the winning layup with five seconds to go in a pulsating 63–61 overtime triumph over St. Joseph's, and scored 28 points in a 63–47 victory over La Salle.

"I remember that play distinctly," said Jones about Erickson's game-winner against the Hawks. "I knew if a man was open, I had trust in my ballplayers that I would hit him. I could name some players that nobody would think of—guys like Eric Erickson, Bernie Schaffer, Joe McGill, Warren Winterbottom, and Sam Iorio weren't considered great All-Americans but they did their job. To have somebody to bang and beat you up at practice and never back down, that's what made you good. They were tough players."

At the beginning of the season, Jones started arriving at games sporting a jaunty blue beret. Soon his teammate joined in. All except Al Sallee, a big, strapping ex-Marine. "He swore up and down, 'there's no way will I wear a beret,'" recalled Kraft. "Nobody said anything to him at all. They just tried to shame him into it."

◄ Villanova coach Jack Kraft celebrates a 63–61 overtime win over St. Joseph's with Wali Jones (right) and Eric Erickson. *(Urban Archives, Temple University, Philadelphia, Pennsylvania)*

THE 'CATS RUN WITH THE BALL (DEFENSE) • 111

And that's exactly what happened a couple of weeks later when Sallee walked into the locker room with a beret perched on top of his 6'8", 225-pound frame and was given a rousing ovation. During the Quaker City Tournament, one of the players asked Kraft why he wasn't wearing a beret. "I said, 'Because you guys aren't playing the way I want you to play. So I don't consider you my team yet.'" Villanova lost to St. Joseph's, then Providence as Ray Flynn, the future mayor of Boston, connected on 16 of 23 shots from the field and finished with 34 points to relegate the Wildcats to fourth place and a mediocre 6–6 record.

"We weren't that bad the first half of the season but we weren't good, either," explained Kraft, whose teams always seemed to improve in January and February. "We had some new guys on the team because we lost Hubie White and Jimmy O'Brien. Whatever the reason—whether major-college basketball was a little too much or whether they felt, 'gee whiz, we've arrived'—I don't know. But you have to try different tactics with different players. So I yelled a little bit and I think that shook them up. The kids thought, 'This guy's doesn't yell, he must be mad.' Well, I wasn't mad, but I was just disturbed."

Soon the 'Cats started playing well. A few games later, Jones walked into the Palestra carrying a beret and said to Kraft, "Now will you wear it?" And so began the legend of "Kraft's Kommandos." "Now we go over to New York for the NIT and we're walking around Broadway," recalled Kraft. "A friend of mine went into every clothing store looking for a blue beret. They all told him, 'We've got maroon, we've got green, but we don't have any blue.' They were all sold out. After about the fourth store, I walked in with him and the manager asked, 'Why is there such a run on blue berets?' 'It just so happens that the Villanova basketball team is all wearing blue berets and all their fans want to do the same,' I told him."

Richie Richman, one of Kraft's backcourt reserves, performed a unique athletic feat early in the 1962–63 season when he played quarterback for Villanova's football team in a 6–0 loss to Oregon State in the Liberty Bowl in Philadelphia's Municipal Stadium in the afternoon of December 16, then hurried to the Palestra and played five minutes in the Wildcats' 73–71 loss to Niagara that night. Terry Baker, the Heisman Trophy winner, ran 99 yards for the only touchdown. Ted Aceto, who later became Villanova's athletic director, also played in that game.

"I don't remember being tired at all," recalled Richman. "We played a football game on the coldest day I've ever seen in my life. It was absolutely freezing. The game was over about 4:30 and I remember saying to our trainer Jake Nevin, 'Jake, they're playing down at the Palestra. Let's get my uniform and let's go.' We called Jack Kraft and he said, 'You shouldn't play, Rich. . . . Take the night . . .,' and I said, 'Coach, I want to play.' I hadn't practiced or played in three weeks, but I was familiar with everything and I'm sure he put me in the game for a couple of minutes as a token."

Actually, Richman's appearance was much more than that. Inserted into the game when Wali Jones fouled out, Richie came up with a big steal with 1:02 left and the score tied, but Niagara eventually got the ball back won the game.

The Wildcats took a 17–8 record into the NIT that year and got by DePaul relatively easy in the first round 63–51 as Jones scored 28 points and Erickson added 18. Then they pulled off another upset, 54–53 over fifth-ranked Wichita. The top-seeded Shockers were led by two of the nation's best big men, Dave Stallworth and Nate Bowman, and Kelly Pete, an excellent guard. Wichita had been held to under 50 points only once, by the nation's No. 1 team, Cincinnati, whom they had beaten earlier.

"We had a tremendous game," recalled Kraft. With about 30 seconds to go, Erickson intercepted a pass and fed Jones, who hit a jumper, was fouled and made the free throw to put Villanova ahead by a point. "Now they have the ball and they're moving it around to get the good shot," said Kraft. "With a few seconds left, Kelly Pete takes the shot and he misses. The ball hits the short side of the rim and bounces down. Their big guys are swarming all over it; they're waiting for the ball to bounce up. But it doesn't bounce up. It hits the dead spot on the floor right in front of Jim McMonagle. And he takes the ball and he just cradles it—he's not going anywhere with it—and the clock runs out."

Complementing Jones brilliantly in the backcourt that year, especially on the fast break, Leftwich averaged 13 points a game. Then he missed his entire junior season after tearing the ligaments in his right knee in an automobile accident in Virginia during the summer. "George had the potential of being a good pro, but then he missed a year and that hurt him tremendously," said Kraft. "Shooting was probably his main forte but he could also jump. He played the wing on our ball defense and he took care of the 6'5" kids. They couldn't get the rebound away from him. He could bring it down and have it before they reacted."

"We compared ourselves with the best backcourt ever to come out of Philly," recalled Jones. "I played against Hal Lear and Guy Rodgers in high school. They were my mentors. Before he broke his leg, George, to me, was one of the best guards playing in college. He had more

things than I had. He could drive, score, rebound. He was bigger, stronger. I knew my game was endurance because I ran cross-country at Overbrook. I could play somebody the whole game full court."

Also instrumental in Villanova's success was Raveling, who had been a ferocious rebounder for the Wildcats before graduating in 1960. When George joined Kraft's staff two years later, he became the first black assistant at a predominantly white major college. Before leaving to become Lefty Driesell's assistant at Maryland in 1968—a career path that eventually led him to head coaching jobs at Iowa, Washington State and Southern California—he established himself as an excellent recruiter. Reaching into previously-untapped areas of the Deep South for players like Howard Porter, Johnny Jones, and Sammy Sims, Raveling revolutionized the racial landscape of college basketball before it became fashionable in many parts of the country, His recruiting philosophy was gradually embraced by the other Big 5 schools that had traditionally drawn most of their players from the Philadelphia area. Soon, some of so-called "lily-white" programs, especially in colleges from the Atlantic Coast and Southeastern Conferences, were falling in step.

"George Raveling was the greatest recruiter in the history of the city," said Dick Weiss, the *New York Daily News* writer. "He probably did more than anyone to open the doors for southern black kids to come north. He had his own underground railroad. He was the first guy that really understood national college recruiting because, basically, recruiting in the Big 5 was done with a subway token. It was regional. He was way ahead of the curve."

A voracious newspaper reader, Raveling regularly took the train from Villanova to Center City Philadelphia to buy out-of-town papers. Not only that, he drove once or twice a month to the New York home of Howard Garfinkel, who established the nation's first recruiting information service. A friend of Garfinkel's in the advertising business would pull sports sections out of newspapers shipped in from across the country. "I can remember many a night sitting down in his living room until one o'clock in the morning copying down names," recalled Raveling. "In those days, that was the only way you could get information on kids."

◄ Johnny Jones, who was one of George Raveling's prized recruits, was the Big 5 MVP in 1967–68. *(Urban Archives, Temple University, Philadelphia, Pennsylvania)*

One night in August 1963, Raveling was visiting one of his best friends, Warren Wilson, in Claymont, Delaware, when they saw on television that "A March on Washington for Jobs and Freedom" was being held the following day at the Lincoln Memorial. "We decided to go down that night, find a motel, and drive down to the monument grounds so we'd know where to go the next morning," recalled Raveling. "As we walked around, this guy struck up a conversation and asked if we'd be interested in volunteering to work. 'We need more security people because the turnout is going to be ten times what we thought,' he said." The next morning, Raveling was assigned to keep order at the podium and found himself standing to the left of the last speaker of the day, Dr. Martin Luther King Jr., in front of 200,000 people.

"I don't think anybody ever thought at that particular moment that this was going to be one of the great speeches in the history of the country," explained Raveling. "So when he finishes, I just happened to say to him, 'Dr. King, could I have that copy?' He turned and handed it to me. He had folded it in half and just as he gave it to me, a rabbi on the other side said something to him and that was the end of it. For years I had it inside of a book in my basement, never knowing that this thing was going to end up being what it was."

About 20 years later, when Raveling was coaching at Iowa, a writer for the *Des Moines Register* asked him if he was ever involved in the Civil Rights Movement. "I said my only real participation was on the March on Washington. I told him I have the speech and he goes bananas. Then he writes the story and all Hell breaks loose. The King family tried to get it from me a number of years ago and I said, 'Fine, here's what we'll do: I'll let you keep it on display anywhere you want as long as you sign a document saying that it belongs to me.' They didn't want to do that. They wanted me to give it to them, which I wouldn't do. I still have it. I actually had a guy offer me three million dollars for it."

Amazingly, Dr. King's famous line "I have a dream," was not part of the original text that day. "He had given the speech previously at a church in Detroit," said Raveling. "Like most public speakers, particularly ministers, he saw that he had the crowd in the palm of his hand. This was the largest gathering of black people in one place in the history of the United States. And so he ad-libbed that part into his speech maybe two paragraphs from the end. The media came up with the title, 'I Have a Dream.' Obviously it was never intended to be part of the content. If you listen to the speech and follow it with the original text, you can see other places where he changed it a little bit. He didn't read the speech verbatim. It wasn't like I thought, 'Oh my God. This is going to be one of the great speeches of all time.' The part everyone remembers was not part of the original intent."

ater in the 1963–64 season, the seventh-ranked Wildcats dropped a 63–59 decision to La Salle in the contest that snapped their 13-game winning streak and ultimately decided the Big 5 title. The game had additional significance, however, because it matched, indirectly, the Walters brothers who had been teammates at Philadelphia's Roman Catholic High School and were now partners in the family plumbing, heating, and air conditioning business. Bob, who played at La Salle, was in his first year as head coach of the Explorers. Joe, a teammate on the same Wildcat team with future St. Joseph's coach Jack Ramsay, was active behind the scenes at Villanova. On the day after the game, Joe was hosting his weekly strategy session with Dudey Moore and Bob McAteer, who scouted the Wildcats' opponents, when a horrific tragedy struck the Walters' Main Line home. Joe's two-year-old son, Jim, who was in an adjacent room, suddenly choked on a piece of an apple. Walters and McAteer both tried rescue efforts and the child was rushed to a nearby hospital, where he died shortly afterwards. A column written by Sandy Grady describing the family basketball rivalry which was scheduled to appear in next day's *Philadelphia Bulletin* was pulled.

he Wildcats remained in the national limelight in 1964 and 1965. They went 24–4 after beating Minnesota to win the 1963 ECAC Holiday Festival. In 1964–65, they returned to Madison Square Garden and finished second in the NIT after eliminating three highly-regarded New York teams playing on their home turf. Leading Villanova that year were Jim Washington, a 6'7" junior forward from Philadelphia's West Catholic High School who would go on to become Villanova's second all-time leading rebounder, and Bill Melchionni, a 6-foot guard who would soon set a Wildcat single-season scoring record (801 points). Washington was Big 5 MVP that season; Melchionni, would be MVP of the Big 5 and the NIT the following year (1965–66), when Villanova finished third after getting an invitation they didn't expect.

Wali Jones tells the story of how Minnesota's Lou Hudson claimed that he never had anybody block his jump shot until Jim Washington did it to him *several* times. A few years ago, Hudson sent a film of the Holiday Festival title game to Jim Washington. "Lou couldn't believe anybody could jump that high," explained Jones. "On the film, Jim Washington was jumping out of the gym. He was just like a monster because they had a big center who had to be 6'10" and Jim just out-rebounded him and beat him with his athleticism." Washington, a member of the Big 5 Hall of Fame, went on to play for ten years in the NBA with St. Louis, Chicago, Philadelphia, Atlanta, and Buffalo.

"That year [1964–65], we had another real good team—Jim Washington, Billy Soens, Petey Coleman and

Leftwich," said Melchionni, who became furious when he learned at the end of the season that school officials had declined a bid to the NCAA Tournament and accepted an invitation to the NIT. "We really belonged in the NCAA and I went crazy. I went running up to Kraft's office and said, 'What are you doing? You can't turn the NCAA down. We've got to compete against the best players.' Then Kraft dragged me over to Art Mahan's office and I yelled and screamed at him. I don't think we would have won it. I just wanted the opportunity to play against the best teams. We were ranked in the top ten during the year—at some point we got as high as fourth. They gave the reason that our last couple of regular-season games were on the road and we would had to play somewhere in Ohio, and we would have missed two weeks of school if we kept playing. We also had a big following in New York. As it turned out, we would have won the NIT, but I got sick in the final game and played only twenty minutes or so."

Two of Villanova's five losses that year were in the Quaker City Tournament, when Wichita got revenge for the NIT upset two years previously and won the semifinal 86–74, and Illinois took the third-place game 74–65. Melchionni will never forget the Wichita game. "That was the first time I really got beat up in a game," he recalled. "Kelly Pete was 6'2", 195 pounds and I thought this guy was just unbelievable. He was the first guy that I ran into that was strong and quick. Every place I went, he elbowed me, hit me. I never experienced anything like that before. It's funny, a couple of years later I was playing for New Jersey and he had bounced around with a couple of teams. He came to the Nets for a tryout and I just killed him."

Wali Jones had taken the young sophomore, Melchionni, under his wing at Villanova and the two quickly became a formidable backcourt combination when Bill moved into the starting lineup late in the 1963–64 season. The Wildcats lost only three regular season games that year—two of them Big 5 games against La Salle and St. Joseph's. They made it back to the NCAA Tournament where they beat Providence and then got derailed by Duke, the eventual NCAA runner-up to UCLA, when Jeff Mullins scored 43 points.

What Villanova fans remember most about the Eastern Regionals that year, however, was the consolation game with heavily-favored Princeton. Bill Bradley put on his typical All-America performance with 30 points and his dazzling passing, shooting, and defensive

▶ Jim Washington was Big 5 MVP in 1965 and finished his career as Villanova's second all-time leading rebounder. *(Urban Archives, Temple University, Philadelphia, Pennsylvania)*

play, but Wali Jones was just unbelievable. Especially when he just took the game over in the last three minutes. Playing the final game of his career, Jones shot 16-for-29 from the field (all but two from long-range), made the last six shots of the game, and finished with 34 points as Villanova pulled away 74–62. After the season, Bradley was honored as the best visiting player at the Philadelphia Basketball Writers' banquet. Alluding to the fact that Villanova beat his Tigers three out of the four games they played during his career at Princeton, Bradley said, "I really thought that we were going to tie the series up until you started shooting the ball, Wali. You weren't supposed to do that."

"I learned a lot from Wali because I used to practice against him all the time," said Melchionni, who also remembers that Jones had an aggravating habit of whacking defenders across the face after throwing up his jump shot. "He did this to me about two or three times in practice with that exaggerated arm motion," Billy recalled. "I'm saying, *'What the hell is it with this guy?'* Finally I said to him, 'Wali, why do you keep slapping me in the face?' He said, 'I'm just following through.'"

"That follow-through has almost gotten me into many fights in the college and the NBA," Jones explained. Guys like Archie Clark, Hal Greer, and Jo Jo White would say, 'Hey, what are you doing slapping me?' One time my best friend, Walt Hazzard, wanted to fight me. He played for the Lakers and I kicked him and hit him in the face on a follow-through. It wasn't intentional. That's because of my jackknife shot, I'd follow through and kick. That's the way I shot because when I was small, I wasn't physically big enough to shoot a regular jump shot. So you had to jerk. You had to put your whole body into it."

"Melchionni was probably the most intense player that I had," recalled Kraft. "He didn't eat before the game. If he did, he would be sick and throw up and still play. He's probably the best shooter that we had." Kraft remembers a game early in Melchionni's senior year when three sophomores were starting and the Wildcats were embarrassed by Army 89–68 in the opening round of the Holiday Festival in Madison Square Garden. That gave us a terrible record—something like two and five," recalled Kraft. "But it was the fact that the young kids were always hesitant to shoot the ball, always looking for Billy. I walked into the locker room and everybody's in there but Billy. I'm going around talking to the kids and all of the sudden in walks Billy. He slams the door and he's hollering at the kids, *'Hey, you guys have to shoot, you've got to grow up, you've got to do this, you've got to do that!'* Maybe that's what I should have been saying, but coming from him it was more effective. He was the captain and it was perfectly within his place to do it. Then we went on and started winning."

▲ **V**illanova's Bill Melchionni, the Big 5 MVP in 1965–66, holds his NIT MVP trophy. *(Villanova University)*

"We were struggling and I wasn't used to losing," recalled Melchionni. "I just walked in there and blew up. I said, 'Basketball is important to me. You guys aren't working hard enough and not playing hard enough.' I always played with a passion. One reason was because of my size. I just didn't have the physical strength to out-muscle and beat people up, so I just worked very, very hard. I just didn't have tolerance for people who didn't work as hard as I did."

The Wildcats really came on strong after that, winning ten of their last eleven regular-season games. Melchionni had a career high 44 points against St. Bonaventure during that run, which was broken only by a 78–70 loss to La Salle in a game in which the Wildcats, astonishingly, out-rebounded the Explorers by 27. With a 15–10 record, they were the last team selected for the NIT. "I don't think we would have been invited if we hadn't done so well the year before," said Melchionni. "They matched us against St. John's in the first round. They thought St. John's, a local team, would quickly eliminate us." Melchionni scored 63 points in the first two games as Villanova upset St. John's in the rematch of the previous season's championship game, 63–61, then nipped Boston College, 86–85, before losing to NYU, 69–63.

After Villanova avenged that early-season loss to Army 76–65 in the consolation game, Melchionni sat in the stands to watch Brigham Young defeat NYU for the championship. The Cougars' big star that year was Craig Raymond, who later played for the Philadelphia 76ers. "When the game was almost over, I started walking out the front of the Garden," said Melchionni, who had scored a total of 109 points. "Suddenly this guy came running out, grabbed me, and said, 'You're going to win the MVP, you can't leave.' And I said, 'Yeah, right.' I just kept walking and he grabbed me and said, 'No, you've got to come back in here. You're going to win the MVP award.' So I went back in and they gave me the trophy." Until then, Maurice Stokes, the great St. Francis (Pa.) All-America, was the only other player who had been named MVP of the NIT without playing in the championship game.

In 1967–68, the Wildcats took an 18–8 record into the NIT and beat Wyoming in the opening round 77–66. "It was on St. Patty's Day and I had pretty good game," recalled Fran O'Hanlon, who was a sophomore guard. "The New York papers played up 'Luck of the Irish' and that type of thing. I remember Johnny Carson doing a monologue on Villanova's students, saying 'The *Beer* Cats are coming.' He said, 'What's Blue and White and lays in the gutter? Villanova *Beer* Cats!'"

In the next round, Villanova faced Kansas and its outstanding guard, Jo Jo White, and lost 55–49. The Jayhawks had eliminated Temple earlier 82–76. "They had a couple of real big kids," said O'Hanlon. "One of them, Dave Nash, was probably 6'11" or 7-feet and weighed 270 pounds. Coach Kraft told me that they have this play where they lob the ball to Nash, 'So when they do that I want you to move over behind him to draw the offensive foul.' On the first play, they throw it and I can always remember Nash catches the ball and lands on my leg and really crushes it. I fall down and he looks at me and lays it up. And I was hurt. After the game, I couldn't walk for a couple of weeks but I kept playing. And coach Kraft was saying, 'Okay, Fran, get him next time.' And I can remember thinking to myself, 'There's not going to be a next time. If they're not going to call this one an offensive foul, I won't get a call all night.'"

One of Kraft's scrappiest players was Frankie Gillen, a 5'10" guard from Philadelphia's Bishop Neumann High School, who played in the back of the *Ball Defense* from 1966–69, and is perhaps best remembered for the way he tormented St. Bonaventure's 7-foot center Bob Lanier. "I remember one time there was a little scuffle underneath the boards and Frankie went in there and gave Bob Lanier a little left to the stomach and then ran like a rabbit," recalled Kraft. "I said, 'What did you run away for?' He said, 'I wasn't going to stay there with that big guy! I got my little jab in and left.' I said, 'You've got a lot of guts hitting a big guy like him.' Frankie was just that type—a pesky player, a pain in the neck to play against. He always liked to talk. He was always thinking of ways to beat you. He was a hustler, aggressive. He would do anything legally to win. He would drive guys crazy."

Villanova and La Salle squared off in the most anticipated Big 5 game in history on February 8, 1969. Not only was it the only city series game that matched teams that were both ranked nationally, it featured the classic matchup between the two best big men to play in the Big 5—Ken Durrett of the Explorers and Howard Porter of the Wildcats, who were co-MVPs of the Big 5 that year. La Salle took command early and won 74–67. "The hype was tremendous," said O'Hanlon, who later played a year in the ABA with the Miami and now coaches

▲ Howard Porter, the Big 5 Co-MVP as a sophomore, is the only Villanova player to record 2,000 points and 1,000 rebounds. *(Villanova University)*

Lafayette. "I can remember going out for introductions and the energy, the atmosphere was better than any game I've ever been in before or since. It was such a hard-fought game but it wasn't a well-played game because the emotions were at such a high level, we tried to do things that we couldn't. When you watch it now, you think, *'Did we play basketball like that?'* It looks so different from today's game."

Porter, a high school All-America from Sarasota, Florida, had been one of Raveling's prized recruits and was already the most publicized sophomore in Villanova's history. "I had never seen a guy in high school who could do what he could do," recalled Raveling. "I called Jack Kraft and said, 'Coach, if we can get this guy I think we could win the national championship and rule the Big 5.'" Of course, the rest is history. "For the most part I never even played against a white boy before in my life," said Porter, who quickly adjusted to big-time basketball. In his very first Big 5 game, the 6'8" center poured in 36 points and grabbed 26 rebounds to spark an 87–62 rout of St. Joseph's. Porter, a member of the Big 5 Hall of Fame, ended up rewriting much of Villanova's basketball history. The only Wildcat to record more than two thousand points and one thousand rebounds in his career, he holds every significant Villanova rebounding record, including the single game mark of 30 against St. Peter's. His career scoring high of 40 triggered the most points ever scored by Villanova in a single game, a 126–96 win over Seton Hall in his junior year.

After the well-publicized La Salle contest, Kraft's 1968–69 Wildcats won five of their last six games to finish with a 21–4 regular-season record and earn another NCAA Tournament bid, where they were immediately eliminated by Davidson. In 1969–70, the Chris Ford era began at Villanova. In Ford's three varsity seasons, the Wildcats compiled a 65–21 record and made three NCAA Tournament appearances. He's still Villanova's single-season assist leader (238), as well as the career record-holder for three-year players (500). The subject of a hotly-contested recruiting war with La Salle, Ford would later share Big 5 MVP honors with Penn's Corky Calhoun in 1971–72 and go on to play and coach in the NBA for more than two decades.

The Wildcats went 22–7 in Ford's sophomore year and finished second to Penn in the Big 5, a result of a 59–55 loss to the Quakers in the first city series game of the season. They upset fifth-ranked St. Bonaventure at the Fieldhouse 64–62, then returned to the NCAA Tournament. There they beat Temple 77–69 (in the first NCAA Tournament game ever between two Big 5 schools) and Niagara 98–73 before losing a rematch to St. Bonaventure 94–74 in the Eastern Regional Finals in

Columbia, South Carolina. But the win proved very costly to the Bonnies, who lost the services of All-America Bob Lanier and, probably, a shot at the national championship.

Early in the first half, Ford missed a shot from the top of foul line and sliced between two defenders as he attempted to follow for the offensive rebound. "As I was splitting them, I got tripped," recalled Ford. "I went like an arrow from the foul line to under the basket and Lanier was standing there gathering up the rebound. My shoulder hit his knee. He came back and played a little bit more in the game but couldn't play in the finals and had to have knee surgery." Ford was hung in effigy when the Wildcats went to Olean the following year. Lanier and Ford later became teammates when Ford joined the Pistons. "He took me out to dinner as soon as I got there," recalled Ford. "It was nice. Everything was forgotten."

Ford's spirited play at Villanova frequently made him a target of opposing fans, especially in the Big 5. On more than one occasion, they showered the Palestra floor with miniature hot dogs during pre-game introductions. "I took it in stride because I was just trying to get the fans involved in the game," said Ford. "I don't think I ever did anything to insult anybody. But it was fun, waving the hands at the fans and stuff like that. It wasn't trash-talking or anything like that."

"I liked Chris," said former St. Joseph's All-America Mike Bantom, who played against Ford both in the Big 5 and NBA. "I actually appreciated his game a lot more than the fans did. I liked the way a guy his size could handle the ball, see the court, find open people, and add rhythm and continuity to the game. I liked the way he wasn't afraid of the crowd, he wasn't afraid of the opposition, he played his butt off. He had a little bit of flair to him back at the time when it probably wasn't very popular, but what he did then is nothing compared to what is going on right now. If you want to call it *hot-dog-gism*, underneath there was a really solid player and he proved it over the years. He became a three-point shooter at the end of his NBA career and managed to get some more time just based on that skill."

In 1970–71, after a 19–5 season punctuated by a grueling twenty-two-day road trip to Kansas, California, Hawaii, and North Dakota, Villanova made it all the way to the NCAA championship game, where UCLA held on for a hard-fought 68–62 win at the Houston Astrodome. Completely overshadowing the Wildcats' other games in the tournament—93–75 over St. Joseph's, 85–75 over an excellent Fordham team coached by former Penn assistant Digger Phelps, and 92–89 in a double-overtime classic over Western Kentucky in the national semifinals—was the incredible 90–47 devastation inflicted on Dick

Harter's previously-unbeaten Pennsylvania team that had won 28 straight games. The Quakers, who finished unbeaten in the Big 5 that year, had won the earlier game 78–70, holding Villanova scoreless for eight minutes in the second half.

How did it all come together for the Wildcats in such a huge game against unbeaten team? "It was nothing that I did," said Kraft. "It was the most perfect game we ever played with our defense. It just looked as though we had six men on the floor because every time they passed the ball we had two men playing it because our kids really moved with agility and quickness—and they moved as the ball was being passed. They didn't wait until it was passed and then get there. We had some other good ones but that game was unbelievable. That was probably the best game that we ever played under my coaching for forty minutes."

No one was more surprised to see Villanova beat the Quakers than the Wildcats' athletic director, Art Mahan. "We never expected to make it to the Final Four," he recalled. "In those days you had to make your own travel arrangements for the tournament. Here we win the game and we don't have a sock packed, nothing. After the game, I went back to Villanova and called our travel agency and the lines were busy. I thought: 'We're not going to make it. We're going to have to go down by bus. We don't even have a hotel room!'" Mahan got on the telephone and called his good friend John Rossiter, the business manager at Penn. "I said, 'John, I'll tell you. I'm not going to say I'm sorry about the game. Have you canceled your plane or hotel reservations?' He said, 'We're so stunned, we haven't canceled anything.' So I picked up his plane reservations, the hotel reservations, the training meal schedule and arrangements. What a break that was, I'll tell you. I mean I would have been fired the next day if it weren't for Rossiter."

Hank Siemiontkowski, playing the game of his life, led the Wildcats to the dramatic win over Western Kentucky with 31 points and 15 rebounds before fouling out in the closing seconds of regulation. That happened when the 6'7" junior bumped into Jerry Dunn while diving for a loose ball, but Dunn missed the free throw that would have given the Hilltoppers the victory. Porter added 22 points and 16 rebounds, including a clutch 15-footer from the right baseline that put the game into overtime. Porter's shot from the corner with 2:44 left in the second overtime—his 2,000th career point—gave the Wildcats the lead for good. Clarence Smith chipped in with 13 points and 11 rebounds. The basketball court was placed on the Astrodome field near second base. "It was particularly hot in there and Western Kentucky full-court pressed with two quick guards pretty much the entire game," recalled Tom Ingelsby, the only sophomore starter in the game. "Being the point guard, I handled the ball against that pressure. I remember playing 50 minutes, then going up in the elevator to get a B-12 shot after the game."

"A lot of people tend to forget that the Western Kentucky game was one of the best college basketball games ever played," said Porter, who outplayed the Hilltoppers' All-America, Jim McDaniels. "As far as I'm concerned, that was really the championship game. Quite a few of my teammates made clutch shots. Jim McDaniels was an excellent ballplayer but they had other great players on that team, like Clarence Glover, the big rebounding guy. They were much bigger than us and they had good guards. We just played a great game."

The following night, Kraft came very close to missing the highlight of his professional career—the ceremony honoring him as National Coach of the Year. "I was looking forward to taking my team out for a nice, quiet dinner because this was going to be our last night together," he recalled. "The executive director of the coach's association called me and said, 'I don't see your reservation for tonight.' I explained that I wasn't going. *But you've got to come!* I don't have to do anything except die and pay taxes, and he said, 'Oh no, you've got to be here, there's no question about that. You're in the Final Four and all the Final Four coaches are expected to attend.' I said, 'We'll, if I'm expected, there not much I can do.' So I asked Dan Dougherty to take my kids out to dinner and when I got to the banquet, and they called my name as Coach of the Year, I thought, 'Oh my God, there's got to be a mistake. I mean here's John Wooden with all his national championships. Ted Owens had a great season with Kansas.' I wasn't prepared and I had to give them an extemporaneous speech. 'I know one thing,' I said. 'It's a great honor to be placed in the same category with the previous winners.' I named some of them. 'And I appreciate that you extended it to me.' I mentioned how lucky we were to get here, especially because of some things that happened in the latter part of the season where if we don't win the game we probably don't even get into the tournament and probably end up in the NIT."

The championship game with UCLA had all the makings of a David vs. Goliath saga. Coach John Wooden's Bruins were shooting for their fifth straight NCAA crown and their seventh national title in the previous eight years. They had lost only once in 29 games that year and were working on a 27-game winning streak in NCAA Tournament competition.

Villanova's coaches knew that they would have their hands full with Sidney Wicks, Curtis Rowe, and Henry Bibby, but they didn't expect a huge game from Steve Patterson, a 6' 9" senior center. Bibby scored 17 points, as expected, but the Wildcats held Rowe and Wicks in check with eight and seven points, respectively. Porter, the Final Four MVP, in particular did a spectacular defensive job on Wicks, the MVP of the previous year's Final Four. Patterson, however, was phenomenal, hitting 13 of 18 shots from the field and finishing with 29 points. He had 20 in the first half as the Bruins built a 45–37 lead. Then in the second half, he hit four of his five field goal attempts to repeatedly thwart Villanova's comeback attempts. Twice Porter hit jump shots to bring the Wildcats within three—the final time at 63–60 on a 15-footer, but that was the closest that Villanova would come. UCLA, amid a chorus of boos, ended up holding the ball to force the Wildcats out of their zone defense. Porter finished with 25 points and Siemiontkowski added 19.

Before the game, Porter told Kraft that he wanted to cover Wicks. "Sidney Wicks was at that time probably the cockiest player I ever played against," Porter explained. "He was an excellent player. He was one of those 6'9" big guys who handled the ball real well, and I wanted him because of his cockiness. I thought that Wicks was the premier player on that team and I felt I could handle him. I felt that I could handle any forward in college basketball and he was considered to be the best. It was time for me to step to the forefront and, fortunately, I was able to do it. In fact we handled both of their forwards."

"The guy that hurt us was Patterson," said Kraft. "He was the one who really killed our ball defense so we had to come out of it and then went into man-to-man. We made him a million-dollar contract. I think he lasted two years in the pros and that was it. That's one of the problems you run into in tournament play. You don't get to see these guys. Of course we did see him against Kansas in the first game but he didn't score that much. Nobody thought we could play man-to-man but we practiced it every day from the beginning of the season. I thought we did an excellent job man-to-man. It brought us back into it. We ended up six points behind but they got a scare. After the game, John Wooden mentioned, 'Boy, you fellows played us really tough. We were fortunate to win.'"

"Just the pure ecstatic experience of us being in the Final Four," recalled Ed Hastings, who was unable to play because of a knee injury. "Here we were, kids from the Philadelphia playgrounds. In our playgrounds we'd always be dribbling around thinking, you know, 'Last shot! Five seconds to go against UCLA in the final game!' That was all we dreamed of and here we were, in reality, in that situation. And we didn't lose by that many points. It was an absolutely winnable game. I don't know if we actually thought we could beat them until later in the game when maybe it was too late."

Eight of the participants in that game played professional basketball—Wicks, Rowe, Bibby, Patterson, Porter, and Ingelsby in the NBA, and Siemiontkowski in

▲ **C**hris Ford was co-MVP of the Big 5 in 1971–72 when he set a Villanova single-season record with 238 assists.
(Villanova University)

Sweden. But the player who lasted the longest was Ford. "Basketball writer Bob Ryan once called Ford 'one of the few players who knows what filling a passing lane means,'" said sportswriter Bob Vetrone. "Chris was probably the least-looking pro prospect in the tournament. He was a good shooter and he hustled, but certainly didn't appear quick enough to play in the pros, but he had a great career." Ford played for more than ten years in the NBA with Detroit and Boston and later was head coach of the Celtics, Milwaukee Bucks, and Los Angeles Clippers.

The euphoria of Villanova's first appearance in the NCAA championship game was short-lived. A few weeks later, the NCAA announced that it was officially vacating the Wildcats' runner-up position because it charged that Porter had signed a professional contract with the Pittsburgh Condors and the American Basketball Association during the season. The NCAA also withheld payment of Villanova's share of $72,000. Even today, some of the facts in the case are cloudy. But

Porter admits that he did sign a document sometime between December and the beginning of the NCAA Tournament.

"I was told that it wasn't binding and it wasn't a contract," he recalled. "When all this occurred, I was in a fog at that time. A lot of that I don't remember or maybe I chose not to remember. But until this day I feel as though I was manipulated by people who were a whole lot shrewder than me. I was really naive about a whole lot of the business aspects. I was in a very vulnerable situation because my mother was sick at that time and I was trying to do whatever I could in order to help. That's when our team wasn't doing very well either. I didn't even know whether I even wanted to continue to play ball. So I got caught up in that and I admit to my wrongdoing." Porter spent seven years in the NBA, three with Chicago and the rest with New York, Detroit, and New Jersey. He is now a parole agent in Ramsey County, Minnesota.

Ingelsby was selected MVP of the 1971 Quaker City Tournament after he scored 28 points, including a pair of free throws with six seconds left, to help defeat Frank McGuire's previously-unbeaten Gamecocks, who had come into the championship game ranked No. 2 in the nation. "The Palestra held 9,200 but we must have had 10,500 people that night," said Ingelsby.

"That's the one game I really always remembered," said Ford, who scored 18 points. "That was probably the loudest I ever heard the Palestra. It was one of those nights when you literally thought the roof was going to blow off. You could feel the place rocking."

"I just remember Kevin Joyce rimming the basket at the buzzer," said Hastings, who chipped in with 13 points for the Wildcats. "He threw up a long jump shot from way out in the corner and their big guy tapped it in *after* the buzzer."

In Kraft's final season, 1972–73, Villanova finished with a 20–8 record. But the Wildcats ended the year with disappointing losses to Penn (78–67) and South Carolina (90–78) in an NCAA Tournament that had begun with a promising 85–70 blowout of East Carolina in the opening round. Ingelsby led the Wildcats in scoring with better than 25 points per game and was MVP of the Big 5. Later, he played two seasons in the ABA with St. Louis and San Diego and a year with Atlanta in the NBA.

▲ **V**illanova's Tom Ingelsby was MVP of the 1971 Quaker City Tournament and Big 5 MVP the following season. *(Villanova University)*

Throughout his 12-year career at Villanova, Kraft had always worked on renewable three-year contracts. In 1973, however, he was told that all coaches would be given only one-year contracts in the future. "That year we had an 11–14 record and I was 52 years old," Kraft recalled. "I said, 'Gee whiz. If I have another bad year they could say *Sayanora* because the old regime had left and a new administration was in.'" By that time, Rhode Island had received Mahan's permission to talk to Kraft. He soon signed a four-year contract with the Rams. "That was a good move for me because not only did it revitalize my coaching career, it gave me a lot more security," Kraft explained. It was also a good move for Rhode Island. In eight years, Kraft enjoyed three 20-win seasons and was named Eastern College Coach of the Year three times.

Chapter 9

• • • • • • •

The Owls Fly High with Casey & Chaney

When Harry Litwack was walking off the floor at the University of Delaware after coaching the last game of his career, a 70–60 loss to St. Joseph's in the 1972–73 Middle Atlantic Conference championship game, one of the first people to shake his hand and wish him well was Mike Bantom, the Hawks' All-America who was about to wrap up his own brilliant collegiate career. "I respected Harry," recalled Bantom. "I grew up watching Big 5 basketball on TV so I knew the history and knew he had done a great job. Early in my career, the team that gave me the most trouble was Temple. I guess it was because the other teams played you straight up, man-to-man. Then I played Temple and that zone would just kill me. I didn't know what to do with it. By our junior and senior years, we had it down and we knew how to attack it. We knew where the holes were, we knew how to move against it and I finally was able to have some pretty good games against them. But I respected him. I respected their coaching staff—Jay Norman and Don Casey—a great deal. They did a great job because they didn't get the best players. We didn't get the best players either, but we were competitive every night and so were they."

Yes they were. And the Owls continued to be competitive under the capable hands of Don Casey, and then John Chaney.

For years, Casey drove across the Ben Franklin Bridge after his own practices at Bishop Eustace High School in New Jersey to catch Litwack's workouts at Temple. Harry was still scheduling many of his practices at night, a custom he began years earlier when he was teaching full-time in the Philadelphia public school system. "I thought Harry had interesting tactics like what they do in the NBA today where they call plays 'Fist up, Fist down,'" Casey explained. "Harry was doing that back in the '50s and '60s. It intrigued me. I'm almost sure that I introduced myself to Harry by going over and watching his practices. Then I used to stop by his office and Harry was very receptive. He gave me his time."

Early in his career, when he became the youngest coach ever to win a New Jersey state championship, Casey had begun to develop relationships with Big 5 coaches who were becoming interested in some of his players, including Bill Melchionni, who would go on to enjoy a great career at Villanova. Soon Casey was bringing his high school teams across the river to scrimmage some of the Big 5 freshman teams.

"Nobody worked harder than Casey," recalled Melchionni. "We were in better shape, better coached than most of the teams we played. We used to scrimmage some of the better Philadelphia schools like Bartram before the season with Earl 'The Pearl' Monroe. These teams would come in and kill us. But Casey wasn't afraid to play anybody and we just got better. He made me a better basketball player. He had a passion for the game and I developed a passion for the game like him." Melchionni learned Kraft's patented *Ball Defense* in high school because Casey had picked it up from the Wildcat coach. "We worked on it more at Eustace than I did at Villanova because Casey had longer practices," added Melchionni, who felt very comfortable playing that defense by the time he got to college.

"Don used to come around and rack my brains," said Litwack. "He would go up to the blackboard, put the Xs and Os on, and ask, 'What would I do here? How does it work there? Why do you use the zone defense?' That's why I recommended him for the job when I was given the go-ahead to hire another assistant. He was winning championships at Bishop Eustace and I could see that he was dedicated. I told Ernie Casale that I thought he was knowledgeable and creative and that he would be a big help to me." One small problem, though: Casey didn't have a college degree. "We had a helluva job convincing the higher-ups to hire him," said Litwack. Permission was finally granted, however, and Casey eventually got his Temple University bachelor's degree by attending classes part-time after being named Harry's assistant in 1966.

Casey remembers the early days at Temple when his salary jumped from $48 a week to $6,000 a year. Litwack purchased the new suit and shoes that he wore on his wedding day with Dwynne in 1964. "My wife and I thought we hit the lottery," Casey said. "I think when I came aboard with Harry as a younger person—as someone outside the scene, I maybe brought a little vibrancy. Harry had to tone me down once in a while. He was a surrogate father to me. The first time I ever saw a Horn and Hardart's restaurant in Center City Philadelphia was with Harry. He and my wife had a nice relationship. 'Don's got to get in here on time,' he used to tell her. I started maturing into a professional person because of him."

Soon after coming on board, Casey jumped in to help with recruiting, a facet of major college coaching about which he knew very little and something that Harry conducted almost exclusively at Mike's Broad Tower. "It was very simple," recalled Casey. "Harry would take kids there and sit them down for sandwiches. I started jazzing it up: 'Let's go to the Pub in Jersey and take the kids out to dinner,' that sort of thing. Harry was a *substance* guy, not a *style* guy. To me, recruiting was style *and* substance. I had to do a little of the 'hubba-hubba' and then bring Harry in to close with the family. Harry had a tremendous identity with parents, the gray hair and all. Once the kids got here, they recognized the solidness of the man."

When the time came for Litwack to step down after the 1972–73 season, Harry let it be known that he wanted Casey to succeed him. "He was a good asset," said Litwack. "He had a good basketball mind. He's proven that in the NBA." Litwack was even prepared to stay on as coach for another year to insure that the transition happened smoothly. "I believe that," said Casey. "The job never opened up for other people for interviews. Harry announced his retirement on a Tuesday and on Thursday I was appointed. What more can you ask for?"

It didn't take the new Temple coach very long to make an impact. It happened in Casey's sixth game— the finals of the Volunteer Classic in Knoxville, Tennessee, when Casey held the ball throughout what turned out to be the lowest scoring game of the modern basketball era in an 11–6 loss to host Tennessee. The Owls had upset Utah State in the opening game but didn't figure to have enough depth to stay with the nationally-ranked Vols. After some early foul trouble, Casey realized that running-and-gunning was not an option. He decided to spend the rest of the game holding the ball just beyond mid-court. Temple scored *one* point in the second half.

The rules at the time said that the offensive team had to pierce the 28-foot line within five seconds. Casey decided to try force the Vols out of their zone defense by putting players on each side of the line and have them toss the ball back and forth to avoid a five-second violation. Instead of coming out and challenging the Owls, Tennessee just sat back in its zone. "It then became a cat-and-mouse game," explained Casey. "We were working on the premise that their defense should initiate action to stop what was going on. If they had come out or even double-teamed the ball, I don't even know what we would have done. It became like, 'who's going to play first?'"

At the half, Tennessee led 7–5. Their fans were furious. "And they still did not come out because the rules didn't force them to come out," recalled Casey. "I can always remember Ernie Grunfeld, the Tennessee All-American, telling me at the time that he was up for the scoring title but his average went right down the tubes. We didn't plan this before the game. It kind of evolved. Tennessee had never played against a zone and they were a big, strong team. They were furious, and you can understand that. But the onus for explanation was on Tennessee: It's your tournament, it's your place, why didn't you go out and get 'em? A couple of scouts came down to see us play and, of course, they came away with nothing. In retrospect would I do it again? I doubt it. But it was early in my coaching career. I was young. We thought maybe that this would jack them up to try to win the game. But the fact is that if you do something like that, you've *got* to win the game."

With their big front line of Joe Anderson, Jerry Baskerville, and Joe Newman leading the way, Casey's Owls swept past Harvard (61–59), Cincinnati (68–64), and California (51–42) to win the final Quaker City Tournament played at the Palestra, in 1973. Anderson, who had a career high of 22 points against Cincinnati—all in the second half—was the MVP. Baskerville, a transfer from UNLV playing in his first game, led the Owls against Harvard with 16 points and 13 rebounds, and he scored the winning basket.

"We started to get it together against Harvard and then steamrolled right on through," recalled Jay Norman, who was Casey's assistant at the time. "Once we got past Cincinnati, it was not that difficult a game with California. We played a very physical team in Cincinnati but our guys just dominated. Cincinnati had some big, strong guys who could shoot from the perimeter but we controlled the interior. Anderson was probably as tenacious a rebounder that has ever been at Temple. Baskerville was quick up and down the floor, very much like Dennis Rodman, who played for the Pistons and Bulls."

"This is like Camelot," exclaimed Casey after the California game, "An 8–2 record and a championship. It's a wonderful feeling."

Not so wonderful, though, for the Eastern Collegiate Athletic Conference, the sponsors of the Quaker City Tournament. Only 3,844 fans attended the championship game. The five sessions that year drew a total of only 12,036 fans—5,000 worse than any other time in the event's 13-year history. The annual Philadelphia holiday tradition came to an end.

Casey's most significant recruit wasn't even a player. It was Jim Maloney, who became his assistant coach and later served under John Chaney before his untimely death from a heart attack at the age of 62 in 1996. Maloney had played at Philadelphia's Roman Catholic High School in the 1950s, then had gone to Niagara University, where he learned the game from longtime Purple Eagles' coach John "Taps" Gallagher. It was as Taps' assistant at Niagara that he recruited Calvin Murphy, one of the finest shooters in college basketball history. Later Maloney served a few years as head coach of the Purple Eagles before moving to the University of Maryland as an assistant to Lefty Driesell. When Maloney expressed an interest in returning to his roots, Casey quickly grabbed him for his staff before the start of the 1973–74 season. "Jimmy was good for me because he understood recruiting," Casey explained. "Coming from Lefty's program he understood the game more and he had a very good knack of spotting players."

Casey was known for his excellent zone defenses, a reputation that extended from coast to coast and a fact quickly discovered by John Nash. As executive director of the Big 5, Nash spent considerable time attempting to convince some of the nation's top teams to visit the Palestra. One day he received a letter from a Pac-10 coach who indicated that he would prefer playing St. Joseph's, La Salle, or Penn. Because his teams had already faced Don Casey's zone, he continued, "We would not be anxious to knock heads with Temple."Casey's coaching tenure lasted nine years and featured outstanding individual performances by three of the Owls' top ten career scorers—Terence Stansbury (second all-time with 1,811 points), Granger Hall (fifth), and Marty Stahursky (tenth), as well as players like Tim Claxton, a member of the Big 5 Hall of Fame who led the Owls in scoring in 1977–78. Casey's teams shared Big 5 championships in four of his last six seasons (1977, '78, '79, and '82). Three of those teams made it to the NIT. The 1980–81 squad advanced to the second round where it lost an overtime heartbreaker at West Virginia 77–76, after pulling off a big upset in an opening round game at Clemson 90–82. The Owls lost

only three regular-season games and came agonizingly close to the NCAA Tournament in 1977–78, only to lose at the buzzer to La Salle 73–72 in the East Coast Conference championship game. They finally made it back to the NCAAs the following season by eliminating Drexel, Lafayette, and St. Joseph's by a combined total of *eight* points in the East Coast Conference playoffs—only to lose in the first round to St. John's, 75–70. But just making the NCAA Tournament back in those days was an accomplishment because the field consisted of only 48, then 52 teams, not the 65-team field of today.

Casey was named Eastern College Coach of the Year in 1978 and 1979 when his teams went 49–9. He is one of the few coaches to receive such a distinction in successive years. His career won-lost record was 151–94. His winning percentage (.616) is second only to Chaney on Temple's all-time list. Yet, after the 1981–82 season when he shared the Big 5 crown with St. Joseph's and finished with a 19–8 record that included an NIT opening round loss at Georgia, Casey was out as head coach.

"It's hard to say what happened," recalled Casey, who had two years left on his contract. "It's a piece of history. At that time I think that [Temple president] Peter Liacouras thought that possibly I could serve the university in a better way—and maybe that meant men's athletic director or assistant AD. And I think that he felt that possibly that John Chaney had a better identification with the Philadelphia area because he played there, coached in high school there, and was head coach at Cheyney State. And then I said, 'No, I want to stay.' And he said, 'Well, you know, we might have to be thinking about a change.' And I think I said, 'Well, I'm getting scared, I want to get my lawyer.' Here I am talking to the former head of the law school." Soon the Philadelphia media learned of Casey's predicament. "Then Peter called me in and said, 'This has gotten out of hand. I was only investigating; it's my right as a president. I thought maybe that you'd be interested in this and you said you weren't. We're going to stay right where we are and fulfill the contract and so forth and so on.' He wrote a nice letter and it ended, but it was a jolt to me."

Meanwhile, Paul Westhead, Casey's squash partner from La Salle, was on the phone urging him to join another Big 5 coaching buddy—Jim Lynam of St. Joseph's—on his staff as an assistant with the Chicago Bulls. "When Paul called, I still was ambivalent and then I talked to a few people who said it's best to move on. In defense of Liacouras, I think he was trying something, which he thought might have been the best and at the same time he was giving me a bone. And I didn't take the bone. I just think it was a situation of change for change sake. I did nothing wrong—we had won 19 games, we had everybody coming back. So I thought if I'm going to make a move, it's a pretty good time to do

◄ Temple's Tim Claxton protects the ball against Villanova's John Olive and Keith Herron during 73–66 victory over the Wildcats in 1977. *(Urban Archives, Temple University, Philadelphia, Pennsylvania)*

it because everything is in order. When I left Temple I left with very mixed feelings. And maybe expressed it one or two times in the papers which was not done very well. Maybe I blasted the university and I shouldn't have done it because, you know, the universities are always bigger. But it was an emotional time. It was embarrassing as it unraveled. First I felt like I was being martyred, then it got uncomfortable. So I think at that point, looking back, that the best decision was made because something else might have happened. It was a blessing in disguise because I've grown since then. I've been all around the country, all around the world. I feel confident now about things. I could deal with it now better than I dealt with it then. I think that it worked out best for both parties."

It certainly worked out well for Casey, who has since spent more than two decades in the NBA. After a short stint with Westhead in Chicago, he became Lynam's assistant in San Diego. Then came head-coaching jobs with the Los Angeles Clippers and New Jersey Nets as well as a stop as an assistant for six years with the Boston Celtics.

"Casey was ahead of his time in a lot of ways," said *Philadelphia Daily News* sportswriter Phil Jasner, who, as a student, had broadcast Temple games with Merrill Reese, the current voice of the Philadelphia Eagles. "He didn't have the resources, the schedule, or the level of

▼ Temple coach Don Casey, with his 1977–78 co-captains Rick Reed (left) and Marty Stahurski. *(Urban Archives, Temple University, Philadelphia, Pennsylvania)*

recruit that John Chaney had, but he got a lot out of a lot of kids. Even now when they talk about the coaching years at Temple, they talk glowingly of Harry, glowingly about John, and it's almost like there are certain pockets at that university that conveniently forget that Don Casey built the bridge." Frank Dolson, the former *Philadelphia Inquirer* sports editor, put it succinctly: "Casey was one of the best coaches the Big 5 ever had."

When Chaney was named to succeed Don Casey in the summer of 1982, the new Temple coach experienced some bittersweet memories. Chaney had been the Philadelphia Public League's Most Valuable Player in 1951, the same year that La Salle's Tom Gola was Catholic League MVP. But times were different then and there were no Big 5 scholarship offers for the Benjamin Franklin High School star—a player regarded by the late Guy Rodgers as "one of the best ball-handlers I've ever seen." Chaney ended up at Bethune-Cookman College, a tiny black school in Daytona Beach, Florida.

"I wanted to play basketball at Temple," he recalled. "But they had only one black athlete in the whole school—Vernon Young, who played football and basketball—and they were only giving out partial scholarships in those days. For one reason or another, I have never found myself looking back too much. It would have been great had I played here for a Hall of Famer like Harry Litwack, but as I teach my kids, once it's over just move on."

Chaney grew up in the projects in Jacksonville, Florida, where his mother was the sole provider for John and his younger stepbrother and stepsister. "One time three of the guys in my group from elementary school came around to our house and said to me, 'Let's go out, man, and have some fun,'" Chaney recalled. "During that time Jacksonville was divided into two areas—the white section was called Riverside, and the section where we lived. If you wanted to go over to the white section you would go in the daytime. You could not travel in that area at night unless you were working because you could be stopped and asked where are you coming from and why are you here, that kind of thing. So these guys came around and I asked my mom if I could go out and she said 'No, you're not going out tonight!' And boy, I started screaming and creating a ruckus. The guys outside were hollering, 'You're nothing but a sissy for listening to your mother.' That even made me angrier because I couldn't go. My mother sent me upstairs to my room with no food to eat and I'm up there grumbling. Meanwhile, those guys went over to Riverside, robbed a store and raped a white girl that night. The next day it was in the papers and my mother showed me that article. At that time you could be electrocuted for doing that in the South. I never saw those guys again. But from

that moment on, I listened to my mom. She always said to me, 'You're only good as the company you keep and that's bad company.' When I asked her how she knew that, she said, 'I can sense the truth. You must remember as long as you live, you can feel truth coming out of a person. You don't have to graduate from high school, but you can feel what's right and what's wrong. That's always been my rod. That's always been my staff.'"

After moving north with his family, Chaney lived about a mile away from South Philadelphia High School but chose to attend Benjamin Franklin High, which was located much further away, near Center City. "During that time Philadelphia was built on little pockets of ethnic Italians, Irish, and blacks, and gangs were thriving," he recalled. "To go to South Philly, I had to walk through neighborhoods of three different white gangs. Once somebody knew that you weren't from their turf, you had problems. Going up Broad Street was longer but easier. Once you got across Market Street you were pretty safe because the area was more commercial. And once you became known as a basketball player, there was respect from the gangs and you could travel anywhere. When you were an athlete you walked with almost like a halo over your head. There wasn't a place in this city an athlete couldn't go once you were established in high school."

An intelligent, multi-talented point guard, Chaney made NAIA All-America at Bethune-Cookman, then played and coached for ten years in the Eastern League, where he was named All Pro six times and earned two MVP awards. As *Philadelphia Inquirer* columnist Bill Lyon was told, "You needed a knife and a gun to take the ball away from him." He played for six months with the Harlem Globetrotters, then began his head-coaching career at Philadelphia's Simon Gratz High School. For six years, he worked for the school's principal, Marcus Foster, "a great man," who later became superintendent of schools in Oakland, California, and was assassinated by a member of the Symbionese Liberation Army in 1973. It was Foster, in fact, who encouraged Chaney to take the Cheyney State University coaching job in 1972, emphasizing to the young coach that he would be able to make more of an impact there.

Chaney quickly established his coaching credentials at Cheyney State, where he led the Wolves to eight NCAA Division II tournament appearances in ten years. He was named NCAA Division II Coach of the Year after winning the NCAA title in 1978. The following year he was awarded the prestigious "State of Pennsylvania Distinguished Faculty Award." However, when the university declined to promote him to full professor, he decided to make the move to the school that had turned him down 31 years earlier. It still wasn't an easy decision, especially since Chaney was 50 years old. "I was apprehensive because I really didn't want to leave Cheyney," he recalled. "You get into a situation when you get a little older and you say, 'Wow! Why am I leaving here?' At the time I wasn't really anxious about leaving to come to Temple. I only wanted to become a professor."

By the time Chaney was inducted into the Naismith Basketball Hall of Fame in 2001, not only had he become Temple's all-time winningest coach, his teams had made a school-record 18 consecutive post-season appearances, including 12 straight trips to the NCAA Tournament. Five of those teams reached the regional finals. Before he arrived, Temple had never appeared back-to-back in the NCAAs. In 1988 he was named National Division I Coach of the Year.

Some experts are convinced that Chaney's *best* coaching was done in his first year in 1982–83, when he had the *only* losing season in his coaching career. The Owls finished with a 14–15 record but came on strong by reeling off six straight wins, only to miss the NCAA Tournament by losing to West Virginia 86–78 in the championship game of the Atlantic 10 Tournament.

"That was probably John's best coaching year," recalled Jay Norman, who served as an assistant under Litwack and Casey, in addition to Chaney. "Each game you had to get the kids back up because they were taking their lumps. But they kept hanging in there."

"Jay is right in saying that, because we went through that year with what we called our 'Two-Guy Team,'" said Chaney. "Then we ended up with a *One*-Guy Team." The *two* guys—Big 5 Co-MVP Terence Stansbury and hot-shooting Jim McLoughlin—were reduced to *one* when McLoughlin ripped up his knee and had to undergo two operations. Then after making an incredible comeback, McLoughlin broke his shooting hand scrambling for a loose ball in the A-10 semifinals against Rutgers. "I never had a losing record in junior high, high school, or anywhere else," explained Chaney. "So

it really was an eye-opener for me that year to find myself in a situation where it had gotten to the point where the youngsters believed that they could not win."

One morning, Chaney arrived at practice to find even the uninjured players in the trainer's room. "They were laying up with headaches and all kinds of problems. I got so angry, I told every one of them, 'Get out!' Even the guys with crutches, I put them standing in a 3-2 zone or a 1-3-1 zone. And I'm working them, passing the ball, saying, 'Drop your crutches. Hold them in one hand. I don't give a damn!' I must have had them out there working for three hours. Every day was the same. And I think that spirit carried us throughout."

The defining moment for Chaney that year—and possibly for his coaching career—came in the opening round of the Atlantic-10 Tournament when Temple eliminated St. Joseph's 88–69. The Hawks had demolished the Owls by 29 points during the regular season and nobody expected Temple to bounce back. "We were beating them by 30 points," recalled Chaney, "and my guys came running off the court at halftime screaming,

▶ **T**emple coach John Chaney was inducted into the Naismith Basketball Hall of Fame in 2001. (*Urban Archives, Temple University, Philadelphia, Pennsylvania*)

'No turnovers!' They finally bought into the idea that you win games because you don't throw the ball away. You don't make mistakes. We ended up with three turnovers in that game, then beat Rutgers with Roy Hinson, their great NBA prospect. At that moment, I realized my message was getting across." Since then, the Owls have consistently been among the nation's leaders each season in lowest number of turnovers.

"**W**hen John came in we were nervous, we were skeptical because it was a change," said Stansbury, who had played the previous two seasons for Don Casey. " I remember that in my second year I finally knew what my role was because Casey had actually said, 'You're the leader. You don't have to score a bunch of points but you just take care of the team and each year we'll build around your knowledge.' Stansbury and his teammates were anticipating more of a freestyle, fast-breaking, one-on-one type of offense under a new coach. "Then when John came, he was a disciplinarian. He had a system that was actually stricter than Casey's. But he had a great philosophy for basketball—not allowing us to skip or lob passes, for example—which we had to adapt to because we wanted to be spectacular, we wanted to run. But the injuries that first year hurt us because I think if all the guys were healthy, we could have adapted his philosophy and probably been more successful earlier. Chaney was the ultimate. John was one of those guys who made you believe that you could be successful. I never forget one of his statements: 'If you keep the game close—nine or ten points with two, three minutes to go, then I'll win it for you.'"

There was also the matter of Chaney's 5 A.M. practices. "I remember him telling us at the beginning that most people were more alert in the morning and it would help us for the rest of our lives if we could get up and be attentive before everyone else," recalled Stansbury. "In the beginning it was difficult

◀ **T**erence Stansbury twice led the Owls in scoring and shared Big 5 MVP honors with Villanova's John Pinone as a junior. *(Urban Archives, Temple University, Philadelphia, Pennsylvania)*

for everybody, but I think the second year he did give us the option—did we want to go in the morning or the afternoon—and we all chose the morning because we liked it. It was a good experience. It really wasn't a problem for me. The good thing about John, he always brought donuts and juice in, so we got free food. But I definitely remember celebrating when I didn't have to do it anymore."

Granger Hall, who had been recruited by Casey, would have certainly been an NBA No.1 draft pick, said Chaney, had it not been for a horrific injury suffered against William and Mary in a freak accident at the Palestra. It happened early in his sophomore year in Chaney's first season in 1982. "I can remember now the pictures showed that knee almost like a hand grenade had almost blown it apart," recalled Chaney. " Nobody hit him or anything like that. He was just trying to go up the floor when he twisted it. But he was a thoroughbred on our ball club. And what a hard worker he was. Just to show the spirit of that kid, he was operated on a Friday and was walking to class on ice and snow on crutches the following Monday." Hall, a member of the Big 5 Hall of Fame, was the Atlantic 10 Player of the Year in 1984–85. A fourth-round draft pick of the Phoenix Suns, he later played professional basketball for many years in Spain.

Chaney's first big-time recruit was Nate Blackwell, a 6' 5" guard from South Philadelphia High School, who would go on to become the first Temple player in history to play in four NCAA Tournaments. He was also the Atlantic 10 Conference Player of the Year and a member of the Big 5 Hall of Fame. "He was one of our special delights," said Chaney. "The toughest job that you have in any program is to get first-class athletes to come in. With him it was so special because he was the top player in the city at the time and he was being sought after by all the other schools because he was the Public League

▼ Temple's Granger Hall came back from a horrible knee injury to make the All Big 5 team three times and be named the Atlantic 10 Conference Player of the Year in 1985. *(Urban Archives, Temple University, Philadelphia, Pennsylvania)*

MVP. That was extra special for me because I was the MVP in 1951. We've had three or four other MVPs since, but he sent the right kind of message to other youngsters that you're trying to recruit and started us off in being a very competitive program." Temple won 108 of 129 games during the Blackwell era. Nate later played for a year with the San Antonio Spurs, then took Maloney's place on Chaney's coaching staff after Jim passed away.

Chaney's message clearly hit home in his second year, 1983–84, when the Owls finished 26–5, raced through the Atlantic 10 with a perfect 18–0 record, shared the Big 5 title with La Salle, and won Temple's first NCAA Tournament game in 25 years, a pulsating 65–63 squeaker over St. John's. Stansbury's 22-foot jumper in the waning seconds was the game-winner. It was set up after St. Johns' Chris Mullin, a 90 percent free-throw shooter, missed the front end of a one-and-one. The Owls quickly moved the ball to half court and called a time out. "We set up a situation to get the ball to Stansbury in the backcourt," recalled Chaney. "He ran through a screen to get it, then beat his man. It was almost like an NBA *three* and he hits it dead in the basket. I'll never forget running off the floor at the buzzer and getting into the dressing room with all the players screaming and hollering."

"That shot helped me make the NBA," said Stansbury, who was drafted in the first round by Dallas that year and played for Indiana and Seattle until 1987, when he went to play for a number of years in Europe. "Being a senior in the NCAA Tournament gave me automatic recognition," added the future Big 5 Hall of Famer.

"The play was designed for either one of us to get open for a shot," recalled Blackwell. "I was a freshman at the time so I'm glad they didn't throw me the ball. That was probably the greatest day of my college career, just realizing that we could play with those types of teams and just knowing that we were getting ready to play North Carolina with great players like Michael Jordan, Sam Perkins, Kenny Smith, and Matt Doherty." The Owls were eliminated in the second round 77–66 by the top-ranked Tar Heels. "We had a great shot at beating them," said Chaney. "Then they went ahead by two points and went into the four-corners to pull us out of our zone. And that's when Kenny Smith and Michael Jordan penetrated to the basket like they always did in those days. But we were looking pretty darn good for a while."

Unfortunately, Blackwell sprained his ankle at practice the night before the game. "The coach wasn't going to let me play," recalled Nate, who got up early the next morning, taped his foot, and ran for Chaney in the

hotel parking lot to show him that he could go. "Believe me, I wasn't ready to play but I toughed it up. I was in so much pain but he gave me the okay to play. Right before half time, I remember stealing the ball from Sam Perkins but because my foot was injured I couldn't beat him to the basket. He ended up fouling me but I should have been able to lay the ball in." With about a minute left, Jordan was taken out for a curtain call. Blackwell just happened to be standing near the Tar Heels' bench. "He came over to me and shook my hand and said, 'You've got a good team.' That's probably the longest conversation I ever had with him. I played against him a little in the NBA but that first time was something special. He was an unbelievable player, probably the player who I most idolized all-time."

Chaney had switched Stansbury from a forward to a point guard when he arrived at Temple and Terence responded by surging ahead of Bill Mlvky, John Baum, and Guy Rodgers to become the Owls' all-time leading scorer at the time with 1,811 points. Stansbury, who was also the Atlantic 10 Conference Player of the Year in 1984, left an impressive legacy at Temple. "But the statistic that I liked the most was actually to play in every single game the four years that I was there," he explained. "That's what I was most proud of. I know you can't play every minute of every game but I only missed seven minutes my entire third year—something that I didn't realize until the end. The coach always told us we were tissue-paper athletes. We tore and broke so easily and he wanted us to be tougher than we were. I kind of adapted to that because I didn't miss one game. There were a few games that I thought I shouldn't have played."

Sometimes it took players a little longer to accept Chaney's system. It all came together for Blackwell during his junior year when the Owls were stunned at West Virginia in overtime, 69–65. "We lost the game mainly because I was off the floor," explained Blackwell. "I fouled out of the game with two offensive charges, which was totally against John's feelings and philosophy. And he gives it to me really bad to the point where I was so upset. I'm crying, he's crying. We're practicing at the Palestra and he makes the team leave. It's just me, him, and Coach Jay Norman, and we're just standing there, me and him, arguing with each other, going back and forth. I'm in tears. He's in tears. I don't ever remember having a disagreement or any arguments with him after

▶ Nate Blackwell, who was John Chaney's first recruit at Temple, is now his assistant coach. (*Urban Archives, Temple University, Philadelphia, Pennsylvania*)

that. After that point in my career I think I began to understand him more. He understood me. But what was real important was that I understood what he wanted from me. I was secure in the fact that he believes so much in me that I was the reason why we lost the game and I could be the reason why we win games. That was an important moment in my career."

Teaming up with Blackwell during Nate's final two years at Temple was Howie Evans, another Public League MVP, who had been coached at West Philadelphia High School by Joe Goldenberg, once a member of Harry Litwack's Final Four teams. Evans had been a shooting guard in high school. At Temple, he and Blackwell often moved from one guard position to another. Whenever they figured they could take advantage of another player, Howie would bring the ball up and Nate would go down and become the shooter, and vice-versa. Evans eventually set all-time Temple records for career and single-season assists, and was one of the Owls' best performers in terms of low turnovers and steals. "Howie was easily one of the best point guards we've ever had," said Chaney. "He had excellent hands. He could pass the ball through the seams from off the dribble, which was exceptional. When Nate graduated, Howie just took over and carried us to the next level. When we've been successful we've always had great point guards. But to have gotten those two guys in succession helped a great deal."

Blackwell and Evans played together for two seasons and helped the Owls finish with a 32–4 record in 1986–87. Temple won 26 of 27 games at one stretch, including an incredible 70–66 win over La Salle when the Owls battled back from a 20 point halftime deficit, much of it created by Tim Legler, who scored the Explorers' first 15 points of the game. Playing with a bloody nose following a collision early in the game, Blackwell had a career-high 33 points and clinched the game with a pair of free throws. There was also a memorable 76–65 win over eleventh-ranked UCLA at McGonigle Hall. "We had to play UCLA three times in order for them to come to our place once," Chaney explained. "That team had seven future NBA players. Our team was a bunch of no names. I used to call them the 'Blank Brothers.' They couldn't shoot a lick but the defense was something else."

◄ Howie Evans is Temple's all-time single game, season, and career assist leader. (Urban Archives, Temple University, Philadelphia, Pennsylvania)

With All-America Mark Macon, a freshman displaying maturity well beyond his years in 1987–88, the Owls found themselves ranked No. 1 late in the season—the first time any Big 5 team ever achieved the top spot in the national polls—en route to a 32–2 record. Opening the season with an impressive 81–76 victory over UCLA at Pauley Pavilion, Temple ripped off 14 straight wins before losing 59–58 at UNLV. They then won 18 more before being eliminated in the NCAA Eastern Regional finals by Duke 63–53 in the Meadowlands. For the second straight year, the Owls went unbeaten in the Big 5. The only city series game that was decided by fewer than 12 points was their 59–56 win over La Salle, which they ended with a 12–2 run.

Joining Macon in the starting lineup was the Atlantic 10 Player of the Year, Tim Perry, a 6'9" center who became Temple's all-time leader in blocked shots and later played for eight years in the NBA with Phoenix, Philadelphia, and New Jersey. There was also Mike Vreeswyk, one of the Owls' best outside shooters. Evans was one of the nation's leaders in assists and steals, and Ramon Rivas, a 6'10" intimidating force at the back end of the Owls' tenacious match-up zone defense, was an excellent foul shooter.

"Tim Perry was the best defensive player I ever played with," said Blackwell. "He blocked more shots and had the best timing of any big man that I can remember. Rivas was our enforcer, a strong man and tough guy. Everyone would try to bump and bruise me up because I was a little skinny guy and they would always put the toughest guy on me. So at some point in almost every game I would say, 'Hey, Ramon. I need you to shake me loose.' And he knew what that meant. He would take a foul, but he would make sure he got the guy real good. It was a sacrifice that he understood that he had to make to send a message to the other team. Vreeswyk was 'Mister Clutch.' Mike never said anything, he never barked, he never tried to be rough, but he just knew that he was going to be here at the end. He could go through a game where he'd go 0-for-10. And then in the last few minutes, he'd make every shot and get the game-winner. It got to a point where we expected that from him. He was a big-time clutch shooter with just a tremendous heart. He had more confidence than any shooter I've ever known because he would miss a lot and it never fazed him." Vreeswyk, a 6'7" forward, is a member of the Big 5 Hall of Fame.

One of Evans' finest performances came in the Owls' first game after they reached No.1 in the national rankings on February 8. It was against Villanova. Evans tied Guy Rodgers' school-record 20 assists and added 17 points including 9-of-10 free throws as Temple won 98–86. "It's a shame, for whatever reason, that Howie was not able to make it in the pros because he was the

◄ Tim Perry is Temple's all-time leader with 392 blocked shots and was a three-time All Big 5 selection. (Urban Archives, Temple University, Philadelphia, Pennsylvania)

kind of guy you loved to watch play," said sportswriter Bob Vetrone. "I guess he wasn't tall enough, he wasn't quick enough, he wasn't this, he wasn't that, he just beat the hell out of you."

The top spot in the national rankings came after Temple shocked North Carolina 83–66 in Chapel Hill in February. "That was the biggest signature win that we could have," said Chaney. "To play on their court where they don't lose and to beat them by such a large margin, I would have to believe that with our tough schedule, that was the most defining moment. After that point, the kids became believers. They weren't arrogant; they weren't conceited; they were very confident, bordering on arrogance. It was the defining moment not only for them as individuals but our defense was unbelievable. That zone worked so perfectly that it became the talk of the nation. At that particular moment I think that's when we grew up to believe that we were number one. And every game thereafter, we just seemed to grow and grow and grow. "

Chaney said that although the 1987–88 Owls were certainly not his most *talented* team, "it was a smart team and a tight-knit team that really played together. We led the country in low turnovers that year. But we didn't beat ourselves. Our kids worked their way out of trouble a lot of times without any kind of acrimony. They had just begun feeling that they were as good as any team in the country, but only because they were good in terms of having great basketball *savvy*, not because they were that talented. That team was easily my best team because they used their heads. They followed orders. They were so disciplined that you could direct them into any kind of battle and felt strongly that you had a chance to win, They were focused; they were strong guys. They would meet themselves and discuss things. I can remember them even saying, 'We've got to listen to coach, even if he's wrong!'"

UNLV finally shattered Temple's hopes of becoming the first team in the school's history to go unbeaten during the regular season. The Owls held the Rebels 32 points under their 91 points-per-game scoring average, but lost the nationally-televised game 59–58 when Anthony Todd drilled a ten-foot jumper in the closing seconds. "People don't know that we had that game won," said Chaney. "But when a pass was thrown down the floor to one of *our* players, someone on their bench jumped up and tipped the ball to one of *their* players to give them possession. So they ended up with the last shot. You could see it on the tape. They just barely touched it and it changes direction and the guy picks it up, calls time out and threw it down to Todd and he scores. The referee was standing there and didn't call it. He was a referee from this area—[Jerry] Donaghy. We talked to Donaghy about it and he felt that his vision was obscured or whatever. It was a heartbreaking game for us but they went on from there to do exceptionally well."

The next heartbreaker came in the NCAA Tournament after the Owls had swept aside Lehigh, Georgetown, and Richmond to reach the Eastern finals against Duke. And just like the North Carolina game in another NCAA Regional final four years earlier, when Temple took the Tar Heels down to the wire, the Blue Devils used their superior depth to pull it out. This time in the person of Quin Snyder, who is now the head coach at the University of Missouri, and Billy King, a 6'6", 210-pound defensive specialist, who is the general manager of the Philadelphia 76ers.

"We got off to a great start—scoring baskets, moving the ball like we wanted to," recalled Chaney. "Snyder was the point guard, the guy who we felt couldn't shoot. We saw him on tapes. He hit all the baskets outside. I kept saying, 'Don't worry about it. Don't go out to get him. He'll start missing.' He didn't miss yet! He and Billy King really won the game for them because King was the one who played Mark Macon. Mark was driving through two or three people trying to make it happen. Billy would force him into help and Mark was missing shots that he made all year. That was probably the toughest game of his life." Macon made only 6 of 29 shots from the floor and finished with 13 points. "They outmanned us," added Chaney. "They were bigger than us and they had the right elements. Their players who were important stayed on the floor. They had a great game plan of doubling Mark Macon and Tim Perry and forcing the other guys to shoot. Our first five guys were adequate and just as good, in my opinion, as their first five. But once I lost one guy out of that five, that changed everything. Ramon Rivas was a big wide body for rebounding and he could stop things inside. He did a tremendous job but got into foul trouble in the first four or five minutes of the game. But Snyder was the player who surprised us all because he scored 27 points."

"I just remember the locker room scene after that game," said Kevin Mulligan, who was covering the Owls for the *Philadelphia Daily News*. "To see a locker room full of kids crying. Watching Tim Perry, who was a real quiet kid, trying to express himself through his tears. They were devastated. They knew they were better than Duke that day. They might have been the best team in the country that year."

Two years earlier, Chaney hadn't known a thing about Macon, even though he was the outstanding high school basketball player in the state of Michigan. One day during the summer before his senior year at Saginaw's Buena Vista High School, Mark and his coach, Norwaine Reed, telephoned Chaney, who recalls the conversation going something like this: "'Coach, I'm coming to Temple.' I said, 'Coming to Temple? What do you mean, you're coming to Temple?' Then his coach got on the phone and said, 'Coach, he's down to four schools on his list—Louisville, Georgetown, Temple, and Carolina, but he's coming to Temple.' I said, 'Why don't you let him come and visit with us? Or why can't I come up there and see him?' He said, 'You don't need to see him!'"

Macon signed the letter of intent without ever visiting Temple's campus. "After he signed, I went to Michigan, met his family, and set up a time when he could visit," explained Chaney. "I also spent time talking with his coach, who put *our* offense and *our* defense into his high school system so that Mark would be prepared when he came in here to be a part of our offense immediately." Macon showed just how prepared he was on his very first visit to Temple. "He came here when we were practicing and the next thing you know, Mark was out on the floor showing our guys what he was doing in high school. And I'm saying to myself, 'I can't believe this.' He was the most unbelievable youngster that I've ever seen. As a freshman he took us to the Final Eight and then he took us to the Final Eight again as a senior. From there we continued to soar as a national team."

Macon led Temple to within three points of an NCAA Final Four berth in 1990–91. The Owls finished with a 24–10 record and shared the Big 5 title with St. Joseph's as city series round-robin competition came to a close after 36 years. Mik Kilgore, a member of the Big 5 Hall of Fame, set the stage for the Owls' city series success by triggering a 70–57 win over Villanova with 21 points and 10 assists. Macon's buzzer-beating three-pointer in the Atlantic 10 Conference semifinals got Temple past West Virginia and into the NCAA Tournament. But the season would again end on a somber note for John Chaney's team as top-seeded North Carolina prevailed 75–72 in another NCAA Eastern Regional final at the Meadowlands. Macon was absolutely superb in that game after the tenth-seeded Owls had eliminated Purdue, Richmond, and Oklahoma State with relative ease. He scored 31 points and grabbed nine rebounds, and finished his career as Temple's all-time leading scorer with 2,609 points.

In 1996, Chaney was devastated when his longtime assistant, Jim Maloney, died suddenly of a heart attack. Maloney's son, Matt, a two-time All Big 5 selection, had graduated from Penn a year earlier and would go on to play for a half dozen years in the NBA with Houston, Chicago, and Atlanta. "Jimmy Maloney was something special," recalled Chaney. "When Jimmy died, he had stacks of books filled with everything that I said. He believed so strongly in what we were doing. The kids loved him because he paid attention to them. He always took the part of me that was lacking and developed it—the compassion that you need to show at times. He was the other half of me. Here I am the driven person, a hard person and he was the guy that always said, 'Hey, don't worry about it, man, the coach loves you. We'll work on that tomorrow.' I'm the guy who would say, 'No, you can't' while he was saying, 'Yes, you can.'"

"Jimmy Maloney lived in my parish in Haddonfield," recalled sportscaster Bill Campbell. "John Chaney called me when Jimmy died. It was two days before his funeral and he said, 'I've written this eulogy. They want me to deliver it, and I'd like to read it to you on the phone, see what you think.' I'll tell you I'm sitting here listening to this eulogy and I'm starting to cry. Finally I interrupted him when he was two-thirds through and I said, 'John, it's great but I don't think you're ever going to get through it.' He said, 'Well, I just gotta do it.' That was the end of the conversation. At the eulogy, the church is jammed. Maloney's casket is right in the middle aisle and John is looking right down on the casket. He gave this unbelievable eulogy about their life together, what they did, scouting trips and all that. It was the greatest eulogy I've ever heard by anybody—TV, Kennedy's funeral, anywhere. At the end of it John's pointing at the casket and he said, 'I've always prayed that I would die before Jimmy because Jimmy could get along without me but there's no way I could get along without Jimmy.' And he walked out. And there was absolute silence for about two minutes—if you didn't have goose pimples. Then he walked down and he walked over and shook hands with Peter Liacouras. Then he sat down. And when he sat down, everybody rose and gave him a standing ovation. I've never seen a more electrifying moment in my life. It was just incredible."

Although he could often be blunt, abrasive, and sometimes quite controversial with his opinions—often a strategically-planned tactic to deflect attention away from his players—Chaney's legacy has little to do with fun and games. "Forget the basketball," said Bill Lyon, the *Philadelphia Inquirer* columnist. "Because in my mind

▶ Mark Macon, the Big 5 MVP in 1990–91, finished his career as Temple's all-time leading scorer. *(Urban Archives, Temple University, Philadelphia, Pennsylvania)*

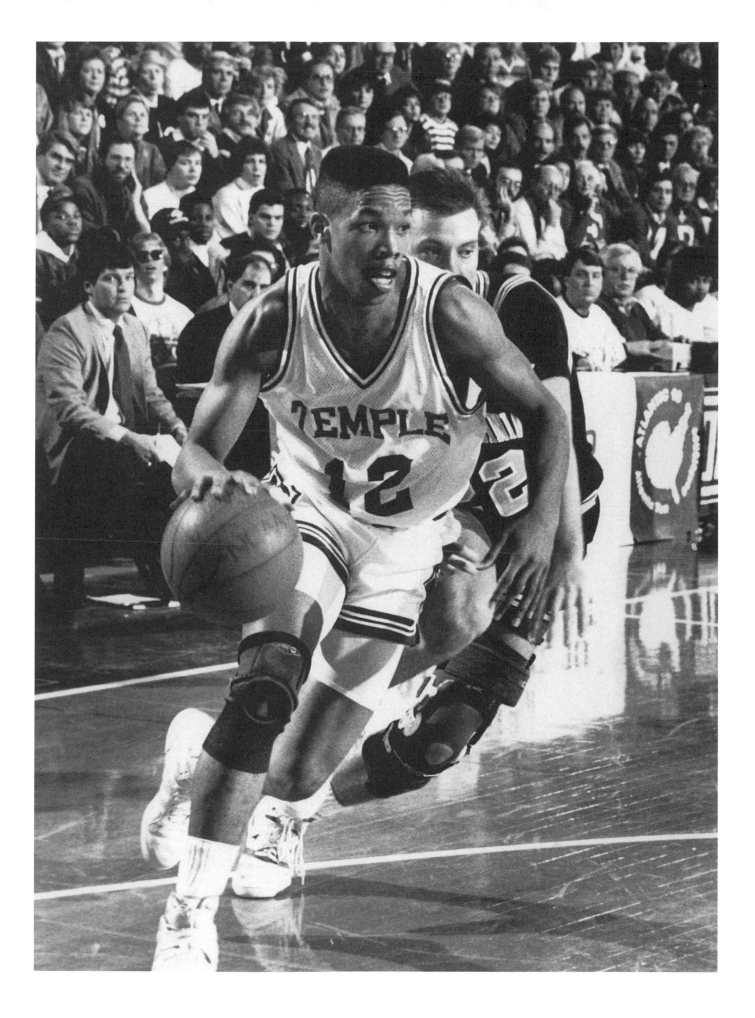

the *least* important thing that John Chaney does is coach basketball. I think he's a savior of souls. There are an awful lot of kids who owe everything that they have to him. Most coaches are protective of their kids but John is really *Mother Hen* protective. He's standing in front of the bullet. The semi is barreling down the highway at one of his kids and he'd knock him out of the way and stand there and let the grill bury him. He's fiercely protective because most of the kids he gets have never had protection and they've all come from pretty hardscrabble circumstances. What greater legacy could any of us leave?"

Chapter 10

• • • • • • •

Another Miracle for St. Joseph's

J im Lynam was relaxing in his recreation room a few years ago when one of his favorite TV shows came on. "I'm a big 60 Minutes fan," he explained. "At the top of the show, they were promoting a piece with Skip Dillard, the former DePaul player, from a jail cell. I just got a chill and sat there and said, 'Oh, my God.' I think it was Mike Wallace who posed the first question. And Dillard said, 'Well, my life was as good as it could get . . . I was in college and we were the best team in the country . . . We thought we were going to win the NCAA championship . . . and I missed a foul shot in the St. Joe's game.'" Dillard was serving an eleven-year sentence at Joliet State Prison after entering a guilty plea in 1988 for a series of armed robberies of gas stations in the Chicago area. "I just closed my eyes," added Lynam. "I watched the piece but I was in half a trance. I must have sat there by myself for about an hour after that show. Something that was so positive and so giving to me personally, to have affected somebody—maybe more than one person—so negatively and you could be totally unaware of that—it just blew me away."

L ynam's thoughts flashed back to that moment in 1981—the highlight of his coaching career at St. Joseph's—when his Hawks upset DePaul, the nation's No. 1 team, in the NCAA Tournament. It was just another example of their "giant killer" reputation that continued long after Jack Ramsay had left for the NBA. Jack McKinney, who succeeded Ramsay, had his share of upsets, but was inexplicably fired eight years later after being named Eastern College Coach of the Year and taking the team to the NCAA Tournament. McKinney was replaced by Harry Booth, another Ramsay protégé, who remained at the helm for four years before he, too, was let go after the 1977–78 season. Then Lynam took over and eventually registered the second-best winning percentage in the school's history before he left for the NBA to assist his mentor, Ramsay.

Lynam actually could have had the head coaching job a decade earlier. He was serving as Ramsay's assistant when Jack came down with his serious eye ailment after the 1965–66 season. Ramsay said to me, 'This is your job,'" recalled Lynam. "I'm 24 years old and I wanted it, but I wasn't sure I was ready for it. What St. Joe's did for me you can't buy or put into words. I had enough common sense about me to say, 'Don't screw them or mess yourself up at the same time.' So I think my indecisiveness was a sign."

Instead, McKinney, who had been Ramsay's freshman coach for five years before going to Philadelphia Textile as head coach for a year, got the call to return to Hawk Hill as athletic director and head coach. Lynam stayed on as his assistant for the next four years before taking the head-coaching job at Fairfield University.

O ne of the major highlights of McKinney's first year in 1966–67 was Cliff Anderson's incredible 32-point and Big 5–record 32-rebound performance that triggered a 96–83 win over La Salle in his final Big 5 game. "Cliff Anderson was the best player I ever coached in college," said McKinney. "He was a tremendous leaping 6' 3" forward who played bigger than anyone you can imagine. We only won 16 games, but he was the reason why. He just carried us."

Steve Donches, the hero from the previous season, finally worked his way into the starting lineup as a senior and had a number of outstanding games, including a 22-point performance against Georgetown. The Hawks won nine of their first ten games and did surprisingly well in the last ECAC Holiday Festival to be played in the old Madison Square Garden. "Everybody figured this would be a quick shot for St. Joe's," recalled Donches, who returned after graduation to his hometown, where he is now vice president of public affairs at Bethlehem Steel Corporation. "Take a bus ride up and

go right back." But the Hawks avenged the previous season's blowout at Brigham Young to upset the taller Cougars, then knocked off Rhode Island before meeting nationally-ranked Providence in the championship game. The Friars had players like Jimmy Walker and Mike Riorden, and the New York tabloids had a field day with headlines such as "THE MAYOR'S BACK IN TOWN." "Jack Ramsay came up for the finals and sat behind our bench," said Donches. "We were winning the whole game and were up by ten points with ten minutes to go. Then we went five minutes without a field goal." Providence won 82–76.

With Dan Kelly—"just a great typical Philadelphia Catholic League guard," according to his coach—scoring from the backcourt, and Mike Hauer taking care of the boards, McKinney won his only Big 5 title in 1967–68. Only a 103–71 loss to La Salle kept the Hawks out of the NCAA Tournament. "Winning the Big 5 made a mediocre season pretty darn good," recalled McKinney. The Hawks also won the Gator Bowl Tournament that year by shocking host Florida and then beating Washington behind the solid defensive play of guard Billy DeAngelis, who was named MVP and would go on to set a single-season team record with 104 steals.

Kelly and Hauer, who are both members of the Big 5 Hall of Fame, dominated the Hawks' offensive statistics throughout their three-year careers, Hauer making All Big 5 three times and Kelly twice. Although he was only fifth on the Hawks' all-time rebounding list, Hauer's work under the boards was something to behold.

"Mike was as strong as they come," said McKinney. "He was only about 6'3½", but he played above his size in ways that defied the laws of basketball. With his timing and position on rebounds, he was uncanny with what he could do. Scoring, he just knew where to be, when to be, and how to be. He had that little

fake that always got guys off balance—just a little hitch of the shoulders or something."

"Inch-for-inch, Mike Hauer was the best Big 5 rebounder *ever*," said sportswriter Jack Scheuer, a Big 5 Hall of Famer himself who has covered college basketball for almost fifty years. "If the ball was there it was his. I would say he was the best rebounder I ever saw."

In 1968–69, McKinney's Hawks lost to Fairfield 77–69 but Jack was not in his familiar position on the bench at the St. Joseph's Fieldhouse to suffer through it. Instead, he was enduring a different kind of suffering as he watched—and *coached* to a fashion—via a telephone hookup with Lynam from his bed in nearby Lankenau Hospital.

"The morning of the game I had a kidney stone that exploded," said McKinney. "I called Jimmy and told him

► St. Joseph's coach Jack McKinney reviews strategy with Mike Hauer (44) and Dan Kelly. *(St. Joseph's University)*

that I couldn't make the game. I said, 'You know what to do. We have the game plan all set.'" A few minutes later, Lynam called back and said that St. Joe's officials had offered to arrange for a telephone hookup. 'You can watch the game and talk to me at the same time,' said Lynam. 'Are you able to do that?' I said, 'Let's give it a try. If it works, it works.' I had passed the kidney stone by game time and was uncomfortable but not in a lot of pain. The game started and I'm sitting in my hospital bed watching it on TV. I'd see something and I'd say, 'Jim, why the hell is so and so doing this? Get him out of there!' The next thing I see, he's out. Afterwards I did say I shouldn't have done that because it was degrading to Jimmy."

Lynam ended up as Fairfield's coach the following year after George Bisacca, the Stags' athletic director, got a taste of the Hawks' spirit that day. "The kids were chanting after the game even though we lost," recalled Lynam. "George has often said to me, 'I couldn't believe it. You guys lost that game but there was just something in that building in terms of spirit.' The loss didn't dim any enthusiasm and that thought stuck in his mind: If you could transmit that to a college campus or some portion of it, you'd be on the way to a successful program."

Two of McKinney's best players turned out to be Mike Bantom and Mike Moody, who played for Speedy Morris at Philadelphia's Roman Catholic High School. Bantom, who became an All-America, averaged double figures in points and rebounds all three seasons at St. Joseph's, and played on the 1972 U.S. Olympic team that was cheated out of the gold medal in the controversial loss to Russia. Moody, an outstanding defensive player, was a Big 5 first team selection in 1973–74.

"Bantom was not a real good player until his senior year in high school," recalled McKinney. "I told Speedy, 'Hey, that big kid's going to be good.' Speedy said, 'He's not good yet, but one more year he should be ready.' I said, 'I'd like to have him right now.' That's when Speedy said, 'Well I've got another kid, Mike Moody, who is going to be a player, also. He never gets headlines or never does enough to be spectacular, but he's going to be a great player.' I didn't know Moody at the time, but then in his senior year I liked him a lot. He was my kind of player—strong and sturdy, and dependable."

"Mike Bantom and Mike Moody was a package deal," said Morris. "A lot of people don't know that. I remember Jack calling me and saying tongue-in-cheek, 'You know Speedy, I don't know what it is. I'm going to church every day, I'm just having trouble getting some players.' He was not interested in Mike Moody. One day I said to him, 'If you take Mike Moody, then Mike Bantom might go.' Jack said, 'I'll take Mike Moody.' I

said, 'Now there's no guarantee.' Then I called Bantom and said, 'St. Joe's just offered Mike Moody a scholarship and he says that he wants to go there.' And Bantom says to me, 'Coach is that just to get me?' I said, 'No, whether you go or not, Mike Moody is going to St. Joe's.' He said, 'I'll go!'"

Bantom had never played organized basketball before he tried out for Roman's JV team as a junior. "I was 6'5" but had absolutely no skills and no experience," he recalled. "Speedy basically taught me how to play. As far as coaches go, he was probably the most influential in forming my philosophy about the game. He had the most impact in my decision to play basketball and also in my belief that I could become a good basketball player. I went from nowhere to somewhere in the space of a year."

"Mike Bantom turned out to be one of the best players we've ever had at St. Joe's," said McKinney. "He carried us to 60 wins in three years. He was wonderful to coach because he just kept getting better. In his senior year I changed him from center to forward because we had another big guy, Kevin Furey, who wasn't mobile enough to be a forward. Furey's best position was center. It was a great thing for us and for Mike because he showed in college that he would be a good a 6'8" or 6'9" shooting forward in the NBA." Bantom played for nine years in the NBA, mostly with Indiana and Phoenix.

"Moody was a great player but was never one to get headlines," added McKinney. "You've seen a lot of players like this—without him, the team is not whole. He averaged maybe ten points a game over three years but he would get four or five steals and he was the best defensive player I ever had. Many times I'd say to Moody, 'You just have to blanket this guy.' We came to expect that of him. He always shut down the good guards."

St. Joseph's set a Palestra single-game record that still stands when it beat Nevada-Reno 128–66 in 1971. "I didn't know there was another Nevada team," recalled Bantom, one of seven Hawks who scored in double figures that night. "But they played like UNLV. They were not playing much defense. They wanted to run up and down and shoot. This was probably the first team that we got into a game like that with. They did not have the talent to play us like that. It just got to be a fun game, a playground game in which we all just scored a bunch of points." Bantom's teammates Bob Sabol and Jim McCollum each had career highs with 20 points.

Between his junior and senior years, Bantom represented the United States in the 1972 Olympic Games and was the team's third leading scorer with 69 points.

Mike Bantom, who twice led St. Joseph's in scoring and rebounding, played on the 1972 U.S. Olympic team. *(St. Joseph's University)*

He also lived close to the scene of the horrifying P.L.O. terrorist attack when eleven Israeli athletes were murdered. "I didn't expect to make this team because they picked guys from the ACC and Big Ten, not guys from the Middle Atlantic Conference," he explained. "I just wanted to measure myself and find out how good I was against the other players in the country." After two weeks of tryouts involving 64 of the nation's top players, Bantom was on his way to Munich. In the gold medal game, the United States, coached by Hank Iba of Oklahoma State, played right into the Russians' hands with a very controlled, slowdown type of game. The Americans trailed with about six minutes left. "That's when we got desperate," said Bantom. "We decided to bust our butts on defense and just run, run, run! The Russians were thinking they had us because I could see them get a little cocky and a little arrogant. When we started pressing and running, I also saw them getting scared. They started to throw the ball away and got a little nervous. That ironclad demeanor they had was suddenly breaking down."

The United States finally went ahead 50–49 with three seconds left on a pair of pressure-packed free throws by Doug Collins, who would later play for the Philadelphia 76ers.

That's when the controversy erupted. It's been well-documented how R. William Jones, the head of the international federation, came out of the stands with one second left and told the official scorer to put three seconds back on the clock. How the Russians were given two extra chances to win after that. "That's similar to David Stern, the NBA commissioner, going down to the Lakers' scorer's table and telling the Lakers' scorer what to do in an NBA game. It just doesn't happen," said Bantom, who has been with the NBA as senior vice president for player development since 1989. "On the play that decided the game, we had two guys guarding this Russian guy and he just flat out pushed them in their backs—the kind of pushing in the back that's obvious and is called by every official. It wasn't a hip-bump, it wasn't a little nudge, it was two hands flat in the back pushed down to the floor. And the guy caught the ball and laid it up. I had never been cheated before. I thought that the good guys always won and things always were fair and I finally realized that, hey, they aren't."

McKinney's best team was his 1972–73 squad which went 22–5 during the regular season, with two of the loss-es coming against Penn and Villanova. The Quakers seemed to have a hex over St. Joseph's. A pair of back-to-back heartbreaking losses to Penn, 54–53 and 55–53, when the Hawks coughed up leads of nine and seven points, respectively, in the closing minutes, cost McKinney shares of Big 5 titles with the Quakers in 1973 and 1974. The Hawks won the 1972 Quaker City Tournament quite impressively, though, beating Rhode Island, Duquesne, and La Salle. Pat McFarland was MVP of the tournament, scoring 18 points and grabbing ten rebounds against the Explorers in the championship game. A Big 5 Hall of Famer who went on to play in the ABA with Denver and San Diego for three seasons, Pat holds the all-time St. Joseph's record for most consecutive games (28) scoring in double figures.

"I remember Pat as being a tough competitor," said Bantom. "First I thought he was just a shooter, but over the course of the four years we played together I grew to respect him a lot more as a guy who would do whatever it took to win. He was a tremendous shooter, but he worked on all the other aspects of his game and made himself into a pretty solid player."

Unfortunately, as was the case in all three of Bantom's years, the Hawks always found themselves matched against one of the East's top teams in post-season tournaments. In his first year, they lost to Villanova's Final Four team 93–75 in the first round of the NCAA Tournament at the Palestra. As a sophomore, it was Maryland winning in the NIT 67–55. The Terrapins finished runner-up in the Atlantic Coast Conference that year and were top-seeded in the Garden. "We played them extraordinarily well for a team as small as we were," said Bantam. "They had a 7-foot front line with guys like Len Elmore. I had no problem guarding Tom McMillen, but they went to the free throw line an extraordinary amount of times. I felt that we should have won that game and probably would have if all things were equal." In 1972–73, it was back to the NCAA Tournament against a surprising Providence team, headed by Marvin Barnes, Ernie DiGregorio, and Kevin Stacom, that made it all the way to the national finals after beating the Hawks 89–76. "They were just a tad better than us," said Bantom. "It was just a bad match-up, bad luck on our part, but we had a great team that year."

His 1973–74 squad gave McKinney the most satisfaction. "It was the year after guys like Mike Bantom, Pat McFarland, and Bob Sabol had graduated and the whole front line was gone," he explained. "One of the pre-season write-ups in a Philadelphia paper characterized our prospects as 'Grim, Grisly, and Gruesome.'"

"I think that might have been the best coaching job I've ever seen in my life," said the team's playmaker Jim

▲ Jim O'Brien drives in to score against St. John's as team-mate Pat McFarland watches during a Hawk win at the Palestra in 1973. *(St. Joseph's University)*

O'Brien, who has been exposed to quite a few good coaches in the NBA. "I remember vividly when they said we would not win four games. There were no overwhelming talents on our team—everybody averaged ten or eleven points—but Jack had taught us, like all the coaches at St. Joe's, the art of team basketball. Nobody really cared who got the credit. It was the best *team* I've ever witnessed, and I've been in this business a long time. To win almost twenty games surprised everybody except the people who were part of that program. We were just going to pick you apart, not make mistakes, get good shots, make it difficult for you to score."

St. Joseph's beat La Salle twice that year, first during the regular season and then for the MAC championship. "I'll always remember that game," recalled McKinney. "Jim O'Brien came over and said, 'They don't know what the hell we're doing, coach!' So I said, 'All right, keep doing it!' O'Brien was high scorer with 19 points as St. Joseph's won 76–71. Moody, playing with a painfully sore rib cage, hit his first five shots from the floor and finished with 16 points as the Hawks built a 17-point lead.

"Jim O'Brien just would not let us lose," recalled McKinney of the Big 5 Hall of Famer. "We would get into a huddle once in a while and he would take over and pump his fist and talk to them. He'd say, 'You freaking guys. You think this team is good enough to beat us? Hell, if they beat us we're going to walk home from here and be so freaking embarrassed. Stop putzing around and play the way we can,' that kind of stuff. You needed a player like that. Jimmy had that quality of leadership. He made you play the best you could."

In a move that could only happen in the Big 5, McKinney and La Salle coach Paul Westhead got together before that 1974 MAC championship game and decided to pool their resources. They flipped a coin to determine whom to send to scout the Pitt–West Virginia game, which would determine the winner's first round opponent in the NCAA Tournament. Westhead won the toss and Joe O'Connor, the Explorers' assistant coach, scouted the game. McKinney agreed to pay his expenses, which probably wasn't one of the greatest investments of all time because Pitt eliminated the Hawks 54–42 in Morgantown, West Virginia.

"That was my favorite team," McKinney recalled. It was also his last team because at the end of the season—after being named Eastern College Coach of the Year—Jack was notified by college officials that he was out as coach of the Hawks.

"To me, the biggest mystery still to this day is why he was fired so unfairly," said sportswriter Frank Bilovsky. "The poor guy had just taken a team that had no right to

go anywhere to the NCAA Tournament and they call him in and he thinks he's going to get a contract extension or a new contract and they fire him. Unbelievable! You couldn't figure out how they were going to win more than twelve games. He wins 19 and we named him Coach of the Year. He really got the ultimate out of his team."

McKinney soon became Larry Costello's assistant with the Milwaukee Bucks, the first of a number of successful coaching stints in the NBA that also included Portland, Los Angeles, Indiana, and Kansas City. In fact, shortly after he was named an assistant coach of the Los Angeles Clippers in February 2000, Kareem Abdul-Jabbar was asked by *Philadelphia Inquirer* sportswriter Frank Fitzpatrick to name the professional coach who had influenced him the most. He immediately mentioned McKinney, who suffered severe head injuries in a bicycle accident early in the 1979–80 season after he had guided the Lakers to ten wins in their first 13 games. Paul Westhead, his old Hawk comrade who had joined the team as his assistant, then took over and coached them to the NBA championship, beating the Philadelphia 76ers in the finals. McKinney "was only with the team about three months but he did an incredible job," explained Jabbar. "He understood the personnel and understood what our potential was. He understood the game and the players."

"I always had tremendous respect for him as an individual and as a coach and for what we accomplished his last year," said Harry Booth, who had served as an assistant under McKinney, as well as Ramsay, for the previous nine years. "Individually, I don't know if any of our players would have started for La Salle that season—maybe Jimmy O'Brien, who was our point guard. But we were able to play so well as a team it really bothered me when St. Joe's chose to get rid of Jack. To the point that I had told him that, if he wanted, I would not be a candidate for the job. He said, 'No, St. Joe's is the place for you.' But it bothered me."

Quite instrumental in helping Booth during this period was Penn coach Chuck Daly. "He's the one that did more to help my confi-

◄ Harry Booth played for Jack Ramsay at St. Joseph's, succeeded Jack McKinney as coach of the Hawks, and later served as a volunteer assistant to Villanova's Rollie Massimino. (*Urban Archives, Temple University, Philadelphia, Pennsylvania*)

dence in the situation," Harry recalled. "He was willing to go out of his way. He came out to the school to meet with me. I felt that I had to defend the school and Chuck sensed that I worried about that. His feeling was, 'Harry, just coach. Just be yourself. You had no control of that situation. You can't change it.' He did an awful lot for me in many ways."

The highlight of Booth's four-year coaching tenure was his 1975–76 team that shared the Big 5 crown with Villanova in a title chase that wasn't decided until the last game of the regular season when the Wildcats won 71–60.

"We were a very young team but our kids had enthusiasm and believed in themselves," explained Booth. The Hawks opened Big 5 competition that year by upsetting a Penn team, coming off a 23–5 season, with four sophomores in the starting lineup. One of the newcomers, Norman Black, sparked the 77–71 victory with 21 points. "What I remembered the most about the Penn game was an early out-of-bounds play where we just threw it up toward the basket," said Booth. "Norm Black came right down the lane and dunked it. It almost seemed like Penn's players looked and said, 'Wait a minute.' At that point the game changed and our kids believed, 'Hey, we can play with them.'"

Guards Willie Taylor, a transfer from Boston College who scored 27 points, and Zane Major completely dominated play as the Hawks beat La Salle 86–75. Then the Hawks' defense took over in a 74–62 win over Temple in a game in which the Owls missed 25 of their 30 field goal attempts in the first half. "Norm Black was a major factor," said Booth. "He had outstanding athleticism, could handle the ball, go one-on-one, and could play defense. I thought he would get better as a shooter." Black, who was twice selected to the All-Big 5 team, finished as the only St. Joseph's player in history to lead the Hawks in scoring average all four years of his varsity career.

A member of the Big 5 Hall of Fame, he also had an uncanny knack for getting open to score on the Hawks' well executed out-of-bounds play. "It seems like it happened 95 times every year," recalled Bilovsky. "Every time St. Joe's would take the ball out under their own basket, we'd say, 'Well Norman Black is going to get a layup.' There'd be some kind of a triple inside screen and Black would get loose underneath. He was a fine player and a good guy who probably didn't get his just due because the team as a whole wasn't that good."

Booth was also responsible for bringing in the two Griffin guards—Luke and John—who were not related. Luke, an excellent point guard who also played on Lynam's 1980 Big 5 champions, was hampered by injuries throughout his career. But he is the only St. Joseph's player ever to lead the team in assists and steals

for four straight years. John, who would later coach the Hawks, was actually discouraged by Booth about coming to the school even though he had been another one of Speedy Morris' solid high school performers. John Griffin was also an outstanding baseball player.

"I thought he was a good basketball player but just felt he would not be able to start at our Division I level," explained Booth, who also coached baseball for a while at St. Joseph's. "My philosophy is if you can't project a player as an eventual starter at some point, you don't recruit him. I tried to get him a scholarship at Drexel and told him from a basketball standpoint, it was best that he go there. I told him you're good enough for a baseball scholarship but if you come here, I want you to focus on that sport. That doesn't mean that you can't come out for basketball. He said to me, 'I'll play baseball. But if you're going to tell me that I can come out for basketball, I'm going to make your team!'"

Not only did Griffin make the varsity as a freshman in 1974, he immediately contributed to a victory in the first road game of Booth's coaching career. "We're one down at Albright with five seconds to go," Harry recalled. "Griffin gets fouled and makes the one-and-one. That showed me that he had an intensity about him. He was a competitor, a student of the game. He brought an awful lot to the program. Later his role became more of a niche player rather than as a starter. But I could see qualities that would make him a good coach."

When St. Joseph's officials began a search for Booth's successor after he was let go in 1978, Jim Lynam's name immediately jumped to top of the list. Lynam had coached at Fairfield for two years and had just completed his fifth season building a successful program at American University. Don DiJulia, a boyhood friend since their elementary school days in Southwest Philly, was in his first term as the Hawks' athletic director. DiJulia would remain in that position until 1981, when he began tours as commissioner of the East Coast and then the Metro Atlantic Conferences, before returning as AD in 1988. DiJulia, who had played for Jack Ramsay's great 1964–65 quintet, remained close friends with Lynam and had served as his assistant at Fairfield and American U. In between, he had worked on the basketball staff at George Washington University. He was also married to Lynam's sister, Pat.

As a young guy, Jim was a natural leader and a feared competitor," recalled DiJulia. "He just had that way about him to motivate and captivate people. I warned the St. Joe's administration that I was married to the family of everybody's candidate. I sought advice and guidance." So did Lynam. "I don't remember it being an easy decision for him, either," said DiJulia. "He

loved American U. and he loved living in Washington."

Lynam's teams went 19–11, 21–9, and 25–8 and finished unbeaten in the Big 5 in 1979–80. But the one game that everyone remembers occurred on March 14, 1981, when the Hawks upset DePaul's No. 1 ranked Blue Demons 49–48 in the second round of the NCAA Tournament, in Dayton, Ohio. Amazingly, they did it with two freshmen— Tony Costner and Lonnie McFarlan—playing key roles. Equally as amazing, Lynam's *former* players almost kept the Hawks out of the tournament.

Gary Williams, now the coach at Maryland, succeeded Jim as coach of American U. and did an excellent job with the team that Lynam had recruited. American had beaten the Hawks 84–83 in overtime late in the season at the Palestra. For the East Coast Conference playoffs, however, the Eagles' best player, Boo Bauers, was out for the year with a knee injury. "Bauers would have had a terrific pro career if he doesn't get hurt," said Lynam. "Actually he was one of the best players I've ever coached on any level."

Playing without Bryan Warrick, who had strained some knee ligaments, and knowing that there would be no NCAA bid to the loser, St. Joseph's battled back from a seven-point deficit to defeat American and win the ECC championship 63–60. The Hawks were placed in the Midwest Regional where they upset heavily-favored Creighton, the Missouri Valley champions, 59–57 when Costner hit a pair of free throws in the closing seconds.

The details of the final frenzied seconds of the DePaul game are engraved in the minds of every St. Joseph's fan. Executing their disciplined "Four-to-Score" slowdown offense and zone defense with precision, the Hawks kept the game close and held DePaul scoreless for the final 6:28. With 12 seconds left and the Blue Demons up by a point, Skip Dillard, the team's best foul shooter, the man they called "Money," went to the line for a one-and-one. He missed.

▲ Five St. Joseph's starters in action against Creighton in the NCAA Tournament (from left) Bryan Warrick, Tony Costner, Boo Williams, Jeffery Clark, and John Smith. *(St. Joseph's University)*

Although the Hawks did have a time out left, Lynam elected to allow his team to move the ball out of the backcourt in what he calls "In the Flow." Besides, he had the utmost confidence in Warrick, his ball-handler. Here, Lynam picks up the story:

"Bryan is up on the foul line checking the shooter in case the ball came back. The rebound went to the right of the basket and with his reaction and quickness, he's the first one who gets to the ball. As he turns to push it up the court, the first De Paul guy comes at him and he puts him away with a dribble move. And the second guy, instead of back-pedaling, was standing there almost nailed to the floor. Bryan put a second dribble move on him. Afterwards, they were raving whether the first move was through the legs or the second one was behind the back. But the one guy fell to the floor with two dribble moves in the space of maybe two seconds and these guys were, maybe, twenty yards apart in the backcourt. They were in such panic at that point.

"So now all of a sudden they're trying to protect a one-point lead. Their players are thinking 'Here they come—that kid just put away two of our defenders.' When Bryan threw the ball to McFarlan, who was going

to have an open jumper 16 feet out in the baseline, two defenders both ran out to Lonnie. Neither of them could guard him anyway. And what that served to do, Lonnie threw it under to John Smith and as John said, 'My big decision was should I lay it up or give it to Tony to lay it up?'" Smith scored the layup. There were still three seconds left. "I had forgotten that they had blown their final time out on their last possession," said Lynam. "We had pressured them on the out-of-bounds and they had to take a time out because they couldn't get it in."

Millions of viewers watched the wild celebration on national television afterwards. While Lynam was embracing one of his teenage daughters, Dei, now a

reporter with Comcast SportsNet TV in Philadelphia, Jim's other daughter, Kath, on a school trip in New York, was waiting in Penn Station to get a train back to Philadelphia. "She and some friends went into bar to see the end of game, but it was over," said Lynam. "They go to a guy sitting at the bar—they can tell he's a little woozy—and asked for the score. 'Yeah,' he said, 'the team, I think it was St. *George*, won.' So they go outside and one of her friends asks, 'Did St. Joe's win?' And my daughter said, 'Well some drunk guy in there said they did, but I don't think so.'"

"People said we were fortunate to win that game," recalled Warrick, who had been an all-state football quarterback at Burlington Township (New Jersey) High School. "But the most fortunate thing for us was that we had the opportunity to see DePaul play earlier in the Palestra against La Salle. We really thought La Salle had a chance to beat DePaul and we had beaten La Salle. So I don't think that there was a man on our team that wasn't confident that we could play with them. Obviously, we didn't feel that we could run up and down with them, but we felt if we controlled tempo, played smart, did the right things, we would have an opportunity. That's what the coach always stressed no matter who we played—make sure we have an opportunity to win the game."

Not surprisingly for someone who grew up watching Big 5 games on Channel 17, Warrick does not consider that win over DePaul as the biggest memory of his college career. "People don't understand that, but without a doubt I've always said it was the Villanova game my sophomore year when we won by one [60–59]. John Smith had a crusher pick. I'm open. I nail the jumper with like eight seconds left. It seemed like we were always underdogs but we won a lot of close games at the buzzer that year."

The Hawks' magic ride through the NCAA Tournament continued the next weekend in the regional semifinals in Bloomington, Indiana, when they edged Boston College 42–41. But the dream ended on Indiana's home court when Bob Knight's Hoosiers won convincingly 78–46 to earn a trip to the Final Four in Philadelphia, where they won it all.

Over the years, Lynam had been offered a number of opportunities to join Ramsay and McKinney in the NBA. "I always knew that I wanted to do it, but I could never find the right time," he recalled. After the 1980–81 season, Ramsay invited him to join the Portland Trail Blazers. "I did some unbelievable soul-searching—I sat out on my deck at three in the morning trying to make up my mind. I was taking my kids three thousand miles from their friends, worried about disrupting my family." Finally, he decided, "If you're going to do it, now's the time." So with the blessing of his family, it was off to Oregon on the start of a NBA career that has carried him to head coaching positions with the Los Angeles Clippers. Washington Bullets (now the Wizards), and Philadelphia 76ers, as well as an assistant's slot with Don Casey at the New Jersey Nets, and, again, with the Trail Blazers. Lynam also served for two years as general manager of the 76ers, succeeding his fellow Hawk, Matt Goukas, in that position.

Jim Boyle, Lynam's buddy who had been his assistant with the Hawks for three years, was immediately named head coach and quickly established a reputation as one of the Big 5's most colorful personalities. "One of the most intriguing guys I've ever met in sports," recalled *Philadelphia Inquirer* columnist Bill Lyon. "To me, he is a Renaissance Man. He has a ton of interests. Unlike most coaches, you can sit down and talk with him four hours straight and never have the subject of basketball come up. He can talk about so many different things because he has so many wide and varied interests. Travel, for one thing. I'll bet there isn't a country in the world that Jim Boyle hasn't been in. He's really interested in other cultures. He has an insatiable curiosity about the whole world and people and how things work. He wants to see other cultures and not just to be a tourist. If he goes to South America, he'll probably go up the Andes and live in a village rather than stay in the Four Seasons or in Santiago. All coaches will tell you, 'I consider myself a teacher.' Jim Boyle is a teacher, but you know what? He's the ultimate *student* because he's always wanting to learn more. Later in life I think that you have to fight becoming fossilized and kind of rigid in your thinking. You're not open to new ideas. But he was. I always admired that about him."

Boyle went 25–5 in his first year as coach and ended up sharing the Big 5 title with Temple after the Owls won 82–77 despite a 29-point effort by Costner. "But for a few points, we would have had three more wins," said Boyle. He's correct. The Hawks dropped heartbreaking road games at Creighton (73–72) and DePaul (46–44), then got eliminated in the first round of the NCAA Tournament by Northeastern (63–62).

"I'm not really surprised that we did so well because I knew we had the best backcourt in the country with Bryan Warrick and Jeffery Clark," explained Boyle about his Big 5 Hall of Famers. "And when you have the best backcourt in the country, you're bound to win a lot of games. I inherited a lot of that team from Jim and they were very well prepared to play basketball." Clark shared Big 5 MVP honors with Villanova's John Pinone.

Costner, who led the Hawks in scoring in 1983–84, had some huge games against Big 5 opponents. In 1983, he triggered an 88–59 blowout of the Owls with 25

▶ **B**ob Lojewski scored 18 points and grabbed 10 rebounds to trigger a 59–57 St. Joseph's win over Penn in 1984. *(St. Joseph's University)*

points and 19 rebounds. As a senior, he went eight-of-ten from the field and nine-of-eleven from the free throw line in an 86–66 rout of Pennsylvania. Another big contributor was Bob Lojewski, who led the team in scoring in 1982–83 and again in 1984–85. "Bob was the quiet leader of the team," recalled Bruiser Flint, who has coached at Massachusetts and Drexel following a good career with the Hawks. "He never looked for the spotlight. He just came out and played every night." So well that Lojewski was eventually named to the Big 5 Hall of Fame.

Midway through the 1982–83 season, the Hawks made the TV highlight shows during a wild 68–58 triumph over Duquesne in Pittsburgh. The trouble started when about 50 disorderly students who regularly sat under the basket dressed as Arabs grabbed the Hawk. Boyle was huddling with his players when he glanced over to the stands. "I waited a second and thought, 'Is this like for sport or are they serious?' It didn't take long to register that this kid's in trouble. I didn't know what to do so I said, 'Yo guys, Get him out of there!' and I sent my team into the stands. The game was televised and the first thing you could see was the Hawk getting beat up. Then you see this chair come flying through the air. One of my guys took a chair and threw a chair at the Sheiks. Then you saw the *St. Joe's Hawks* going in to rescue *the Hawk*." Naturally, ESPN played up the incident and the next morning when the team arrived back in Philadelphia, Boyle was summoned to the president's office. "I walked in and Father Donald MacLean said, 'Well coach, I just want to let you know I was proud of what you did.' Here I thought I was going to get fired and I ended up getting a pat on the back." Duquesne officials disbanded the "Sheiks" shortly afterwards.

The most satisfying season of Boyle's nine years as coach came in 1985–86 when his first recruiting class won 26 of 32 games and again shared the Big 5 championship with Temple. Only a 74–69 loss to La Salle, led by Tim Legler's 22 points, kept the Hawks from winning the title outright.

"Looking back, I knew my first team had won 25 games," said Boyle. "I thought, 'I hope I can do as well with my first recruiting class,' and this group ended up winning 26 games." Geoff Arnold, "one of the best team leaders that you could dream of," was Boyle's first recruit. Others in that group included Maurice

▲ James "Bruiser" Flint (14) and Geoff Arnold, shown cele-brating a Hawk victory, were best friends who competed for playing time with each other throughout their careers. *(St. Joseph's University)*

Martin, Wayne Williams, and Dave Slattery. Bruiser Flint joined the team a year later, and Rodney Blake came on board in 1985. Martin was high scorer in all three of the Hawks' Big 5 victories that year with a total of 59 points, including 26 in the 65–63 squeaker over Temple. The future Big 5 Hall of Famer also played well when the Hawks won the Far West Classic in Portland, Oregon, by shocking Kansas State in overtime, Oregon State, and then Iowa in the championship game. "I think people finally realized just how good Martin was in that tournament," recalled Flint. "He played four

positions, he rebounded, he scored, I mean he did everything."

Arnold and Flint spent their careers at St. Joseph's competing with each other for playing time at point guard. "We were roommates in college but I actually thought of not going to St. Joe's because I would be going up against him," explained Flint. "We were good friends and we had known each other since we were ten years old. But he was one of the people who sold me on coming here. 'Don't worry about that stuff. We'll play together. You'll get time. I'll get time. We've got great guys here,' he said. Geoff made me better. We went at each other in practice. I knocked him down. He knocked me down. I picked him up. He picked me up. When practice was over we went back to our room and ate together. I'd cheer for him. He'd cheer for me. We had to compete against each other in practice for play-ing time, but when everything was said and done he was still my boy. We hung out every day and today he's still one of my best friends." So much so that Flint later took Arnold to Massachusetts as his assistant coach. When Bruiser got the Drexel University job, Geoff came back to Philadelphia with him.

Blake, one of the top shot-blockers in the history of college basketball, led the nation with 111 rejections in 1987–88. He finished his career as Hawks' all-time record-holder in blocked shots and field goal percentage, and as the second all-time NCAA Division I shot blocker with 419. "He was probably one of the nicest people I've ever been around in my life," said Flint. "Almost to a detriment. I thought at times that I wanted him to be a little bit nastier."

Boyle's most memorable Big 5 game came on December 12, 1987, when Ivan "Pick" Brown raced the length of the court and hit a 15-foot bank shot at the buzzer to beat heavily-favored Villanova 53–52. "I remember everything about that game," Boyle explained. "We had to play *at* Villanova and to this day I don't like the fact that we had to go there and they never came to ourfield-house. It didn't seem quite fair or reasonable. In fact, it might have been a contributing factor for circumstances that led to me leaving the school. I went in there with a little chip on my shoulder. Near the end of the game, they went dunk, steal-dunk, steal-dunk, fastbreak-dunk."

After Boyle called a timeout, St. Joseph's defense took over and held on for a couple of possessions. Suddenly Villanova's seven-point lead was cut to 52–51 with four seconds to go. Then Villanova's Doug West missed a pair of free throws. The Hawks got the rebound; Brown got the outlet pass and scored at the buzzer. "Pick Brown was 1-for-15 before making that shot," recalled Phil Martelli, who served as assistant coach under Boyle and John Griffin before taking over the reins of the Hawks in 1995. "It wasn't the most pleasant of games. There wasn't a lot of friendship being exchanged."

Boyle had been JV coach at Widener University when Martelli was a freshman. Phil played a few games for him before moving up to the varsity and the two remained friends. When an opening for assistant coach popped up on Hawk Hill in 1985, Martelli applied for the job and was hired. "I remember always having my eyes wide open because you never knew who could walk through the office—whether it be Jim Lynam or Matt Guokas or Jack Ramsay," recalled Martelli. "I was a St.

Joseph's fan my whole life. I believed wholeheartedly in the passion that this school brought to the game. To me it was like a kid-in-the-candy-store type of an approach."

Griffin gave up a lucrative Wall Street career to succeed Boyle as the Hawks' head coach in 1990–91, the final year of the Big 5 round-robin. He remained in that position for five years. "John Griffin brought an attitude that 24 hours wasn't enough time in the day," said Martelli. "He really worked himself tirelessly and he worked all of us the same way. But it was a joy because you knew that he was doing exactly the same thing. There were no shortcuts. We were going to get out of our funk by working hard, by coaching hard, by recruiting hard. I really admired John because he had a lot going on and he had a lot of ways to make a lot of money. But this was clearly his passion."

The Hawks shared the final Big 5 title with Temple in 1990–91 by upsetting the Owls and La Salle and beating Penn in the last three city series games played as part of the round-robin. Bernard Blunt, the Hawks' top career scorer with 1,985 points, and a three-time All Big 5 selection who would later be inducted into the Big 5 Hall of Fame, sparked the 66–60 upset over Temple with 20 points and 14 rebounds. Only an early-season 83–82 loss to Villanova at the Spectrum, when Marc Dowdell grabbed a crucial rebound and made a pair of free throws with 5.4 seconds left, kept St. Joseph's from winning the title outright.

It was quite fitting that the final Big 5 championship should be decided by a one-point heart-stopper between St. Joseph's and Villanova. Especially since these bitter arch-rivals had clashed in the very first Big 5 game way back on December 14, 1955.

▶ **P**hil Martelli (right) served as an assistant to Jim Boyle and John Griffin (left) before becoming the Hawks' head coach in 1995. *(St. Joseph's University)*

Chapter 11

• • • • • • •

La Salle's Speedy, Lefty, and "Shakespeare"

Jim O'Brien, the coach of the Boston Celtics, remembers struggling with his foul shooting as a young sophomore at Philadelphia's Roman Catholic High School. "My father said, 'Why don't you go to the new coach and ask him to help you with that?' And I said, 'He's the varsity coach, Dad. I don't want to bother him.' He says, 'You really need to. Go up to him and tell him you're struggling.' And I did. I went to Speedy Morris on a Friday afternoon, I said, 'Coach, I'm Jim O'Brien.' He said 'I know who you are.' I explained my problem. He says, 'Where do you live?' I told him and he said, 'I'll pick you up tomorrow at 9 o'clock in the morning.' The next morning he took me up to the grade school where he coached in Manayunk. He stood me on the foul line and without any basketballs we spent a good half-hour shooting foul shots. He really gave me my first indoctrination into visualization, just visualizing the technique in our minds, seeing the ball go through the basket. I never had a problem with foul shooting again in my life. I dramatically improved because he simplified things and made me believe in myself. Here I wasn't even on the varsity, and for Speedy to come from Manayunk to 7th and Olney to pick me up on a Saturday morning when I'm sure he had a helluva lot of better things to do, really said something about the commitment he made to us."

After Tom Gola helped restore some stability to the La Salle basketball program, his successors—Paul Westhead, Dave "Lefty" Ervin, and William "Speedy" Morris—continued the tradition of just that kind of personal commitment to their players that has characterized so many Big 5 coaches over the years. In addition to returning to the national spotlight on various occasions, the Explorers were blessed with the three players who dominated the Big 5 at the beginning of the decades of the '70s, '80s, and '90s—Ken Durrett, Michael Brooks, and Lionel Simmons. Lionel and Michael are still the Big 5's all-time leading scorers. All three were No.1 NBA draft picks, but unfortunately, all of them had promising professional careers curtailed by knee injuries.

Westhead was the unexpected choice to succeed Gola, who had strongly endorsed his assistant, Curt Fromal, for the position. A Jack Ramsay protégé, Westhead was working as Jack McKinney's assistant at St. Joseph's and was widely considered to be his heir apparent. "We were all very disappointed when he left after our freshman year to take the job at La Salle," Mike Bantom recalled. "We had hoped that he would be a part of our lives here." Not only was Westhead succeeding La Salle's "Living Legend," he had to sell himself to a veteran team headed by Durrett, clearly one of the nation's elite superstars, who would go on to be Big 5 MVP for the third straight year. The defining moment of Westhead's coaching career came quickly—in Paul's very first week of practice.

"I'm probably so naive I don't know what's going on," recalled Westhead, who guided the Explorers to a 20–7 record that year. "We're doing a basketball drill where you play the dribbler and the offense sets a pick so you either have to go under the pick or through the pick. It's not an easy situation. So I'm teaching them the classic hard-nosed Bobby Knight approach that you just fight the dribbler. You're relentless. After I demonstrate it, the players are trying to do it. Three or four of them are running right into the pick and stopping. And one of them said, 'Hey, we can't do this. You just can't do it!' So everybody's stopped for the moment and Durrett was just standing in line. It wasn't his turn but he comes over and hands the ball to a player and he says, 'Let's do the drill.' And he gracefully goes right in front of the pick and executes the drill perfectly. Then he turns to me with all the players standing there and says, 'Like that, coach?' That was Durrett's way of saying, 'We're going to do it with this guy. Let's give this guy a chance.' It was also a sign that Kenny Durrett could do anything he wanted. The other guys were probably right. They *couldn't* do it. But he was just marvelous."

Like just about everyone else, Joe Juliano of *The Philadelphia Inquirer* was most impressed by Durrett's ver-

satility. "He could score on the inside or from the outside," the sportswriter recalled. "Before the days of Julius Erving, he could hang and float to the basket in a style reminiscent of Elgin Baylor, a perennial all-pro. He was a determined rebounder, combining toughness with leaping ability."

Durrett's greatest game came midway through his senior year at the Palestra. With La Salle fans chanting their customary "Dooooo-rett, Dooooo-rett," Ken outplayed Western Kentucky's All-America Jim McDaniels and scored a Palestra-record 45 points to help the Explorers upset the fifth-ranked Hilltoppers 91–76. "We had a week off for exams and I flew down to Bowling Green and scouted them myself," recalled Westhead. "I came back and told the players, 'We can't run with this team. We're going to hold the ball.' It's one of the few times in my life I ever thought that, let alone try to do it. I said, 'If we score a basket we'll press. But other than that we're going to play very conservative.' The game starts and we get an opening tip and score a basket and press, steal the ball and score, and press. And the next thing I know, I look up and it's 17–2."

Three weeks later, Durrett was having another spectacular game against Canisius at the Palestra. Suddenly, late in the first half, the horrific happened. "He had the ball and was coming down as graceful as he normally does," Westhead explained. "He kind of faked right, went left and his leg went. It wasn't like a dramatic collision or like he got hit in the front and hit in the back. It was just a freak thing." Hampered by torn knee ligaments, Durrett was never the same player afterwards. He still finished as the nation's second leading scorer with a 27-point average, but hobbled through the Explorers' 70–67 loss to Georgia Tech in the opening round of the NIT. The fourth player picked in the NBA draft, his pro career with Cincinnati, Kansas City-Omaha and Philadelphia lasted four years. "Before he got hurt he was awesome," said Westhead. "Afterwards, he was there, but he was kind of a shadow of his dominating force." Penn's Bob Bigelow played with Durrett in the Charles Baker League a few years into his pro career. "I couldn't believe how good he was with the bad knee," Bigelow recalled. "I said to myself, 'How good could he have been with *two* knees?' I mean he could have been one of the all-time greats. No one had more athletic ability." Durrett died of an apparent heart attack in 2001. He was 52.

La Salle's most memorable Big 5 game that year was the one when Durrett did *not* play. It came against Villanova three days after Kenny's injury. No one gave the Explorers a chance against the Wildcats, who would later go all the way to the NCAA championship game. Bobby Fields put La Salle up for good with a three-point play and Jim Crawford clinched it with a layup as the Explorers pulled off one of the biggest upsets in Big 5 history, 73–69. "I can still remember Kenny sitting on the bench with his head down as the introductions were going on and literally tears were coming out of his eyes," said Westhead. "It was the game that he wanted to play because it was

◀ La Salle's All-America Ken Durrett, a three-time Big 5 MVP, scores two of his Palestra-record 45 points against Western Kentucky in 1971. *(Urban Archives, Temple University, Philadelphia, Pennsylvania)*

▲ **P**aul Westhead's first team at La Salle in 1970–71 included a nucleus of (from left) Bob Fields, Jim Crawford, Ken Durrett, Ron Kennedy, and Greg Cannon. *(La Salle University)*

the final dramatic Porter–Durrett match-up. I can still remember the pure joy on the faces of those players in the locker room. The tears from Fields and Ronny Kennedy as he almost single-handily picked the team up. That game was most satisfying to me and certainly the most dramatic Big 5 game of my career." Although Fields was frequently overshadowed by Durrett, the 6' 3" guard from Chicago contributed significantly to the Explorers with his leadership, some clutch shooting and aggressive defense. He went on to play for a year in the ABA with Utah and is a member of the Big 5 Hall of Fame.

Westhead, who also taught part-time in La Salle's English department, was certainly one of the most colorful coaches in the Big 5. A Shakespearean scholar who had written his master's degree thesis at Villanova on *Titus Andronicus*, he frequently used analogies from the Bard to discuss basketball strategy. Once at a banquet, for example, he quoted from *Macbeth* to describe the Explorers' fast break: "If it were done when 'tis done, then't were well it were done quickly."

Westhead's practices and game-day activity often reflected his keen interest in Zen philosophy. Like the

time in 1976–77 when the Explorers upset Villanova 71–70 as Darryl Gladden calmly sank two free throws with one second left. Before he went to the line each team called a time out—La Salle to get its bearings and Villanova, to "ice" Gladden. "There really wasn't much to say because we were down with one second to go," recalled Westhead. "I was a little bit into my Zen stuff and I had guys doing layup drills and shooting free throws in preseason practice with their eyes closed. My whole point to them was that much of shooting was muscle memory. If you shot enough free throws, it would go in because your muscle memory would take over. You wouldn't really need to see it. That was back in October. Now it's February and we hadn't done that in months. We're about to go back on the court and Gladden looks at me and says, 'With or without?' I said, 'Excuse me?' He said, 'Do you want me to shoot these with my eyes open or with my eyes closed?' He's busting me. I turned to my assistants, Joe O'Conner and Lefty, and said, 'There's no doubt in my mind that we're going to win this game.' And he just buried those free throws."

Westhead's 1974–75 team was his best. Headed by future Big 5 Hall of Famers Bill Taylor, the only senior in the starting lineup, and Joe Bryant, the team's leading scorer, the Explorers jumped out to a 16–1 record and went unbeaten in city series play. Their only loss in that span was to Canisius at the buzzer. They beat Southeastern Conference champion Alabama and Southern Conference titlist Furman, as well as highly-regarded teams like Texas Tech, Memphis State, and Clemson. The 67–65 win over Penn, triggered by Bryant's 25 points, ended the Ivy League champions' record 12-game Big 5 winning streak. The Explorers won back-to-back tournaments early that season, the Dayton Invitational and the Sugar Bowl Classic. But the title in New Orleans was dampened when Dr. Gene Gallagher, La Salle's team physician since 1964, collapsed and died of a heart attack during its opening-game win over Furman. La Salle was ranked as high as seventh by the Associated Press before fading down the stretch and losing unexpectedly to Syracuse 87–83 in overtime in the first round of the NCAA Tournament at the Palestra to finish with a 22–7 record.

"They were a special group of guys," Westhead said. "Joe Bryant was, in some respects, like Kenny Durrett. He became the Pied Piper. If he had a great game, he could win it for you. He was a very talented guy who won big games for us and yet always had that little flair about him. Billy Taylor was kind of a silent performer. You didn't notice him but the next thing you knew, he had 25 points." Bryant, the MVP of the Sugar Bowl Classic, played only two years at La Salle but made the All Big 5 team both times. A first-round draft pick of Philadelphia, he played in the NBA for eight years with the 76ers, San Diego, and Houston before coaching and playing for a decade in Italy, Spain, and France. His son, Kobe, is now an NBA All Star with the champion Los Angeles Lakers.

The Westhead era at La Salle included a pair of future Big 5 Hall of Fame members from New Jersey. Crawford led the team in scoring and rebounding in 1971–72. Charlie Wise, the Big 5's MVP in 1975–76, scored a career high 29 to trigger the Explorers' only city series win that year, 75–72 over Villanova. "As explosive and demonstrative as Michael Brooks was," recalled Westhead, "Jim Crawford was the opposite. He was silent and quiet but lethal against other teams. In his early days, he was so quick and such a great jumper that

sometimes he would shoot the ball from 12 feet out and purposely miss because he then could explode, get it, and put it back." "I did have jumping ability," explained Crawford, who had been recruited by Tom Gola, his boyhood idol, out of Camden Catholic High School, where he coaches today. "Paul taught me every time I shot the ball I should assume that I was going to miss. Therefore, I was always ready to follow up."

Westhead still talks about the spectacular play made by the 6'4" Crawford, who was known as "Skyman," during La Salle's big upset over Villanova in 1971. "Howard Porter was a man among boys taking his classic 18-foot jump shot," Paul explained. "He lifted up like he was above everybody. You didn't see it, but coming off to the side as Howard releases the ball, Jim Crawford goes flying up in the air and *Whack*! He puts the ball in the fifth row."

Wise, who later played professionally in New Zealand, reminded Westhead of former guards Darryl Gladden and Greg Cannon—"tough hard-nosed guy who would lead your team, punch the ball through difficult situations, and help you win." Gladden pulled out a number of games for the Explorers, none more dramatic than his two free throws in the last three seconds to beat Villanova 71–70 in 1977. His 27-foot jump shot at the buzzer beat Temple 73–72 in the 1978 ECC championship game.

Tony DiLeo, a transfer from Tennessee Tech, made the big play to set up Gladden's heroics. The 6-foot guard, who is now the Philadelphia 76ers' director of scouting, tied up Villanova's Keith Herron after the 6'6" Wildcat forward had grabbed a rebound in the closing seconds. "During a time out, I said, 'I'm just going to go up and try to knock his arm as far as I can so he can't tip it,' DiLeo recalled. "I went up and went for the ball but I really knocked his arm and the ball went to Darrell."

Then there was one of the Big 5's most underrated backcourt combinations—Kevin Lynam and Greg Webster—who played together for eight years, four of them at Archbishop Carroll High School, in suburban Philadelphia. Webster came to La Salle on a partial golf scholarship. Lynam came *not* highly recommended by his brother, Jim, who was one of Westhead's teammates at St. Joseph's. But Kevin did receive a glowing endorsement from Bill McDonough, who had coached both players in summer leagues. "I called my friend Jim, and asked, 'What about your younger brother?' recalled

> ▶ **C**harlie Wise was MVP of the Big 5 in 1975–76 when he sparked La Salle to its only city series triumph with a career high 29 points against Villanova. *(La Salle University)*

Westhead. He said, 'He's a good kid and he's a pretty good player, but he's not good enough to play in the Big 5.' I didn't disbelieve Jim, but maybe it was because we had a scholarship and we needed a guy who could shoot the ball. I pursued it and he decided to come. Kevin was a lot like Jimmy Crawford. He didn't say much but, boy, he could play and he could make big shots. Webster turned out to be a tough little point guard. At the time, they said he's too small and a better golfer than he is a basketball player, but he was a terrific player. That was the best combination I ever got without doing anything other than making a phone call."

Kevin Lynam, who made All Big 5 in his senior year, had no problem playing in the shadow of his more-prominent brother, who by now was coaching the archrival Hawks. "I always looked up to him for his accomplishments," explained Kevin, who was 18 years younger than Jim, the oldest of eleven children. Kevin was number ten. "He was at the top of the mountain and we were always trying to get to his bootstraps, always trying to beat him one-on-one, and that kind of thing. It wasn't like I was trying to top him or anything like that." Kevin's biggest moment at the Palestra came early in his senior year when he drilled a jump shot at the buzzer to beat Villanova 84–83 in a triple overtime marathon that went well past midnight.

"We were the perfect complement to one another," recalled Webster, who converted two consecutive one-and-ones in the last minute to help seal La Salle's first win ever over Notre Dame, 62–60 in 1980. "Kev was a great shooter and scorer and I was a much more natural point guard. My game was defense and directing people. It made it easier because we had defined rolls. Just from years of playing together, by the time we got to La Salle, we intuitively knew each other's moves so well that we knew exactly what one another was going to do."

Recruiting Michael Brooks, however, was a far more challenging matter for Westhead. At Philadelphia's West Catholic High School, Brooks had gone from being the *last* man on his freshman team to a *starter* on the varsity as a sophomore. But going into his senior year, the future Big 5 Hall of Famer still played in relative obscurity. That's because a few blocks away at West Philadelphia High, Gene Banks was grabbing all the headlines as the most sought-after player in the nation. "All the La Salle alums who talked to me were all excited about Gene Banks," recalled Westhead. "I tried to make inroads into that situation and got absolutely nowhere. His high school coach, Joey Goldenberg, was a good friend of mine: *'Oh, you know, Paul, I'd like to help you out, but basically Gene isn't interested.'* I can remember the La Salle people were befuddled why such a terrific program, with the tradi-

tion of people like Tom Gola, couldn't get involved with Gene Banks."

Westhead and his coaches then shifted their focus completely to Brooks. " La Salle showed the most interest from the beginning," he recalled. "We literally went to every game that Michael played in his senior year. We got to know his mom, his family, the people at West Catholic. When he began showing how good he was, it was too late for a lot of schools to come in and try and sweep him away." Late that season, West Catholic played in a tournament in Cumberland, Maryland. "It was about a six-hour ride from Philly," said Westhead. "I got in my car and arrived there with two seconds to go in the game. Michael was on the free throw line and he made a foul shot to win it. Afterwards, I went down into the locker room, said hello to him, and said, 'Great foul shot!' He said, 'Thanks a lot, coach.' I went back in my car and drove six hours home. A twelve-hour ride for two seconds. That signifies what we were willing to do to show him that we really cared."

At the beginning of his La Salle career, recalled Westhead, Brooks was a talent in the process of exploding. "And I mean that in a good sense," the coach explained. "He was bubbling with talent and it was almost out of control. From his freshman through his sophomore year, you never really knew what was going to happen when you put him out on the court. He was like a dynamo. He would just run, jump, score, twist, turn. He might make seven or eight baskets in a row before the opposition even saw him, he was doing it so quickly. Yet, on the other hand, he might throw the ball into the stands or foul people, or do something that he never had a chance to think about because it was already done. He would act before he thought which, in the game of basketball, if you have enough talent, frequently that's not bad. Because you're acting before the other team even knows what you had on your mind. As his career blossomed, Michael began to figure things out and play with more control and pace, but never giving up his explosiveness. That's what really made him the great player that he was."

That talent also allowed Westhead to unveil the "System," which became his coaching signature throughout his NBA career in Los Angeles, Chicago, and Denver, as well as with George Mason and Loyola Marymount Universities. Paul had picked up the concept from Sonny Allen, who was running the System at Southern Methodist University. After La Salle beat the Mustangs in the 1976 Volunteer Classic, Westhead brought the SMU coach to Philadelphia to explain it to his team. "We tried to get our players to just run relentless fast breaks and beat people with our speed," said Westhead, who frequently referred to his System as "Showtime." "Sometimes we had terrific success with people like Michael Brooks who just outran people. It was very accommodating for players like Kurt Kanaskie and Kevin Lynam, who could get down the court and spot up. If you go fast enough, it exploits teams that just aren't ready to be in a good defensive mode. Therefore, you get good quick open shots. It's one of the things that will get you hired or get you fired because when it works it's really good, but when it doesn't work it's really bad. If you have players who are really committed to it, and can shoot and rebound, you can beat anybody. If you have players who can't make open shots and just won't run hard enough, you won't."

The System backfired on La Salle in the first round of the 1978 NCAA Tournament against Villanova when the Wildcats won 103–97 at the Palestra. "That game typified both the good and the bad," said Westhead. "It was an explosive, fast game. We were running and scoring and causing all kinds of problems for Villanova. The downside is that Villanova, who much preferred to play a tighter game, more of a halfcourt defensive battle, got caught up in it and found some success in running against us. Normally when a team that is not accustomed to doing it gets caught in that game and it's like a little fool's gold. They start playing the speed game and they say, 'Hey, this is easy!' But over the forty minutes it catches them like a marathoner going out too fast. By mile 21 he can hardly walk, let alone finish the race. That particular game typified what we were about. We did exactly what we wanted to do. We got Villanova in a speed game and it just turned out that we lost."

Brooks and Banks faced each other only once during their college careers, with Banks getting the edge in scoring 24 to 16 and Brooks winning the rebounding battle 16 to 13. That game, won by Duke 91–81 at the Spectrum in 1978, was played in such a raging blizzard that La Salle almost didn't get out of Syracuse, where they had lost to the Orangemen two nights earlier. Their flight finally touched down in Philadelphia at 5 A.M., only hours before the afternoon game was scheduled to begin. The following season, when Duke was ranked No. 1 in the nation, the Blue Devils beat La Salle 66–42 in Durham, but Brooks was forced to sit the game out with a thigh injury.

The first Duke—La Salle contest featured another sideshow—Westhead's "Box and None" defense. The gimmick worked so effectively that the Explorers were able to cut a 15-point deficit down to five before the deeper and more talented Blue Devils pulled away. With about ten minutes to go in the game, Westhead sent Kanaskie up court to try to steal the ball. If he missed, he was to stay there. He never came back down on defense, so at that point, La Salle was playing four guys against five. Then when the Explorers got possession,

either after a make or a miss, they'd throw the ball down to Kanaskie. "Let's say we made a basket," explained Westhead. "Duke would put the ball in play and walk it down in a methodical manner. Kanaskie would play the ball-handler full-court. Somewhere before reaching the mid-court line, he would make an attempt to steal the ball. He *had* to steal the ball. It wouldn't be like, *I'll wait until this guy fumbles around and I'll try and steal it.* He would run at him like a matador and a bull, and if he had the good fortune to steal it, we'd love that. But if he missed, we didn't care because we wanted him to separate himself from the ball. So it works and we cut into the lead." With about 4:30 left in the game, Kanaskie attempted again to steal the ball. It didn't work and Kurt ended up standing 20 feet behind the Duke dribbler, who was not moving. As Westhead recalled, "Kurt yells down to me because the ball's coming in our direction, 'Coach, coach, let me go back and play defense. We have a chance to win this game!' I said, 'Kurt, you stay where you are, I *command* you to stay there. You never wanted to play defense anyway.' This defense, as crazy as it was, was working. In the last three minutes or so we went back into a standard defense and eventually lost the game, but it was interesting and humorous because here was this guy dying to play defense."

"That's a true story because, defensively, I didn't have a clue," said Kanaskie, who is now the coach at Drake University. "I really enjoyed playing for Paul because he just let us play. It takes a lot of guts to sit on the bench and let your players go up and down and play that quickly and have no control of what really happens, because once the game started we just shot as quickly as we could. I thought it demonstrated great confidence in his players." Westhead considered Kanaskie one of the "toughest, hard-nosed players" he ever coached. "When you aren't very quick, not very fast, not very physically strong, you better play hard," said Kanaskie, the most accurate single season free-throw shooter in La Salle's history.

One time in a game eventually won by Temple, the Owls were up by eight points and playing conservatively late in the first half when Westhead deployed his "Box-and-none" and sent Steve Baruffi down court. The Owls didn't bite and continued to pass the ball around against four defenders. Westhead sent another player down and Temple still didn't attempt to score. Then a third player went down and finally when it was five-on-two, Temple's Ricky Reed tried to drive the basket and promptly bounced the ball off his knee out of bounds. "I felt sorry for Don Casey because this was a full house and everybody starts booing Temple," said Westhead. "The whole tempo of the crowd changed when we did this. Afterwards, Casey says, 'I do the best thing. I win the game. I out-coach you and everybody's booing me. What the hell's going on?'"

Lefty Ervin, who had served as his assistant for seven years, replaced Westhead in 1979–80 when Paul resigned to join the Los Angeles Lakers. The Explorers went 22–8 before losing to Purdue 90–82 in West Lafayette, Indiana, in the first round of the NCAA Tournament. That was the last year the NCAA permitted teams to host NCAA regional games on their home courts. Led by All-America Joe Barry Carroll, the Boilermakers went all the way to the NCAA Final Four that year. "That was my best team," Ervin said. "Brooks was so phenomenal and we had three of the smartest guards in the country with Kanaskie, Lynam and Webster. Stan Williams was an unbelievably underrated 6'7" power forward; Mo Connelly at 6'7" was flat-out a great shooter, and we had Don Word, a 6'5" jumping jack, coming off the bench."

▼ **D**ave "Lefty" Ervin, who played for La Salle, served as assistant under Tom Gola and Paul Westhead before becoming the Explorers' head coach in 1979. *(La Salle University)*

Kanaskie helped engineer the Explorers' two biggest wins that year over Notre Dame and Alabama. "As a Catholic kid growing up, I always wanted to play for Notre Dame," Kurt recalled. "I'd practice in the back yard using the names of famous players like Duck Williams and Austin Carr." Kanaskie hit seven of eleven field goal attempts and made a crucial free throw with nine seconds left to clinch La Salle's upset over the eighth-ranked Irish 62–60. Kanaskie also made a spectacular play at the end to beat Alabama 82–80 at Tuscaloosa. With five seconds to go, the ball was inbounded to Kurt. "He starts up the right side and thirteen thousand people are going nuts," recalled Ervin. "One of Alabama's guards cuts him off and he goes behind his back to the left side. Another guard swipes at the ball and Kurt goes behind his back again, this time with his left hand. He gets it over half-court and from 38 feet shoots a jump shot that went *swish*. Alabama's coach, C. M. Newton, came up to me and said, 'That was one of the greatest plays I ever saw.'"

"To be able to win at the end like that was something special because we dedicated that game to Jim Wolkiewicz," said Kanaskie, referring to the co-captain

of La Salle's 1977–78 team, along with Joe Mihalich. Although he later recovered, Wolkiewicz was fighting for his life at the time in a Philadelphia hospital. He had been shot as an innocent bystander in a bar a few days earlier.

Early that season, Brooks put on the most spectacular offensive show ever displayed by a Big 5 player in a road game. It came during a triple-overtime 108–106 loss to Brigham Young in the championship game of the Cougar Classic in Provo, Utah. Michael scored 28 straight La Salle points during one stretch and finished with 51. When Brooks was announced as the tournament's MVP, 22,000 fans rose and gave him a prolonged standing ovation. Michael stood there, tears rolling down his cheeks, then slowly turned to face each of the four sides of the cavernous arena as the applause cascaded down. "I'll never forget that scene," said Ervin. "People were crying. I took a team back there a few years later and they were still talking about it."

By the time his La Salle career ended, Brooks was a consensus All-America and National Player of the Year. Twice he was named Big 5 MVP. He also shares the distinction with Lionel Simmons, Villanova's John Pinone, and Temple's Mark Macon as the only players to make All Big 5 *four* times. "He showed me some moves I didn't know existed," said Villanova's Alex Bradley. Between his junior and senior year, Brooks played on the U.S. team that won the gold medal in the Pan American Games, where he earned the praise of coach Bobby Knight. "If I were allowed to start my own team tomorrow the first person I would pick is Michael Brooks," Knight wrote afterwards in a letter to La Salle's sports information director Lawrence Fan, "a great kid and one hell of a basketball player." Later, Brooks captained the 1980 U.S. Olympic team. Unfortunately, that squad never had the

▶ La Salle All-America Michael Brooks was National Player of the Year and MVP of the Big 5 in 1979–80 and was named captain of the 1980 U.S. Olympic team. *(La Salle University)*

opportunity to showcase itself in Moscow because of the U.S. boycott over the USSR's invasion of Afghanistan. Brooks went on the play for eight years in the NBA with San Diego, Indiana, and Denver but never achieved his full potential because of knee injuries. He later played and coached for many years in Europe.

In 1983, Ervin guided the Explorers to their first post-season victory in 28 years when they beat Rick Pitino's Boston University team 70–58 in an NCAA preliminary round game at the Palestra. La Salle hadn't won in the NCAA or NIT since 1955 when it beat Iowa in the NCAA national semifinals. Ironically, there was a Greenberg in La Salle's lineup both times—Charley in '55 and his nephew, Chip, in '83. The Explorers lost to Virginia Commonwealth in the next round of the NCAA playoffs despite an outstanding performance by Chip Greenberg's backcourt running mate, Steve Black. The 6'4" sophomore scored 23 of his 31 points in the second half of the 76–67 loss to Virginia Commonwealth. "Chip Greenberg was one of the greatest complements to my game," explained Black. "We were meant for each other. We didn't even have to look at each other and Chip would hit me with at least two alley-oops a game. We'd catch the defense sleeping."

"Chip had the best set of hands of any guy I ever played with, even in the NBA," said Tim Legler, who went on to become the most accurate three-point shooter in La Salle's history. "He just was amazing at stripping the ball from people. If he got his hands on the ball, a loose ball or something, it was his. You could guarantee that." Although he was only 6'4", Greenberg led the Explorers in scoring *and* rebounding in 1985–86.

Black, a member of the Big 5 Hall of Fame, was hampered by ankle and foot injuries throughout his career. "Oh, what a great shooter he was," said Ervin. "Abso-

◄ **S**teve Black led the nation's freshmen in scoring in 1981–82 and set a Big 5 record the following season with 40 points against Temple. *(La Salle University)*

lutely one of the best. If he didn't have weak ankles, he would have been a great NBA player." Black, who later played professionally in Europe for eight years, led the nation's freshmen in scoring in 1981–82. He had 28 points to lead the Explorers to their only city series win that year, 76–75 over Penn in his very first Big 5 game.

After being named MVP of the 1982–83 Milwaukee Classic, Black and his La Salle teammates traveled to Western Kentucky, where they beat the Hilltoppers 62–56 for one of the Explorers' rare victories in Bowling Green. Early in the game, Black sprained his ankle. He stayed on the bench but couldn't walk. Late in the second half, Greenberg got fouled, fell and broke his shooting hand. "I told the referee that Chip can't shoot," said Ervin. He said, 'You can put anybody on your bench in to shoot for him.' I look over and see Stevie Black sitting there with a sprained ankle that might be broken. I said, 'Stevie, can you get to the foul line?' He said, 'Yeh, I think I can.' His teammates carry him to the foul line. He stands on one foot and makes two shots." While this was unfolding, Western Kentucky coach Clem Haskins moved over next to Lefty at mid-court and said, 'I can't believe what you're doing here.' I said, 'I know,'" replied Lefty. 'Isn't this unbelievable, Clem?' But then Stevie had to stay in the game and play. We fouled immediately and they carry him back off the court and we win the game."

Black and Temple's Terence Stansbury waged two of the most memorable individual battles in Big 5 history. "We couldn't stand each other on the court but loved each other off the court," explained Black. "When we played each other it was like looking in the mirror." Black got the upper hand the first time as a sophomore by scoring a Big 5 single-game record 40 points, but the Owls won 84–79 before 17,583 fans at the Spectrum. Stansbury guarded Black and had 33. "That was a war," said Black. "I felt like I couldn't be stopped that night." The following year, the Explorers tied Temple for the 1983–84 Big 5 title by pulling out a double overtime 80–79 win. Stansbury sent the game into overtime with a 28-foot shot at the buzzer and Black put La Salle ahead for good with a 15-foot baseline jumper. "That was one of the greatest games the Palestra has ever seen," said Black. "It was like a heavyweight battle, a classic, a chess match." The Explorers had beaten Villanova and Penn earlier that season. Playing on a bad ankle that hampered him all year, Greenberg had 18 points and nine assists against the Wildcats. Albert "Truck" Butts triggered the win over the Quakers with 25 points.

Ralph Lewis, a junior from Philadelphia's Frankford High School, came out of nowhere to lead the Explorers in scoring and rebounding and win the Big 5 MVP award that year. "The greatest walk-on since Neil Armstrong," said La Salle's assistant coach Joe Mihalich. Lewis played in the Sonny Hill League for Steve Black's dad, Bob, who recommended him to Ervin. "He was a 6'6" stallion who just improved every day," said Lefty, who guided La Salle to a 20–11 record that included a 75–71 loss to Pitt in the opening round of the NIT. "Ralph Lewis was the hardest worker I played with at La Salle," said Legler. "He won every single sprint in practice. He always wanted to be first in every single drill." Lewis, a Big 5 Hall of Famer, worked his way into the NBA, where he played for three years with Detroit and Charlotte. "Lewis epitomized what you see in a Big 5 player," said Greenberg. "If you looked at our team coming out of high school, I would probably say that Ralph was the seventh or eighth guy you would think would ever make it in the NBA."

With their top seven players expected to return—and another future Big 5 Hall of Famer joining the team as a freshman—hopes were sky-high for the Explorers in 1984–85. In addition to Black, Greenberg, and defensive specialist Gary Jones in the backcourt, La Salle had a formidable front line. Lewis and 6'7" Larry Koretz flanked Butts, a rugged 6'9" veteran center who provided a dozen points and rebounds a game. Joining the team was Legler, a 6'5" freshman who would later become a Big 5 Hall of Famer. Two weeks into pre-season practice, however, La Salle learned that it would not have the services of Butts. Earlier, the NCAA had declared him ineligible for his senior season because he had played a second year of prep school after his 20th birthday at Frederick Military Academy, in Virginia. La Salle appealed the ruling, but it was thrown out by a federal court in Philadelphia. Although there were a few bright spots—Black and Lewis combined for 45 points to trigger a 74–69 win over St. Joseph's— La Salle struggled to a 15–13 record. "We were irreparably harmed," said Ervin. "We would have won 25 games that year. Butts would have been a top draft pick. His physicality was absolutely NBA."

"The person I felt most sorry for was Lefty because he worked his butt off assembling this team," said Black. "This was the team that was going to put him on the map because we would have been nationally ranked. Butts was our enforcer. Losing him took the air out of us." Indeed it did. The Explorers were upset in overtime by Army in the first round of the Metro Atlantic Tournament that year. They suffered the same fate at the hands of Holy Cross the following season, when they finished with a 14–14 record. Despite a late season win over 15th-ranked St. Joseph's behind Legler's 22 points, Lefty was done as La Salle's head coach after that.

LA SALLE'S SPEEDY, LEFTY, AND "SHAKESPEARE" • 169

Time was critical in quickly finding a successor to Ervin early that spring in 1986. That's because La Salle was deeply involved in recruiting one of the nation's hottest prospects, Lionel Simmons, who had been leaning toward the Explorers. But Temple, with Bill Cosby lending an influential hand, and Villanova, riding the crest of its national championship, were making late bids for the South Philadelphia High School star. Athletic director Bill Bradshaw realized that La Salle couldn't afford wasting three or four weeks to find a new coach. Besides, he had a good candidate in the wings—Bill "Speedy" Morris—who had just completed his second year as the Explorers' first full-time women's coach by taking them to their first NCAA Tournament. Morris had been a legendary coach at Philadelphia's Roman Catholic High and Penn Charter School for 16 years before that. After convincing La Salle's president, Brother Patrick Ellis, of the urgency of the situation, Bradshaw gave an impassioned speech to the university's athletic committee, explaining how Morris had turned the women's program around and warning that the Explorers could lose Simmons if they decided to initiate a lengthy search for a coach instead of hiring Speedy.

"I left the room and the committee voted fourteen to one to search," Bradshaw recalled. "When I came out, Brother Pat said to me, 'Boy, Bill, it's a good thing you gave such a great speech. Imagine if you didn't. It would have been fifteen to zero.'" Bradshaw then urged La Salle's president to overturn the athletic committee and hire Speedy. "I was very much attracted by his whole coaching style, but there was some question about his not having a college degree," said Brother Ellis. A number of advisors and trustees were consulted and Morris was hired the next day, making him the only Division I coach to make the transition from a women's to a men's program. Shortly thereafter, Lionel Simmons announced his college decision. He was becoming an Explorer. It was a perfect match from the beginning.

From that point until the 1991–92 season—the year after the Big 5 round-robin ended—Morris equaled Ken Loeffler's post-season record by guiding the Explorers to either the NIT or NCAA Tournaments six straight seasons. He is the only La Salle coach ever to take three straight teams to the NCAA playoffs. Only three other Division I coaches won a hundred games in their first four seasons as quickly as Speedy, who was voted Eastern College Coach of the Year in 1990. The Explorers went 30–2 that year, not only an all-time school record, but

◀ **R**alph Lewis grabs a rebound against Holy Cross as Larry Koretz watches. Lewis was Big 5 MVP in 1983–84. (*La Salle University*)

the most wins by any major college that season. La Salle lost only six of 64 games during Simmons's final two years, and its 22-game winning streak in 1989–90 still stands as an all-time school record.

By the time the 1986–87-basketball season rolled around, Bradshaw had become athletic director at DePaul University. Before he arrived in Chicago, however, he pulled off a maneuver that has probably never been done in college athletics. As the AD officially representing each school, he signed *both* copies of the contract agreeing to the details of the basketball game between the Blue Demons and Explorers scheduled to be played at the Palestra the following January. "I found some unfinished business in my briefcase when I was flying to the press conference announcing my appointment as DePaul's AD," Bradshaw recalled. "One of the items was this contract that had been signed by Bill Bradshaw *from La Salle*, but had not been signed by anyone from DePaul. It outlined the referees and the TV and radio details, but I discovered that it included some things that weren't too fair to DePaul. For example, I realized that both officials had been assigned from the ECAC, so I changed the contract and made it a split crew." This meant that an official from the Midwest would be assigned to join a referee from the East. By the time DePaul came into the Palestra to face the Explorers, the Blue Demons were 16–0 and ranked third in the country. "I remember one of those split crews making an intentional foul call on La Salle at the end of the game that Speedy wasn't too happy with," said Bradshaw. "But I sat there and quietly thought, *pretty good timing*." DePaul won the game 58–54.

The Explorers went all the way to the NIT championship game in Speedy's first year. Just being invited to the tournament, where they became the first La Salle team in 35 years to win an NIT game, was a surprise, especially since they had been eliminated in the first round of the Metro Atlantic Tournament by Fairfield. "We were all but dead after that game," recalled Legler, who had scored 25 points and played the best game of his career earlier that season in a 79–72 loss to No.1 North Carolina. "We were ready to go home for spring break."

Playing in his first post-season game as a freshman, Simmons calmly drove the length of the court and sank a jump shot in the final six seconds to eliminate Villanova 86–84 in the opening round at duPont Pavilion. La Salle then won at Niagara 89–81. Simmons fractured his nose late in the first half but came back to finish with 23 points. Craig Conlin, the Explorers' all-time field goal percentage leader, chipped in with 20 against the Purple Eagles. La Salle then played its best defensive game of the season and defeated Illinois State

70–50 at the Palestra, as the "I-Train" scored 18 points and grabbed 15 rebounds. The Explorers were even more devastating in a 92–73 win against Arkansas-Little Rock in the semifinals at Madison Square Garden. La Salle made its first five shots of the game, all three-pointers. Larry Koretz, the only senior in the starting lineup who never missed a game in four years, hit two. Then Rich Tarr and Legler connected and the Explorers were off to a 12–2 lead. Legler finished with 26 points and Tarr, who did an outstanding job all year at point guard, finished with a career high 23.

With 30 bus-loads of fans coming from La Salle and hundreds of others traveling by automobile and train to the Garden, the Explorers saw their Cinderella dream finally end with a 84–80 loss to a good Southern Mississippi team in the championship game. La Salle connected on only three of its first 18 shots and missed 12 field goal attempts in a row after coming back to take its only lead of the second half 44–43. The Explorers trailed by ten points with 2:39 left but refused to give up. "I remember that game pretty vividly," said Legler. "We were down two with the ball and 30 seconds left. We drew up a play to get a three-pointer, but we ended up throwing the ball away and never got a shot off. We had the ball underneath the basket and set a screen. Richie Tarr came up to the left wing and caught the ball at the three-point line. He jumped up to shoot, but at the last second he thought he saw Lionel under the basket. As he jumped to shoot, he passed it to Lionel. But Lionel was turning to block out and get a rebound because he thought Richie was shooting the ball." The ball ended up in the hands of a Southern Mississippi player, who was fouled and made both free throws. Simmons, who had 34 points, and Tarr, who added 14, both made the All Tournament team.

The Explorers won 24 and 26 games, respectively, the next two years. Each season ended with NCAA opening-round losses, first to Kansas State, then Louisiana Tech. In 1987–88, they won all 17 Metro Atlantic Conference games, becoming the first team in league history to go unbeaten. In 1988–89, only Temple prevented the Explorers from winning their first outright Big 5 title in 14 years. They did grab a share of the crown, however. First, they beat St. Joseph's 81–57—their widest victory margin over the Hawks since the Gola era. Then they defeated Penn en route to the Jostens Tournament title as Simmons scored 32 points

and, finally, Villanova in overtime when Lionel grabbed 21 rebounds.

By then, Morris had discovered a new weapon that had just been legalized by the NCAA the year he got the men's job. At first, recalled *Philadelphia Daily News* sportswriter Dick Jerardi, "Speedy hated the three-point shot. But he looked around and saw the kinds of players he had. He saw how the game was evolving and, of course, he later became known as a guy who loved the three." With players like Tarr, who led the Explorers in that category the first year, Legler, Simmons, Jack Hurd, Doug Overton, and Randy Woods, it's no wonder that Speedy started playing a more wide-open game. "Speedy just got better and better as time went on," said Jerardi. "He understood that the game had changed and that's hard for a lot of coaches. His teams were always fun to watch. They always ran and pressed."

And scored! Never better than New Year's Eve, 1990 when Woods (46) and Overton (45) set an NCAA record with 91 combined points as La Salle beat Paul Westhead's Loyola Marymount team 133–118 in Los Angeles. "My philosophy is 'Never up, never in,'" explained Morris. "I still have a philosophy that you should only take shots that you can make, but we were blessed with some really great shooters and when you have people like that, you've got to get them shots."

La Salle's most accurate long-range shooter was Legler, who surprised everybody by going on to play for six different teams in the NBA. As a member of the Washington Bullets in 1996, he captured the league's three-point title by connecting on an amazing 52 of 75 shots during the competition at the NBA All Star game. "I remember the first time John Chaney saw Tim Legler take a jump shot," said Bradshaw. "Like a guy who's been around a race track and discovered a colt, Chaney just turned around and looked at me—I don't know where I was or who we were playing—and said, 'Will you look at how that young man squares up and shoots that ball?' It was almost like Apollo Creed looking at the tape of Rocky when he was hitting the side of the beef with his left hand and all the guys around him were yelling and screaming, and he went, 'Oh my God! Will you look at him square those shoulders.' And for the first time I looked at Legler differently, not having the trained eye and instincts that Chaney has. He saw that talent in a kid coming off the bench, a little-used freshman who years later wins the NBA three-point contest."

Hurd also won a number of games for La Salle with his three-point shooting. The most pulsating came late in his freshman year, 1988–89, when he scored 19 points and clinched a 101–100 win over 12th-ranked Florida State in a nationally televised game at the Palestra. "Jack was a clutch player," recalled Morris. "Even as a freshman he was not afraid to take a big shot. If he missed a shot,

he wasn't afraid to come right back and take another one. I remember Florida State scored eight in a row late in the game to cut our lead to one point. Hurd had missed two straight shots. Then he came down and hit a three-pointer, came back and got fouled and made both fouls."

Simmons had another one of his spectacular games with 36 points and 10 rebounds. Overton, who holds La Salle's all-time records in steals and assists, had 17 points and directed the offense superbly against the Seminoles. "That was the breakout game for me," recalled the 6'3" guard, who had been playing in Simmons' shadow. "That game put me on the map on the national scene." Both Hurd and Overton are in the Big 5 Hall of Fame. Overton made the All Big 5 team three times and went on to play for nine years in the NBA with Washington, Denver, Philadelphia, New Jersey, Orlando and Boston. "You could tell from the first day he walked into the gym that Doug was a very confident young man who really believed in himself," said Morris. "He's probably the most humorous kid I ever coached, a very funny kid. He would lighten up the team on many a road trip."

Simmons was the National Player of the Year in 1989–90. Lionel scored his career high of 40 at Manhattan and finished with 3,217 points, making him the third highest Division I scorer in history. He was named MVP of *five* mid-season tournaments, including the 1989 Sugar Bowl Classic when the Explorers beat Ohio State and Florida. La Salle swept the Big 5 for the first time in 15 years, edging both Villanova and Temple by a point. Randy Woods had 13 of his 15 points in the second half and clinched the 71–70 win over the Wildcats with a pair of free throws with 2.1 seconds left. Simmons had 23 points in the 63–62 win over the Owls as Overton sealed it with two free throws right before the buzzer.

"Lionel just made us all better," said Overton, who recalled that he and his Explorer teammates were quite relieved when Simmons decided to forgo the NBA and return to La Salle for his senior year. "We were concerned whether he was going to leave and there was no doubt in our minds that we were going to have a great team when he came back. When I first got to La Salle I really didn't know if I had the goods and the skills to play in the NBA. But after playing with Lionel and seeing how driven he was, I wanted to get better and realized that I had a chance to follow him."

"Everybody knew that Lionel was good, but no one

could have predicted that he's be the player he turned out to be," said Morris. "But every year he got better. His numbers are just unbelievable. He had a tremendous work ethic, he was unselfish, and he was a good defender." Morris once told sportswriter Frank Bilovsky that Simmons reminded him of Tom Gola, Ken Durrett and Michael Brooks all rolled into one—with a little Dr. J thrown in. "His catlike quickness around the basket reminds me of Brooks," explained Morris. "His rebounding reminds me of Gola. And the way he's handling the basketball and bringing it up reminds me of Durrett. And with Durrett, if he doesn't tear up his knee his senior year, you're talking in the same vein as Julius Erving."

Simmons played professionally in Sacramento for seven years. "I'm convinced that he would have had a solid ten- or twelve-year NBA career if his knees didn't go bad," said Jerardi. "He was in the Larry Bird–Charles Barkley mold as a passing forward. He had over a hundred assists the year he was National Player of the Year. That just shows how smart and how savvy he was about the game."

At one point during Simmons' career, La Salle won 55 of 56 Metro Atlantic Conference games, losing only to St. Peter's at the buzzer at the Palestra. Only an early January 121–116 loss to Loyola Marymount kept eleventh-ranked La Salle from its first unbeaten regular season during Lionel's senior year. Overton's former high school teammates at Philadelphia's Dobbins Tech—Hank Gathers, the NCAA's leading scorer the previous year, and Bo Kimble—electrified the Philadelphia Civic Center crowd that night, only two months before Gathers died tragically during a game in California. His death happened during the Explorers' 106–90 win over Siena in the semifinals of the MAC Tournament. La Salle's players were devastated when they heard the news, especially Overton and Simmons, who had played with and against him in the Public League.

"I don't know if people realize how close Lionel and Doug were with Hank," said Morris. "They worked out and lived with each other all summer. It was like losing a member of their family. I said to the young people, if they don't feel like playing, it's up to them and I'll understand." La Salle was scheduled to play Fordham for the conference title. Soon Rams' coach Nick Macarchuk was on the phone with Speedy. "He called me in my hotel room and said, 'Look, you guys finished first. If you don't want to play, there'll be no forfeit and you win.' That was a real classy thing to do. We met a couple of hours later. I let them get their thoughts together and they said that they wanted to play. Which I thought that they would do, anyway."

La Salle beat Fordham 71–61. But the season came crashing to a bitter, disappointing end when the

◀ **La** Salle's Lionel Simmons, a three-time Big 5 MVP, was National Player of the Year in 1990. *(La Salle University)*

Explorers blew a 19-point first-half lead and lost to 17th-ranked Clemson 79–75 in the second round of the NCAA Tournament after eliminating Southern Mississippi easily in the opener. Led by two 6'11" future NBA No. 1 draft picks, Dale Davis and Elden Campbell, the Atlantic Coast Conference champions held La Salle scoreless for almost seven minutes in the second half. "That was the most disappointing loss I've ever coached because it was a game that we had won," said Morris. "It wasn't that we came out flat or turned the ball over. We just couldn't make a shot. We had a great first half and they couldn't handle our press. I was dead sure we could beat Connecticut in the next round so we would have been in the Final Eight playing Duke. Who knows what would have happened, but it would have been great."

Connecticut beat Clemson at the buzzer in the next round before losing a last-second heartbreaker to Duke. The Blue Devils then were beaten by UNLV for the national title. "I was positive that La Salle had Final Four talent that year," said sportswriter Dick Jerardi. "That team was actually good enough to contend for the national title." Ironically, two years later, the NCAA Committee on Infractions ordered that all of Clemson's victories in that 1990 tournament be forfeited because the Tigers had used an ineligible player.

"I thought Speedy was just remarkable that year," said Joe Mihalich, the long-time Explorers' assistant who is now head coach at Niagara University. "That was the best coaching job that I've ever seen. I just marvel about how he motivated all the players and how he pushed the right buttons. We were at Fairfield one time and we got the stat sheet at halftime. Lionel Simmons had something like 18 points, nine rebounds, a couple of blocked shots, and a couple of assists. And Speedy chewed him out! He said, 'You're not playing like an All-American.' It was great because that was exactly what Lionel needed to hear. It motivated him and he played even better. Speedy just had a knack for doing the right thing at the right time."

Overton's importance to the Explorers was never more obvious than in his senior year, 1990–91, when La Salle jumped out to a 16–5 record. "The night before the St. Joe's game, about two minutes before practice ended, he went down with a severely sprained foot," recalled Morris. Overton missed the next seven games and La Salle dropped four of them. "If he stays healthy, we win the MAC and go to another NCAA Tournament," said Speedy. Overton came back for the Explorers' first round game in the NIT, but

Massachusetts pulled it out 93–90 in Amherst with a three-pointer at the buzzer. Doug was the hero in both of La Salle's Big 5 victories that year. He had 35 points in the overtime win over Penn and then combined with Woods for 53 against the Wildcats.

Speedy's final 20-win season came in 1991–92, the year after the Big 5 round-robin ended. Randy Woods, a future Big 5 Hall of Famer, won Big 5 MVP honors and finished as the nation's third-leading three-point shooter and fourth highest scorer with 27.3 points a game. But just like the formal Big 5, La Salle's glory days were over—at least for a while.

▲ **D**oug Overton, a three-time All Big 5 selection, is La Salle's career leader in assists and steals. *(La Salle University)*

Chapter 12

• • • • • • •

The "Ivies" in the Final Four

No Big 5 team dominated a decade as the University of Pennsylvania did under the coaching of Dick Harter, Chuck Daly, and Bob Weinhauer in the 1970s. The Quakers won or shared seven Big 5 titles in that decade and were nationally-ranked seven times. At one stretch, they lost only once in 22 Big 5 games. They never lost an Ivy League game at the Palestra in that period under Harter or Weinhauer. They won 80 percent of their games overall (223–56) and almost pulled off one of the biggest miracles in college basketball in 1979 when they upset North Carolina on the way to becoming only the second Ivy League team ever to make it to the NCAA Tournament Final Four.

As a youngster in Punxsutawney, Pennsylvania, Chuck Daly had already decided what he wanted to do when he grew up. "I told my mother in ninth grade that I wanted to be a college coach and make ten thousand dollars a year," he recalled. Chuck transferred from St. Bonaventure to Bloomsburg State College, where he graduated with a teaching degree in speech. In 1954 he started his coaching career at Punxsutawney High School and immediately began attending every clinic he could find. "We'd be sitting around until 3 or 4 A.M. talking to coaches like Clair Bee, Nat Holman, Frank McGuire, and Press Maravich," Daly said. Maravich's son, Pete, was one of the demonstrators. So was Joe Naimath at clinics at Aliquippa. Wilt Chamberlain was working as a waiter at Kutcher's, in Monticello, New York.

Daly also became a regular at clinics conducted by Duke coach Vic Bubas. When the Blue Devils played in the NCAA Final Four in Louisville, Chuck flew down, bought a seat from a scalper, and watched the tournament from the last row at Freedom Hall. Shortly afterwards, when one of Bubas' assistants left to become head coach at Connecticut, Vic offered Daly the job. The man he replaced was Fred Shabel, who would later become Penn's athletic director. It was Shabel who hired Daly as the Quakers' head coach when Dick Harter left to go to Oregon.

In 1964, his first year as a Duke assistant, Chuck found himself back at the Final Four, this time in Kansas City, where the Blue Devils finished runner-up to unbeaten UCLA. "I love to tell this story to coaches," said Daly, who took a cut in salary to join the Blue Devils. "I go from the last row in Freedom Hall—with a scalper's ticket, to boot, when I didn't even have a hotel room, to sitting on the bench at the Final Four in one year!"

Shabel soon started to weave an indelible thread through Daly's career. Six years later, he helped Chuck make the decision to become head coach at Boston College. "The next thing I know, Fred moved from the coaching position at Connecticut and talked to me about taking that job," Chuck recalled. "But I decided it wasn't for me at that time. Then after my second year at Boston College, one of my assistants, Bob Zuffelato, who later became the BC coach, called Fred about the Penn job. I'm in my office one day and the phone rings. It's Fred and we're talking about Bob and he says, 'By the way would you be interested?' I said, 'As a matter of fact, I would be.' We ended up with an interview."

Before Daly was hired, however, Digger Phelps, who was then coaching at Fordham, said that he was offered the position at Penn. "When Harter left to go to Oregon, Shabel wanted me back and I went down to interview with him," explained Phelps, who is now an analyst on ESPN. "It was a done deal. But I knew Notre Dame was going to open and I just knew if I waited, that was the job I really wanted. About a week went by and I called Fred and said 'No.'"

When he was finally offered the job, it was not a difficult decision for Daly to make. For one thing, it hadn't been easy replacing Bob Cousy, a Boston icon, as coach of the Eagles. "BC had joined the Big East and had become a very good basketball school," Chuck explained. "But, frankly, there was Bruins' hockey, college hockey, the Celtics, baseball, football. You were lucky if your basketball team in Boston could make the seventh or eighth sports page. It was very difficult to recruit because of that strong influence of other sports. And the Big 5 at that time was an incredible basketball league. People don't realize what it meant to be part of the Big 5."

Daly's first move at Penn was to bring in a young new assistant, a defensive specialist named Rollie Massimino, who had recently guided tiny Stony Brook on Long Island to an unbeaten regular season and the university's first appearance in the NCAA Small-College Tournament. The two had become friends during Daly's Boston College days when Rollie was a high school coach in Lexington, Massachusetts. It didn't take Massimino long to have a profound influence, not only on the Quakers, but eventually on Villanova's basketball program and, ultimately, the entire Big 5.

But neither Daly nor Massimino was quite ready for the intensity of the Big 5 when the Quakers took the floor in 1971 for their first city series game before 9,224 screaming fans at the Palestra. When it was over, Temple's wily coach Harry Litwack had again performed magic with his matchup zone as the Owls snapped Penn's 48-game regular-season winning streak 57–52. "It's like everything else in life," recalled Daly. "Until you get in the eye of the storm, you don't realize the intensity. We were left with an outstanding club by Dick Harter. There wasn't any question about the talent. One of the things that I said to Rollie when I hired him as my assistant, 'Let's not screw this up.' But the zone defense is a great equalizer in college basketball—at least it used to be before the three-point shot, before the clock. You had to work so hard to get a shot and usually it was from long-range. If you didn't get second shots, you had no chance against the zone."

From that time on, Daly never missed a Big 5 game. "You watched every one," he said, "because those games, in a lot of ways, were bigger than the leagues you were in—except the league took you somewhere, whereas the Big 5 games didn't. And you found out that it was just incredible to win a game in the Big 5, no matter who was playing whom." Teams like Temple, Daly thought, were from a technical standpoint the most difficult to play against in the Big 5. "The St. Joe's and La Salle's were

▲ **C**huck Daly won or shared four Big 5 titles in six years as head coach of the Quakers. *(University of Pennsylvania)*

more difficult to play against for passion reasons," he added. "They could play the underdog role and they used junk defenses. But they played with such a passion that became a whole other problem. The Big 5 games were highlights on your schedule, the days you marked in advance because you knew you weren't going to sleep well either before or after unless you won."

Daly's Quakers did not lose again in the Big 5 for the next three years. Their 12-game winning streak in city series games, in fact, has never been surpassed. They won or shared four Big 5 titles in Daly's six years at the helm and had four seasons in which they won at least 21 games. And no Penn coach has ever matched Daly's record of four straight NCAA Tournament appearances. Unfortunately, the Quakers always seemed to run into one of the nation's top teams in the post-season. Teams like Providence, which beat Penn 84–69 in 1974. "I remember driving to the basket in that game," said Ed Stefanski, who is now the player personnel director for the New Jersey Nets. "I thought I did a pretty good job getting Marvin Barnes off his feet, and I dished it to John Jablonski. I thought Jabbo had a wide-open lay-up. By the time he went up for it, Marvin was already down, up, and had blocked the shot going the other way. I knew we were in big time trouble. He was a phenomenal basketball player."

Daly's only other regular season loss besides Temple that first season came at Princeton, 69–56. His first trip to the NCAA Tournament resulted in victories over Providence (76–60) and Villanova (78–67). Then the Quakers ran up against another powerhouse North Carolina team in the Eastern Regional finals and lost 73–59 in Morgantown, West Virginia. "Rollie and I were not real experienced in NCAA playoffs and we worked our guys probably a little too hard the day before the game," said Daly. "When I look back on it, at the time it was devastating."

Later that day, between halves of the second game, Hot Rod Hundley invited Daly to be his guest on CBS-TV. "We get ready to go on and he says, 'I'm standing here with . . .'and there's silence. He forgot my name. I said, 'Don't worry about it Rod, it's Chuck Daly.' Then I said, 'And my alumni just forgot my name, too!'"

Corky Calhoun, the Big 5 Co-MVP that year, and Craig Littlepage, who would later coach the Quakers, played for both Harter and Daly. Each player noticed significant differences in their coaching philosophies. "With Dick Harter, it was more like he had his system and he pushed that system," Corky explained. "It was very successful so you really couldn't question it. Chuck Daly would take a look and try to draw out the best part of each person. His system blended around the individuals as opposed to the individuals blending into the system."

"Chuck brought a level of flexibility to his whole approach," recalled Littlepage. "Things did not seem to be quite as tightly structured as they were previously. With Dick, everything was scheduled on a minute-to-minute basis, more calculated in terms of practice, of what was done in the games, and what was done with recruiting. And one of the great things that I remember about Chuck was his willingness to delegate and the degree of autonomy that he gave to Rollie Massimino. Giving Rollie authority and input in team matters, I thought, was a stroke of brilliance on his part."

Midway through his junior year, Littlepage was surprised to learn how much input *he* actually had. The Quakers had been rolling along smoothly in their first ten games under Daly, with only that Temple loss spoiling an otherwise perfect record. Then, in their first game ever in Jadwin Gym, they were ambushed by Princeton, primarily because they could not handle the Tigers' defensive pressure. "Princeton just pressed us all over the place and took the ball away from us," explained Littlepage, who had been a backup center until moving into a starting position in the frontcourt at the beginning of the year. "We were going to be playing them a few weeks later in a rematch at the Palestra, and I had this crazy thought: *Why don't I bring the ball up*

against their center and completely nullify that pressure defense? I could handle the ball pretty well and would probably make pretty good decisions." Littlepage suggested it to Rollie, who discussed it with Chuck, and suddenly, said Craig, "Here I am, the 6'6" center, bringing the ball up against Princeton. Basically we accomplished what we wanted and blew them away."

Bob Bigelow, a 6'7" forward from Boston who blossomed into a Big 5 Hall of Fame player in his senior year, was recruited by Daly when Chuck was coaching at Boston College. "I told him I wasn't interested," Bigelow recalled. "I told him I wanted to go to Penn." Bigelow

▼ **B**ob Bigelow blossomed into an excellent all-around player in his senior year at Penn. *(University of Pennsylvania)*

had been recruited by Harter and actually made his college decision after Dick had left for Oregon. Two weeks later, Daly got the job, "which was fine with me," said Bigelow, who had also played against Massimino's high school team in New England. Bigelow, who later played for four years in the NBA with Kansas City, San Diego, and Boston, actually did not have a great career at Penn until his senior year. "Chuck really liked me as a player and liked my hard work ethic," he recalled. "But I was kind of his whipping boy in practice because he felt that I could take the heat. I had some moments but nothing really worked all that smoothly. By my senior year I finally figured out what they were trying to do. I was more a run-and-gun offensive type player and they were playing it more close to the vest. But that wasn't all that bad, either, because I had a chance to learn some of the other parts of the game. I became a very good defensive player, I became a passer, and got better court sense because I had to learn to play with others. That actually helped develop me as a better all-around player, which probably made me more appealing to the pros."

Daly's obsession with his personal appearance is legendary. "The first time I met Chuck in the early sixties I was overwhelmed by the wardrobe," said Bill Raftery, who was coaching at Fairleigh Dickinson (Madison) at the time. "And he's impeccably dressed to this day. There was a degree of professionalism on the sideline—this was his office and he was going to look the part. Chuck used to take three outfits to every game—wear one in, change into another, then put his suit on for the game."

Bob Weinhauer replaced Massimino on Daly's staff when Rollie took the Villanova job in 1973. The new assistant frequently joined Daly for lunch in Center City Philadelphia during the season, often when the streets were messy with dirty slush and snow. "By the time we got from the car to the restaurant, I'd have slush stains all over my shoes, slush up and down my pants," Weinhauer recalled. "You'd look at Chuck and it's like his shoes were just shined. He never got snow or slush on his shoes. Sometimes we thought he took them off and he walked barefooted. Chuck always set the proper example for us in dress, how to behave, how to react to different situations."

Raftery also was impressed with Daly's administrative skills. "I don't know if there's anybody better at the psychology of the game. He was a great observer of people and I think that's what made him extraordinary. He's one of those guys that you might fool him once. But down the road he's going to figure it out. He had a sensational ability to cut to the chase—nothing extraneous, very little verbiage at practice. He delegated his duties. He always wanted to surround himself with a great staff and he always had exceptional people. He was ahead of his time. I don't think he ever felt uncomfortable if somebody was smarter or knew the game better because I think he felt that he had his own package and wasn't concerned about somebody upstaging or intruding."

After his playing days at Penn, Ray Carazo worked as an assistant to Harter and Daly for three years, then got the head-coaching job at Yale in 1975–76. The team that he inherited was mostly comprised of seniors and wasn't very good. "We only won six games all year," Carazo recalled, "but we upset Penn 46–44 late in the season at the Palestra. It was the greatest damn night of my life. They were fighting for a NIT spot. We only had three wins going into the Palestra and when I came back, they had signs, 'WELCOME BACK, RAY.' St. Joe's was playing Villanova in the second game and the place was sold out." Despite the loss, Daly's Quakers finished with the best overall record (17–9) in the Big 5 that year. But for the only time in Big 5 history, no city team played in a post-season tournament.

Although they performed well during the regular season, none of Daly's next three teams went past the second round of the NCAA Tournament. One bright spot for the Quakers during that time was John Engles, a 6'8", 230-pound center from Staten Island, New York, who still played well enough to make the Big 5 Hall of Fame despite blowing out a knee in a collision with La Salle's Charlie Wise during his junior year. "What a tremendous beast he was," said Bigelow. "He could run all day. He had terrific hands. Once he got into the lane, it was hard getting him out. He and Ron Haigler were both very good low-post players who really complemented each other well. Sometimes when you get two guys like that, they're like oil and water, but Chuck and the guys had them going high post-low post and designed an offense around their two skills. Ron was the slight, skinny scorer who could fit through the cracks, and John was the bull in a china shop, who just ran everybody over."

By now, Daly was getting restless because of the new NCAA rule that allowed freshman to play in varsity competition everywhere *except* the Ivy League. Financial aid was also getting tighter, making it increasingly more difficult for his staff to recruit quality athletes. Over the years, Daly had brought in two highly-regarded assistant coaches. First came Weinhauer, who Chuck remembers as "a very strict, firm, tough-minded coach." Then Bob Staak, who later enjoyed considerable success at Xavier and Wake Forest and as an assistant coach for more than a dozen years in the NBA, took Carazo's place as freshman coach.

Andy Geiger was Penn's athletic director. One day

into Andy Geiger's office and were informed that Chuck was on the way to the NBA. "Bobby Staak and myself are sitting side by side," recalled Weinhauer. "Andy looks across the table and he says, 'And *Bob*, you're going to be the acting head coach.' Well, there's two Bobs sitting there and he never really said which Bob he meant. We kind of looked at each other and he finally said, 'You, Bob Weinhauer, you're going to be the next acting coach. However, don't you tell a soul today. You guys are going to go to practice today and act normal and you're not allowed to tell your wife or your family or anybody because tomorrow we're going to meet with the players and tell them and then we'll have a press conference.'"

After practice, both coaches went home. "Finally at 9 or 10 o'clock at night, I invited Staak over," said Weinhauer. "We stayed up until 4 A.M., planning practices and deciding what we're going to say to the players." The next day, after talking to the team for five minutes, Weinhauer canceled practice and made a quick phone call to Big 5 Hall of Famer Ron Haigler, one of the most prolific scorers in Penn's history. The two-time Big 5 MVP quickly agreed to become his freshman coach. Haigler, a high school All-America in Brooklyn, played for Chuck Daly from 1972–75. He led the Quakers in rebounding three times and scoring twice. "The thing that always impressed me about Ron," recalled teammate Bob Bigelow. "In the heat of the game, I never saw him get flustered. I never heard him swear. He just had that amazing Zen calmness about him. He just minded his Ps and Qs and worked on his wonderful low post-mid post, 15-foot offensive game. In the Big 5 games, he'd just run around and do his thing and he'd always score his 19 points."

Daly said to him, "You know Andy, if we ever went to a scholarship program—which Penn would never do—we would be easily in the top fifteen every year because we could attract that kind of quality player." Obviously Daly knew that wasn't going to happen. "Then we had an eighteen-game winning season and the alumni weren't happy," he recalled. "I wasn't looking for another job but this opportunity with the 76ers came along. I went into it blindly for the same amount of money as I was making here and didn't know where it was going to take me." So in November 1977, ten days before the start of the season, Daly suddenly resigned to become Billy Cunningham's assistant with the Philadelphia 76ers.

Later that afternoon, Daly's two assistants got called

Weinhauer never asked Geiger why he was chosen

▲ Ron Haigler, a two-time Big 5 MVP, returned to Penn as an assistant to Bob Weinhauer. *(Urban Archives, Temple University, Philadelphia, Pennsylvania)*

over Staak, but he vividly remembers the contract negotiations with his athletic director. "By this time I was making about $17,000," Bob recalled. "Andy said, 'I'm going to give you $23,000.' That was a lot more money than I was making, but I sat there and I looked right at him and said, 'No Andy, I want $25,000.' And he said, 'Okay,' but it was like, 'Okay, but *don't* ask for more.'" Six games into the 1977–78 season, Geiger took the interim title away and gave Weinhauer a three-year contract.

It was a lifelong dream come true for the new Quakers' coach, who had been frustrated when he lost out to Mike Krzyzewski for the Army job, then couldn't even get an interview with Drexel when the Dragons hired Eddie Burke. A graduate of Cortland State in New York, he had spent most of his career teaching and coaching at Massapequa High School on Long Island. When he joined Daly's staff four years earlier, he had four children and another one on the way. In high

school he was making approximately $20,000 a year. "I came to Penn for $13,200," Weinhauer recalled. "Here I am coaching at the University of Pennsylvania and my children in school qualified for the free lunch program."

Weinhauer had learned the intricacies of big-time college coaching quickly under the tutelage of Carazo and Daly. "Ray really became my mentor for the first two years," he explained. "Coming out of high school, I had not a clue about recruiting. He taught me about recruiting and about dealing with college athletes. Not that Chuck didn't, but working side by side in an office as big as your bathroom, Ray and I worked together sometimes 16 hours a day on the telephone talking to guidance counselors, coaches, and parents."

Weinhauer was impressed with Daly's understanding of the academic pressures facing the Penn players. He also learned a valuable lesson about Chuck's work ethic. "I spent the first summer at Penn living by myself, " he recalled. "Ray Carazo and I would go to games all over the state and sometimes not get home until 1 or 2 o'clock in the morning. Then we'd be in the office at 8:30. I fell behind one time in my telephone calls and I told Chuck that I was having trouble making connections.' He said to me, 'Bob, you know there are 24 hours in a day and you've got to use all 24 hours.' I never forgot that. He was absolutely correct. When you're in a college coaching game, there are 24 hours in a day and if you want to be successful, you better use all 24 of them."

Bob also found Daly to be ahead of most of the other college coaches, especially as far as his offensive mindset was concerned. "Chuck was way beyond me. I just sat there and soaked up as much as I could. He was extremely bright. He had great offensive concepts, very good defensive concepts and I thought tremendous rapport with the players. I used to call it the ability *never to paint yourself in a corner when dealing with the players.* He had rules and yet he knew when and how to bend them if they had to be bent. Sometimes when you come from a high school setting, you're very set in your ways and there's very little deviation. I tried to learn some of that deviation, that ability to bend a little bit more. Not necessarily break, but bend and have an understanding in what the players' needs were."

After dropping three of their first five games—to Virginia, Villanova, and Oklahoma—the Quakers celebrated Weinhauer's inaugural season by bouncing back to win 14 of their next 15. Then they overcame an eight point deficit to beat St. Bonaventure 92–83 in the first game of the NCAA Tournament, as Kevin McDonald climaxed one of the finest offensive seasons ever achieved by a Penn player with 37 points. McDonald, who once outscored Moses Malone in a high school all-star game, had been Big 5 MVP the previous year. But Duke came back in the second half to win the next round 84–80 as Mike Gminski turned the game around with some spectacular blocks.

"With six minutes to go, we had an eight point lead," recalled McDonald. "We had all the momentum. We had them on the ropes. Then there was a decision on part of the coaches to go into a semi-stall. We were told to only take uncontested lay-ups and three times we went in for what appeared to be uncontested lay-ups. But Mr. Gminski had other ideas. He blocked all three shots and all three of them were converted at the other end. Now instead of being eight points up, we had a two-point lead with entirely too much time left on the clock."

After that season, Weinhauer attended the first NCAA Final Four of his life, in St. Louis, where he watched the Blue Devils lose the championship game to Kentucky. The new Penn coach sat down and wrote a letter to each of his returning players. He challenged them, explaining that their goals should not only be to win the Big 5 and Ivy League titles, not only to return to the NCAA playoffs, but to get to the Final 4.

That's exactly what happened in 1978–79—much to the surprise of the nation, but not to Bob Weinhauer,

▲ Kevin McDonald, the Big 5 MVP as a junior, scored 37 points against St. Bonaventure in the NCAA Tournament in 1978. *(Urban Archives, Temple University, Philadelphia, Pennsylvania)*

nor the Penn students. "They had a big chip on their shoulder the whole year about not being ranked," recalled *Philadelphia Daily News* columnist Rich Hoffman, who was sports editor of the *Daily Pennsylvanian* at the time. "It was a gigantic issue for everybody on the campus." Especially when the Quakers beat Temple, the No.15 team in the nation. The following week, Penn still wasn't ranked and the Owls actually moved *up* a slot. "That just infuriated people," said Hoffman.

The Quakers went into the NCAA Tournament still unranked in the national polls. They were seeded ninth out of ten teams in the Eastern Regionals and, predictably, the underdog in every game. That's because they had lost six regular season games— including a 110–86 blowout by a San Diego State team headed by a scrappy playmaker named Tony Gwynn. Later they were upset by a mediocre Villanova team 89–80 when Tom Sienkiewicz scored a career-high 39 points.

"But we knew we were pretty good," recalled Weinhauer. "At the beginning of the season, we beat two ACC teams, Virginia and Wake Forest. We went out to California undefeated (5–0) and lost in two overtimes to Iowa. They were good, so there was certainly no shame in losing that game. We also lost to Georgetown (78–76)

▲ **B**ob Weinhauer guided the Quakers to the NCAA Final Four in 1979, with James "Boonie" Salters as one of his key players. *(Urban Archives, Temple University, Philadelphia, Pennsylvania)*

on a Saturday afternoon Eastern regional TV game at the Palestra. Georgetown was ranked number ten in the country and I said after that game, 'If they're number ten, then we're number ten-A.' After clinching the Ivy League title at Cornell, we went down to Columbia and lost. I'll never forget all their fans chanting, 'FIRST ROUND LOSERS. . . FIRST ROUND LOSERS.' That kind of stuck with us a little bit, but again, I used to tell them that when you go into a tournament, it's a whole new ball game. There are no underdogs. Everyone is good; otherwise they wouldn't be there.'"

Penn had a fascinating starting lineup that year: Matt White, a 6'10" walk-on center who was an accomplished classical pianist; Tim Smith, a 6'5" forward from West Philadelphia whose handwritten letters describing his basketball ability were ignored by every Big 5 school except Penn; Tony Price, the MVP of the Eastern Regionals who outscored Magic Johnson and Larry Bird in the Final Four; Bobby Willis, a quick, left-handed point guard with a great knowledge of the game, and the only non-senior in the starting lineup, and James "Booney" Salters, a 5'11" guard considered

by Weinhauer to be "the smartest floor general I've ever been around."

The Quakers jumped out to a 41–29 halftime lead in the preliminary round game against Jim Valvano's Cinderella Iona team in Raleigh, North Carolina. But the Gaels came storming back behind the play of Jeff Ruland and trailed by only 59–58, with 4:50 left in the game. Price finished with 27 points and 12 rebounds and 6'9" freshman Tom Leifson hit four clutch free throws down the stretch to help the Quakers pull away to a 73–69 win. "Anybody who was backing up White was going to get a lot of playing time because Matt always picked up his three fouls sometime in the first half," explained Weinhauer. "Then I would bring Matt back and tell him, 'Don't worry about fouling out because we're going to play you until you foul out.'" Vincent Ross, a 6'8" sophomore, was also in that mix once in a while. "If we needed athletic ability and defense, it was Vince. If we needed offensive help it was Tommy Leifson." White later played professionally in Spain.

Price again was the hero with 25 points and nine rebounds two days later when Penn pulled off perhaps the most stunning upset in Reynolds Coliseum history, knocking off the nation's No. 3 team, North Carolina, 72–71. Tony sealed the victory with 2:12 left and the Quakers ahead 66–65. After grabbing a rebound, he threw a length-of-the-court pass to Salters, who made a spectacular layup and subsequent free throw despite being fouled brutally on the play. The game was played less than 20 miles from the Tar Heels' campus. The fans couldn't believe their eyes, especially when St. John's eliminated Duke in the other game on a day forever mourned in the Atlantic Coast Conference as "Black Sunday."

"Early in the game the officials called us for some quick fouls," recalled Weinhauer. "I said to one of them, 'Hey, don't you get intimidated by this crowd or that team because we're not.' Of course he didn't like that and he gave me a dirty look but he didn't give me a technical. Near the end of the game when Booney had a breakaway, was knocked down, and had to get up and make the foul shots that put us further ahead, Dean calls time out. As the players were going back on the floor, I walked down to the scorer's table and said to the timer, 'Now, do me a favor. Make sure that you start the clock on time.' He looked up at me and said, 'Coach, when you got up by one point, if I could have run the

▶ **T**im Smith was ignored by every Big 5 school but Penn, but led the Quakers to a string of upsets in the 1979 NCAA Tournament. *(University of Pennsylvania)*

as the final 84–76 score indicated. Price was again top scorer with 20 points. Smith and Salters had 18 and 15, respectively, as the Quakers raced to a 17-point halftime lead over a team which came into the game with a 26–3 record and one of the nation's best big men, 6'11" All-America center Roosevelt Bouie. "Our guys were so good it was scary," said Weinhauer. "I didn't have to say a thing. Matt White wasn't afraid of anybody in the world. He was so big and strong, he didn't know how strong he was. We got such an insurmountable lead that they couldn't get back at us."

In the Eastern Regional final, Price and Smith put on a spectacular offensive show by combing for 27 of Penn's 35 second half points as the Quakers edged St. John's 64–62. Salters clinched the game with a pair of free throws with 23 seconds left and Ross picked off a desperation full-court pass as time ran out. "The toughest game of the whole group," said Weinhauer. "Both teams were not supposed to be here."

St. John's coach Lou Carnesecca was Joe Lapchick's assistant when Weinhauer used to watch their practices. Lou also spoke at Bob's high school basketball banquet. "Now here I am in a game against a guy whom I look up to as one of my idols. We played cautiously, knowing that any mistake could be the mistake that kept you out of the Final Four. I thought our kids played well and his kids played well and we got lucky enough to win the game at the end."

The Quakers were on their way to the Final Four in Salt Lake City. It was not a happy journey. The 101–67 loss to Michigan State in the national semifinals was almost anticlimactic, as was their 96–93 overtime loss to De Paul in the consolation game. The Big Ten champions ran their fast break to perfection, held the Quakers scoreless for one stretch of 8:44 in the first half, and

▲ Tony Price outscored Magic Johnson and Larry Bird in the 1979 NCAA Tournament. *(Urban Archives, Temple University, Philadelphia, Pennsylvania)*

clock out, I would have.' Of course, he's a North Carolina *State* guy. He didn't want to see anything good happen to Wild Blue Heaven there."

Next up for Penn was Syracuse, in Greensboro, North Carolina. The Quakers ran the No. 8 Orangemen right off the floor in a game that was not nearly as close

built a 40–8 lead barely fifteen minutes into the game. Two nights later they won the NCAA championship over Indiana State 75–64, in the first of the classic Magic Johnson–Larry Bird match-ups.

"To tell you the truth, I thought we were going to win," said Weinhauer, who had obtained a film of North Carolina's earlier game with Michigan State from Dean Smith. "We looked at that film and evaluated it, but we didn't have the ability to realize how quick they were jumping *off* the floor. North Carolina had beaten them and I really thought we could do the same thing. I really thought we did a good job on Magic. But we didn't do a good job of scoring after we got the ball inside against their match-up zone defense. We got it where we wanted to go but we did not convert and we just dug a hole for ourselves. There were a lot of missed layups." At half-time, the score was 50–17.

"What you do after a game like that," said Weinhauer, "is a lot of soul searching: *was there something that we did that wasn't right in preparation?* That hung with me for a long time. That really bothered me because I felt that I let the players down, I felt that I let the student body down and that we let the university down in that we didn't compete the way we knew we were capable. If we were capable of beating North Carolina and Syracuse, we were certainly capable of competing on even terms with Michigan State. The one thing you want is to be competitive in that setting. That was the one disappointment that I had in all my years of college coaching. I felt that we did not compete in that one particular game the way we were capable of."

Even though the Quakers' season came to an abrupt and inglorious end, recalled *Philadelphia Inquirer* columnist Bill Lyon, "the Penn kids can still look back and say, 'We were part of history,' because, with Magic and Larry, that was the Final Four that turned college basketball around. If you're doing a timeline, that's the weekend that college basketball took off."

Was there any resentment in the Ivy League over Penn's trip to the Final Four? "Oh absolutely yes," said Shabel, who is now vice chairman of Comcast-Spectacor, in Philadelphia. "The Ivy League, Harvard, Yale, Princeton, particularly, always resented the level that Penn played at. All you have to do is look at the history of Penn and Princeton dominating the league. So, they resented it, and some of the people in those academic leadership positions could not handle it when Penn would go deep into the NCAA. *Penn going to the Final Four? Are you kidding me?* Sitting up there at Harvard or Yale in particular, they had great difficulty and would beat up on the Penn leadership. So a Penn president was always defending Penn's basketball success."

Weinhauer was named Eastern College Coach of the Year and saw his Quakers climb all the way to 14th in the national rankings. He pulled off another upset in the NCAA Tournament the following year by shocking George Raveling's Washington State team in the opening round 62–55. Weinhauer's 1980–81 team went 20–8, but lost at West Virginia 67–64 in the NIT. That's the year that every team in the Big 5 finished with a 2–2 record, the only time that's ever happened. The *Philadelphia Daily News* commemorated the occasion by printing the standings *five times*, each with a different team on top.

After the 1981–82 season, which ended with a 66–56 loss to St. John's in the first round of the NCAA Tournament, Weinhauer resigned to become head coach at Arizona State, taking one of his assistants, former Philadelphia 76ers guard Doug Collins, with him. Bob left with the distinction of being the only Penn coach in history to lead the Quakers to a post-season tournament (including four NCAA appearances) every year he was in charge.

Penn had brought in Charles Harris as its new athletic director. It was also becoming tougher for Weinhauer to work with the admissions office. "Our interaction was not as good as it could be," Bob recalled of his relationship with his new boss. Ironically, a few years after Weinhauer took the Arizona State job, the Sun Devils hired a new athletic director. His name? Charles Harris. Soon afterwards, Weinhauer was off to the NBA, where he has since served in various coaching, broadcasting, scouting, and front office capacities with the Los Angeles Clippers, Atlanta, Milwaukee, Minnesota, Philadelphia, and Houston, where he won a NBA championship as the club's general manager.

Waiting in the wings was Craig Littlepage, who had become one of the youngest top assistants in major college basketball when he joined Rollie Massimino's staff at Villanova immediately after graduating from Penn in 1973. The two had become close friends when Rollie worked for Chuck Daly. After spending two years with the Wildcats, Littlepage joined another former Quaker assistant, Ray Carazo, at Yale for a year. Then he spent six seasons at Virginia under Terry Holland, the man whom he would eventually succeed there as athletic director in 2001, making him the first black AD in the history of the Atlantic Coast Conference.

Littlepage couldn't have asked for a more auspicious beginning. In his very first Big 5 game, the new Quakers' coach found himself going head-to-head with his mentor, Rollie Massimino. Penn had not beaten Villanova in six years, but the Quakers pulled off an electrifying 84–80 upset over the ninth-ranked Wildcats when Anthony Arnolie made ten consecutive free throws in

the final 2:29. "We went into that game probably as well prepared as any team that I've been associated with," said Littlepage. "We played a near perfect game. We had a bunch of no names, pretty much, who put together a classic Big 5 effort." And what did the teacher say to the pupil afterwards? "Quite honestly, I think we were both speechless. I do remember shaking hands with Rollie and he said, 'Way to go, babe!'"

The Quakers also won their next Big 5 game, beating La Salle 78–72. "We were in a commanding position in Big 5 at that point," recalled Littlepage. "But we might have been reading our press clippings a little bit too much. In all honesty, I think we were a tired basketball team by mid-January and kind of limped in the rest of the way." Penn finished with a 17–9 record but was denied a share of the Big 5 title when Temple pulled out a double overtime 61–53 win in John Chaney's Big 5 coaching debut. The Owls sent the game into overtime on one of Chaney's patented "Jack in the Box" plays. Terence Stansbury caught a length-of-the-court pass, wheeled, turned, and hit a jumper at the buzzer. Littlepage called it "a bitter and disappointing loss."

Littlepage decided to rebuild with youth rather than go with the experienced veterans the following year. The Quakers finished with a 10–16 record, playing one of the nation's toughest non-conference schedules that included teams like Southern Cal, Oregon State, and SMU. The strategy paid off in 1984–85 when Penn broke even during the regular season (13–13) and captured the Ivy League title. Moreover, the Quakers came very close to becoming the first No. 16 seed ever to upset a No. 1 in the NCAA Tournament.

"I thought we were a pretty good team," recalled Littlepage. "We had a 6'7" center in Bruce Lefkowitz, great guard play, speed, and quickness. When we got the match-up with Memphis State, I was thinking to myself, '*God, this is great. We can beat these guys!*'" With ten minutes left in game, the Quakers were leading Keith Lee, William Bedford & Company by six points. Fans in Houston were buzzing about a monumental upset, especially when the Tigers' big men ran into foul trouble and had to go to the bench. "Things were going along perfectly according to plan," said Littlepage. "We were going to spread the floor, play efficiently on offense, and maybe mix things up on defense." But when Memphis State's big people had to be replaced by smaller, quicker, more athletic players, Penn's speed and quickness advantage was suddenly nullified. "It was one of those

unintended consequences. We were doing so well against their big team. We were controlling the tempo, but when they went with the smaller lineup, the lead quickly dissipated and they turned the game around. I was so proud with the way that our guys responded to a big challenge in a situation where nobody gave them any credit. We played just an unbelievable game." The Tigers won 67–55 on their way to the Southeast Regional finals, where they lost to Villanova, the Cinderella NCAA champion that year.

During his three years as coach, Littlepage grappled with the same problems that had plagued Bob Weinhauer in trying to compete for the top-level athletes. So much so that the Quakers did not have a player on the All Big 5 first team after Booney Salters made it in 1979–80 until 1992–93, when Jerome Allen and Matt Maloney were selected. Not only were the admissions standards still getting tougher; there were larger concerns about financial aid. When Littlepage played at Penn, the total cost of his education was about $4,000. The need-based aid he received, combined with summer employment and on-campus jobs, basically provided the equivalent of an athletic scholarship. By the time he began coaching, however, the cost had gone up to about $18,000. "All of a sudden there was a very big differential with what need-based aid would provide in comparison with a scholarship," he explained. "That was a struggle. It seemed like every week we were dealing with a different issue related to somebody's financial aid package, their summer job, their campus job, or how much debt they were going to accumulate at the end of four years. There were days when it just wasn't a lot of fun. There was only so much that we as a coaching staff could do. But nonetheless, because of my love for the university and the Big 5, it was a good time for me, so they were enjoyable years."

Before the 1985–86 season, Penn's athletic situation changed significantly. Shabel had been promoted to a vice president at the university and Littlepage decided to take the head-coaching job at Rutgers University. A few days before former Quaker basketball player Paul Rubincam was appointed to succeed Shabel, Penn's president, Sheldon Hackney, interviewed Lehigh University coach Tom Schneider and hired him on the spot to succeed Littlepage. Schneider was no stranger around the Palestra. He had worked as an assistant to Weinhauer and Littlepage before moving up to Bethlehem to become head coach of the Engineers.

Led by the excellent shooting of Perry Bromwell, a transfer from Manhattan, Schneider enjoyed his best season in 1985–86 when the Quakers went 15–11 and beat La Salle 86–80 for their only Big 5 triumph. As a freshman, Bromwell had hit three jump shots down the stretch to help the Jaspers nip Penn 74–73 in the Music City Classic in Nashville. A year later, he walked up to Schneider at the Penn Relays and said he wanted to transfer. Perry would go on to become the Quakers' all-time best three-point shooter.

Penn beat La Salle again 66–61 in 1987–88, as Tyrone Pitts, the team's leading scorer, had 21 points and 10 rebounds. The game turned when 6'7" freshman Ben Spiva, "probably the best player I ever recruited," according to Schneider, took a charge from Lionel Simmons in the waning seconds. Unfortunately for the Quakers, Spiva decided to transfer to Memphis State in his hometown after the season. Schneider said the best player he ever coached at Penn was Lefkowitz, the 6'7" center who led the team in rebounding and field goal percentage all four years of his career. "He was a coach's nightmare in practice and a referee's nightmare in games because he bumped into everybody," Schneider explained. "But once they turned the lights on, this kid wanted to play. He had great hands, great court savvy, and really knew how to play the game."

Schneider's most memorable Big 5 triumph came in his final season as coach in 1988–89 when Penn shocked nationally-ranked Villanova 71–70. The Wildcats had come within one game of making the Final Four the previous year. "Rollie was devastated," recalled Fran Dunphy, who had become Schneider's assistant that year. "Maybe that was the reason that Villanova decided to play only two games with the Big 5."

"I had eight freshmen on that team," said Schneider. "I walked out during warm-ups and saw that they had like three guys who were 7 feet tall. I said to myself, 'Temple and Villanova are complaining about playing us. What the hell are *we* doing playing these guys?'" Jose Tavarez, one of the freshmen, scored on a putback in the last minute to give Penn a three-point lead, then won it when he made the front end of a one-and-one with two seconds left.

Dunphy, who played on La Salle's great 1968–69 team, had earned a solid reputation during his career as an assistant coach in a number of major college programs. He worked under his former high school coach, Dan Dougherty, at Army, and Gary Williams at American U. He also spent a total of five years at La Salle, where he assisted Lefty Ervin during Lefty's first and last seasons as head coach, and later served under Speedy Morris for three years. But the job Dunphy really wanted back in 1986 was to be La Salle's athletic director when Bill Bradshaw resigned to go to DePaul University. "When they decided to go in a different direction, I was devastated," Dunphy said. "I thought it would be a perfect opportunity. I knew I had to make a move. I was frustrated."

That opportunity came two years later when

Schneider hired his good friend. But it took some convincing. "I knew Dunph for a thousand years," recalled Schneider, a graduate of Bucknell who had grown up in Washington D.C. "It got to a point where I thought I needed somebody who really knew Philadelphia. Ed Stefanski said, 'Talk to Dunphy.' So Fran and I had a few beers and talked and he said that he didn't want to come to Penn. There was just something about the Ivy League and all that. So I called him back two weeks later and he took the job."

When Schneider left to become head coach at Loyola (Maryland) after the 1988–89 season, Dunphy was sitting in the wings to replace him. "If I'm still at La Salle, I don't think I'm getting this job," he recalled. "It was just the right time at the right place and Paul Rubincam took a flyer on me."

"Fran wasn't the unanimous choice," recalled Rubincam. "But I had known him and watched him operate. We never had long conversations, but I would watch him interact with people and could see over the course of that year that he was just solid. I said to the search committee, 'I like what I see here. I like the way he handled himself. I like his work ethic and I think he'll fit in fine even though he's a La Salle man and we're turning down a Penn person for the job.'" Some people on the committee wanted former Louisville star Butch Beard, who was an assistant with the New Jersey Nets at the time. Others wanted Fran McCaffery, the former Penn guard who is now head coach at North Carolina-Greensboro, or Pete Carroll, who was P. J. Carlissimo's assistant at Seton Hall.

Dunphy struggled the first few years. "We didn't knock them dead," he recalled. "I had a three-year contract and to be honest with you, when I first got the job I would have taken a three-*day* contract. Our first year we were 12–14. The next year we were 9–17. And now I'm going into the last year of my contract. We had gotten Jerome Allen as a recruit the year before and Rubincam came in to me and said, 'Here's a new three-year contract.' I said, 'Let me get this straight. We just went 12 and 14 and 9 and 17 and you're going to give me a new three-year contract?' He said, 'Yes. I trust in you and I think you're going to do a good job. I like how you approach things. I like the direction of the program. You'll be fine.'" And that's just what happened. The following season—the year after the Big 5 round-robin ended, Dunphy guided the Quakers to a 16–10 record. Then came three straight Ivy League championships and records of 22–5, 25–3, and 22–6. Penn's glory days had returned. "I'm very grateful for Paul's trust in me," said Dunphy. "You don't see that very often."

Fran O'Hanlon, the former Villanova guard who is

now coaching at Lafayette College, credits Dunphy with keeping him in the game. "Without Dunph, I'm not here," said O'Hanlon, who helped install the motion offense at Penn when he assisted Dunphy for six years. The two became close friends during their Big 5 playing days. "In this profession you don't get many opportunities to go from high school to college. They ask, 'What's your recruiting contacts? What's this? What's that?' Dunph said. 'I don't care. We go way back and I feel comfortable in having you as my assistant.'"

"I had never coached the motion offense before," recalled Dunphy. "I had always used a pattern offense. I told Fran that I want to give the kids some freedom to play. I said, 'Show me what it is.' He said, 'I can't show you, I can't write it down. I can put it in but I can't show you.' I said, OK, I'll be learning it just like the kids are learning it.' He did a great job. He's a terrific basketball coach and a good man and a good friend as well. It was a good partnership. He was certainly a head coach in an assistant coach's body. I learned a lot of basketball from him in those years."

So did the Big 5. From both Frans.

Chapter 13

• • • • • • •

The 'Cats Reach the Promised Land

It was halftime of the 1985 NCAA Southeast Regional championship game against No. 1 seed North Carolina and things were not going well for Villanova. As the players filed into their locker room, Rollie Massimino could sense that the Wildcats were struggling. He stood in the middle of the room with his tie off and his shirt hanging out. "What I want more right now than getting to the Final Four, more than anything else, is a big dish of pasta with greasy clam sauce," he rasped. His players looked up in disbelief. "We kind of looked at each other like, 'There's something wrong with this man,'" recalled Harold Pressley, the Wildcats' 6'7" defensive specialist. "Then we went out and beat North Carolina by twelve to go to the Final Four."

A few days later, Villanova pulled off one of the greatest upsets in college basketball history by beating Georgetown 66–64 to become the only NCAA champion in the formal history of the Big 5. Which came as no surprise to former Penn coach Chuck Daly, the man responsible for bringing Rollie Massimino in as his assistant 13 years earlier.

"Rollie was a character," recalled Daly. "The first time we talked, I could tell what a great coach he was, what a terrific background he had. Plus a lot of Italians have this in sports—a way of identifying family life—the Lasordas, the Fratellos, the LaRussas—there's something about their style that works and I thought it was a good contrast. I always try to hire people for what I needed at that time. I rarely hired someone I knew very well. I wanted new ideas. I always felt I needed at different times, different personalities at different places. So in Rollie's case, his personality was different and his basketball was sound. I thought we had a great relationship."

And, occasionally, a stormy one. "We'd have three-hour meetings to prepare for practice—arguing, screaming, hollering," explained Daly. "Then we'd go out and run a mile together every day in Franklin Field. But we had a great time, great fun."

Massimino, who was making $19,000 a year at Stony Brook, took a $6,000 pay cut when he accepted the Penn job. "With a wife and five kids and a broken-down station wagon, I couldn't afford to live in Cherry Hill, New Jersey," he said. "So they gave me two months more salary up to $15,000. I eventually got that up to $19,000, then when I came to Villanova, I made $17,000."

Daly and Massimino still laugh about the time when they walked out on the Palestra floor for their first Big 5 game. "We were playing Temple and the place was mobbed," Massimino recalled. "We were underneath the basket on the back side near our locker and he said, 'Rollie, isn't it worth $5,000 just to see this?'" "The place was absolutely electric," added Daly. "He nudged me as only Rollie can do and said, 'It was worth the pay cut!'"

"In his own way, Rollie was very demonstrative and flamboyant," said former La Salle coach Paul Westhead, "throwing his jacket, stomping up and down the sidelines, huffing and puffing. But Rollie was a very clever, calculating coach. Nothing was ever easy against Rollie because for all of his flamboyance, he was very calculating in what he was trying to do against you. Rollie always had gamesmanship going. He was always trying to outmaneuver you."

Like Jack Kraft, his predecessor, Massimino was not Villanova's first choice back in 1973. Herb Magee, who had taken Philadelphia Textile College to the NCAA Division II championship, was given strong consideration. So was Dan Dougherty, the former St. Joseph's player who was Kraft's assistant when the Wildcats went to the Final Four. "Dan absolutely could have had the job," recalled Joe Walters, who was heading the search.

"You can probably say that I verbally agreed to take it," said Dougherty, who was in his second year as Army's coach at the time. "I went back up to West Point planning on resigning and the people there talked me into staying. I had a tough decision to make. At that time I thought we were just starting to turn it around. We had a good recruiting class coming in. I thought I could do the job. It didn't work out that way. I don't look back and cry over it, I just look back and wonder." Two years later, Dougherty was replaced by Mike Krzyzewski.

Meanwhile, Daly was on the phone with Joe Walters strongly pushing his assistant, raving about Rollie's capabilities as a defensive coach. "Chuck couldn't say enough about him," explained Walters. "We interviewed him and right away he sold himself."

Massimino started at Villanova the same time that Bill Raftery, the former La Salle player, became coach at Seton Hall. "Rollie and I went from being good friends to no friends to good friends again," recalled the CBS-TV basketball analyst. "Seton Hall played Villanova for 85 years, but they had to stop the series because the two of us were going to kill one another. Silly stuff like '*Who called a time out late?*' or '*Who didn't shake hands?*' Once there was a fight in a game and we ended up going jaw-to-jaw afterwards." Later when Villanova became a member of the Big East Conference, Raftery was president of the league's Coaches' Association. "That meant you were coach of the last-place team and nobody disliked you," Raftery explained. "At the league meeting, Dave Gavitt, the commissioner, said, 'since you're the president, I want you to introduce Rollie.' As they tell the story, I said:

"*YouknowVillanovaisintheleaguethisisthecoachRollie Massimino.*'

"Now we finish our morning meeting and we go out to the golf carts. I'm looking for my clubs and I find them in the same cart with Rollie. Dave put us together. So we called each other everything an Irishman calls an Italian and an Italian calls an Irishman and we end up winning. We beat everybody. Now we have a great relationship."

Massimino's first recruits were Joe Rogers, a guard from nearby Archbishop Carroll High School who had been MVP of a preliminary game at the Dapper Dan Classic in Pittsburgh, and John Olive, an all-state 6'7" forward from Bishop Eustace in New Jersey. Both signed the same afternoon. They eventually joined two other

freshmen, Chubby Cox and Larry Herron, the first of three brothers to play for the Wildcats, in the starting lineup. "They called us 'teenyboppers' and we really struggled that first year," recalled Rogers. "But Coach Massimino was full of energy and enthusiasm. It was terrific from my perspective because he gave younger kids a chance to play." Playing a tough independent schedule, Villanova finished 7–19 and went winless in the Big 5. Rollie picked up a new nickname, "Daddy Mass," and Olive's teammates selected him the club's MVP.

With Whitey Rigsby, a guard from New York City; Reggie Robinson, a forward from nearby Radnor High School, and Larry Herron's brother, Keith, coming on board in 1974–75, Villanova's top seven players were now either freshmen or sophomores. The Wildcats improved slightly. They were 9–18 overall and 2–2 in the Big 5, but the season was highlighted by that ugly loss to Oregon during a 20-day road trip that also included stops at the Kentucky Invitational, Hawaii, and Southern Cal.

In 1975–76 the Wildcats started to turn things around with a 16–11 record and a share of the Big 5 title. "The fans were getting a little restless with Rollie at that time, but we all bought into his program and loved him as coach," said Rogers, who triggered Massimino's biggest win up to that point, a 69–67 upset over Penn, coached by his mentor, Chuck Daly. Rodgers won it with a 25-foot jump shot at the final buzzer. With the score tied and four seconds showing on the clock, the Wildcats called a time out. Hal Grossman, who had officiated dozens of Rogers' freshman games, was one of the referees. "Hal says, 'What the hell does he have you doing, Rog?' I said to Hal, 'One of the Herrons, who do you think?' He says, 'Why don't you just take the shot and end the game?' I said, 'Yeah, right! He would die!' Hal was always great with on-the-court kibitzing with the players. So he said, 'OK Rog, let's get this thing over.' I come up the court and there's no time left, so I just pulled up and shot because time was wasting. The last guy who thought I was going to shoot it was Eddie Enoch, who was covering me. I'm sure Chuck Daly never mentioned my name during the time-out."

Beginning in 1974–75, Massimino's teams beat St. Joseph's four straight times, and no one was happier than Rogers, who grew up within a stone's throw of Hawk Hill. He used to deliver *The Philadelphia Bulletin* at 54th and City Line, and rode his bicycle almost every day through St. Joe's campus. His idol was Jimmy Lynam, and Massimino always referred to the game with the Hawks as 'Joey's Game.' One of the highlights of Rogers' senior year in 1976–77 was Villanova's 92–78 victory at the Spectrum. It was the first Big 5 game ever

played away from the Palestra and it drew 12,138 fans, far below capacity. "I just dribbled the ball, made some foul shots, and got the ball to the Herrons so they could shoot," Rogers recalled. "But I would have much better preferred to play the game in the Palestra."

Massimino took the Wildcats to his first post-season tournament, the NIT, at the end of that season. "That was the turning point of the program," Rollie recalled. "Mike Fratello, one of my assistants, was with me. We were sitting in my office waiting for five or six hours. We were crying, *'We've got to get an NIT bid.'* The NIT committee finally called and said, 'Maryland won't go to Old Dominion. Would you go there and play?' I said, 'We'll go *anywhere* to play.'"

Villanova had to overcome a 17–1 deficit in the opening round at Old Dominion before winning 71–68. After beating Massachusetts in the quarterfinals at Madison Square Garden, Massimino took Rogers to the post-game press conference. "The New York writers asked me this, that, and the other thing and finally said, 'Joe, What do you feel about playing in the Garden?' I said, 'Listen, I grew up in Philadelphia. The Palestra is the Mecca of basketball.' Rollie kicked me under the table and said, 'What the hell are you saying?' He grabbed me after the conference and said, 'This is New York. You're in the Garden. You can't say that.' I said, 'Coach! Who cares about the Garden? I'm from Philly.'"

The Wildcats dropped the semi-final game to St. Bonaventure 86–82 then grabbed third place by upsetting Alabama 102–89 to finish the

◄ **V**illanova's Rollie Massimino is the only Big 5 coach to win a NCAA championship. *(Urban Archives, Temple University, Philadelphia, Pennsylvania)*

year with a 23–10 record, the first of Rolllie's nine 20-win seasons. Keith Herron was limping around at the pregame meal before the Alabama game. "Man, I'm sore," he told Rogers. "Don't give me this 'I'm going to limp through it' business," replied Rogers. "This isn't just a consolation game. This is the last game of my career, so you're either playing or not playing!" Herron went out and scored 35 points, his career high. "I could barely walk," he recalled. "It was just one of those games where I got into a zone and everything was falling. It suddenly seemed that I had two good ankles even though my ankle was swollen to an incredible size. I loved playing in Madison Square Garden. There was just something about New York that inspired me." Herron, who played at Mackin High School in Washington D.C., will never forget how he was recruited by Massimino. "Rollie came down to see me in an all-star game," Keith explained. "He jumped out of the stands and said, 'Keith. You played well, but DEFENSE, you've got to move the feet.' All these coaches were around and he was actually showing me how he wanted me to stand and move my feet on defense. This got to me. He really touched me. I loved Rollie's energy. I could tell that he was a people person." Herron would go on to lead the Wildcats in scoring for four straight years and play another four seasons in the NBA with Atlanta, Detroit, and Cleveland.

The following year, Massimino's Wildcats made their first NCAA

◄ **K**eith Herron led Villanova in scoring four times and was named to the All Big 5 team in three of those years. (*Urban Archives, Temple University, Philadelphia, Pennsylvania*)

▶ **A**lex Bradley, Villanova's first three-year captain since 1952, set a number of Wildcat records as a Freshman All-America. (*Villanova University*)

Tournament appearance and overcame a big deficit to beat La Salle 103–97 in the opening round at the Palestra. Sportswriter Frank Bilovsky was sitting at the press table near Villanova's bench. "Early in the game it was like 20–6," he recalled. "La Salle was hitting everything in sight and Rollie calls a time-out. He sits the team down and calmly—as calmly as I've ever seen Rollie—said, 'Look guys. They can't keep shooting like that. They're making every shot right now but they can't keep it up. We're going to get back into this game two-by-two. We're going to catch 'em, we're going to beat 'em. Don't worry about it. They just can't keep shooting like that.' It was the most reasoned time-out I ever saw Rollie have. Then he sends the team back out on the floor, and he turns to Mitch Buonaguro, his assistant. We used to call him 'Little Rollie.' He grabs Mitch and shakes him and says, 'Jesus Christ, they're making every God damn shot!' That defined Rollie to me. This is a guy who could have made his players as rattled as he was. Instead he calmed them down, then grabbed his assistant and let his true feelings hang out."

Villanova advanced to the Eastern Regionals in Providence and upset Indiana 61–60 as Rory Sparrow made one of the half-dozen game-winning shots of his career. Duke, led by Mike Gminski, then eliminated the Wildcats 80–72, putting the game away early by turning numerous Villanova mistakes into a commanding 21–6 lead. Sparrow, a 6'2" Big 5 Hall of Fame guard who played excellent defense, finished high on Villanova's all-time charts in scoring, shooting accuracy, and assists. He went on to play for a dozen years in the NBA, much of it with the New York Knicks, and is now the league's director of basketball operations.

The Wildcats probably wouldn't have made it to the NCAA Tournament that year had it not been for the outstanding play of Alex Bradley, a 6'6" freshman who made an immediate impact as an inside force. Bradley's unbeaten Long Branch High School team had been rated No. 1 in New Jersey in his senior year. "He was the first guy we ever had who could rebound and dunk in one motion," recalled Rigsby. Bradley scored 19 points to trigger a 69–68 win over Penn in his very first Big 5 game. Later, he was the MVP of the Eastern Eight Tournament as the Wildcats got by Penn State, Pitt and West Virginia at the Pittsburgh Civic Arena, which was virtually a home court for the Panthers and Mountaineers. "Our play during that tournament was based on pure emotion and determination," said Bradley, who would help lead the Wildcats to three NCAA Tourney appearances in his four-year career. "I enjoyed the pressure that was placed upon me as a freshman. It made me play harder."

That's one reason why Bradley and Massimino hit it off so well. "He surrounded himself with people who played hard." explained Bradley, who became the first three-year Villanova captain since 1952. "He was a disciplinarian, as most people could tell by his style of play. It was not just 'Chuck'n and Duck'n,' the term he used to describe running up and down, throwing the ball up, and scoring two hundred points a game. He was more of a controlled tempo type of coach. You could not play for coach Mass and not give 100 percent because he really drives you. Whether you liked it or not, you end up playing harder. He was at times a little too much of a perfectionist, but that was his style. He was equally as concerned with his players academically and made sure that guys attended class every day. In a sense, he was kind of a father figure to all of us in terms of expecting that we carry ourselves off the court in a certain manner." Bradley probably would have made the All Big 5 team three straight years had it not been for a broken thumb suffered early in his senior season at a Holiday Tournament at Texas-El Paso. A member of the Big 5 Hall of Fame, he still finished his career as one of Villanova's top-ten scorers and rebounders, and went on to play a year for the New York Knicks.

Jim Lynam, the former St. Joseph's coach, remembers the first time his Hawks played Massimino's Wildcats in 1979. "He had the better team but we ended up winning the game when Luke Griffin, a very good point guard but a marginal shooter, banked a jumper from about 19 feet," said Lynam. "After the game at the little St. Joe's party, who is sitting at my table having a beer at the end of the night but Rollie. I didn't invite him, I know that, but I'll tell you this. Had the tables been reversed and I had the best team and his point guard, who can't shoot, banked a jumper from 19 feet to beat me, that's one place I wouldn't have been. I would never have been at a Villanova party sharing beers with a victorious coach." Massimino's recollection of that gathering is a little different.

"Lynam said, 'Why don't you come over,'" Rollie recalled. "'We're meeting at a party someplace.' I said, 'Okay, I'll come.' He never thought I would. I came."

A number of observers, including Massimino, feel that Villanova's 1982–83 team was better than the group that won the NCAA title two years later. "That team had a chance to win a national championship because we were very good," said Massimino. "Without a doubt, that was probably our best team from top to bottom," agreed John Pinone, who was winding up a brilliant career in which he won or shared Big 5 MVP honors three times. "We were deep, we were experienced. It was probably more talented than the team that won it. We could have easily been in the Final Four that year but we did not have one of our better games against Houston."

Ed Pinckney, the Big 5 MVP the year the Wildcats won the NCAA crown, agrees that the championship 1984–85 squad would not have beaten the Pinone/ Stewart Granger/ Mike Mulquin team. "I mean it would have been a 30-point blowout," he explained. "That team could beat anybody. Granger was a great point guard. Pinone was just a tremendous player and leader. Mike Mulquin didn't get a lot of playing time but was very instrumental in us winning the North Carolina game as well as others during that year. He was 6'8", very athletic, and ran like crazy." Granger, a member of the Big 5 Hall of Fame, started 95 consecutive games for the Wildcats and is second on Villanova's all-time assist list. He was a first round draft pick of the Cleveland Cavaliers and also played in the NBA for New York, Chicago, and Atlanta.

Pinckney is one of only two players to lead the Wildcats in rebounding all four years. The 6'9" center, who is now the analyst on the Miami Heat NBA broadcasts, had two memorable performances within a ten day span during his sophomore year in 1982–83. First he avoided a charge and nailed a baseline jumper with one second remaining to give Villanova a 72–71 win over La Salle to help Massimino win his first outright Big 5 title. He followed that up by outplaying Georgetown's Patrick Ewing with a 27-point, 22-rebound effort as the Wildcats picked up their first-ever Big East Conference win over the Hoyas 68–67. Ewing was held to eight points before fouling out.

"If you ask anybody about me in school, they will tell you that I was pretty quiet," recalled Pinckney. "I never really talked much about what we were going to do out on the court, but for the Georgetown game they had a small pep rally at the Jake Nevin Fieldhouse. Well, I opened my big mouth. I said, 'We're definitely going to win this game. There's all this talk about Ewing. I'm going to handle Ewing.' I remember saying to myself before the game, *What did I get myself into?*' After we ended up winning, I could remember thinking, 'Wow, we finally possibly may get some respect in this league and in Philadelphia.'

▶ **S**tewart Granger played in four NCAA Tournaments and is second on Villanova's all-time assist list. *(Villanova University)*

Then we end up going up to Boston College and losing by ten."

Later that season, the Wildcats had to fly to Chapel Hill out of Atlantic City in a raging blizzard. For the first time ever, they beat top-ranked North Carolina 56–53 despite Michael Jordan's game-high 20 points. Pinone led Villanova with 14 points while Pinckney added 11 points and 11 rebounds. "Beating the number one team in their own gym proved that we were legitimate," said Pinone, the Wildcats' captain. "In my junior year, Kentucky had beaten us pretty good on national TV, so there were people out there who were still asking, 'How good could we be.' Now they knew we were a legitimate contender for a national championship."

Unfortunately, the Wildcats ran up against Hakeem Olajuwon's powerful Houston team in the NCAA Midwest Regional finals and lost 89–71. "I knew we were in trouble early in the game," recalled Harry Booth, the former St. Joseph's coach who was working as a volunteer assistant for the Wildcats. "Stew Granger was 6' 3" and Clyde Drexler came down on a fast break. Granger held his position in the lane and I thought *'We're going to get a charge.'* Drexler jumped right over him and dunked it. I said, 'Uh oh!'"

In addition to winning 90 games during Pinone's career, Villanova appeared in the NCAA Tournament in each of John's four seasons. The 6'8" center, who later played for a season in the NBA with Atlanta before spending seven years in Spain, led the Wildcats in scoring four times, thus becoming the second Villanova freshman ever to do so. "Back then, I played almost all the time with my back to the basket," explained the Big 5 Hall of Famer, who was known as a fearless competitor. "The physical part was the easy part. It was a different adjustment because I had to play against guys who were bigger and better athletes, guys who were talented, who could jump. But our system was designed to try to put pressure on the defense by getting the ball inside."

In 1985, the year that they won it all, the Wildcats almost didn't even make the NCAA Tournament. Villanova won only 18 games during the regular season and had been humiliated in its final game at Pitt 85–62. The Wildcats trailed by 13 at halftime of that nationally-televised game and Massimino had seen enough of his team's lack of effort. "I knew that we had a chance for the NCAA tournament if we could just win one or maybe two games," he said. I told them at halftime, 'I'm going to give you guys three minutes to play.' After three minutes they weren't playing any better and I took them all out. "I remember saying to myself, 'Ah, he's not going to take us out. There's no way,'" recalled Pinckney, who later played for 12 years in the NBA, six of them with Boston. "I just remember being very disappointed in that game and thinking, 'We're not going to be in the tournament now. We're going to go to the NIT.' But the Wildcats came back to beat Pitt 69–61 in the opening round of the Big East Tournament. Even though they were ousted by St. John's 89–74, the win over the Panthers was just enough to sway the NCAA Selection Committee.

With their beloved trainer Jake Nevin suffering from Lou Gehrig's disease and offering inspiration from his wheelchair, Villanova faced perhaps its most difficult game in the opening round against Dayton on the Flyers' home court. The Wildcats were forced to play there even though they were seeded eighth, one spot ahead of their hosts. Unlike many preliminary games that were sparsely attended, Villanova faced a hostile standing-room-only crowd of Dayton fans. With the score tied, time running out, and the Flyers holding the ball for the last shot, Pressley reached in, grabbed it, and threw the length of the court to Harold Jensen, who laid it up for the deciding basket in the 51–49 win. Jensen, a 6'4" sophomore from Trumbull, Connecticut, came off the bench to play the six greatest games of his career in the tournament.

The Wildcats again found themselves underdogs in the next round against Michigan, even though the Big Ten champions were loaded with freshmen and sophomores. "A lot of Villanova guys took

▶ **E**d Pinckney lines up behind his coach, Rollie Massimino, and Villanova trainer Jake Nevin. Pinckney was MVP of the Big 5 in 1985, when he led the NCAA champs in scoring and rebounding. *(Urban Archives, Temple University, Philadelphia, Pennsylvania)*

◄ Harold Pressley (21) and Ed Pinckney in action. Pressley, the Big East Defensive Player of the Year in 1986, started a record 106 consecutive games for the Wildcats. *(Villanova University)*

offense to that," recalled Pinckney. The Wildcats went eight minutes without scoring at one point but still controlled the game and won 59–55.

The Southeast Regional semifinals were held in Birmingham, Alabama, where Villanova faced Maryland, a team that had nipped them 77–74 in College Park earlier in the season. "I remember Lenny Bias just dunking all over my head," said Pressley, who later played for four years in the NBA with Sacramento and now does TV and radio analysis of Kings' games. "He had a couple of monster dunks in the tournament game but we were able to hold them off." Villanova won 46–43. "We were just all over Bias the entire game," recalled Pinckney. "Every time he got the ball, everybody was communicating with one another saying, *'He's on the left-hand side! He's fighting inside! You can't leave him open!'* Defensively, we did everything. We played a 1-2-2, we played a 2-1-2. We played match-up zone. We played man-to-man on the way back and then we would drop into a three-quarter-court press. Rollie threw the book at them."

Then came the 56–44 win over North Carolina. The team that almost didn't even make the tournament was in the Final Four. Inspired by Massimino's culinary dissertation, the Wildcats played well in the second half, especially on defense. "Coach had a great ability to keep people relaxed," explained Craig Miller, the Wildcats' sports publicist at the time. "It wasn't life and death with him. Unless you were part of the inner circle, that was a side of Rollie that not a lot of people got to see."

The Wildcats went into the national semifinal against Memphis State feeling very confident. The Tigers had beaten Pennsylvania 67–55 in an opening round game that was much closer than the score indicated. Villanova had handled the Quakers easily back in December 80–67 when Pressley and Pinckney each scored 19 points. Memphis State beat Boston College to get to the Final Four. "We were hoping that Boston College would win that game," said Pinckney. "It could have been an All Big East Final Four." Villanova eliminated the Tigers 52–45.

April 1, 1985. Playing as close to a perfect game as humanly possible before a standing-room-only crowd of 23,134 at Kentucky's Rupp Arena, Villanova shocked Georgetown 66–64 to win the NCAA title. The Wildcats connected on 22 of their 28 field goal attempts and missed only one of ten shots in the second half. They converted 22 of 27 shots from the free throw line including 11 of 14 during the pressure-packed final two minutes. Villanova's 78.6 per cent field goal percentage was even more amazing, considering it came against the nation's top defensive team. Playing a zone defense, the Wildcats held Ewing, Georgetown's 7'1" All-America, to 14 points on a sub-par 7-for-13 shooting night. As a team, Georgetown made only 29 of 53 field goal attempts.

John Thompson's Hoyas had beaten Villanova twice during the regular season, 52–50 at the Spectrum and 57–50 in Washington. They quickly jumped to a 20–14 lead but the Wildcats battled back, "two-by-two," as Massimino liked to say. When Pressley followed up his own missed shot with four seconds left, Villanova led at intermission 29–28. "I remember Georgetown holding the ball for the last shot of the half and thinking that's a moral victory for Villanova," recalled Rigsby, who broadcast the game. "I thought that was the only victory Villanova was going to get that day. Georgetown was so much bigger and stronger and better."

With 10:41 left in the second half, Georgetown regained the upper hand 42–41. The lead changed hands five times after that, with Villanova holding the largest margin at 53–48. The Hoyas regained the lead 54–53 with 4:50 left. Then they immediately spread the floor and went into a slowdown offense before Dwayne McClain and Jensen turned the tide for the Wildcats. McClain came up with the biggest steal of his career, and with 2:36 to go, Jensen calmly nailed an 18-footer from the right wing to give the Wildcats the lead for good at 55–54. Pickney then blocked a baseline layup attempt by David Wingate, who led the Hoyas in scoring with 16 points. Ed was fouled as he retrieved the ball, sank both free throws, and extended Villanova's lead to 57–54. With 18 seconds left, it was 65–60 and a pair of Georgetown layups wrapped around another Wildcat free throw proved meaningless. Pinckney was named MVP of the Final Four and was later joined by Jensen, McClain, and Pressley in the Big 5 Hall of Fame. For McClain, like Pinckney, it was a storybook ending to a brilliant college career. McClain, the talented 6'6" guard from Worcester, Massachusetts, won five games for the Wildcats with last-second shots and finished among the all time Villanova leaders in both scoring and assists. He played for a season in the NBA with Indiana, then spent many years playing in Australia.

Basketball fans everywhere were shocked by Gary McLain's startling admission two years later in a *Sports Illustrated* article: the Wildcats' point guard, who scored eight points in the title game against Georgetown, claimed that he used cocaine and marijuana during his

playing days and sold cocaine during his junior year. McLain entered a drug rehabilitation program in August 1986, about a year after he graduated.

Bob Vetrone, who had broadcast the semifinal win over Memphis State, was rooming with former Villanova coach Al Severance during the tournament. "The morning of the championship game," recalled Vetrone, "I didn't want to disturb Al so I went downstairs, made some telephone calls, and shot the breeze with some Villanova fans in the coffee shop. I got back upstairs and Al Severance had died shaving. This was a friend of mine who had helped me very early in my career at the *Bulletin* and some of the players had Al in class because he was still teaching. That was an emotional bittersweet moment, going from such a low that morning by finding one of my first really good friends in the business dead, and then within a span of 15 hours watching Villanova win a NCAA championship."

"When we went out to practice," recalled Booth, the volunteer assistant, "I remember Rollie getting the players together and telling them—it was such a motivational speech—'Tonight Al Severance will be on the opponent's basket and he'll be knocking away shots and he's going to help guide our shots in.' And he was serious.

Then he told the kids that he wanted them to go back to their rooms after our pre-game meal and not even talk to their roommate, but just function on their own and envision us winning the championship. That whole day, how he could turn a negative into a positive, was amazing."

That Booth was even working for Massimino was quite a surprise. The two had never been particularly close. There had been an incident at the annual Villanova–St. Joseph's alumni luncheon during Booth's second year as coach when Harry got up to speak, ripped off his shirt and tie, and displayed a T-Shirt reading BEAT VILLANOVA. "I think that may have antagonized him a little bit, but we never had words," explained Booth. "I'm not going to say we were close at that point. Rollie had his unique personality and certainly I was fiery. Out of that incident there was some concern that we could get along." Two years after leaving the Hawks, Massimino invited Booth to join his staff.

Ironically, when he was Chuck Daly's assistant at Penn, Rollie was basically a man-to-man coach who disdained zone defenses. During their first season together, the Quakers played Paul Westphal's nationally ranked USC team at the Kodak Classic, in Rochester, New York. "We had not spent much time working with the zone," recalled Daly. "Rollie used to call it, 'Hands-up Harry.' He would say, 'I don't want to play that Hands-up Harry.' So at halftime, I switch to the zone, we win the game, and it became a very strong defensive weapon for us. The interesting part was Rollie goes on to win an NCAA championship with the zone, and then he would go lecturing all over the country about zone defenses."

Pressley was named Big 5 MVP and Big East Defensive Player of the Year in 1985–86. He set a Villanova record for blocked shots in a game (ten) against Providence. But he saved his best effort for Georgetown by connecting on 14 of 17 field goal attempts for 34 points and grabbing 12 rebounds as the Wildcats came from behind to pull out a 90–88 double-overtime thriller in a nationally-televised game at the Spectrum. Pressley, who always played well against the Hoyas, sealed the win when he dove on the floor to tip the ball away from Georgetown's Charles Smith and flipped it to Dwight Wilbur, who laid it up. "I just knew that we had to win that game to make the NCAA Tournament," Pressley recalled. "It was diving on the floor, it was getting your legs burnt up, putting your body in front of big guys for charges—no matter what it was, we had to do it." The Wildcats finished with a 23–14 record and beat Virginia Tech in the first round of the NCAA Tournament before the dream of defending their national championship ended with a 66–61 loss to Georgia Tech.

The Wildcats came within a game of another Final Four appearance in the NCAA Tournament two years later when they upset heavily-favored Arkansas (82–74), Illinois (66–63), and Kentucky (80–74) before being eliminated by Oklahoma (78–59) in the Southeast Regional finals, in Birmingham. Sparked by the surprising play of 7'3" sophomore Tom Greis, the tallest player in Big 5 history, Villanova had finished the regular season with a 21–12 record. Greis was MVP of the Jostens Classic in December after scoring 21 points to lead the Wildcats to an 83–80 win over La Salle in the semifinals. Gary Massey came off the bench for a career-high 21 points to trigger an 83–70 victory over Wake Forest in the championship game. Greis also had nine blocked shots in a 64–58 win over a big Georgetown team headed by Alonzo Mourning and Dikembe Mutombo at the Spectrum.

"Tom Greis was unbelievable that year," recalled Jay Wright, who was in his first season as an assistant to Massimino. "He had a very frustrating freshman year. He came in kind of slow and out of shape. Pat Croce (later the president of the Philadelphia 76ers) took him in and worked him out all summer. He came back in the greatest shape of his life and had the best year of his career."

Wright had been assigned by Massimino to scout La Salle's games before the Jostens Classic—something that Rollie usually didn't entrust to one of his first-year assistants. "Most of the time you had to be with him for a number of years before he would give you a scouting assignment," Jay explained. "It was a big responsibil-

ity in his eyes." Massimino's assistants like Steve Lappas and John Olive took their assignments seriously and carefully kept track of their won-lost records in games they scouted.

A few days before the La Salle game, Wright walked into Massimino's office with his scouting report. "He just ripped it up," Jay recalled. 'This is wrong . . . they don't run this cut like that . . . they don't do that.' He said, 'Go back and watch more tape . . . you don't know . . . you don't have it down . . .' I was in shock because I spent days watching every La Salle game film and everything. I came out of the office and Steve and John said, 'Don't worry about it. He always does that. He's just testing you. He just wants to make sure that *you're* sure about what you're talking about.' Then Rollie gave some of La Salle's game tapes to Lappas and Olive and said, 'Here, you watch it with him. He doesn't know what he's doing.' I was crushed. I was like, *'Oh my God. I let everybody down.'* Then we all came back in the second time and he was a lot more receptive. It *was* just a little test to see that I was sure that I knew what I was talking about."

Massimino always let his assistants go over their scouting report in front of the team before the game. "I remember thinking, 'This is like a dream. I'm in the Palestra. I'm doing a scouting report and I'm talking to the team before the Villanova–La Salle game,'" recalled Wright. "Then we won the game. I remember Steve, John, and Steve Pinone all hugging me after the game. It was a big deal to get your first win as a scout."

Wright is now Villanova's head coach. He replaced Lappas before the 2001–2002 season.

In the first round of the 1987–88 NCAA Tournament, Doug West had a game-high 22 points and Kenny Wilson, a 5'9" junior guard from Jersey City, New Jersey, scored all of his 17 points in the second half to trigger the win over Arkansas. Mark Plansky and Pat Enright were the heroes in the triumph over Illinois. Plansky, the only holdover from the '85 NCAA championship team, scored 10 of his 16 points in the final 2:19. He sank two deciding free throws with four seconds left as the Wildcats battled back from a ten-point deficit. Enright, a 5'11" walk-on from Ridgefield, Connecticut, was in the game only because West got kicked in the head and suffered a concussion late in the first half. After Kendall Gill made a shot to put Illinois ahead by ten points with less than three minutes to go, "Gill got into Enright's face and was boasting that they were going to win," recalled Craig Miller, Villanova's publicist. Then Villanova started fouling, Illinois started missing free throws, and with 29 seconds left, Enright won it with a three-point play. Fittingly, he did it with a neat pump fake from the right baseline that thoroughly confused Gill, who fouled him on the play. Enright was an unlikely hero. He had transferred to Villanova after being cut from the team at Marymount College in Massachusetts. Then he was turned down twice by Massimino before Rollie finally put him on the team midway through the 1985–86 season.

The Wildcats got all the incentive they needed for their semifinal matchup with sixth-ranked Kentucky during their pre-game meal. They overheard coach Joe B. Hall in the next room telling his Southeastern Conference champions that Villanova should be a breeze because the Wildcats did not have a single player who could make Kentucky's team. West and Plansky led the way with 20 and 16 points, respectively, as an inspired bunch of Villanova "no names" led by as many as 13 points in the second half and held off the *other* Wildcats. Defensively, Massey played a box-and-one on Rex Chapman and completely shut down Kentucky's top scoring threat.

When the Wildcats arrived in Birmingham, they tried to make hotel reservations for an extra night in case they beat Kentucky. "You can only have the rooms for the first night because the Kentucky people have everything booked for both nights and we're sold out," they were told. "Coach Mass was really ticked off and he let them know about it," recalled Wright. "He said, 'What are we going to do? If Kentucky loses, they're not going to want to stay there.' The hotel people still said they couldn't do anything." Villanova finally got to stay in Kentucky's rooms after they won the game. Louisville also got ousted from the tournament by Oklahoma. "It was amazing," said Wright. "The hotel just emptied. All you could see was a long line of cars with Kentucky license plates on the highway heading out of town."

With another trip to the Final Four on the line, Villanova surprised heavily-favored Oklahoma with a deliberate four-corners offense and actually led at the half 38–31. The Big Eight champions got back into the game with an 11–0 run midway through the second half. The Wildcats trailed by only 57–54 with 5:28 left, but the Sooners put them away by scoring 13 straight points. Trailing by 12 points with 1:35 left, Massimino cleared his bench. West kept Villanova close with 18 points, including seven-for-eleven from the field, and Wilson added 15.

West, a 6'6" guard from Altoona, made the All Tournament team. The Wildcats' two-time scoring leader later played in the NBA for more than a dozen years with Minnesota and Vancouver. "I loved watching West play," said *Philadelphia Inquirer* sportswriter Joe Juliano of the Big 5 Hall of Famer. "He was really a fantastic player, but not a *spectacularly* fantastic player. He was what they'd call a stat sheet filler. You'd look up and swear the guy didn't do anything and all of the sudden you'd look at the stat sheet and he'd have 18 points, eight rebounds, four assists, and a couple of steals."

Villanova's national reputation helped the Wildcats land another "Philly guard" before the 1988–89 season from, of all places, deep in the heart of Texas. "Villanova was very hot and I wanted the East Coast experience in Philadelphia," said Chris Walker, a 5'11" point guard from Houston, who ended up leading the Wildcats in assists three straight seasons. "When I played in high school I was a lot of flash and dash, scored a lot of points and shot all the time. When I got to Villanova, coach Massimino really showed me how to play. I had to understand that Lance Miller and Greg Woodard were scorers and my job was to get them the ball, play defense, and run the team."

Even though he didn't start until midway through his first season and even though he missed the Big East and NCAA Tournaments that year because of a broken foot, Walker was named to the All Big 5 team after his freshman and sophomore seasons. And Chris didn't even know it! "Nobody ever told me," he recalled. "I guess it was my junior year when I looked into the book one day. I said, 'That's got to be a mistake.' Truth be known, I had no idea what the Big 5 was when I came to Philadelphia. But once I understood what it meant, there was no way I wanted to lose those games."

It didn't take the point guard from Texas long to find out what the Big 5 was all about. In his very first game at the Palestra, Penn roared out to an 11–0 lead and shocked the heavily-favored, 17th-ranked Wildcats 71–70 behind Walt Frazier Jr.'s 25 points. "Rollie just let us have it," said Walker, who is now an assistant to Steve Lappas at Massachusetts. "I thought that they were a cupcake, but there was a different intensity that those Penn guys brought for one game. They played their hardest and their best against Villanova."

Walker's teams never beat La Salle during his four years at Villanova. In fact, a dramatic comeback by the Explorers that resulted in a 71–70 victory during his sophomore year cost the Wildcats the Big 5 title. "I'll never forget that game as long as I live," said Walker. "We were up the whole game. And later we're on our way to Hawaii and James Bryson was a freshman at the time, a young boy, and he was crying, crying, crying up a storm, saying, 'How are we going to win the Big East if we can't beat La Salle?' Everybody's going, 'Shut up!

▶ **D**oug West twice led Villanova in scoring and set Wildcat records for single-game three-point shooting. *(Villanova University)*

Shut up,' and he's crying, 'We can't beat La Salle . . . we can't win in the Big East!'"

The Wildcats didn't win the Big East that year, but a 70–60 win over St. John's in the opening round of the conference tournament got them an NCAA bid. They were quickly eliminated by Louisiana State, behind Shaq O'Neill and Chris Jackson 70–63. In 1990–91, the last year of the Big 5 round-robin, Villanova returned to the NCAA Tournament. Lance Miller made a pair of free throws at the end to give the Wildcats a 50–48 win over Princeton, but North Carolina wore them down 84–69 in the next round.

It was the 14th time that a Big 5 school had been eliminated by either Duke or North Carolina in the NCAA Tournament.

It was also Rollie Massimino's last post-season tournament with the Wildcats. Two years later the Big 5's only coach to win an NCAA championship was on his way to UNLV. Lappas took his place and guided the Wildcats to the NIT championship in1993–94. Asked years later on one of his rare visits back to the Main Line campus why he decided to leave Villanova, Rolllie replied, "I really don't know why." Does he regret his decision? "I don't know. I mean I love this place, I really do."

Actually, that wasn't the first time Massimino considered leaving Villanova. After the Wildcats won the national championship, friends held a roast for him at the Adams Mark Hotel on the outskirts of Philadelphia. People like Jim Valvano, the late North Carolina State coach, and Billy Cunningham, of the Philadelphia 76ers, were there. "Afterwards we adjourned to get a couple of beers," recalled John Nash, who had left the Big 5 to take a job with the 76ers. "It was well chronicled that Rollie was considering the New Jersey Nets job and that was the night he was going to have to make a decision, although I'm not sure everybody knew that. I was with those guys until 2 A.M. and I left because I had to go to work the next day. When I left, he *was* going to New Jersey, and we were all congratulating him. Somewhere between 2 A.M. and 6 A.M., he changed his mind and decided to stay at Villanova. Whether it was for altruistic reasons, whether it was for the security of college versus the pros, who knows? But he was really doing some soul-searching that night."

Chapter 14

• • • • • • •

What Went Wrong?

Late in the fall of 1990, Dan Baker weaved his way through traffic from his office on the University of Pennsylvania campus to the Main Line for a meeting with the Rev. Edmund J. Dobbin, the president of Villanova. As the Big 5 executive director, it seemed as if Baker had been spending most of his time the past few years engaged in athletic shuttle diplomacy, struggling to maintain the fragile relationship among the five institutions. His efforts had not gone unrewarded. The schools had just completed the fifth year of the longest contract in Big 5 history—ten years, a deal that Baker had painstakingly hammered out in 1986. The unprecedented length of the agreement was a quid pro quo after the Wildcats and Temple had insisted on taking the Big 5 games out of the Palestra to their home campuses. Now Baker had been tipped off by a couple of presidents and athletic directors from other schools that Villanova wanted to abruptly end the round-robin city series for the first time in 36 years. Hence the hastily arranged meeting. "Because we had a ten-year agreement I kept thinking to myself, there was no way," recalled Baker as he approached Villanova's campus. "I continued to hope that this was just idle speculation and maybe something being manufactured at the coaching level."

Baker soon found out differently.

"After some small talk, Father Dobbin told me, 'Dan, it just doesn't look like Villanova is going to be able to play all the Big 5 games anymore.' And I think I said, 'Well what do you mean anymore?' And he said something like, 'I don't see how we can play all the games next year.'" Father Dobbin, who was in his third year as Villanova's president, explained that the NCAA had just reduced the total number of games a member could play by one game, to 26. Moreover, the Big East was adding Miami in 1991–92, bringing the total of required conference games up to 18 and, in effect, leaving the Wildcats with the net loss of *three* games that they had the previous season. The Big East also required members to reserve one game for the annual Big East–Atlantic Coast Conference Challenge, and another date for a national TV game with an intersectional opponent. In addition, there were usually opportunities for other regional TV appearances and an invitation to a Christmas tournament in Hawaii, as well as next year's opening game in Houston as part of Rollie Massimino's tradition of playing a game in the hometown of one of his seniors—in this case, Chris Walker, who grew up in that Texas city.

"Mathematically, it's just getting to the point where it's impossible," added Father Dobbin. "I counted that schedule backwards and forwards and I knew it left them little flexibility," said Baker. "But it still could have been done. My first reaction was, 'Well, Father, if you do feel that way, you're certainly entitled to your opinion and you have to do what's in the best interest of your school. It still seems to me that we have five years to go on a ten-year agreement. How about making this decision after the agreement's over and the contract's fulfilled?' And he said, 'Well remember, Dan. There is a clause in the contract that says that we can discuss the contract in the context of any changed circumstances. And I believe that adding another team in the Big East—increasing the number of games in our commitment to our league schedule—that is a change and it allows me to bring it up.'" Baker then suggested playing the full round-robin schedule in 1991–92 and gradually phasing in a reduced schedule of Big 5 games afterwards. But the answer was "no." Villanova would only play two city series games each season. After 36 years, the Big 5 was done. At least as we knew it.

Actually that wasn't the first time that Villanova attempted to reduce its commitment to the Big 5. In 1960, when the first renewal of the five-year agreement was being negotiated, Villanova's athletic director Frank Reagan said that his university's Athletic Council had recommended that four of the Wildcats' games in the 1961–62 season be played in the Fieldhouse on campus,

211

thus reducing Villanova's participation in Palestra twin-bills to seven or eight games. The other athletic directors responded quickly: "Full participation in the program is required of Villanova University or some adjustment will have to be made in the financial statement," they said. The Wildcats compromised and played in nine doubleheaders that year as well as in a season-ending city series playoff. St. Joseph's and Penn made 13 appearances, La Salle 12, and Temple ten.

Art Mahan, who was Villanova's athletic director from 1961 to 1978, recalls that there were rumblings of discontent about the Big 5 on the Main Line as far back as the early 1970s. That's when university officials for the first time unveiled plans for a new fieldhouse on campus, plans that were shelved in favor of two academic facilities that were later constructed, the Connelly Center and The Mendel Science Center. Word leaked out that Villanova had engaged a consultant to evaluate the feasibility of playing all of its basketball games on campus. "That put us in a bad light," recalled Mahan: "'We hear that you guys are pulling out of the Big 5.' I said, 'I don't think in my time you'll ever see it. I don't think it's a big worry.' I would have hated to drop out of the Big 5 and go back and try to get a schedule for our Fieldhouse. Hey, we couldn't get anybody to come to our Fieldhouse. It was a tremendous asset when we were able to tell a big-name team that we were sharing the Palestra. When you only have two thousand to three thousand seats it's tough to play a top schedule. So everybody had a vested interest in the Big 5 and didn't want to spoil it."

Villanova students were often unhappy about making the 17-mile journey to the Palestra, a factor that led to Villanova's request to play the second game of doubleheaders whenever possible—especially since the campus dining halls closed at 6:30 P.M., making it virtually impossible to make it for a 7 P.M. opener. In addition, Mahan recalled that Villanova officials were never really satisfied with the annual financial payout that they received from the Big 5, even though there were considerable expenses for things like security and maintenance of the Palestra. "I said, 'okay, Father, if you want to move back here, look whom we're playing. We're now getting some kind of a national name and that's not at our Fieldhouse, that's from playing at the Palestra. Everybody benefits. Even if you only break even, just the publicity the program gets you, from an enrollment standpoint, makes it worthwhile.' Don't forget, today we operate at capacity but in those days, you wanted those students. That's how I always tried to justify football. I'd say, 'hey, do you know what Madison Avenue would pay for this type of advertising?' So when you looked at the dollars and cents—whether it was twenty-five

thousand dollars or a hundred thousand dollars—it wasn't an awful lot."

Was the end of the Big 5 round robin inevitable? After all, times *had* changed. Our lifestyles were different. In a couple of generations, college basketball had grown from a relatively inexpensive operation dominated primarily by small Catholic colleges in the eastern part of the United States, to a huge, wealthy, multifaceted international business now controlled by the larger state universities, conference affiliations, *and* television. Large antiseptic arenas with luxury suites replaced smaller, cozier Palestras with bleachers. No longer were Big 5 institutions able to steal national championships with talent recruited exclusively from the Philadelphia Catholic or Public leagues. In fact, no longer could institutions anywhere expect to compete nationally if they restricted recruiting to their local areas with limited budgets.

But the Big 5, which hosted as many as 30 doubleheaders a year, was still a Philadelphia treasure. St. Joseph's athletic director Don DiJulia recalled that college basketball people throughout the nation marveled at its uniqueness and made numerous attempts to duplicate it in their areas. "New York tried it five times," he explained. "I remember George Raveling saying that he tried to get something going in the Los Angeles area when he was coaching at Southern Cal." So did Penn's athletic director Steve Bilsky when he was running the athletic department at George Washington University. "I tried to get my colleagues in Washington to understand just how special the Big 5 really is," explained Bilsky, who saw a potentially similar situation with nearby schools like Navy, Georgetown, Maryland, and American University. "You had the natural makings of something like the Big 5. The problem there was that John Thompson wouldn't play anybody and Maryland wouldn't play those teams if Georgetown wasn't going to play them. So you had the politics, which is more the reason why the Big 5 is so special because there are others cities that have four or five Division I schools in their midst. But the only city that was ever able to capture something like this was Philadelphia."

When the Big 5 started in 1955, World War II and Korea were still fresh in the minds of most Americans. The Cold War was red hot but the space race had not yet begun between the United States and the USSR, who jostled for global supremacy. Alaska and Hawaii were still U.S. territories. It was the Age of Innocence, *Happy Days*, if you will, in the eyes of many Americans. The Civil Rights Movement was in its infancy and a war hero named Eisenhower was serving as president. Philadelphians were about to experience only their second Democratic administration after 50 years of Republican rule with the election of Mayor Richardson Dilworth. The city had just recently lost its American League baseball team, the Athletics, to Kansas City, and the National Hockey League would not come to town for another dozen years when the Spectrum was built. When the Big 5 began, Penn's athletic department consisted of two dozen full-time people. By the time Paul Rubincam took over as athletic director in 1985, that number had swelled to 130. When Temple went to Final Four in 1958, the Owls had twelve members in their athletic department. When John Chaney took Temple to the NCAA Elite Eight in 2001, it had 107 employees.

DiJulia could sense things starting to change in the late 1970s, when many colleges began to experience serious financial difficulties and college athletics in general began to undergo a revolution of sorts. "Higher education was coming out of some cost-containment eras," he recalled. "Coeducation was new on many campuses and the culture and fabric of Philadelphia was different. People weren't going to the games like they used to." Indeed, an overwhelming majority of Big 5 fans for the first two decades lived within Philadelphia city limits. Now they had moved to the suburbs and weren't coming to the Palestra as frequently. "Then," said DiJulia, "the questions started to rise up: Does it make sense for St. Joe's to play Rider and La Salle to play Duquesne in a doubleheader? If you just looked at it from a business standpoint, a practical standpoint, as much as my heart and other hearts were there, you could logically say: 'You know what? This doesn't make sense.' If somebody had their own facility, you either had to change how people shared in all this—whatever it was—or just look at it again differently." The doubleheader format among all the Big 5 schools remained intact until 1984–85, when Temple and Villanova moved most of their home games to campus.

"There was much more congeniality and good fellowship in my day," recalled former Penn athletic director Fred Shabel. "There wasn't a lot at stake compared to what developed later. There wasn't enough money being distributed in those days to put people in a position where they had to be a little selfish for their institutions. I've got to believe that the political climate changed later when all of a sudden you got into a different type of decision-making with television and the big conferences. Suddenly, the potential of larger gate receipts at the Spectrum took some of the issues to another level."

"Our society lived a different lifestyle twenty years ago," explained John Nash, who was Dan Baker's predecessor. "For one thing, we played all of our Saturday doubleheaders at night. News was on TV at 11, not 10. Phillies games at Connie Mack Stadium started at 8:05, not 7 P.M. Palestra doubleheaders started at 7 but if the first game went into overtime, the second game might not start until 9:30. Now you're looking at games ending at 11:30 or 11:45. You couldn't take grade school kids. I thanked my parents for letting me go because they would say, 'you're not going to be home until midnight.' They had the benefit of being able to turn the game on and see where I was and gauge how much time it was before I got home. Back in the '50s when the Big 5 started, everybody went home, had dinner, then went to the games. Fast food places didn't exist. Maybe they had a hot dog as a snack, or popcorn, but you went to watch basketball, you didn't go to eat. Just look at the size of the concession stand at the Palestra. Today we've become accustomed to going to the game at the arena and eating dinner there."

The most significant factors in the changing landscape of college basketball were interrelated—the emergence of athletic conferences, which made it absolutely necessary to become affiliated with a league, and the awesome impact of television. The landmark year was 1979, when ESPN, the nation's first national cable TV network, and the Big East Conference were born within months of each other. Both left an indelible impact on the Big 5. Especially when Temple, then a member of the East Coast Conference, declined an invitation to become a charter member of the Big East and Villanova was selected to replace the Owls.

"That was something that we thought was absolutely mind-boggling," recalled John Nash, when Temple declined the invitation to join the Big East. Nash was the Big 5's executive director at the time. Then when the Big East turned to Villanova, the Wildcats' athletic director, Ted Aceto, had reservations. "He asked me what I thought," said Nash. "I finally had to tell him I thought it would be in their best interest. I'm not sure where Rollie was in all this. He may have been worried about it because although everyone felt that the Big East would generate more visibility, Rollie had been pretty successful in the Eastern 8."

When Dave Gavitt, the former Providence coach, was putting the Big East together as the conference's founder and first commissioner, he started with a core group that included St. John's, Georgetown, Syracuse and Providence. "We really did have a *big market* strategy," he recalled. "We wanted to have at least one school in each of the big Eastern cities—feeling that was the only way really to get television and other people's attention, if we somehow tied them all together. At the same time we did not want to leave out hotbeds like Syracuse or Providence—smaller cities where teams had done well and had a great following." Gavitt found some initial hesitation, particularly from Syracuse, when he began conversations with the schools in the spring of 1978. "Syracuse was concerned that they not be the only non-Catholic school in the league," he recalled. "We felt out a number of schools as to their level of interest. One of them was Temple, another being Rutgers because we wanted more than one school in the New York metropolitan area. Both really had the same answer. They felt that they wanted to be in a league with Penn State because of football, so they both declined. Holy Cross also had an opportunity to come in but didn't. That's how Boston College got in."

Gavitt then moved quickly to invite Villanova, but the Wildcats were committed to the Eastern 8 for one more year. "We knew that Villanova would ultimately come with us so we went with seven members that first year," he explained. Seton Hall and Connecticut completed the original alignment, with the Wildcats joining the league the following season. "If Villanova had said 'No,' we clearly would have gone to St. Joe's. They both had great basketball traditions and programs and I personally had pretty strong ties to both schools. The overall Villanova athletic program, particularly in track and field, was so strong. It mirrored what Georgetown and Providence were doing as well, and that kind of weighed in on Villanova's side. We were hesitant to go to a second Philly school." Temple and St. Joseph's eventually ended up in the Atlantic 10. So did La Salle, after the Explorers played for nine years in the Metro Atlantic Conference and for three disastrous seasons in the Midwest Collegiate Conference.

Being situated in a corridor of the country containing 25 percent of the nation's television homes was a tremendous advantage to the Big East, recalled Gavitt, who once played basketball for Dartmouth against Paul Rubincam's Penn team. Before the Big East was formed, schools operating independently usually found it extremely difficult to get their games on television. Two years earlier, in fact, Rutgers had a great team and went to the Final Four. St. John's was also very good, but when the two New York metropolitan area teams faced each other in the NCAA Eastern Regionals in North Carolina, they couldn't clear the game on television in New York City. "There's no question that we had a big market strategy and television was a part of it," said Gavitt. "And there was also no question that we were certainly helped by the emergence of ESPN. But we really made our own mark by creating our own television network. That's kind of a segue to some of the problems that related to the Big 5. We certainly weren't looking to harm the Big 5 in any way. That was never our intention

because I grew up appreciating the Big 5. Those doubleheaders were just great. But we did indirectly cause some problems because we had to have access to our games for television. We couldn't be part of a Wednesday night 7–9 doubleheader at the Palestra if we needed the game between Villanova and Georgetown at 8 P.M. to go on our network. And we needed so many games in each market. We couldn't clear games at 7 P.M. because of the game shows that all the local stations carried, so we needed tip-off times that didn't work with doubleheaders."

Television problems also became more complicated from a financial standpoint when some Big 5 members found that contracts negotiated by their conferences, like the Big East and Atlantic 10, took precedence over existing local TV commitments. In 1989–90, Philadelphia's PRISM was in its 13th year of televising Big 5 games. It had begun carrying them for $750 a game in 1978–79 and now was paying a rights fee of $16,000 for each contest. But it warned that the schools could expect a sizable reduction in revenue if the Big 5 could no longer guarantee the premium cable TV outlet exclusivity when it carried a city series game. The problem had arisen when the Atlantic 10, which owned the television rights of all of its members' home games, wanted to place La Salle's game at Temple on ESPN because it offered national exposure. ESPN subsequently refused to carry it, however, because it did not want to black it out in PRISM's trading area, as it had agreed to do in two previous instances.

The Big East's other issue with Villanova concerned the Wildcats' antiquated arena. "We basically told them after a couple of years that they couldn't play in the Fieldhouse anymore," said Gavitt. "We didn't tell them that they had to build a place; we just said that the Fieldhouse was not an adequate site for Big East games. We couldn't have Patrick Ewing or Chris Mullin or Ed Pinckney breaking a leg with somebody on the baseline, and you couldn't televise games out of there with the camera requirements. So we kind of drove them off campus. They played some games in the Palestra and some in the Spectrum. It probably did light the fire for them to build the Pavilion. But they weren't the only school. The same message was sent to Boston College and to U-Conn."

Because of the Big East TV requirements, Gavitt understood that it would be increasingly difficult for the Wildcats to continue to be a full partner in the Big 5 doubleheader program. "But the city series was totally different than that," he explained. As far as any problems Rollie Massimino had with Big 5 games, "my position with him was that he should play them. I never felt that Villanova shouldn't be a full participant in the city series. I also felt that even though Villanova and Temple both were going to have their own arenas, the city series should have been played either at the Palestra or at the Spectrum. It should have been a program unto itself—and could be doubleheaders rather than stand-alones in some cases. I think Rollie was feeling—and as a coach I can understand this—he was in a different position than anyone else in the Big 5 because the Big East was so tough. So once Pitt and Miami came in the league, he's got 18 really tough games and then he adds four more on top of that. Then he's at 22 and he doesn't have a lot of places to get well in terms of getting to the NCAA Tournament. That probably was what caught his attention. In fairness, I think that John Chaney had some reservations, too. A long time before it was really fashionable, he stepped up and played the world. He took on all comers and he probably felt a little bit that he was kind of a sitting duck, too, in the city series games."

It is no secret that Massimino did not want to play all the city series games. Dick Vitale once described on ESPN how Rollie had told him just that because all of the city teams were gunning for him and the Big 5 games were just too tough. Dan Baker and Massimino had a number of discussions on the topic. "He would try to explain how playing all the Big 5 games, now that Villanova was in the Big East, made it extremely hard for him because those Big East conference games were so difficult," recalled Baker. "He said that a lot of other Big East conference teams were playing automatic W's with their non-conference games. And were, in fact, encouraged to do so by the conference. He maintained that one year Tom Schneider's Penn team had upset Villanova and that loss kept Villanova out of a tournament." In fact, the only time Schneider's Quakers beat Villanova, 71–70 in 1988–89, the Wildcats finished with a 16–15 regular season record and went to the NIT. Emphasizing again how "special" the Big 5 was, Baker pointed out to Rollie that the NCAA Selection Committee would be more inclined to take Villanova over other Big East teams with better records most years because they would take into account that the Wildcats played the more difficult schedule and had more quality wins.

John Chaney was able to maintain the best of both worlds for his Atlantic 10 Conference basketball program. He balanced the desire for a national schedule with occasional network television appearances with a commitment to continue to play all of the Big 5 schools every year—even after the Owls moved their games out of the Palestra. Of course, the Atlantic 10 required only 16 regular season games in 1991–92, two fewer than Villanova's Big East obligation. "When I first came in

here, this school was playing locally—the Drexels and Lehighs and teams like that," Chaney recalled. "I wanted to get this school on the map so I gave Al Shrier a list of fifty of the top programs in the country. I said, 'Go out, call them on the phone and get back to me. I'll play them two-for-one, whatever, but I want to bring us into the limelight.' I knew then that TV was the most important aspect of the game. Beating the other guys on the block was not that important to me because I could see what was coming."

Chaney realized that recruiting locally was becoming a major problem because most of the better players from the Philadelphia area were heading elsewhere. "It got to a point where I said to myself, *Hey, I can't stay here and recruit!* The most important recruiting device is recognition, and recognition comes from national TV. When you call a youngster or a parent and want to know if you can come in and visit, you don't want them saying, 'Temple? Where are they?' That's what happened to me. When I called, 'I'd have to say, 'well we play in the Big 5 with teams like Villanova, La Salle and St. Joe's.' They don't know what the Big 5 is outside of this area. They knew who Villanova was when they won the national championship so you could always attach yourself to them. But it wasn't going to get you very far because no one knew the history and tradition of the Big 5."

Villanova's move to the Big East was a brilliant move for its basketball program, explained Chaney, primarily because, in addition to the huge financial benefits, the Wildcats gained so much national exposure from the conference's television contracts. "That in itself gave way to the recruitment of youngsters from the outside," explained Chaney. "Remember, when Rollie won the national championship, he didn't have one player from the Philadelphia area. So I'm saying to myself, I'm a black coach here in the city and people were saying 'Oh, he's a black coach. He's going to get all the players now. They're all going to Temple.' I didn't get one. Not one, until I was here the second year and got Nate Blackwell. I wanted that kid in the worse way because he was from South Philly. And I was from South Philly. I knew his father. But that in itself gave me the idea that if I wanted to get this program in a national way. I didn't have to give up the Big 5. But outside of my initial responsibility of so many games in the A-10, I had to also look at the Big 5 as four other difficult games, and at the rest of my games being tough and against big time schools."

Chaney was one of the first coaches who recognized the secret of getting into the NCAA Tournament. "The biggest and most important aspect of this business is to get into the door," he explained. "Whether you win the first or second round, the door now opens and seven-comes-eleven from there. So I said the only way I can do that is follow the formula that the NCAA set up. If you don't look at how you're chosen and be guided by that, you will find yourself wallowing around in a quagmire. The way they rate and select teams is a good, great schedule, a good won-and-lost record, and how you finish. That's the last taste of the lollipop for the NCAA. If you end up on a winning streak, the NCAA says, *My goodness. That's great! We know we have a team that's going to be representative.* That became the rule because I started it. The rule came later. The NCAA developed the idea, *You're not getting any more points for playing Division II teams and coming in here with twenty-five wins and twenty of them against the Little Sisters of the Poor.* Other people were arguing that they won 23 games, and we were getting into the NCAAs with 17 wins. But they were quality wins and a great schedule. Now we could go out and recruit against the big timers."

Never was the importance of national recognition more obvious to Chaney than when he tried to recruit Jason Ivey out of Alabama in 1992. "This was in the month of July when I called," Chaney explained. "His mother picked the phone up and I said, 'I'm Coach Chaney from Temple University. I'm trying to recruit your son.' She said, 'You're from Temple? Where is Temple?' So I said, 'Well we're a great metropolitan school in the Philadelphia area and we have a great program.' She said, 'I haven't heard of Temple' and then said 'Wait a minute. Will you hold on?' Wimp Sanderson, the Alabama coach, was calling her on the other line and this was Wimp Sanderson territory. He was also trying to recruit her son. She said to him 'I have another coach on the line.' He asked who. She said 'Coach Chaney.' He said, 'You don't want your son to go up there to Philadelphia. It's snowing up there.' And Wimp says, 'I'll be there in two minutes.' He's 50 miles away. So now she gets back on the phone and says, 'Did you say your name was Coach Chaney from Temple?' And in the background I could here Jason Ivey saying, 'Mom. Let me have that phone! That's Coach Chaney from Temple!' She says, 'I'm sorry but my son is not coming up there. It's snowing up there.' Now here it's July and she says, 'We don't have the money to buy winter clothing.' And Jason says, 'Mom, give me that phone!' He takes the phone and we end up getting this youngster from down in Gadsden, Alabama. That just shows that recognition is your key to recruiting. That opens up the door. From then on you have a chance to sell your program nationally." Ivey later joined the coaching staff of Dean Demopoulos when Chaney's longtime top assistant became the head coach at Missouri-Kansas City.

The other Big 5 schools also found themselves pressured by the lure of television and influenced on occasion by visions of greater financial rewards. Lefty Ervin, the former La Salle coach, remembers being approached by Bill Bradshaw, his athletic director, one summer day in 1980. "Bill comes up and says, 'Lefty, you know the date you have for Delaware on the schedule? Guess what. This would really be wonderful. Missouri called and offered us a TV game and they're going to give us $40,000.' I said, Bill, 'You want me to play Missouri *at* Missouri instead of Delaware? You're asking me to take a *win* off my schedule?' He comes back 20 minutes later and says, 'Guess what, Lefty. They're going to give us $50,000.' Tom McCarthy, one of our vice presidents, writes a letter and says, 'in your contract, we will write a little addendum that you did this for the school.' I didn't see any of the 50 grand and the big Missouri loss is still mine, but I took one for the school. We played pretty well and lost by nine. We never had a chance."

The Big 5 schools never got rich from the basketball program at the Palestra. Cash shares, distributed evenly to each of the teams in the years when all ten of the city series games were played at the Palestra, ranged from a low of $3,859 in 1958–59 to a high of $55,513, way back in 1973–74. In 1983–84, the final season in which *all* of the Big 5 games were played at the Palestra, each school earned $53,853.

That was a far cry from the pre–Big 5 days, especially for La Salle, Temple, and St. Joseph's. "Josh Cody told us that each school got only $85 from Madison Square Garden for the games they played in the last year of Convention Hall doubleheaders," recalled former Penn publicist Bob Paul, the man who helped start it all. "And he thought it was wonderful!" So did the Big 5 in 1962–63, when WFIL radio paid a whopping total of $800 to each school for the rights to broadcast 27 doubleheaders.

Ticket revenue was never as high as would be expected, primarily because 50 percent of the fans attending a typical Palestra event usually purchased their tickets at the half-price rate offered to students, faculty, and staff. The largest gross sale in Palestra history was $44,000 for the opening doubleheader of the 1983–84 season, matching La Salle–Vermont and St. Joseph's–Villanova.

In 1964–65, the Big 5 enjoyed its best attendance ever for the ten city series games at the Palestra, averaging 8,604 fans per game. The following season, the payout to each school jumped more than $20,000 to $49,547. When the athletic directors agreed to a new five-year contract that year, they authorized John Rossiter, the business manager of the University of Pennsylvania, to investigate the possibility of increasing the seating capacity of the Palestra. But they quickly killed the project a few months later when Rossiter reported back that such a study would cost $10,000. Rossiter served as the Big 5's executive secretary until Nash was hired in 1975.

The Big 5's highest attendance *overall* came in 1982–83, when an average of 10,131 fans watched the city series games. Included were the two biggest crowds in Big 5 history—18,060 who saw Villanova beat St. Joseph's at the Spectrum (at the time the largest crowd ever to watch a basketball game in Pennsylvania), and 17,583 for a Temple win over La Salle.

When Nash joined the Big 5 in 1975, he soon learned that the coaches were beginning to feel that for recruiting purposes it was necessary to play in a building other than the Palestra once in a while. "That's when we made the decision to take some big games to the Spectrum against teams like Notre Dame, South Carolina and Duke," he recalled. "Sometimes coaches would take recruits to a 76ers game and show them the 76ers locker room and say, 'we play here.' It wasn't because anybody was dissatisfied with the Palestra, it was just when a kid got to see Pauley Pavilion or Clemson or some of the other big venues, the coaches felt there was a need to combat that. Even though the coaches wanted to do this, they always criticized the Spectrum when they played there. In hindsight, I'm not sure if it was a good or bad thing to do. I don't think there is anything quite as enjoyable as the Palestra."

Jim O'Brien, who was playing at St. Joseph's at the time, recalls that some of the better Philadelphia-area high school players like Gene Banks and Andre McCarter were beginning to drift out of town, lured by the more intense recruiting of the higher-profile national programs. "We would always talk about how great it was to play at the Palestra," O'Brien explained. "Then you got out and saw that there was life outside of Philadelphia basketball. You go to another place like Duke, like Gene Banks did, or out to UCLA, where McCarter went, you'd see that they have bigger places and all the fans will be rooting for you. They won't be rooting against you. It was just a product of basketball becoming a bigger thing in the United States. There was more pressure on big-time programs to get the best players. If they happened to be in Philadelphia, you couldn't fault anybody for going away."

It is doubtful, though, if the move to the Spectrum was a sound financial decision. "At one time the thinking was if you're not going to draw 13,000 fans, don't use the Spectrum," said Rubincam, the executive director of the Big 5. "If you had a crowd of over 13,000 people, it really made financial sense to play the game there." The first Big 5 game ever played outside the Palestra was at the Spectrum between Villanova and St. Joseph's on

February 19, 1977. It drew 12,138 fans. There were seven Big 5 promotions at the Spectrum after that and, except for the two record-setting dates mentioned earlier, the Big 5 never drew more than the 11,456 who attended a doubleheader featuring Villanova–Penn and La Salle–Temple in 1980. Three of the crowds, in fact were under 10,000 with the smallest (8,946) for Temple–Villanova in 1985.

When the schools abandoned the Palestra and started playing Big 5 games at their home sites, however, average attendance for the ten city series games dropped considerably. The first game played on a campus, at Temple's McGonigle Hall, against Penn on December 8, 1986, drew only 1,892 fans. The highest average attendance in the next five years before the round-robin format was eliminated in 1990–91 was 5,814 in 1988–89. The best crowd that year was 8,722 for the St. Joseph's-Villanova game, at the Palestra. It was the poorest average for any one season dating all the way back to 1960–61, when the Big 5 games averaged 5,285. Only in the first two years of the Big 5—in 1955–56 and 1956–57 when city series games averaged 3,707 and 2,602 fans, respectively—were the crowds smaller.

Even though their home games were now being played elsewhere, the coaches always made sure to stop at the Palestra when they were showing recruits around town. "I remember Rollie always wanting keys to the Palestra because he wanted to bring recruits through the building without the other people knowing who he was bringing in," explained Nash. "And Chuck Daly, probably because he just liked to tweak him, set up this system whereby Rollie had to call the security office at the university to get somebody to open the Palestra. Rollie was certain that that meant that Penn would know who Villanova was recruiting. Seldom were Penn and Villanova recruiting the same kid, but we used to have arguments about that."

In an attempt to address concerns by Villanova that the Wildcats were drawing a higher percentage of fans to the Palestra, Baker initiated a "Unit System" in 1985–86 by which Big 5 teams no longer received equal shares of the revenue. Instead they were compensated proportionally according to a formula that assigned a higher point value to more attractive opponents. Monmouth College, for example, was awarded one point whereas a Big 5 rival or a nationally-renowned team like Duke received five points. Ironically, this system that was developed to appease Villanova actually benefited St. Joseph's, La Salle, and Penn more because those schools continued to play most of their home games at the Palestra. St. Joseph's received the largest payout, $63,677, in 1985–86 when the Hawks hosted only eight games but their schedule included attractive contests with Villanova, Duke, and West Virginia as well as two games against Temple. La Salle played eleven games at the Palestra that year and was awarded $56,793. Penn earned $55,477 in 1986–87 when the Quakers' eleven Palestra opponents included Notre Dame, Villanova, St. Joseph's, Princeton, and Vanderbilt. That also was the first season of a three-year companion deal to the new Big 5 contract, the Palestra Basketball Agreement, which Baker negotiated for Penn as well as for La Salle and St. Joseph's, who continued to share the revenue and expenses for games played on the Quakers' campus. In 1989–90, La Salle moved its home games to Philadelphia's Civic Center Convention Hall and St. Joseph's returned to Hawk Hill for most of its games. Big 5 basketball at the Palestra was over except for an occasional city series contest. In 1990–91, the final year of the round-robin, only two of the city series games were played at the Palestra—both Penn home games.

The biggest victim of the demise of the Big 5 was La Salle because the Explorers had the smallest home-court capacity of all. Hayman Hall held fewer than a thousand fans before that facility was expanded to four thousand seats and renamed the Tom Gola Arena in 1998, long after the city series round-robin had ended. In the meantime, the Explorers remained at the Civic Center until 1996, when that arena closed and they were forced to move to the First Union Spectrum for two seasons.

When the Big 5 schools went more national with their recruiting programs, some people tried to downplay the importance of the city series games. "That was bull," recalled Ed Stefanski, the former Penn player. "I remember interviewing out-of-town kids on TV after their first Big 5 games. The kid would say, 'I had no idea how intense these games were.' Even the national recruits from out of the area who came in here felt that way. If you're a player, you want to play those games. Coming from the Philadelphia Catholic League and having grown up with the Big 5, it was a religious war for me. But for these guys out of state who didn't realize it, once they figured it out, they loved it. They knew that when those games started, you better put your helmet on and strap it tight because the Big 5 games were still very, very aggressive."

John Pinone, who played just when Villanova was joining the Big East, said that the Wildcats were unfairly accused of not caring for the Big 5. "Did the Big 5 probably mean more to the kids who were in Philadelphia? Absolutely. Did it mean more to me to come back and beat U-Conn. in my own back yard? Absolutely. Our whole season wasn't made because we beat Penn or

something. We wanted to win the Big 5 just as much as we wanted to win the Big East. I can't speak for the other schools—maybe St. Joe's considered our game bigger than whomever they were playing next. Maybe it's true, I don't know. Maybe they did place more importance on the Big 5 than we did. We didn't have a lot of kids from the Philadelphia area, which we caught a lot of grief about, also. There was a reason for that. We recruited them. Sometimes academically we couldn't get them in or sometimes they just didn't want to go to Villanova. It wasn't for a lack of effort. We were on some kids' short list. They just chose not to come. I think that was unfair criticism of the program. To an outsider who didn't live in the area, looking back now, I don't think college coaches really give a hoot where they're from. If a kid can play and he qualifies and he can help the team win, who cares where he's from?"

Baker's most gratifying accomplishment was the ten-year contract he negotiated in 1985, an agreement that essentially saved the Big 5—at least for a while. It all came about after the Rev. John Driscoll and Dr. Peter Liacouras, the presidents of Villanova and Temple, announced intentions to move all home city series games, as well as contests with the more attractive opponents, to their respective campuses. Villanova had just constructed the 6,500-seat Pavilion and Temple wanted to showcase McGonigle Hall, which had a capacity of 3,900. "The other three schools felt very strongly that these games should be played at the Palestra," recalled Baker. "They were concerned that the Big 5 would lose something if the games were moved. On the other hand, Father Driscoll and Peter Liacouras felt that their basketball programs would be best served by playing home games at campus sites. They made it very clear that if this concession wasn't granted, that they were prepared to leave."

Baker met individually with each athletic director, then collectively with all the ADs and presidents. "It was my assessment that unless we were willing to change the venue, Villanova and Temple weren't bluffing," recalled Baker. "They would pull out. So then I came back to Father Driscoll and said, 'Father, you're asking an awful lot because La Salle, Penn, and St. Joseph's feel just as justified in their desire to maintain the Palestra as the home site.' I said, 'You are going to have to give something up to gain this concession.' He looked at me: 'Dan, what do you have in mind? What can we give up?' I said, 'Well, here's what I think you can do. And I can't guarantee that I can sell this but I would do my best as a negotiator to try to find some common ground.' Peter Liacouras was very helpful in this, too, in trying to come up with the common ground."

Baker suggested that the length of the new contract

to be increased to ten years, which was unprecedented because the Big 5 had historically operated on five-year agreements. "I expressed to both Father Driscoll and Peter Liacouras that some of the schools were even concerned that maybe Temple and Villanova wanted to get out and just didn't want to play the other schools, period! But Father Driscoll said, 'No, that is not the case. We want to play the games. We need to be able to play them in our home arena.' So I said, 'Then if you're willing to commit to a city series full round-robin for ten years, then here's the other part: we have to come up with a way to maintain the great atmosphere of the Palestra.'" Visiting teams have been traditionally allocated one hundred tickets for their fans, usually far up in the corner of the arena. Baker suggested instead that the visiting team would get 20 percent of the capacity; in the case of Villanova's Pavilion that would amount to 1,300 of the 6,500 seats. In addition, one hundred tickets had to be right behind the visiting team bench.

"Father Driscoll and Peter Liacouras agreed," said Baker. "Then I had to sell the other schools. There was some reluctance on their part at first. But I told them—and they knew from their own discussions with these presidents—that the threat was very real. That was the gist of the agreement that began with the 1986 season and was supposed to run through 1995." Then Baker fashioned the "Palestra Basketball Agreement" among the Explorers, Quakers, and Hawks that enabled the doubleheaders to continue for another three years. In all, it was a major diplomatic accomplishment for the executive director of the Big 5, who later became the coordinator of broadcast relations at Drexel University's athletic department.

The events leading to Villanova's decision to end the Big 5 round-robin began one day in 1990 when Ted Aceto, the Wildcats' athletic director at the time, walked into the president's office. "He said to me, 'Father, we're going to have to cancel next year's nationally-televised game with North Carolina,'" Father Dobbin recalled. The game was worth $180,000 to Villanova. "I said 'Oh, no, we're not!'"

Villanova's president says that he didn't consult with many people before making his decision to slice the Wildcats' participation in the Big 5 to only two games a year. "I'm thoroughly familiar with Villanova athletics and also with the strategic planning of the university," he explained. Father Dobbin and Aceto took the matter to the University Senate, the institution's governing organization composed of faculty, administrators, and students. "They studied it and sent us a recommendation on the issue, favoring the decision that we made. At the same time I took it to the Board of Trustees' athlet-

ic committee—the full board doesn't get involved in things like this—and that committee made a recommendation collaborating our decision. But I didn't go through any extensive consultation. I didn't have to. To me it was a no-brainer. I'd say the consensus was almost unanimous. The only people that felt badly about it were usually Philadelphians. But even they would say, 'My emotions tell me this, my mind tells me we're doing the right thing.'"

Father Dobbin said that the decision was not made just for athletic or financial reasons. "It had to do with the strategic positioning of the university," he explained. "We had made a commitment with our strategic plan around that time to really emphasize the national visibility of the university and our basketball program was a major vehicle for that. As great a tradition as the Big 5 was, we got no visibility for it outside of this area. I'd be traveling and it would be hard for me to find out the results of a Big 5 game. Even money was not the main issue. Much more important than the money was our national name recognition. Villanova now draws student from every state and many foreign countries.

"Rollie Massimino had nothing to do with this decision," said Father Dobbin. "Basically he was even not in the loop initially, largely because we knew he wouldn't have a problem with it. Ted Aceto and I started talking about this and I brought it right to the Board of Trustees' athletic committee. We discussed the issues. In fact, one of our own senate committees had already made a report to us about it. So there was input, but the coaches were really not driving this at all. It had to do more with positioning the university, not just the basketball team. And our presence in the NCAA Tournament was jeopardized every year because we were on the bubble. We were playing one of the toughest schedules in the country. It was a very difficult situation, but, honestly, I don't think I had a conversation with Rollie during this whole thing."

The announcement to the media was made on May 14, 1991. Father Dobbin says he "fully expected" the negative backlash. Even Philadelphia's Mayor Ed Rendell, a graduate of Villanova's law school, wrote a letter asking him to reconsider. "We took a hit from a public relations perspective," he recalled. "I was a new president at the time. They'd hear my New York accent and would presume that I don't appreciate the Big 5. In fact, I even told them that I was a freshman at Villanova the year before the Big 5 started, so it wasn't as if I was not aware of the tradition. I had followed Villanova basketball since Paul Arizin was here in the '40s." One of Father Dobbin's students when he was chairman of the mathematics department at Malvern Prep was Penn's coach, Fran Dunphy. Dunphy's coach at Malvern, Dan

Dougherty, taught geometry there at the time and frequently played faculty pick-up basketball games with Villanova's future president.

When Baker got the Big 5 officials together to discuss the issue, Father Dobbin was quite surprised by their response. "The meeting of the presidents and athletic directors was not at all cantankerous," he explained. "To tell you the truth, one thing that surprised me in a positive way was how understanding the other presidents were. As emotionally concerned as they were [that] some schools would be hurt more than others, the presidents of the other schools reached consensus on it. I'm not saying that it was their preference, but they reached the unanimous vote in a very friendly atmosphere. Then several of them told me, 'Let's face it. If we were in the same circumstances, we'd do the same thing.'"

Father Dobbin was most surprised by Penn's reaction. "Penn was very emotional about it," he said. "Not in a negative way—they weren't nasty at all. But Penn thought more about it than I thought they would have. Of all the schools, I would have expected that from La Salle and St. Joe's. Of course, Temple was very much sympathetic, largely because they were also part of moving out of the Palestra just before my time. Peter Liacouras was very supportive of our decision. But at the same time, I wouldn't have expected Penn to care, but they cared very much."

Afterwards, someone suggested to Baker the possibility of bringing Drexel University into the Big 5. When he asked the other athletic directors if they wanted to consider having the Dragons replace Villanova to maintain the round-robin, he was instructed to test the waters and inquire if PRISM would be willing to pay the same rights fees for televising city series games. "They said absolutely not," Baker recalled. "They said that Drexel is not a nationally-prominent basketball school like Villanova, and if they were to replace Villanova in four of the ten telecasts it would equate to less viewership and less money from sponsors because the package wouldn't be as attractive." Drexel had been appearing periodically in Big 5 doubleheader programs since the

1962–63 season. The Dragons played against PMC (now Widener), Haverford, and Rider at the Palestra that year with the Big 5 paying all expenses and guaranteeing Drexel up to $100 a night.

So beginning in 1991–92, the Big 5 schools played only two city series games a season on a rotating basis. All of the institutions except Villanova continued to schedule games with each other every year, even though only two of them counted in the official Big 5 standings.

Massimino has never divulged what he said to Villanova officials while the issue was being deliberated, but still feels that he was the scapegoat. "I'll tell you quite frankly, I was unfairly blamed," he said. "I had nothing to do with the final decision. That was done on the administrative level, the presidential level, and I just did what I was told to do. I didn't create that scenario. It really, really upset me because it wasn't me. Obviously I talked, but I don't make those decisions. I'm the basketball coach."

"There's no way Massimino could have ever controlled the administration's decision to stay or get out," said Joe Walters, the retired vice chairman of Villanova's Board of Trustees. The same went for Rollie's successor, Steve Lappas. "When he was hired," explained Walters, "they told him, 'This is the way it is.' He had no control over bringing it back."

"The saddest story for me in the whole thing was Rollie," recalled sportscaster Al Meltzer. "There were a lot of bitter feelings there with all the accusations. I think he was kind of forced out of town. I don't think he could go to a restaurant without somebody hassling him because there was always a Big 5 alumnus around. How could you avoid them because the Big 5 was a treasure? When it broke up, somebody had to take the fall and it was Rollie. Actually, it lasted longer than maybe we had any reason to expect. Considering where it came from and where basketball is today, 36 years is a very long time."

Epilogue

It's not the same and the doubleheaders are long gone, but Penn's athletic director, Steve Bilsky, is among the legions of former players and fans who were ecstatic when Big 5 schools resumed the round-robin format in 2000-01—even though only a few of the games are being played at the Palestra.

"It's important** to keep the Big 5 together," said Bilsky, who worked tirelessly with Baker, Rubincam, DiJulia, and others to restore the traditional round robin. "Leagues now are very short-term and, for a variety of reasons, schools are changing conferences all the time. If your conferences are thriving, that's great. But things change. The Big East exists today, but ten years from now you'll look at that conference and there may be different schools in it. Maybe it will be a football conference or maybe there won't even be a Big East. Conferences like the A-10 will probably change, but the Big 5 is kind of an anchor that's not going to change. We're all going to still be in Philadelphia so why would you *not* want to keep that going?"

And how *did* Villanova return to the Big 5?

"No one has ever noticed the perfect symmetry between the conditions under which we made that decision in 1991 and the conditions under which we made the decision to return," said Father Dobbin, a year or so after the full city series round-robin resumed. Back then, the NCAA reduced the number of games a team could play by one, and the Big East added Miami, thus requiring members to play two more conference games. In 2000, the same thing happened in reverse. The NCAA permitted teams to add another game to their schedule and, coincidentally, the Big East went to two divisions, thus reducing the required number of conference games by two.

The Big 5 *is* back. But it will never be the same!

• • • • •

Acknowledgments

Writing *Palestra Pandemonium* fulfilled a long time dream, but wouldn't have been possible without the enthusiastic assistance of some good friends and professional colleagues who share my affection for the Big 5.

Special thanks for their memories, their encouragement, and their resourcefulness in digging up valuable background information go La Salle University's Bob Vetrone, Sr., the Godfather and historian of the Big 5; Frank Bilovsky, who covered college basketball for many years for the *Philadelphia Evening and Sunday Bulletin*; Jack Scheuer of the Associated Press; Joe Juliano of the *Philadelphia Inquirer*; and Kevin Mulligan of the *Philadelphia Daily News*.

The cooperation extended by Paul Rubincam, the Executive Director of the Big 5, as well as his predecessors Dan Baker and John Nash, is greatly appreciated. Athletic directors Don DiJulia of St. Joseph's University and Steve Bilsky of the University of Pennsylvania were particularly helpful, as were Al Shrier, the special assistant to the athletic director of Temple University, and publicists Larry Dougherty of St. Joseph's University, Mike Sheridan of Villanova University, and Carla Shultzberg of the University of Pennsylvania.

Margaret Jerrido, the head of Urban Archives at Temple University's Paley Library, provided photographs and clips from the *Philadelphia Bulletin* and clips from the *Philadelphia Inquirer*. Martin J. Hackett and Mark Lloyd opened the Archives of the University of Pennsylvania for a glimpse of the minutes of Big 5 meetings. Everyone associated with producing the annual Big 5 *Yearbooks* and the basketball media guides distributed by each of the Big 5 schools contributed a wealth of invaluable information that served as my primary resource. Also useful in my research was *Pride of the Palestra: Ninety Years of Pennsylvania Basketball*, written by Paul J. Zingg with Howard Gensler and Elizabeth A. Reed, and *The Philadelphia Big 5: Great Moments in Philadelphia's Storied College Basketball History*, by Donald Hunt.

Others who helped in various ways include: Peter J. Dougherty (publisher and senior economics editor at Princeton University Press), Dr. Tom Brennan, Joe Chase, Kevin Currie, Essie Davis, Don Delaney, Jim DeStefano, Beth Devine, Andy Dougherty, Fran Dunphy, Larry Eldridge, Jan Geale, Joseph Grabenstein, F.S.C., Charley Greenberg, Jim Gulick, Herb Hartnett, Ralph Howard, Phil Jasner, Rich Kochanski, Joe Lunardi, Mike Kern, Ken Mugler, John McAdams, Jack McCloskey, Speedy Morris, Ken Mulderrig, Whitey Rigsby, Tommy Sheppard, Evan Towle, Mike Tranghese, Paul Vigna, Rich Westcott, Ted Wolfe, and Gail Zachary. Whether it was providing essential information, offering suggestions, or doing some serious arm-twisting, *Palestra*

Pandemonium wouldn't have been nearly as complete without their assistance.

Credit for the quality of the manuscript, of course, belongs to my editor at Temple University Press, Micah Kleit, a consummate professional. His timely advice and guidance, useful recommendations, and fine-tuning expertise were absolute revelations to a newcomer to the world of publishing. So, too, was the support of Ann-Marie Anderson, the brilliant marketing director of Temple University Press, and Naren Gupte, the talented production editor at P. M. Gordon Associates.

Finally, a special word of appreciation to my dear wife, Joan, for her patience and understanding, especially when I frequently allowed myself to become totally preoccupied with this project. Her inspiration and advice were a tremendous help. So was her careful proofreading, often done late at night with my son, Greg, who also bailed me out by transcribing tapes of some lengthy interviews when I found myself facing difficult deadlines.

Southampton, PA
2002